15/6

J. Munsey Turner
Didsbury College
Bristol
Oct-1955

SELECTIONS

FROM

THE LITERATURE OF THEISM

SELECTIONS

FROM

THE LITERATURE
OF THEISM

*EDITED, WITH INTRODUCTORY AND
EXPLANATORY NOTES*

BY

ALFRED CALDECOTT

D.LIT.(LOND.), D.D.(CAMB.)

PROFESSOR OF MENTAL AND MORAL PHILOSOPHY, KING'S COLLEGE, LONDON,
EXAMINER IN PHILOSOPHY OF RELIGION IN THE UNIVERSITIES OF CAMBRIDGE
AND LONDON; LATE FELLOW OF ST. JOHN'S COLLEGE, CAMBRIDGE

AND

H. R. MACKINTOSH

D.PHIL.(EDIN.), D.D.(EDIN. & OXON.), TH.D.(MARBURG)

PROFESSOR OF THEOLOGY, NEW COLLEGE, EDINBURGH
EXAMINER IN THEOLOGY IN THE UNIVERSITY OF LONDON

THIRD EDITION

EDINBURGH
T. & T. CLARK, 38 GEORGE STREET

PRINTED IN GREAT BRITAIN BY
MORRISON AND GIBB LIMITED

FOR

T. & T. CLARK, EDINBURGH

LONDON: SIMPKIN MARSHALL, LIMITED
NEW YORK: CHARLES SCRIBNER'S SONS

FIRST EDITION 1904
SECOND EDITION . . . 1909
THIRD EDITION 1931

CONTENTS

PREFACE

———◆———

THIS volume has been prepared with the aim of bringing together within a small compass some of the leading positions in the philosophy of religion. It is agreed on all hands, in our day, that no one, except here and there an original genius, can expect to be in line with twentieth-century thought who dispenses himself from reference to the positions held by great minds. It is by training his mind in their high thoughts that he can expect to win power and insight for himself. Such training may be extended indefinitely, and the vastness of the field tends, no doubt, to discourage many from ever entering upon it—they attain to belief, or disbelief, on authority, or by reference to some single influence with which they have been brought into contact, quite casually perhaps. But in the range of religious arguments there are some which are of cardinal importance, and among the men who have given to the world their meditations there are some who are acclaimed as masters. The volume contains a selection of such principal arguments, and our only doubt as to its value lies in the possibility that our choice, restricted for space as it is, may not have been the best that could have been made.

We have also in view the increasing number of University students for whom this study is prescribed, or who choose it for themselves. The nineteenth century saw a withdrawal of the philosophical treatment of religion from the

curricula of British Universities and Theological Colleges—
partial in Scotland and some Nonconformist Colleges in
England, complete in the English Universities and the
Theological Colleges of the Church of England. The cause
lay, no doubt, in the tacit acceptance of a truce between the
Theological and the Philosophical Faculties in face of a
supposed conflict. But this is now changing fast. In June
1903 the University of Cambridge admitted Philosophy of
Religion as a subject (optional) in the advanced stage of
study for Theological Honours. The reorganised University
of London placed it at the outset as a regular subject for
the new Divinity degree. Further recognition in Theological
training is sure to come, and then it will remain only that
the Philosophical Faculties admit it on their side. At lectures students will be constantly referred to certain great
thinkers and certain great arguments, and it will not be
possible for many of them to own all the books referred to by
their lecturers. This volume is offered as a first collection,
which may serve them in their preliminary stage.

For both the general reader and the University student
the collection is designed on the ground that it is necessary
for them to read standard writings at first-hand. No pondering over abstracts however accurate, or over compendious
summaries however judicious, can dispense with resort to
the originals. This is desirable for many studies, but it is
indispensable in a subject touching life in so many points as
is done by religious belief. The form of presentation cannot
be sundered from the subject-matter. We have every confidence that few who thus come into contact with arguments
in their original forms will regard this volume as other than
an introduction to the literature, to be followed up as
opportunity allows and taste directs.

The Selections might have been left to speak for themselves, but it seemed that introductory and explanatory
notes, with references for further reading, would be of

service. Both editors have looked over these notes, but each is responsible only for those accompanying the Selections to which his name is attached.

As we have referred to first-hand study, we have almost to make apology for placing so many translations on our brief list. But this is not, in our judgment, to depart from that aim ; in a faithful translation an English student is closer to the mind of thinkers who wrote in Latin or German than he would be if he were struggling to follow them in languages which he himself *thinks in* only with effort and hesitation. We have to express our cordial thanks for permission to print our texts from the following standard translations :—*Descartes*, to the widow of the late Professor Veitch of Glasgow (Messrs. Blackwood); *Kant*, by the late Professor Meiklejohn (Bohn's Library, Messrs. Bell & Sons); to Dr. Abbott (Messrs. Longman); to Dr. Bernard, Dean of St. Patrick's (Messrs. Macmillan); *Schleiermacher*, to the Rev. John Oman, B.D. (Messrs. Kegan, Paul & Co.) ; *Comte*, to Mr. Frederic Harrison (Messrs. Longman); *Lotze*, to Miss E. E. C. Jones, Mistress of Girton College (the present publishers) ; *Janet*, by the Rev. William Affleck, B.D. (the present publishers). New translations are made for *Anselm* and *Thomas Aquinas* (with many suggestions from the Rev. W. O. Sutcliffe, Principal of St. Edmund's House, Cambridge), and for *Spinoza* and *Cousin*, by the Editor; for *Ritschl* we use the translation of the Editor, as already published in the *Justification and Reconciliation* (the present publishers). We desire also to thank Professor Fraser for permission to use his text of *Berkeley*, the Clarendon Press for this text and that of *Martineau*, the Cambridge University Press for that of *John Smith*, and Mr. John Murray for that of *Mansel*.

A. C.
H. R. M.

25th *March* 1904.

PREFACE TO SECOND EDITION

THE reception of this Selection has amounted to a general approval of the Editors' conception of what was desirable, both as to the arguments chosen and as to the writers. This is true of the opinions of critics, and the use of the book in college classes by friends and by ourselves has confirmed the endorsement.

Various suggestions of the pieces have been offered, but none of them with sufficient force to justify the displacement of a present piece in its favour. That an omission of anything from Leibniz and Hegel would be objected to we quite expected, but after consideration we still find ourselves unable to discover a selection, such as our limits require, which would state a leading position in a way fully representing the argument itself, or illustrating the general standpoint of either writer. We have therefore made no change. But we take advantage of a new edition to make a few verbal emendations, and a few additions to the bibliographies.

PREFACE TO THIRD EDITION

———◆———

In this edition we have omitted the Selections from *Janet* and *Martineau*. Our very cordial thanks are due for the three new Selections : to Mrs. O. Ward Campbell (the literary trustee of Professor Ward) and the Cambridge University Press for Selection XIV. ; to Professor Sorley and the Cambridge University Press for Selection XIII. ; and to Professor Otto, of Marburg, and the Oxford University Press, for Selection XVI., as also to Professor Harvey for the Translation. The bibliographies have again been revised.

A. C.
H. R. M.

King's College, London.
New College, Edinburgh.
January 1931.

xi

NOTE

IT is due to the memory of a promising Scholar to say that this collection was first planned by me in association with the late William Johnston, B.D., of Edinburgh and Glasgow, Professor at Cheshunt College. In the week in which we were settling down to the work Johnston was thrown from his bicycle in Theobald's Park, and died within twenty-four hours, at the age of thirty-eight years. We lost in him one who had pondered over theological and philosophical problems from his boyhood, and from whom much was to be expected in his maturity. My colleague joins me in inscribing to his memory this recognition of his connexion with this volume.

A. C.

INTRODUCTION

——◆——

WHAT is the Philosophy of Religion? We take it to be the application of ultimate principles of thought to the religious experiences of mankind. To suppose that there is only one philosophy of religion is, therefore, to suppose (1) that there is only one system of ultimate principles, and that it is known; and (2) that religious experiences are capable of being brought into a coherent whole, and are not incongruous and irreconcilable. No doubt most writers make both these assumptions; but they do so by the simple method of taking their own principles to be the only system, and the religious experiences they are aware of to be the only religious experiences. But so long as the literature of philosophy teems with varying systems, and the literature of religion with varying religious experiences, it is obvious that we are not in possession of a single philosophy of religion.

In presenting a selection of views it is not supposed that the reader will be seeking a single one for exclusive adoption. No one is likely now to become a Cartesian or a Berkeleian pure and simple. And at the present day, when the greatest of modern attempts to construct such an absolute philosophy, that of Hegel, has few whole-hearted supporters, if any, and the leaders who have succeeded him fall into several groups or schools, it is plainly indispensable that we should study and compare all the most worthy presentments which are offered to us. By means of such a comparison a way may be won, not to some exclusive selection, nor to a merely casual eclecticism, but at least in the direction of the unifying principles which philosophy is ever seeking. It is as a first aid for such study that the following selections have been made.

In looking back, accordingly, over some six centuries of European religious philosophy, we invite the reader to adopt the view that he will always be in contact with living thought. There are, indeed, some thoughts which served their day, and have perished; they failed to affect the stream, and left no contribution to the common stock. But there are others which touched the issues in a living way, and brought into evidence some vital factor. They were expressed in an investiture of temporary forms, no doubt, yet there was in them an imperishable substance. It is these which we have intended to select, of course; we take each answer to express something vital in reference to some primary problem, and we believe that in pondering over them material will be gained which is indispensable, even now, for the construction of a system which is to be comprehensive. In each case, certain philosophical principles were in operation, and certain religious experiences in view. If space had allowed, it would have been the business of editors to bring these forward. But what could not be done fully we have endeavoured to do in a modest way by our Notes. For further study resort must be made to the standard editions of the authors, and we have suggested a few books to which a first resort might be made for elucidation or criticism.

We have not been able to cover the whole ground of religion as concerned with God, the Soul, and the World. In selecting, we have chosen the primary topic, the Existence and Nature of God, for the principal part of our space. We have not accepted the invitation of the Psychological School now rising into some prominence, especially in France and America, to take the believer's mind as the primary object of investigation in religion. To do so would be to misrepresent the course of the history, and to presume that that course had been misguided. But this has not prevented us from including some selections in which it is the nature of religious belief rather than its object which is the problem dealt with.

When we look at our list we confess to some searching of heart at the absence from it of anything to represent either Leibnitz or Hegel. The prominent recognition of Force and Activity in Nature and Mind by Leibnitz, as compared with Descartes, Spinoza, and Berkeley, and the claim for constructiveness in Transcendental method made by Hegel, as compared with Kant, render these omissions very serious. We must, however, content ourselves with the pleas, that in the case of Hegel we could discover no suitable selection ; that in both cases the state of opinion as to the significance of their systems on the Theistic side is unsettled ; and, further, that both of them can be studied to greater profit after such preliminary discipline as is offered in the selections we have chosen.

A final word to the reader who makes his first acquaintance with the diversity of judgments upon the doctrine of God, as set in the clear daylight by men of the highest mental and spiritual faculties who agreed in sincerely regarding it as the supreme task of their life to explain it. We would ask him by no means to feel depressed, and disposed to abandon his pursuit of the ideal of philosophical inquiry that there is for religion, as for all else, one universe, one ultimate type of human soul, and one God over all and in all. Rather, let it brace him to take his share in the common task, which is, to bring these varying thoughts into inherent reconciliation with all the highest visions of reason, and with all the noblest sentiments of the soul.

SELECTIONS FROM THE LITERATURE
OF THEISM

I.

THE ONTOLOGICAL ARGUMENT.

ANSELM (1033–1109).

ANSELM, a native of Italy who died Archbishop of Canterbury, can be regarded as the first great Schoolman, if we take Johannes Scotus (Erigena) as a ninth-century pioneer, and allow for Anselm being more Platonist than his successors. During his cloister days at Bec, in Normandy, Anselm, at the request of some of the Brethren, wrote out a meditation on the Essence of the Divine Nature, known as the *Monologium*. In this he set forth the necessity for there being something which is best and greatest and highest of all things, and independent of all things save itself. Reviewing the *Monologium*, some time afterwards, he was dissatisfied with the fact that the proof seemed to be too elaborate, too much a complex construction of arguments; and, further, that in it the Divine Being was considered only in relation to the created world. He wondered whether or not some argument could be found which should be at the same time simple and self-sufficient. After long deliberation and frequent inclinations to abandon the search, one day, *quodam die*, when weary with the effort, in the midst of his mental disquiet, the very object he was beginning to despair of presented itself, *se obtulit quod desperaveram*. This new

I

thought he at once wrote down, and presently he gave it in a finished form in the *Proslogium*, or Allocution on the Existence of God. From this brief narrative it is plain that, whatever affinity there may be between Anselm's proof and an earlier form of the same thought given by Augustine, with Anselm it is independent; and his formulation has a distinctive character which has won for it a place of its own in the history of Theism, not unworthy of standing on the threshold of the second thousand years of Christian thought. Remembering that Anselm's mood is *fides quærens intellectum* (his own expression), we should not duly appreciate his attitude if we wholly omitted the *excitatio mentis ad contemplandum Deum* with which he opens. The following are the closing aspirations :—

Lord, teach me to seek Thee, and show Thyself to me as I seek, for I cannot seek Thee unless Thou teach me, nor find Thee unless Thou show Thyself. May I seek Thee in longing for Thee, and long for Thee in seeking; may I find Thee in loving Thee, and love Thee in finding. I confess, Lord, and I offer Thee thanks, that Thou hast created in me this Thy image in order that I may remember Thee, and think on Thee, and love Thee. But this image of Thee is so worn by the pressure of my faults, and obscured by the fume of my sins, that it cannot accomplish its purpose unless Thou renew it and reshape it. Lord, I strive not to penetrate Thy lofty nature, for in no way do I compare my understanding with it; but I desire in some degree to understand Thy truth, believed and loved already in my heart. For, indeed, I do not seek to understand in order that I may believe, but I believe in order that I may understand. For this also I believe, namely, that unless I believe I shall not understand.

Proslogium, c. ii. *That God really exists; although the Foolish man said in his heart, " There is no God."*

Therefore, Lord, Thou who givest understanding to faith, grant to me that as far as Thou knowest it to be expedient

I may understand that Thou art, as we believe, and that
Thou art what we believe Thee to be. Our belief is this—
Thou art a Being than which no greater can be conceived,
quo nihil majus cogitari potest.[1] Is there, indeed, no such
nature because *the Foolish man hath said in his heart, There
is no God* ? (Vulgate, Ps. xiii. ver. 1 ; A.V., xiv. ver. 1). But
certainly that very man, when hearing the term, understands
what he hears ; what he understands is in his understanding,
even though he does not go on to understand that such
a Being exists. For there is a difference between having a
thing in the understanding and understanding that the thing
is in existence. When, for example, a painter prepares in his
mind what he is about to produce, he has the conception in
his understanding, but he understands that what he has not
yet produced is not yet in existence. When, however, he
has painted his picture, he both has it in his understanding, and also understands that the thing which he has now
produced is in existence. Even the Foolish man, therefore,
is convinced that something than which no greater can be
conceived is in his understanding, because when he hears
this he understands it, and whatever is understood is in the
understanding.

Now certainly that than which no greater can be conceived
cannot be in the understanding alone, for if it were only in
the understanding it could then be further conceived to be
also in reality, which would be a greater thing.[2] Therefore,

[1] Anselm's word *cogitare* is translated "conceived," "thought,"
"thought of" ; the word "imagine" being less appropriate to the
intellectual character of the operation in this connexion. *Intelligere*
is translated by "understand."

[2] In *majus* Anselm includes *melius*. In c. ii. of the *Monologium* he
says, "I do not mean greatness in space, like a body, but greatness in
goodness and worth, like wisdom." So that what he means is that a
thing which is both in our thought and also in reality is a better
thing, a thing of more value, than if it were in our thought only : a
picture painted has worth beyond that of a composition which remains

if that than which no greater can be conceived were only in the understanding, there would be something still greater than it, which assuredly is impossible. Something, therefore, without doubt, exists than which no greater can be conceived, and it is both in the understanding and in reality.[3]

c. iii. *That God cannot be thought non-existent.*

And certainly this greatest possible exists so truly that it cannot be thought not to exist. For we can think that there is something which cannot be thought of as non-existent, and so is superior to anything that can be so thought of. So that if that than which no greater can be conceived can be thought of as non-existent, it must at the same time be the highest object of thought and not the highest—which is an inconsistency. Therefore, there so truly is something than which no greater can be thought, that it cannot be thought of as non-existent. And this Thou art, O Lord our God.

So truly art Thou, O Lord my God, that Thou canst not be conceived not to be. And rightly so; for if any mind could frame the conception of something superior to Thee, the creature would be transcending the Creator, and passing judgment upon Him; which is most absurd. And, indeed, all else that exists can be thought of as non-existent,

only in the artist's imagination; a moderately well-governed city is of higher value than a perfect Utopia. There is advantage in re-reading the whole argument with the word "better" or "superior" instead of "greater."

[3] This is the pivot for Anselm. An image of a picture may be only mental; this is inferior to a picture which has been produced, and therefore has existence both in imagination and in reality. But Anselm's new thought lies rooted in the view that has occurred to him, that the inferior and limited status cannot be attributed to ultimate Perfection; of that there cannot be a conception limited to pure mentality; it is indispensable for the supremacy of the conception, that we attribute the supreme status, existence *both* in the mind and *also* in reality.

save Thee alone. Thou, therefore, alone, most truly of all things, and therefore most of all things, hast existence. For whatever other thing exists, exists less truly, and therefore it has less of existence, than Thou hast.

But if this is a demonstrable necessity, how can it be possible for even the Foolish man to deny the existence of God? Anselm finds that the denial is not real, but verbal; the *thought* of God cannot be misapprehended and rejected, but the *word* may be used without the thought, or to signify some other thought. The conclusion is—

Whoever understands that God so is (as above considered) cannot think of Him as non-existent. I offer Thee thanks, good Lord, I offer Thee thanks, for granting that what by Thy gift I formerly believed I now by Thy illumination so understand, that even if I were to be unwilling to believe in Thy existence yet I could not but know it by my understanding.[4]

In the next chapter Anselm briefly indicates that from this necessary thought of God it follows that He is the Source of all other existence, and of all goodness, and of all happiness.

This new argument was at once made matter of keen scrutiny in the monasteries and schools. It was immediately challenged in a brief *Liber pro Insipiente adversus Anselmi in Proslogio ratiocinationem*, by Gaunilo, of the Monastery of Marmoutier, near Tours. Gaunilo disallows the explanation of Atheism by reference to verbal misuse, and holds that either the understanding is fallible and may fail to prove the existence of God or else there is no necessary proof of God at all; he disallows also the analogy between the relation of a picture unpainted to the picture painted and the relation between the *quo majus nihil* in conception and in reality. To the main argument, that the highest possible excellence will not be there unless existence is included, Gaunilo objects that he cannot admit

[4] Anselm is so confident in the cogency of his argument that he is prepared now to defend Theism on intellectual grounds alone, apart from the prior operation of faith.

any inference from an object of thought to an object of reality; unless you prove, he says, that your best possible is the best possible thing among existing things, you have proved nothing. You cannot transfer from the region of thought to that of existence. Then he produces his famous illustration—

Some say that there is somewhere in the Ocean an Island which, as it is difficult, or rather impossible, to discover what does not exist, is known as the Lost Island. It is fabled to be more amply supplied with riches and all delights in immense abundance than the Fortunate Islands themselves. And although there is no owner or inhabitant, yet in every way it excels all inhabited lands in the abundance of things which might be appropriated as wealth. Now, let anyone tell me this, and I shall easily understand all that he says. But if he then proceeds to infer : " You can no longer doubt that this most excellent of islands, which you do not doubt to exist in your understanding, is really in existence somewhere, because it is more excellent to be in reality than in the understanding only, and unless it were in existence any other land which does exist would be more excellent than it, and so that which you have understood to be the best of islands would not be the best,"—if, I say, he wishes in this way to compel me to assent to the existence of this island, and to suppose that there can be no more doubt about it, either I shall consider that he is in jest, or I shall know not which I ought to consider the more foolish, myself if I grant it to him, or him if he thinks that he has, with any certainty at all, proved the existence of that island. He must first have shown me that its very excellence is the excellence of a thing really and indubitably existing, and not in any degree the excellence of a something false or dubious in my understanding.[5]

---

[5] Dr. J. H. Stirling says (*Gifford Lectures*, x.) that in his under-graduate days he had illustrated the objection he then felt to Anselm's argument by reference to Milton's Garden of Eden and

Gaunilo closes with a cordial tribute to the value of the rest of the Proslogium, intimating that the very point in dispute is rightly aimed at, though the argument is weak, *rectè quidem sensa sed minus firmiter argumentata.*

Anselm did not fail to take up the challenge in a brief *Liber apologeticus contra Gaunilonem.* The pith of the reply is—

(In c. i.) . . . If that than which nothing greater can be conceived can at all be conceived to exist, then it must exist of necessity. For it cannot be conceived as existing except without any beginning; but that which can be conceived to exist, but does not exist, can be thought to have a beginning of existence. It is not possible, therefore, that the *quo majus nihil* could be thought to be, and yet actually not be. If, therefore, it can at all be conceived as existing, it must exist of necessity.

(In c. iii.) (As to the Island) I confidently say that if any-one has found for me something existing either in reality, or in thought alone, to which he is able to apply my argument, besides the *quo majus nihil*, I will both find for him that lost island, and I will give it to him and secure him against its ever being lost again. We see clearly now, that the *quo majus nihil* cannot be thought non-existent, because it exists on an assured ground of truth, otherwise it would not exist at all. Finally, if anyone says that he thinks that it does not exist, I say that at the very moment when he is thinking this, either he is thinking of something than which a greater cannot be conceived, or he is not thinking of it. If he is not thinking of it, he is not thinking that that does not exist of which he is not really thinking at all. But if he is thinking of it, assuredly he is thinking of something which cannot be thought not to be. For if it could be thought non-existent,

Thomson's Castle of Indolence, without having heard of Gaunilo's Island. In his later development he accepted, with reservations, Anselm's argument in its principle.

it could be thought to have a beginning and an end; but this is impossible. He, therefore, who really thinks of it, is thinking of something which cannot even be thought of as non-existent. But he who is thinking of this, does not think that it is non-existent, otherwise he would be thinking what cannot be thought. It is impossible, therefore, to think of the non-existence of that than which nothing greater can be conceived.

It will be observed that Anselm declines to start, as Gaunilo invites him to do, among objects which are contingent, and have beginnings and endings. He had done this in the *Monologium*, where he had followed the upward path from contingencies to necessary Being. But he had been unsatisfied with this, and it is his new discovery that he can go direct to necessary Being. The new position is, then, that the perfect is also existing, and necessarily so; if you are thinking of perfect Being, you are thinking of necessarily existing Being; and from this you may proceed downwards to all other existences.

The reader is sure to have a mixed impression from this argumentation. He feels that there is set a clear opposition between two things, and yet that a unity is aimed at. Thought and existence are set apart, but the right of passing from one to the other is claimed. He will therefore not be surprised to find that for five hundred years not a single cordial and whole-hearted welcome was accorded to this method of Theistic proof by any thinker, in the front rank at least, although the impressiveness of its aim was such that it never passed out of view. By Descartes it was again placed in the front, whether spontaneously or by revival of Anselm's endeavour is uncertain. After Descartes it received prominent notice, usually to be rejected, sometimes to be treated with a deference which remained otiose (*see* Caldecott, *Philosophy of Religion*, pp. 28, 139). But Wolf, who had great influence over academic philosophy and theology in Germany, incorporated it with the cosmological and teleological arguments into the "Three Proof System" which Kant found in vogue. Kant (*see* Selection VII.) severely criticised it, but discerned its intention, and acknowledged that in the Three Proof System it was indispensable, and was indeed the keystone. Hegel set in clear light the distinction between the aim and the form of the argument—"the content was right, but the form defective"; if Anselm and Descartes were trying to pass from thought to existence, they were open to hostile assault: but for Hegel the true position was that in God, in the Infinite or the Absolute, this opposition is transcended by unity; and it is this which is the true ultimate, and this at which Anselm and Descartes were aiming, and he praised them for bringing into clear consciousness this highest of oppositions, and trying to unite them. This view is endorsed by the modern Spiritualist school in France. The distinction between aim and method of proof must be kept in view in considering any judgment passed upon the Ontological argument, *e.g.*, in passing from Ueberweg's summary condemnation to Erdmann's approval. Lotze's characteristic attitude is manifested in his replacing the attempt at logical proof by reference to the immediate certainty of "living feeling," to the inner experiences which declare it to be "intolerable" to believe that our ideal perfection is "an idea produced by the action of thought, but without existence, power, or validity in the sphere of reality" (*Microcosmus*, IX. c. iv.). Dr. E. Caird's estimate (*Journal of Theological Studies*, vol. i. No. 1) amounts to a pronouncement that Anselm's thought is in its essence on a line with that of Platonism, the Christian doctrine of the Logos, and Hegelianism,—a line of summit peaks indeed.

References.—Our translation is from Gerberon's Paris edition of 1721, compared with Migne's revised text. Expositions and criticisms of Anselm's argument are given in nearly all histories and philosophies of Theism. Special attention may be advised to E. Caird (above cited), Pringle-Pattison, C. C. J. Webb, and A. A. Cock (article in Aristotelian Society's *Proceedings* for 1917).

II.

SOME POINTS IN SCHOLASTIC THEOLOGY.

FROM THOMAS AQUINAS (1227–1274).

MODERN philosophy of Religion has characters of its own, but no one living in the atmosphere of the twentieth century is likely to suppose that it started *ex vacuo* with the Renaissance. The leaders of the new philosophies—Bacon, Descartes, Spinoza, Locke—do, indeed, make protestations of being adventurers on untried lines, and seem to have worked under an exaggerated estimate of the novelty of their procedure. But the lines on which they had been nurtured soon became evident in various strands which run through the fabric of their thinking; even on the philosophical side we can look back for origins. If this is so for the innovators in philosophy, it is obvious that for the Reformers in Church doctrine and Church order, absorbed as they were in these problems, the results of previous philosophy of religion would continue to suffice; and it did so, until the stress of conflict as to doctrine and organisation was relaxed, and leisure began to be found by Churchmen for taking account of what was being said in philosophy. So that for theologians, both Romanist and Protestant, the mediæval results of religious philosophy ran on for some time without important modification, and in the new field of philosophical speculation these results continued to have important influence. Far from regarding Scholasticism as a by-path, we take it to be on the main line of European thought, and some direct acquaintance with it not to be foregone by the student in search of first-hand knowledge all round.

From amongst the Schoolmen there need be no hesitation, apart from the interesting Anselmic speculation, in selecting the system of Thomas Aquinas. A superficial reason for doing this is obvious in the fact that it was the system which had found its way to official recognition by the Roman See before Western Christendom became divided, and it was therefore dominant in the Schools and Universities in which both the Reformers and the new philosophers were educated. But there is no good ground for regarding this recognition as due to any other source than a straightforward and honest interpretation on the part of the Curia of Rome. The theory of both Conciliar and Papal decisions need not be gainsaid, namely, that they did not create doctrine, but formulated what competent men were thinking; they were not dictating to the Christian community, but exhibiting to it its own mind. In selecting the system of Aquinas, both for exposition of Christian dogmas and for philosophy of religion, the official recognition may be taken to signify that his was the method which the Christian community of Western Europe found most congenial. It was the most comprehensive of them all; more elements entered into it; it appropriated previous thought from more sides than any other did. There was the central line of its Peripatetic Aristotelianism, but there were also Platonic features derived from Augustine, and even Neo-Platonic features from Dionysius. And also for its central factor, its Aristotelianism, a claim can fairly be made when we look back over the course of the centuries between the Athenian Schools and the rise of modern speculation, that it presented the most readily appreciated intellectual instrument for general employment, within the sphere of Latin Christianity at least. Hence, although we might usefully set out typical passages from Duns Scotus to illustrate Theism based philosophically on the Will, or from Bonaventura for a Mystical Philosophy, or from William of Ockham for Scepticism as to Reason and withdrawal of religion within the confines of positive Revelation, we offer as the most useful for historical study some select points from the system of Thomas Aquinas.

Thomas was an Italian, but he does not in any special sense represent Italy. The great Orders knew no national limits, and Thomas was a Dominican. He passed from the School of Naples to those of Cologne and Paris, and his most influential teacher was a German, Albertus Magnus, who had himself studied at Padua and Bologna. From Albertus, whom some competent judges regard as the master

in more than a pædagogic sense, Thomas learned to use
Aristotle, chiefly in the *Physics* and *Metaphysics* ; and he
acquiesced in allowing to the great Greek the title of " the
Philosopher," *par excellence.*   Thomas wrote commentaries on
Scripture, and various monographs, and then his systematic
intellect was concentrated on the presentation of a single
system of Theology and Philosophy ; this appeared in two
forms—(i.) *De Veritate Fidei Catholicæ contra Gentiles* (1261–
64) (usually referred to as the *Summa contra Gentiles*) ; and
(ii.) the great *Summa Theologica,* which he did not live to
finish.

The topics on which selections are given are—(i.) Reason
and Faith ; (ii.) Canons of Predication in reference to God ;
(iii.) the Demonstration of the Existence of God ; (iv.) Personality of God ; and (v.) Evil, in relation to God.

§ 1. REASON AND FAITH.

(From *Summa contra Gentiles*, Bk. I. c. iii.)

IN THOSE THINGS WHICH WE ASSERT OF GOD, THE WAY OF TRUTH IS TWOFOLD.[1]

Since all ways in which truth is manifested are not
identical, but " it belongs to the man of learning to
endeavour to secure faith in each case only in so far as the
nature of the case admits," as the Philosopher has well said

---

[1] The first recognition of a twofold way of truth for religion, as
either Natural or Revealed, of which the later Mediæval Schools made
so much use, cannot be traced ; but it so obviously expresses the
situation in which Christian thinkers found themselves that we feel
that it was inevitable that the distinction should be brought to the
front when it was.   Albertus, as the first who had to grapple with the
metaphysical works of Aristotle unaccommodated to Christian use,
was perhaps the first to see clearly that some Christian doctrines must
be withdrawn from Aristotle's range and placed in a sphere of their
own.   The same situation had, however, already become clear to the
Jewish Aristotelian, Maimonides (d. 1204), whom it is known that
Albertus studied ; and also to the Arabian philosophers, especially to
Averroës (d. 1198), who had to deal with the not very congruent subjects

(*Ethica*, ɪ. c. 2),[2] and as Boetius also brings before us (*De Trin.* c. 2),[3] our first need is to show which way is applicable to the manifestation of the truth we are dealing with.

In those things which we assert of God, the way of truth is twofold. For there are things true of God which surpass every faculty of human reason—that He is three (*trinus*) and one, for example. But there are others which are within the scope of natural reason, such as, that He exists, that He is one, and others of that kind; these have been demonstratively proved by philosophers, following the light of natural reason. It is quite clear that among the things which can be known about God some wholly exceed the grasp of human reason.[4] The first principle of the whole of the knowledge

of Aristotelianism and Islam. It may here be noted that in thinking of Revealed Religion the Schoolmen had in view both Islam and the Greco-Roman religion, and that within that sphere they had to distinguish Christianity from these : in most of them the distinction adopted was simply that between true and false claimants to the title. Cf. Jastrow, *Study of Religion*, and Illingworth, *Reason and Revelation*.

It is frequently supposed that when Faith and Reason come into conflict, Aquinas, whether purposively or not, invariably imposed sacrifices upon Reason alone. This cannot be proved : for there are important points on which theologians feel that the sacrifice was imposed upon theology. And in cases where both could run together, it can be shown that Reason had the leading part.

[2] The Philosopher.—The unqualified appropriation of the term to Aristotle is a mark of the character of what this School understood by philosophy or reason in the main.

[3] Boetius or Boethius (470–525), a Neo-Platonist himself, became by means of his translations of the Logical writings the best-known medium of Aristotle before direct access to his other works was recovered.

[4] The doctrines which Aquinas passed over to the region of Faith were those of the Holy Trinity, the Incarnation and Redemption, Sin, the Resurrection of the flesh (he held from Plato the *natural* immortality of the soul, and tried to read it into Aristotle), the last Judgment, the Church and its Sacraments. Duns Scotus added the Beginning of the World and the Immortality of the Soul ; William of Ockham carried over the whole of Theism, and, indeed, Ethics as well.

which reason gains concerning anything is the understanding
of the substance of that thing, because, as the Philosopher
teaches, a demonstration should begin with *what a thing is*;
it is necessary, therefore, that the measure of understanding
the substance of a thing, should be the measure of all that
is known about that thing.   Wherefore, if human intelligence
grasps the substance of a thing, say, of a stone or a triangle,
nothing which can be understood about that thing will be
beyond the scope of human reason.   But this is certainly
not our case in the things concerning the Deity.   For
human intelligence cannot by its natural strength achieve
the apprehension of His substance, because in our intelligence,
according to the manner of our present life, cognition begins
with data of the senses.   Those things, therefore, which do
not fall within the range of the senses cannot be apprehended by human intelligence, except in so far as cognition
of them is gathered from the data of our senses.[5]   But
things of sense cannot lead our intelligence to the point of
seeing in them what the Divine Substance really is (*quid sit*),
since they are effects which only inadequately manifest their
cause.   Our intelligence, however, is led from things of sense
into Divine knowledge, to the extent of knowing that God is
(*quia est*), and other things of that kind, such as are rightly
attributed to the first principle of all things.   There are therefore

[5] The dependence of human intellect on sense-knowledge was not
waiting for Hobbes and Locke to proclaim it; what they did was to
assert it against an exaggerated Intellectualism, and, in Hobbes' case
at any rate, to carry it forward to a similar exaggeration.   In so doing
they were repeating what the degenerate Peripatetics had done before
them.   It is this modified reference of our knowledge to the humble
materials of our sense-experiences which determines Aquinas upon his
opposition to metaphysical Ontologism and his claim for a region of
Faith.   But Aquinas held that it was only materials which the
senses supply: they are only passive; the intellect is active, and by
that activity perceives these sense-data, forms them into images, and
finally constructs from them universal notions.

some things knowable about God which are open to human reason, but there are others which wholly surpass its power.

Further, the same result is apparent when we consider the gradations of things intelligible. For of two men, of whom one has intelligence capable of perceiving things more subtilely than the other can do, the one whose intelligence is more lofty understands many things which the other cannot in any way grasp. A rustic, for example, can in no way grasp the refined points of philosophy. Again, the intelligence of an angel excels the intelligence of man more than the intelligence of the best of philosophers excels that of the least uneducated person; for the latter difference lies within the range of the human race, whereas angelic intelligence lies altogether beyond it. An angel, indeed, knows God from the consideration of effects of a nobler order than those open to man, by so much as the substance of the angel, by which he is led to know God by natural knowledge, is superior to the things of sense, and even to the soul itself, which form the means by which human intelligence attains to the knowledge of God. And the Divine intelligence surpasses that of angels even more than the angelic intelligence surpasses that of man. For the Divine intelligence by its capacity is adequate to the Divine substance, and therefore God understands perfectly what He is Himself, and knows everything which can be understood about Himself. But an angel cannot know what God is, by natural knowledge, because his own substance, by which he is led to such knowledge, is an effect inferior to the power which has brought him into being. Therefore it is not everything which God understands of Himself that an angel can grasp by natural knowledge, nor can human reason suffice to apprehend everything which lies within the scope of the natural knowledge of an angel. As therefore it would be a sign of the greatest madness for an uneducated man to assert those things to be false which are put forward by the

Philosopher, simply because he himself cannot grasp them; so, and much more, would a man be at the height of folly to suspect as false the things revealed by the ministration of angels, simply because they cannot be fathomed by human reason.[6]

Further, the same conclusion follows from the deficiency we daily find in our way of knowing things. We are ignorant of most of the properties of the things of sense, and cannot find a complete reason, in most cases, for the properties we have ascertained. Much more, therefore, is reason an inadequate instrument of inquiry into that most excellent substance which surpasses all objects intelligible to man. The saying of the Philosopher endorses this when he asserts that "our intelligence is related to the highest among beings which are most manifest in nature, as the eye of the bat is related to the sun" (*Met.* ii. i.).[7]

Holy Scripture brings its testimony to this truth. For it says, "Can you, forsooth, comprehend the traces of God and discover the omnipotent to perfection?" (Job xi. 7); and, "Behold, God is great, overcoming our knowledge" (xxxvi. 26); and "We know in part" (1 Cor. xiii. 9).[8] We must

[6] Here it may be supposed that we have some of the vain speculations which have caused prejudice against Scholastic writings; a few words may be of service. Aquinas in his treatment of Angelology resorts as much to Dionysius as in his Physics to Aristotle. But it is no idle part that these speculations play in the thought of Aquinas, and he ought not to be condemned by those who adopt Evolution as a comprehensive conception. For he held to development in the sphere of mind, and indeed, in a subtle way of his own, even as between matter and mind; and it was natural that he should at times speculate on what might be conceived to be the modes of mental life in beings of a higher grade than that of the human race.

[7] This is another reason for believing in beings endowed with intellectual faculty, arising from our own confinement to sense-given data.

[8] The method of the *Contra Gentiles* of clenching the argument with Scriptural confirmation by means of single texts, detached and uncriticised, shows that this method was no invention of post-Reformation preachers, as is sometimes supposed.

not, therefore, with the Manicheans and some infidels, reject as false everything which is spoken of God, although it cannot be fathomed by our reason.

In chap. iv. Aquinas gives some considerations for the need for religious truths, even of the demonstrable order, being accessible to ordinary men otherwise than by study and reflection; and in chap. vii. he explains his position that the truths obtained by Reason are not contrary to those offered to Faith by Christian Revelation (in opposition to the Arabic admission that contrariety was possible between truth of reason and truth of faith).

(*Summa contra Gentiles*, Bk. i. c. vii.)

THAT THE TRUTH OF REASON IS NOT OPPOSED TO THE TRUTH OF THE CHRISTIAN FAITH.

Although the truth of the Christian Faith surpasses the capacity of human reason, yet those things which reason has inherently in possession cannot be contrary to the Christian truth.

For those things which are naturally inherent in reason are most true, in so much that they cannot even be supposed false; nor, on the other hand, is it right to suppose false what we hold by faith on the strength of Divine confirmation. It is only the false which is contrary to the true, as is obvious when we consider their definitions : it is, therefore, impossible for a truth of the faith to be contrary to those principles which reason knows by nature.

Also, anything which passes into a learner's mind from a teacher is contained within the knowledge of that teacher, unless he is teaching fictions—which it is impious to suppose of God. Now the knowledge of principles naturally known by us has been divinely implanted, for God Himself is the Author of our nature. Therefore those principles are included within Divine Wisdom. Anything which is contrary to such principles must therefore be contrary to Divine Wisdom, and cannot be from God. Therefore the things which

2

we hold through faith, by Divine revelation, cannot be contrary to natural knowledge.

Further, if reasons oppose one another, our intelligence is fettered, and cannot move on to the knowledge of truth. Should opposing cognitions be sent to us by God, our intelligence would be hindered from obtaining knowledge of the truth : this could not proceed from God.

Still further, things which are natural cannot be changed so long as nature remains.   But contrary opinions cannot at the same time be in the same mind.   Therefore, no opinion or faith is sent by God against natural knowledge.   And therefore the Apostle says, "The word is near thee, in thy heart and in thy mouth ; that is, the word of faith which we preach" (Rom. x. 8).   But because faith surpasses reason it is taken by some to be contrary to it, which it cannot be. The authority of Augustine endorses this, who in the second book of his *Super Genesim ad literam* (c. xviii.) says, " What truth makes clear can in no way be contrary to the sacred books either of the Old Testament or the New."

From which it is plainly gathered that whatever arguments are set against the documents of the Faith cannot issue from first principles planted in our nature and known of themselves.   They cannot have the force of demonstration either, but are either probabilities only or sophistries, and so are susceptible of explanation.

In chap. viii. he adds a commendation of the employment of Reason by the religious mind.   In the sphere of natural knowledge we shall find, he says, *vestigia, similitudines* ; it is itself a beneficial exercise for our mind ; and it is also a source of great delight—what we may note as a testimony to the happiness experienced in the pursuit of knowledge by one of the greatest intellects of our race.   Here, too, we may again notice his resolute adoption of *order* and *system* ; for him, Natural Knowledge cannot be disconnected from Revealed ; it can be employed as material to which Revealed truths give form,

§ 2. THE KINDS OF KNOWLEDGE OF DIVINE THINGS.

Passing from the distinction between things of Faith and things of Reason or Knowledge, Aquinas proceeds to formulate distinctions *within* the region of Knowledge. In this he maintains his general allegiance to the Peripatetic principle that all "knowledge" is through things of Sense, and not absolute; but he applies it to the theological problem on the lines of a remarkable book of the fifth century which specially deals with theological knowledge, the *De Divinis Nominibus*, ascribed, with manifest inappropriateness, to Dionysius the Areopagite, of Acts xvii. 34. The work is a fifth-century production reflecting Neo-Platonism: with the other writings of the same unknown author it was a favourite with Mystics of the Middle Ages; and Aquinas had derived some modifying influence from it upon his own mainly Peripatetic mode of thought.

(*Summa contra Gentiles*, Bk. i. c. xxx.)

WHAT NAMES MAY BE PREDICATED OF GOD.

We can consider what may be said of God, and what may not be said; and of the former class, what may be said of Him alone, and what of Him and other things also.[9]

For since it is possible to find in God every perfection of the creature, but in another and more excellent manner, whatever names denote perfection absolutely and without defect are predicated of God and of other things also, such as goodness, wisdom, being, and others of that kind. But whatever names denote perfection in a manner peculiar to

[9] The threefold division is important : *non dicenda de Deo*, such as courage, which implies liability to danger and the overcoming of fear ; *dicenda de Deo solo, e.g.* self-existence, eternity ; and *dicenda de Deo et de aliis rebus, e.g.* (1) such qualities as wisdom, which is attributable to both man and God though in different degrees ; and (2) such as are predicable of Him only after the way of analogy or metaphor, *e.g.* hearing, sitting upon His throne.

created things cannot be said of God, except by way of
metaphor and similitude, according to which predicates true
of one thing are usually adapted to some other thing; as
when a man is called a stone, on account of the hardness
of his intellect. Of this class are all names imposed for
the purpose of designating a species of created being, as
man and *stone*; for to each species there is due its own
mode of perfection and being. Similarly also, whatever
names designate the properties of things such as are caused
by the principles proper to their species can only be spoken
of God by metaphor. But names which express perfections
of this kind in a more excellent manner, by which they are
appropriate to God, are spoken of God alone; such as the
summum bonum, the first Being, and others of that kind.
I say, further, that some of these names imply perfection
without defect so far as concerns that which the name was
intended to signify; but, so far as concerns the mode of
signification, every name is defective, for by a name we express
a thing in the way in which we grasp it by our intelligence.
. . . Names of this kind can therefore, as Dionysius (*De
Divinis Nominibus*, cc. i. and v.) teaches, be affirmed and
denied of God. They may be affirmed by reference to the
purpose of the name; they may be denied by reference to
the mode of signification. Moreover, the mode of super-
eminence in which such perfections are found in God cannot
be signified by the names imposed by us except either by
negation, as when we say that God is eternal or infinite;
or by relation between Him and other things, as when He
is called the First Cause or the highest Good. For we cannot
grasp what God is, but only what He is not, and how other
things are related to Him, as is obvious from what has been
said above.[10]

[10] Aquinas's class of *dicenda de Deo solo* does not rise to the lofty
range of knowledge claimed by philosophies of the Absolute. His
allegiance to Peripateticism, with its lowly origin in sense-data

(From *Summa Theologica*, Part I. Quæst. xiii., *De Nominibus Dei*, Art 5.)

.   .   .   .

It is impossible that anything can be predicated of God and of created beings in the same sense (*univocè*).[11] For every effect, since it has not an equal value with its cause, takes the likeness of the cause, not adequately, but in a defective manner. So that what is divided and multiple in the effects is simple in the cause and in one mode only; for example, the sun from one single power of its own produces manifold and various forms in things. In the same way, all the perfections of things which are in

prevents his allowing any claim for knowledge of God *per se* : it is at its best *per creaturas* : hence his opposition to Anselm's Ontological argument, for instance. But even in the sphere of knowledge which starts with sense-given data, there is a region in which there are attributes proper to the Deity, only these are not absolute ; they are, as he says in the above extract, either negative of creature-attributes, or relative to them. This position marks out Aquinas as occupying the middle position between the Sceptics on the extreme left hand, and the Mystics and speculative Rationalists on the extreme right. In determining his position Aquinas mediated between the Neo-Platonism of the pseudo-Dionysius (whose work *de Nominibus* was before him), and such Aristotelianism as was known to him.

From the *dicenda de Deo et de aliis rebus*, Aquinas proceeds to bring out the use of analogy and metaphor, protesting against insistence upon identity of meaning with as much force as against absence of meaning. By retaining this class, in this sense, Aquinas guards himself against the peril of the relapse into silence which, on his theory of knowledge, awaits those who deny any function for analogy or metaphor in thinking about the Deity.

[11] *Univocè*, that is, when a word is used with an identical significance in all its applications ; *æquivocè*, without any bond or connection between the meanings (*e.g.* a *pen* of sheep and a quill *pen*) ; and *analogicè*, when there is a ground of comparison amid differences (*e.g.* the *tide* of passion) ; if the ground is very slight we have *metaphoricè* (*e.g.* the *wings* of imagination).

them in division and in multiplicity, pre-exist in God in
unity and simplicity. . . . And so, when the word *wise* is
spoken of a man, it in a certain way circumscribes and grasps
the thing signified; but it is not so when it is spoken of
God : in His case it leaves the subject spoken of ungrasped
and surpassing the signification of the name. So that it is
clear that the word *wise* is not spoken in the same way
of man and of God. And so for other names. No name,
therefore, is used in the same sense of God and of created
beings.

And yet it is not used in entirely different senses, as some
have maintained. For if this were so, nothing could possibly
be known or demonstrated of God from observation of created
beings without incurring the fallacy of equivocation. And
it would be as much against the Philosopher who proves
many things demonstratively concerning God (*Phys.* viii.
and *Met.* xii.), as against the Apostle who says (*Rom.* i. 20),
" The invisible things of God are rendered intelligible by means
of those things which have been made." We must reply,
therefore, that names of this kind are applied to God and
to created things, according to analogy, that is, proportion.

.   .   .   .

Some things are spoken of God and the creature, therefore,
neither in entirely different senses, nor in entirely the same
sense, but analogically. We have shown (in Art. I.), that we
cannot name God except by means of predicates drawn from
His creatures; and thus whatever is said both of God and
His creatures is said inasmuch as there is some relation
between the creature and God as its principle and cause,
in whom there pre-exist, in a more excellent manner, all the
perfections of things.

This method of treatment guides the official Natural
Theology of the Roman Church. It has enabled those trained
in her schools to regard with some complacency those whose
perplexities have obviously been due to attempts to force all

predications within a single category, whether with sceptical results or with positive results of a partial character and therefore a precarious tenure.

§ 3. THE DEMONSTRATIVE PROOFS.

Aquinas opposes the claim for direct or intuitive knowledge of the Deity apart from Faith : He cannot by natural light of Reason be known *per se*. He examines and rejects the claim for innate ideas as made by John Damascene, and the Onto- logical argument of Anselm, himself resting on Aristotle and on St. Paul (Rom. i. 20), and on his theory of knowledge generally. But, on the other hand, against those who make even the existence of the Deity a matter of Faith, he insists on its demonstrability by inference upwards ; the relation to Faith being that the Divine existence, made known by means of natural reason, gives not *articuli fidei sed prœambula ad articulos*. His demonstrative proofs are thus given :—

(*Summa Theologica*, Pt. I. Quæst. ii. *An Deus sit ?* Art. 3).

That God exists can be proved in five Ways :—

1. The first and most evident Way is the argument from Motion.[12] For it is certain and agrees with what our senses inform us that in this world some things are in motion. But anything which is moved, is moved by some other thing ; for nothing is moved except in so far as there is in it the

[12] This is Aristotle's famous proof of the First Mover (*Physics*, Bk. VIII., and *Metaphysics*, Bk. XI.). *Motus* is the term used, the κίνησις of Aristotle. It is of wider significance for both Aristotle and Aquinas than merely change of place. It signifies the coming from potentiality into actuality, mediating between δύναμις and ἐνεργεία. Aristotle has four kinds of change : of substance, by genera- tion and decay ; of quantity, by increase or decrease ; of quality, by "passion" ; of change of place (*Metaphysics*, XI. (or XII.) c. 2 : the last three are the three possible kinds of motion. We have had it confirmed by Newton in the sphere of motion that motion continues as it is and rest continues as it is, unless a cause of change is intro- duced : so in everything. How could the potential become actual of itself ?

relation of potentiality with that towards which it is moved but one thing moves another in so far as the former is in actuality, for to move is nothing else than to draw anything from potentiality into actuality. But nothing can be brought from potentiality into actuality except by means of something which is already in actuality. Fire which is actual heat makes wood which is only potentially hot become actually hot, and by this means moves and alters it. Moreover, it is impossible for the same thing to be in potentiality and in actuality at the same time and in the same respect; it could be so only in different respects; for what is actually hot cannot be at the same time potentially hot, although it is at the same time potentially cold. It is impossible, therefore, that in the same respect and in the same manner anything should be both moving and moved, or be self-moved. Everything therefore which is moved must be moved by something else. If therefore that by which the first thing is moved should itself be moved this must be by motion from some third thing, and that third thing by some other in its turn. We cannot here proceed to infinity, for in that way there would be no first source of movement and consequently no other moving thing at all, because secondary moving things do not move except as they are moved by the first source of movement; a stick, for example, does not move except it is moved by a hand. We must then arrive at some first source of motion which is moved by nothing else : and such a source all men understand to be God.[13]

[13] As Aquinas puts it, we see that his argument lies open to the charge that it gives only that inference to a First Cause which is now known as "Deism." He reaches only an initial Cause and does not bring out permanence of operations. Aristotle was for permanence, because his *datum* was eternity of motion, the maintenance of a world in actuality which would fall into mere potentiality but for the permanent Cause. But the doctrine of Creation *ex nihilo* had been taken as necessary for concordance with Biblical doctrine since Augustine in the Christian Schools, (as it was also in the Jewish Schools, cf. Mai-

2. The second Way is from consideration of efficient Causes. In things of sense we find an order of efficient causes; but it is not found, nor is it possible, that anything is the cause of itself, for this would mean that it is prior to itself, which is impossible. Finally, it is not possible in efficient causes to go back to infinity, for in all series of efficient causes first comes the cause of the intermediate, and the intermediate is the cause of the last whether the intermediate be many or only one. If then the Cause is removed so is the effect. Therefore, if there have not been a first among the efficient causes neither will there be a last, nor an intermediate. But if we proceed with efficient causes to infinity, there will be no first efficient cause, and so no last effect, nor any intermediate efficient causes; which is plainly false. We must therefore posit some first efficient Cause : and all men call this God.[14]

3. The third Way is taken from consideration of the possible and the necessary, and proceeds as follows. Amongst things we find some which are capable of existing or not existing, for they are found to be generated and to be corrupted, and therefore can either exist or not exist. It is impossible, however, that all the things of this kind should always be in existence, because what is capable of not existing, at some time does not exist. If, therefore, all things are capable of not existing, there was a time when there was nothing in existence. But if this is true, even now there would be

monides) and Aquinas made some attempt to twist Aristotle into meaning it. The prominence of this first method, by proving an originating Cause only, kept the doctrine of the Divine Immanence in the background in subsequent Natural Theology, until Spinoza and Malebranche inaugurated its revival. At the same time, this is only one of the five Ways of Aquinas, and his third, fourth, and fifth Ways imply immanent operation.

[14] This second argument for efficient Causes is simply the argument of Aristotle in his *Metaphysics*. Its limitation is of the same kind as that of the first argument.

nothing in existence, for the non-existent does not commence to exist except by virtue of some other thing which is already existing. If ever, therefore, there were nothing in exist-ence, it is impossible that anything should commence to exist : and so there would be nothing in existence now : which is obviously false. Therefore it cannot be that all things are merely capable of existing ; there must be among things some thing which is necessary.

Moreover, every necessary thing either has a cause of its necessity from some other quarter, or it has not. But it is not possible to proceed in infinity in things necessary which have a cause of their necessity, just as was proved for efficient causes. We must, therefore, posit something which has its necessity, not from some other quarter but *per se*; and which is itself a cause of necessity to other things. And this all men call God.[15]

4. The fourth Way is the consideration of the grades or stages which are found in things. For we find in things something more or less good and true and noble, and so or other qualities of this kind. But "more" or "less" are spoken of different things, according to their different degrees of approach to what is greatest of all : as that thing is the hotter which more nearly approaches that which is hottest. There is, therefore, something which is most true and most good and most noble, and consequently is being in the highest degree (*maxime ens*) : for what is true in the highest degree is also being in the highest degree, as is said in the *Meta-physics*, Bk. II. But whatever is called highest in any kind of being is the cause of all other things which are of that kind ; as fire, which is the highest of the class of hot things is the cause of all hot things, as is said in the same book.

[15] Some modern Romanist theologians, aware of the limitation to Deism involved in the first two arguments, lay most stress on this third, the argument from the Contingent to the Necessary, which provides for Immanence.

There is, therefore, some being which to all beings is the cause that they exist, and that they are good, and so for every perfection. And this we call God.[16]

5. The fifth Way is the consideration of the government (*gubernatio*) of things. For we see that some things which have no power of knowing, such as natural bodies, work for ends (*propter finem*), as is manifest from their constantly, or at least frequently, working in the same way for the attainment of that which is best; which shows that they arrive at their end not by chance but from intention. Now such things as have no power of knowing do not tend towards an end unless they are directed by some being which has know-

[16] For this Way Aquinas refers to Aristotle explicitly, but it comes really through Neo-Platonist commentators on Aristotle. It is suggested by the Platonic theory of Ideas, and was used by the Stoics and also by Augustine; Anselm, Abelard, and Alexander all employed it. It is the philosophy of Nature which regards all things as compacted of matter and form, and ranged in scale accordingly. For Theism the question is whether Reason can arrest its course without taking into cognisance pure Matter beyond the visible foot of the scale and pure Form beyond the visible summit. The affirmative answer to this would not imply a transcendent Theism only, for the theory relates every form to the proximate form below it in one direction, and to the proximate form above it in the other : so that there is profound significance in regarding the pure Form as itself the true formative principle from the lowest depth of nature to its highest height. If the several graduated forms are regarded as permanent we have, of course, the view of Nature which has prevailed in our recent pre-Evolution days. But loyal Thomists may repudiate that phase of thought, and claim that it is Evolution that is his fundamental view: indeed he himself states it, and states it apart from all the other arguments, in the Preface to Book IV. of the *S. c. Gentiles*, before entering upon the doctrine of God as Holy Trinity.

In future Theism the purport of this *Via*, therefore, will fulfil a function more prominent than could be the case when Nature was regarded as a congeries of disconnected and independently created species of being : and the character of the Theism arrived at will be the more profound in consequence. Cf. Bradley, *Appearance and Reality*, c. xxiv. (Degrees of Truth and Reality), who here acknowledges special debt to Hegel; and G. T. Ladd, *A Theory of Reality*, c. xv. (Spheres of Reality).

ledge and intelligence, as an arrow is directed by an archer.
There is therefore some intelligent Being by which all natural
things are directed towards ends.   And this we call God.[17]

§ 4. PERSONALITY OF GOD.

not a very good title)

We shall not expect to find in Aquinas the full conception
of Personality, either human or Divine, to which the nineteenth century attained, but we can see that he secures much of
it if he proves that to the Supreme Being we must attribute
Intelligence, Will, Goodness, and Happiness.   This is as far
as he takes Natural Theology : he remits the farther exposition to Revealed Theology, where he treats of the doctrine of
the Holy Trinity, and where alone he uses the term " Person."
For Intelligence he gives seven arguments, of which we
print five.

(*Summa contra Gentiles*, c. 44.)

INTELLIGENCE.

Argument 2. Intelligence must be attributed to the Deity
if there is to be a reference of things moveable, not only to
a first mover which moves itself, but to a mover which is
wholly unmoveable.   For the first mover is the universal
principle of motion.   Therefore, since everything that causes

---

[17] As here stated it seems scarcely the deeper teleology of immanence, but only the popular inference of an intelligent cause being
required to keep in regularity of action things which have no cognition
and therefore no view of ends and no intentions.

This may be thought a surprisingly meagre treatment for the great
teleological argument which had already been so forcibly expressed in both Greek and Latin literature.   And it is sometimes said
that the Schoolmen took little interest in this Proof, owing probably
to their cloistered life and remoteness from study of nature.   But it
may be pointed out that Aquinas at least knows what he is doing, and
does not look to Teleological argument for proof of existence, but for
proof of intelligence—all that he obtains here is *aliquid intelligens*,
which alone would not describe God.   The argument is made prominent for this purpose in the proof of intelligence (*see* p. 29).

motion does so by means of some form which it has in view when it sets up the motion, the form which the first mover has in view must be a universal form and a universal good. But universal forms cannot be found, except in intellect. The first mover, therefore—which is God—is intelligent.[18]

complicated argument.

cf vii.

Argument 3. Further. In no series of things which cause motion is it found that a thing which causes motion by means of intelligence is the instrument of a thing which causes motion apart from intelligence, but much the reverse. All things in the world which cause motion are referred to the prime mover—that is, God—as instruments to the principal agent. Since, therefore, we find in the world many things causing motion by means of intelligence, it is impossible that the first mover should be without intelligence. It is necessary, therefore, that God have intelligence.

Argument 5. Again. No perfection is lacking to God which may be found in any kind of being (as proved in chap. 28), although it does not follow from this that His nature is in any way composite (as shown in chap. 18). Now, among the perfections of things the most important of all is that a thing should be of the order of intellect, for by this it is itself all things in a certain way, having in itself the perfections of all things. God, therefore, has intelligence.

Argument 6. Moreover. Everything which aims at some end in a fixed way, either prescribes to itself that end, or finds that end prescribed to it by something else ; otherwise it would not aim at this end rather than at that. Now things in nature aim at fixed ends, for natural utilities are not obtained by chance, which of itself would only bring them about in rare instances, and by no means invariably, or even

---

[18] The Intelligence here proved is correlative to the universal Forms in which Aquinas believes. In Argument 7 (below) the procedure is parallel ; the datum there is particularised forms, from which we pass upward to pure forms, and therefore to an Intelligence to which pure Forms are proper.

in many cases.   Since, therefore, things do not prescribe them
selves an end, the end must be set before them by another,
who is the founder of nature.   But this (by chaps. 13 and 37)
is He who gives being to all things, and is of Himself necessary
being : whom we call God.   Now He could not prescribe an
end to nature unless He understood.   God, therefore, has
intelligence.[19]

Argument 7.   Further.   Everything imperfect is derived
from something which is perfect ; for perfect things are
naturally prior to the imperfect, as actuality is to potentiality.   But the forms existing in particular things are
imperfect because they are particularised and have not all
the perfection of the universal form.   They must therefore
be derived from some forms which are perfect and not
particularised.   But such forms can only be of an intellectual
order, for no form is found in its universal scope except in
the intellect : consequently these must be intellectual if they
are substantial, as they must be in order to be operative.
Therefore it is necessary that God, who is the first substantial
source of action from which all other things are derived,
have intelligence.[20]

On Will.

Will, with Aquinas, has a more exclusive relation
to Intellect than much modern treatment assigns to it.

---

[19] This is an employment of the Teleological argument.   Although
he has also included it as a distinct " Way " of proving the *existence*
of the Deity (see p. 27), we noted how little he had to say of it in
that connection.   But here it avails as an argument for certain
conclusions as to the *nature* of the Deity.   That this latter is its
proper function is now a commonplace of Theism.

[20] These arguments for Intelligence exemplify the now familiar
method of demonstrating Personal Theism.   The Causal connexion
having been established, whatever is seen to be in the effect
must be included in the Cause : and as perfection is a character of the
Cause, all that is carried up is elevated to perfection, *via eminentiœ.*

For him, Will is the acceptance by the mind of what is presented by Intellect, and it is contrasted with Appetite, which is similarly related to Sensibility. It is *Appetitus intellectivus*: the *bonitas* is presented by Intellect, and what Will has to do is (1) to accept this, and (2) to initiate action. Sometimes it seems as if he meant what is more like Feeling, simply a something arising spontaneously when Intellect presents an object; but this is not his fundamental position, he has separate functions for Will and Feeling. The close attachment of Will to Intellect differentiated Aquinas from Duns Scotus, whose advocacy of the primacy of Will made him the precursor of the Voluntarists and Pragmatists of the present time.

(*Summa contra Gentiles* c. 72.)

GOD HAS WILL.

Argument 1. From the fact that He has intelligence it follows that He has Will. For since a good apprehended by the intellect is the proper object of the will, it is necessary that the good so apprehended be willed, in so far as it is of this character: but the term "apprehended by the intellect" is used in reference to an intelligent being: it must therefore be that a being that understands good, in so far as it is of this character, is endowed with will. But God understands good: for since He is intelligent in perfection, as has been proved, He understands being in its relationship to good. He therefore has Will.

Argument 4. To understand is a source of delight in proportion to its degree of perfection. But God understands, and with the highest degree of perfection (as shown before, c. 44). With Him, therefore, understanding is at the height of delight. But a delight for the understanding comes by means of the will, just as a delight for the senses comes through appetite. In God, therefore, there is Will.

Argument 5. A form, when presented to the mind by means of the intellect, does not move anything or cause anything except by the mediation of a will directed to an end and a good, by which someone is moved to act : therefore the speculative intellect does not initiate motion, nor does the pure imagination, apart from the valuation of good and ill. But the form of the Divine intellect is a cause of motion and of existence in other things, for He acts upon things by means of intelligence (as will be shown later on). He must therefore have Will.

Argument 6. Also it is in virtues which are active and have intelligence that Will is first found : for Will applies every potentiality to its own act. For we understand because we exercise will, we imagine because we exercise will, and so of other things. And it has this effect because its object is an end, although the intelligence moves the will not after the manner of an efficient and moving cause, but after the manner of a final cause, by setting before Will its object, which is an end. Therefore it is especially fitting that the First Mover have Will.

Argument 7. A thing is free which is the cause of itself (*sui causa*) ; and so a free thing has the character of that which is *per se*. But Will first has freedom in acting : for in so far as anyone acts voluntarily he is said to effect the action freely. It therefore specially belongs to the First Agent to act by way of Will, because it specially belongs to Him to act *per se*. . . .

After another Argument, the chapter closes with the usual scriptural confirmation.

The testimonies of Holy Scripture confirm this attribution of Will to the Divine Being : for it is said, " All things which the Lord hath willed hath He accomplished " (Ps. cxxxiv.) ; and " Who hath resisted His will ? " (Rom. ix.).[21]

---

[21] On the relation of Will to Intellect a battle-royal was waged in the Schools. Duns Scotus was the protagonist for the supremacy of Will : Indeterminism. How important the question at issue is for Theism is obvious : if Intellect is of inferior status, its claim to be

On Feeling.

Aquinas follows Aristotle in his treatment of Feeling. In so far as emotion is passive it belongs to our sensibility, which is in alliance with our body; in it our mind is determined from without, and therefore in this sense, as "passion," it is amongst the *non dicenda de Deo.* But emotions have a purely mental side — *formal* is the term, meaning formal in relation to the passive side as *material;* and with this distinction in view we must inquire again whether or not they are attributable to the Deity.

(*Summa Theologica,* Part I. Q. xx. c. 1.)
Is Love in the Deity?

Intellectual power does not cause motion except by the mediation of appetitive power, and as in us general Reason causes motion by the mediation of particular reason (as is said in *De Anima,* iii.), so the intellectual appetite which is called "Will" causes motion in us by the mediation of the sensitive appetite: therefore the proximate moving power over the body in us is the sensitive appetite. Wherefore some bodily change always accompanies an operation of the sensitive appetite, and especially some change in the region of the heart, which is the first principle of motion in an animal, as the Philosopher says (*De Partibus Animalium,* ii. and iii.).[22] So, therefore, operations of the sensitive appe-

referred to the Perfect Being lapses, or at least is weakened: and we are confronted with a doctrine of a supreme Indeterminate Will, and Divine Laws become Arbitrary Decrees. Aquinas attributes Will to the Divine Being, in its association with Intellect or Reason: for him Divine Laws are expressions of Divine Reason.

[22] This taking over of Aristotelian tradition as to the heart being the seat of bodily activity, illustrates, of course, the absence of recourse to investigations in the physical sciences, which is notorious in the Mediæval Schools. In psychological analyses what they received was of more enduring value, and they were in a position to carry them further by their own reflections. These brief extracts from Aquinas are only indications of how they handled psychological questions.

3

tite in so far as bodily changes are annexed to them are named "passions," but acts of the will are not so named. Love, therefore, and joy, and delight, are "passions" in so far as operations of the sensitive appetite are signified, but not in so far as operations of the intellectual appetite are meant: and it is in the latter way that they are found in God. Wherefore the Philosopher says (*Ethica*, VII.) that "God rejoices by a single and simple operation": and for the same reason He loves without "passion."

In the passions of the sensitive appetite we have to deal with something as it were material, namely, a bodily change, and something as it were formal, namely, that which springs from the appetite: *e.g.* in Anger (as is said in *De Anima*, I.), the material is the kindling of the blood around the heart, or something of that kind; but the formal is the appetite for vengeance. But, again, in some of these emotions on the side which is formal there is implied some imperfection, *e.g.* in Desire, which is for a good not in possession, and in Sadness, which is for an evil possessed: and the same is true of Anger, seeing that it implies Sadness. But some emotions imply no imperfection, *e.g.* Love and Joy. Since, therefore, none of the emotions can be predicated of God according to this material side, neither can those which imply imperfection on the formal side, except by metaphor, according to some similitude in their effect, as said above. But such emotions as do not imply imperfection are correctly referred to the Deity, *e.g.* Love and Joy; yet without "passion," as proved above.

The operation of Love always tends in two directions, namely, toward the good which is desired for some one, and toward the person for whom the good is desired. For, properly speaking, to love anyone is to desire good for him; therefore, in so far as anyone loves himself he desires good for himself, and so seeks to unite that good to himself, so far as he can. And so far Love is called a uniting power (*vis unitiva*), even in God; but without implying composition in Him, for that good which He desires for Himself is not anything else than Himself, who is good by His own essence, as above shown. But in so far as anyone loves another person he wishes good to him, and so deals with him as with himself, taking the good befalling the other person as if it befell himself. And so far Love is called a combining power (*vis concretiva*), because it draws another person to oneself, and one bears oneself towards him as towards one's own self. And so, also, Divine Love is a combining power—omitting all idea of composition in God—in that He wills good things to others.[23]

§ 5. EVIL IN RELATION TO GOD.

In default of space for showing how Aquinas treated either the Creation or the Government of the world (Cosmology), or the Nature of the Soul (Psychology), we add only his method of dealing with the question of Evil in relation to Theism.

He holds that all conscious activity has good in its aim ; evil cannot be willed : it is privative of good, and has neither independent reality nor a positive ground of being, and therefore it cannot be referred to an absolute principle. On the other hand, the Good is good *per se*, and not *ex institutione* ; and finite Good finds its necessary explanation in the perfect Goodness of the Perfect Being, in whose essence the *perseitas* of Goodness is grounded.

(*Summa contra Gentiles*, c. 39.)
THAT EVIL CANNOT BE IN GOD.

Being and goodness, and all things in which we refer to essence, have no admixture of anything from outside them-

---

[23] The references to the Good in the foregoing arguments amount to an anticipation of the Moral argument which has since been drawn apart and exhibited in independence (see, especially, the Selections from Kant and Martineau). Even in modern treatises on Natural Theology composed on Thomist lines, this argument is not set out as an independent one : and the term "Moral Argument" is allotted to the argument from Consensus.

selves, although that which is good may have something besides its being and its goodness. For there is nothing to prevent that which underlies one perfection from underlying another perfection also, as a body may be both white and sweet. But everything is enclosed within the confines of its own nature (*ratio*), so that it can take nothing extraneous into itself. But God is not only good but Goodness (as shown in chapters 37, 38). There cannot, therefore, be in Him anything which is not Goodness, and so Evil cannot possibly be in Him.[24]

Further, whatever is opposed to the essence of anything is incompatible with that essence while that essence remains : *e.g.* irrationality or insensibility is incompatible with a man unless he should cease to be a man. But the Divine essence is Goodness itself, as has been shown (c. 37). Evil, therefore, which is the opposite of the good, can have no place in Him; unless He should cease to be, which is impossible, since He is eternal, as before proved.

Again, since God is His own Being, nothing can be predicated of Him as though He participated in anything, as is evident from the foregoing reasoning (c. 38). If, therefore, Evil is predicated of Him, He will be said to possess it, not by participation, but by essence. But Evil can be predicated of nothing in such a way as to be its essence; for

---

[24] In chapter 37 it is shown that God is good by identifying goodness with perfection which had already been established as Divine ; goodness is a mark of Divinity as the highest object of desire and as the supreme reality, and as the universal Cause of being : in chapter 38, that God is His own goodness (1) as Himself the author of His own actuality, which is one of the marks of goodness ; (2) as Substance and therefore the source of His own goodness ; and (3) as Simplicity, and therefore good, not by participation in some other goodness than His own, but having goodness in His own essence. From these positions, the argumentation of chapter 39 follows by applying them to Evil as the privation and opposite of Goodness.

to such a thing being, which is good, would be lacking, as above proved (c. 37). And in Evil there cannot be anything intermixed from outside, just as in the case of goodness. Therefore Evil cannot be predicated of God.

Also, Evil is opposed to Good. But the nature or essence of Goodness consists in perfection ; the essence of Evil, therefore, is imperfection. But defect or imperfection cannot be in God, who is truly perfect, as above shown (c. 28). Therefore Evil cannot be in God.

Besides, anything is perfect according as it is actual; therefore, it will be imperfect according as it is deficient in actuality. Evil, therefore, is either privative, or it includes privation, or it is nothing. But that which is the subject of privation is only a potentiality, and potentiality cannot be in God ; therefore neither can Evil.

Moreover, if that is good which is desired by everything, therefore Evil, in so far as it is the undesirable, is what is avoided by every nature. But what is opposed to the operation of anyone's natural appetite, is violent and contrary to nature. Evil, therefore, is for each thing violent and contrary to its nature by reason of its being evil, although it may be natural to it according to some part of its composition, in things which are composite. But God is not composite, nor can anything in Him be violent or contrary to nature, as has been shown. Therefore Evil cannot be in God.

This is confirmed by Holy Scripture : for it is said, " God is light, and in Him is no darkness at all" (1 John i.) ; and, "Far be impiety from God, and iniquity from the Almighty" (Job xxxiv.).

As British students are so little accustomed to resort to the actual words of even the chief among the Scholastics, now that these two Selections are before them—brief as they are —a few words may be added on the general value of the Scholastic philosophy of Theism.

The Schoolmen were not philosophers at large in search of

beliefs; they were Christian theologians. For them the Scriptural and Ecclesiastical doctrine of Divine things was the possession of the Church of which they were members, and was accepted by their own faith. In their Dogmatics, or Supernatural Theology, they unfolded that doctrine; but first they looked into Nature by means of the Greek philosophy (as they knew it), which to them meant the natural light of reason, to see what could be found there and by what instrumentality. *An Deus sit?* meant for them not Does the God of Abraham exist? not Does God as Holy Trinity exist? but, Does the system of nature when explored, does reason when forced into explicitness, show a Divine Being? And if so, with what attributes? If not with all the richness of Christian Doctrine, then how far towards that richness? And similarly for the World, and for the Soul and Human Society.

We know quite well how particularist their philosophy was: that in the main line of Albert and Thomas Aquinas it was Aristotelianism, in part direct in part as passed to them by the Arabian philosophers, with more or less of Neo-Platonism through Dionysius and Augustine; and that on other lines, more of Platonism on one hand, or more of Scepticism on the other, was what they were working by. And their Christian theology had also its particularist limitations. Their task of combining the dogmata of faith and the deliverances of natural reason fell within these limits; and to that part of it which formed their Natural Theology the limits can be without difficulty assigned by the historian. But within these limits their work was of noble proportions. In raising their theologico-philosophical structures they were fellow workers with the architects of the great Gothic Cathedrals and Monastic Churches of that very age. And though Modern thought passed into fresh fields by rejecting considerable masses of their work, yet in such main issues as those indicated in our Selections, the rejections were much less extensive than is commonly supposed, and many of their leading thoughts persisted under new guises, and persist still. Allowing for particularisms, they stamped indelible features upon the philosophy of Theism, as the broad presentment of what the religious mind believes about God, and Nature, and the Soul. And though no absolute beginning for our study can be made at any point of the stream of thought, we feel confident that the student will endorse our decision to commence this set of Selections with Anselm and Aquinas.

References.—Both the *Summa contra Gentiles* and the *Summa Theologica* are included in the edition of S. Thomas's Works issued by Pope Leo XIII., with a prefatory Encyclical. From this edition the Fathers of the English Province of Dominicans made a translation (1911–22). There is also an English translation by J. Rickaby, S.J., under title, *Of God and His Creatures,* annotated (1905). Copies of old editions are procurable at second-hand booksellers' : the *Gentiles* for a few shillings, the great *Summa* for about two pounds. We mention this because few English students have ever seen either of these works of capital importance, and they suppose them to be inaccessible except in expensive folios.

The Scholastic Theology, as taught in Roman Catholic colleges, is developed in various directions to include important modern ideas, *e.g.* by Boedder and Rickaby, and M. C. D'Arcy, S.J., *Thomas Aquinas,* 1930, and notably by Cardinal Mercier. There are standard histories by Kleutgen, Stöckl, Hauréau, and de Wulf ; in English by H. O. Taylor, *The Medieval Mind* (1925), and W. H. V. Reade, *Philosophy in the Middle Ages* in the Cambridge Medieval History, vol. v. c. 23 (1926). P. H. Wicksteed's *Dante and Aquinas* (1913) is a guide to the literary aspect of scholasticism.

III.

THE EXISTENCE OF GOD.

DESCARTES (1596–1650).

IN Descartes we have a metaphysical Theism : the being of God a necessity as the ground of unity in a dualistic universe; the activity of God the source of the dual series of changes and of their interaction; or, in reference to knowledge, belief in God as the basis and guarantee for confidence in the validity of the thoughts of imperfect and finite thinking beings. In the *Meditations on First Philosophy*, including the Existence of God and the Immortality of the Soul, published in 1641 (æt. 45), we have an orderly exposition of the chief features of his system. In Meditations I. and II. he has doubted whether anything is more than a passing object in his mind until he came to his *Cogito ergo sum* : here he has been able to find a point where he could use the verb *esse*, could speak of existence. But how is advance to be made? In Meditation III. he is trying to discover what other existences or coexistences there are. The point of his philosophy is that he finds this in the existence of Deity. The thought of Deity has always been present to him; it has hovered in his mind as a possible source of deception even : so that his search takes the form of inquiring whether Deity exists; and if so, whether His existence can be a source of deception, or is a sure ground of certainty.

It is not possible to ascertain how much Descartes was influenced by Theology and how much his mind was philosophical *simpliciter*; but if we use philosophical terms we can put it that when he starts away from *Cogito* as the one sure intuition of the unity of thought and reality, he has no expectation of discovering further reality in the region of the finite, imperfect, or contingent : doubt is always possible there. His expectation of achieving anything lies in going direct to his consciousness of the Infinite and Perfect; if the unity of thought and reality is there also, much else may follow.

MEDITATION III.

OF GOD: THAT HE EXISTS.

I will now close my eyes, I will stop my ears, I will turn away my senses from their objects, I will even efface from my consciousness all the images of corporeal things; or at least, because this can hardly be accomplished, I will consider them as empty and false; and thus, holding converse only with myself, and closely examining my nature, I will endeavour to obtain by degrees a more intimate and familiar knowledge of myself.[1] I am a thinking (conscious) thing, that is, a being who doubts, affirms, denies, knows a few objects, and is ignorant of many,—[who loves, hates], wills, refuses, — who imagines likewise, and per-

---

[1] Descartes has doubted without reserve until he was arrested by the conviction of his own existence : his existence as a conscious being disclosed in every moment of consciousness : the thinker, the very doubter, exists while he thinks and doubts. Various interpretations of the *Cogito* are before the world. We commend to the reader the following :—

Descartes finds that *I am conscious involves I am* is a judgment which he makes at every moment whenever he turns his thought upon consciousness. It is not an inference, but a spontaneous judgment. But he sees in it far more than the momentary experience ; he sees in it a something which is universal ; not in the false sense, as if the universal lay side by side with the particular experiences, but in a penetrative sense, so to speak, as in them all. There is a *universale* (myself) *in rebus* (my experiences).

Here is a criterion for belief in existence secure against the powers of doubt. And it is existence in just the sense which *thought* requires. No individual fact, no mere datum of experience, but an intuition of a universal truth. Whatever belief can be linked to this, or better, can be seen to be involved in it, exists in the same high sense. This he proceeds to work out.

ceives;[2] for, as I before remarked, although the things
which I perceive or imagine are perhaps nothing at all apart
from me [and in themselves], I am nevertheless assured that
those modes of consciousness which I call perceptions and
imaginations, in as far only as they are modes of consciousness, exist in me. And in the little I have said I think I
have summed up all that I really know, or at least all that
up to this time I was aware I knew. Now, as I am
endeavouring to extend my knowledge more widely, I will
use circumspection, and consider with care whether I can
still discover in myself anything further which I have not
yet hitherto observed. I am certain that I am a thinking
thing; but do I not therefore likewise know what is required
to render me certain of a truth? In this first knowledge,
doubtless, there is nothing that gives me assurance of its
truth except the clear and distinct perception of what I
affirm, which would not indeed be sufficient to give me the
assurance that what I say is true, if it could ever happen
that anything I thus clearly and distinctly perceived should
prove false; and accordingly it seems to me that I may
now take as a general rule, that all that is very clearly and
distinctly apprehended (conceived) is true.

Nevertheless, I before received and admitted many things

[2] *Penser* with Descartes represents the whole sphere of consciousness, "all the operations of the will, intellect, imagination, and senses
are thoughts" (*Reply to Second Objections*). But in his view the
fundamental mode of consciousness is thinking,—the others are
subordinate, and he is not concerned to find a metaphysical or theological explanation for them as he is for thinking. It is, however,
to be observed that some French advocates of Voluntarism, which
makes Will and its cognates more fundamental than Intellect, consider that this runs back to Descartes. It may be so, but if it is, then
Descartes was misinterpreted by both friends and foes for two centuries. A refutation of this view of Descartes is given by L. Susan
Stebbing in *Pragmatism and French Voluntarism*, Girton College
Studies, No. VI. (1914), which also contains a criticism of Bergson's
position. The reader must refer to the whole works of Descartes if he
desires to follow that path : our selections bring out the Descartes
who impressed himself on succeeding historical development.

as wholly certain and manifest, which yet I afterwards found to be doubtful. What, then, were those? They were the earth, the sky, the stars, and all the other objects which I was in the habit of perceiving by the senses. But what was it that I clearly [and distinctly]* perceived in them? Nothing more than that the ideas and the thoughts of those objects were presented to my mind. And even now I do not deny that these ideas are found in my mind. But there was yet another thing which I affirmed, and which, from having been accustomed to believe it, I thought I clearly perceived, although, in truth, I did not perceive it at all; I mean the existence of objects external to me, from which those ideas proceeded, and to which they had a perfect resemblance; and it was here I was mistaken, or if I judged correctly, this assuredly was not to be traced to any knowledge I possessed (the force of my perception, Lat.).[3]

But when I considered any matter in arithmetic and geometry that was very simple and easy, as, for example, that two and three added together make five, and things of this sort, did I not view them with at least sufficient clearness to warrant me in affirming their truth? Indeed, if I afterwards judged that we ought to doubt of these things, it was for no other reason than because it occurred to me that a God might perhaps have given me such a nature as that I should be deceived, even respecting the matters that appeared to me the most evidently true. But

---

* Words within square brackets mark additions made by Descartes himself when revising the French text : the *Meditationes* appeared originally in Latin.

[3] Descartes has started with a dualism between himself and objects external. He has been accustomed to hold the doctrine called "representative perception," that ideas of sensible things are *copies* of those things ; and he now sees that this does not help him to obtain certainty ; for if all that he knows is only a copy, what is the guarantee of there being an original at all? No study of the copies can avail to give him a knowledge of originals.

as often as this preconceived opinion of the sovereign power of a God presents itself to my mind, I am constrained to admit that it is easy for Him, if He wishes it, to cause me to err, even in matters where I think I possess the highest evidence; and, on the other hand, as often as I direct my attention to things which I think I apprehend with great clearness, I am so persuaded of their truth that I naturally break out into expressions such as these: Deceive me who may, no one will yet ever be able to bring it about that I am not, so long as I shall be conscious that I am, or at any future time cause it to be true that I have never been, it being now true that I am, or make two and three more or less than five, in supposing which, and other like absurdities, I discover a manifest contradiction.[4]

And, in truth, as I have no ground for believing that Deity is deceitful, and as, indeed, I have not even considered the reasons by which the existence of a Deity of any kind is established, the ground of doubt that rests only on this supposition is very slight, and, so to speak, metaphysical. But, that I may be able wholly to remove it, I must inquire whether there is a God, as soon as an opportunity of doing so shall present itself; and if I find that there is a God, I must examine likewise whether He can be a deceiver; for, without the knowledge of these two truths, I do not see that I can ever be certain of anything. And that I may be enabled to examine this without interrupting the order of meditation I have proposed to myself

[4] The introduction of mathematics, based here on the validity of the law of Contradiction, reminds us that Descartes had not cleared his mind of everything, as he seemed to think. When he had secured his start many principles came into force again which he does not pause to criticise. Causality, for example, including necessity of the cause being at least adequate for the effect, and some other principles he recognises, and admits to rank as Axioms by reason of their standing the test of clearness and distinctness to his mind, and he covers them with the expression "the natural light."

[which is, to pass by degrees from the notions that I shall find first in my mind to those I shall afterwards discover in it], it is necessary at this stage to divide all my thoughts into certain classes, and to consider in which of these classes truth and error are, strictly speaking, to be found.

Of my thoughts some are, as it were, images of things, and to these alone properly belongs the name *idea*; as when I think [represent to my mind] a man, a chimera, the sky, an angel, or God. Others, again, have certain other forms; as when I will, fear, affirm, or deny, I always, indeed, apprehend something as the object of my thought, but I also embrace in thought something more than the representation of the object; and of this class of thoughts some are called volitions or affections, and others judgments.

Now, with respect to ideas, if these are considered only in themselves, and are not referred to any object beyond them, they cannot, properly speaking, be false; for, whether I imagine a goat or a chimera, it is not less true that I imagine the one than the other. Nor need we fear that falsity may exist in the will or affections; for, although I may desire objects that are wrong, and even that never existed, it is still true that I desire them. There thus only remain our judgments, in which we must take diligent heed that we be not deceived. But the chief and most ordinary error that arises in them consists in judging that the ideas which are in us are like or conformed to the things that are external to us; for assuredly, if we but considered the ideas themselves as certain modes of our thought (consciousness), without referring them to anything beyond, they would hardly afford any occasion of error.

But, among these ideas, some appear to me to be innate, others adventitious, and others to be made by myself (factitious); for, as I have the power of conceiving what is called a thing, or a truth, or a thought, it seems to me that I hold this power from no other source than my own nature; but if I now hear a noise, if I see the sun, or if I feel heat, I have all along judged that these sensations proceeded from certain objects existing out of myself; and, finally, it appears to me that sirens, hippogryphs, and the like, are inventions of my own mind. But I may even perhaps come to be of opinion that all my ideas are of the class which I call adventitious, or that they are all innate, or that they are all factitious, for I have not yet clearly discovered their true origin; and what I have here principally to do is to consider, with reference to those that appear to come from certain objects without me, what grounds there are for thinking them like these objects.[5]

The first of these grounds is that it seems to me I am so taught by nature; and the second, that I am conscious that those ideas are not dependent on my will, and therefore not on myself, for they are frequently presented to me against my will,—as at present, whether I will or not, I feel heat; and I am thus persuaded that this sensation or idea (*sensum vel ideam*) of heat is produced in me by something different from myself, namely, by the heat of the fire by which I sit. And it is very reasonable to suppose that this object impresses me with its own likeness rather than any other thing.

[5] He divides ideas into innate, adventitious, and factitious. To the factitious there are plainly no objects corresponding, unless by accident; these we make for ourselves, and we can alter them at pleasure. The adventitious are such as come to us through our Senses: we are accustomed to suppose objects for these, but this may be only our supposition, no certainty is secured by mere contemplation of objects of this kind; but as Descartes held the doctrine of "representative perception," he allows to these some power of showing us objective reality. The innate ideas are such as we neither make for ourselves nor have thrust upon us, so to speak: they are in us potentially, ready to be evoked when our intellectual faculty is called into activity. (See later, Meditation V. *ad init.*) The innate ideas of which he will make most explicit use are infinity and perfection, causality and substance, matter and mind.

But I must consider whether these reasons are sufficiently
strong and convincing. When I speak of being taught by
nature in this matter, I understand by the word nature
only a certain spontaneous impetus that impels me to believe
in a resemblance between ideas and their objects, and not a
natural light that affords a knowledge of its truth. But
these two things are widely different; for what the natural
light shows to be true can be in no degree doubtful, as, for
example, that I am because I doubt, and other truths of the
like kind: inasmuch as I possess no other faculty whereby
to distinguish truth from error, which can teach me the
falsity of what the natural light declares to be true, and
which is equally trustworthy; but with respect to [seemingly]
natural impulses, I have observed, when the question related
to the choice of right or wrong in action, that they frequently
led me to take the worse part; nor do I see that I have
any better ground for following them in what relates to
truth and error. Then, with respect to the other reason,
which is that because these ideas do not depend on my will,
they must arise from objects existing without me, I do not
find it more convincing than the former; for, just as those
natural impulses, of which I have lately spoken, are found
in me, notwithstanding that they are not always in harmony
with my will, so likewise it may be that I possess some
power not sufficiently known to myself capable of producing
ideas without the aid of external objects, and, indeed, it
has always hitherto appeared to me that during sleep they
are formed by some power of this nature without the
aid of aught external. And, in fine, although I should
grant that they proceeded from those objects, it is not a
necessary consequence that they must be like them. On the
contrary, I have observed, in a number of instances, that
there was a great difference between the object and its idea.
Thus, for example, I find in my mind two wholly diverse
ideas of the sun; the one, by which it appears to me

extremely small, draws its origin from the senses, and should be placed in the class of adventitious ideas; the other, by which it seems to be many times larger than the whole earth, is taken up on astronomical grounds, that is, elicited from certain notions born with me, or is framed by myself in some other manner. These two ideas cannot certainly both resemble the same sun; and reason teaches me that the one which seems to be the most immediate is the most unlike the real sun. And these things sufficiently prove that hitherto it has not been from a certain and deliberate judgment, but only from a sort of blind impulse, that I believed in the existence of certain things different from myself, which, by the organs of sense, or by whatever other means it might be, conveyed their ideas or images into my mind [and impressed it with their likenesses].⁶

But there is still another way of inquiring whether, of the objects whose ideas are in my mind, there are any that exist out of me. If ideas are taken in so far only as they are certain modes of consciousness, I do not remark any difference or inequality among them, and all seem, in the same manner, to proceed from myself; but, considering them as images, of which one represents one thing and another a different, it is evident that a great diversity obtains among them. For, without doubt, those that represent substances are something more, and contain in themselves, so to speak, more objective reality [that is, participate by

⁶ Here Descartes sees that the doctrine of "representative perception" fails him: it is only by "blind impulse" that he believes in external objects at all.

In reference to ideas of *bodies*, it will be seen that Descartes finds that most of the content of our ideas of them is composed of ideas only: there is " but little " that might not be so referred, namely, Extension ; yet for that little, reality must be recognised. This is sufficient to lead him when he has found his Theistic principle, his Substance, to acknowledge a substantiality for corporeal bodies, at least so far as to make them independent of the perceiving mind. But see note ⁹.

Ideas are copies of more or less complete perfection.

representation in higher degrees of being or perfection] than those that represent only modes or accidents; and again, the idea by which I conceive a God [sovereign], eternal, infinite, [immutable], all - knowing, all - powerful, and the creator of all things that are out of himself,—this, I say, has certainly in it more objective reality than those ideas by which finite substances are represented. *is th' g reason*

Now, it is manifest by the natural light that there must at least be as much reality in the efficient and total cause as in its effect; for whence can the effect draw its reality if not from its cause? and how could the cause communicate to it this reality unless it possessed it in itself? And hence it follows, not only that what is cannot be produced by what is not, but likewise that the more perfect—in other words, that which contains in itself more reality—cannot be the effect of the less perfect: and this is not only evidently true of those effects, whose reality is actual or formal, but likewise of ideas, whose reality is only considered as objective. Thus, for example, the stone that is not yet in existence, not only cannot now commence to be, unless it be produced by that which possesses in itself, formally or eminently, all that enters into its composition [in other words, by that which contains in itself the same properties that are in the stone, or others superior to them]; and heat can only be produced in a subject that was before devoid of it, by a cause that is of an order [degree or kind] at least as perfect as heat; and so of the others. But, further, even the idea of the heat, or of the stone, cannot exist in me unless it be put there by a cause that contains, at least, as much reality as I conceive existent in the heat or in the stone: for, although that cause may not transmit into my idea anything of its actual or formal reality, we ought not on this account to imagine that it is less real; but we ought to consider that [as every idea is a work of the mind] its nature is such as of itself to demand no other formal

4

reality than that which it borrows from our consciousness, of which it is but a mode [that is, a manner or way of thinking]. But in order that an idea may contain this objective reality rather than that, it must doubtless derive it from some cause in which is found at least as much formal reality as the idea contains of objective; for, if we suppose that there is found in an idea anything which was not in its cause, it must of course derive this from nothing. But however imperfect may be the mode of existence by which a thing is objectively [or by representation] in the understanding by its idea, we certainly cannot, for all that, allege that this mode of existence is nothing, nor, conse-quently, that the idea owes its origin to nothing. Nor must it be imagined that, since the reality which is considered in these ideas is only objective, the same reality need not be formally (actually) in the causes of these ideas, but only objectively: for, just as the mode of existing objectively belongs to ideas by their peculiar nature, so likewise the mode of existing formally appertains to the causes of these ideas (at least to the first and principal) by their peculiar nature. And although an idea may give rise to another idea, this regress cannot, nevertheless, be infinite; we must in the end reach a first idea, the cause of which is, as it were, the archetype in which all the reality [or perfection] that is found objectively [or by representation] in these ideas is contained formally [and in act]. I am thus clearly taught by the natural light that ideas exist in me as pictures or images, which may in truth readily fall short of the perfection of the objects from which they are taken, but can never contain anything greater or more perfect.[7]

[7] Here he resorts to the category of Causality as a form of con-structing knowledge. That he has not subjected it to criticism or doubt is only an indication that he stood on the threshold of modern philosophy, and that much lay before those who should come after him.

The purport of this paragraph is not difficult to apprehend; but the

And in proportion to the time and care with which I examine all those matters, the conviction of their truth brightens and becomes distinct. But, to sum up, what conclusion shall I draw from it all? It is this—if the objective reality [or perfection] of any one of my ideas be such as clearly to convince me that this same reality exists in me neither formally nor eminently, and if, as follows from this, I myself cannot be the cause of it, it is a necessary consequence that I am not alone in the world, but that there is besides myself some other being who exists as the cause of that idea; while, on the contrary, if no such idea be found in my mind, I shall have no sufficient ground of assurance of the existence of any other being besides myself; for, after a most careful search, I have, up to this moment, been unable to discover any other ground.

But among these my ideas, besides that which represents myself, respecting which there can be here no difficulty, there is one that represents a God; others that represent corporeal and inanimate things; others, angels; others, animals; and, finally, there are some that represent men like myself. But with respect to the ideas that represent other men, or animals, or angels, I can easily suppose that they were formed by the mingling and composition of the other ideas which I have of myself, of corporeal things, and of God, although there were, apart from myself, neither men, animals, nor angels. And with regard to the ideas of corporeal objects, I never discovered in them anything so great or excellent which I myself did not appear capable of originating; for, by considering these ideas closely and scrutinising them individually, in the same way that I yesterday examined the idea of wax,

terms used require some study of scholastic terminology, especially *formal; object* and *subject* (which have been altered since Kant). See Veitch, *Notes* 3 and 7, Fleming's *Vocabulary of Philosophy*, and art. on "Latin and Scholastic Terminology" in Baldwin's *Dictionary of Philosophy.*

I find that there is but little in them that is clearly and distinctly perceived. As belonging to the class of things that are clearly apprehended, I recognise the following, namely, magnitude or extension in length, breadth, and depth; figure, which results from the termination of extension; situation, which bodies of diverse figures preserve with reference to each other; and motion, or the change of situation; to which may be added substance, duration, and number. But with regard to light, colours, sounds, odours, tastes, heat, cold, and the other tactile qualities, they are thought with so much obscurity and confusion, that I cannot determine even whether they are true or false; in other words, whether or not the ideas I have of these qualities are in truth the ideas of real objects. For although I before remarked that it is only in judgments that formal falsity, or falsity properly so called, can be met with, there may nevertheless be found in ideas a certain material falsity, which arises when they represent what is nothing as if it were something. Thus, for example, the ideas I have of cold and heat are so far from being clear and distinct, that I am unable from them to discover whether cold is only the privation of heat, or heat the privation of cold; or whether they are or are not real qualities: and since, ideas being as it were images, there can be none that does not seem to us to represent some object, the idea which represents cold as something real and positive will not improperly be called false, if it be correct to say that cold is nothing but a privation of heat; and so in other cases. To ideas of this kind, indeed, it is not necessary that I should assign any author besides myself: for if they are false, that is, represent objects that are unreal, the natural light teaches me that they proceed from nothing; in other words, that they are in me only because something is wanting to the perfection of my nature; but if these ideas are true, yet because they exhibit to me so little reality that I cannot even distinguish the object represented from non-being, I do not see why I should not be the author of them.[8]

With reference to those ideas of corporeal things that are clear and distinct, there are some which, as appears to me, might have been taken from the idea I have of myself, as those of substance, duration, number, and the like. For when I think that a stone is a substance, or a thing capable of existing of itself, and that I am likewise a substance, although I conceive that I am a thinking and non-extended thing, and that the stone, on the contrary, is extended and unconscious, there being thus the greatest diversity between the two concepts,—yet these two ideas seem to have this in common, that they both represent substances. In the same way, when I think of myself as now existing, and recollect besides that I existed some time ago, and when I am conscious of various thoughts whose number I know, I then acquire the ideas of duration and number, which I can afterwards transfer to as many objects as I please. With respect to the other qualities that go to make up the ideas of corporeal objects, namely, extension, figure, situation, and motion, it is true that they are not formally in me, since I am merely a thinking being; but because they are only certain modes of substance, and because I myself am a substance, it seems possible that they may be contained in me eminently.[9]

[8] Descartes holds to an absolute distinction between perceptions and conceptions, between ideas of modes or accidents and ideas of substances. He has come to see that the representative theory is almost valueless for perceptions, but he continues his allegiance to it for conceptions such as infinity and eternity : these are not confused but clear, not obscure but distinct ; they may be depended upon.

[9] He comes very near to dissolving the independence of external objects. The "little reality" has become only "substantiality"; and even that may belong to myself, and only be accredited to them, as it were, by transference. His dualism nearly disappears here. Some

There only remains, therefore, the idea of God, in which I must consider whether there is anything that cannot be supposed to originate with myself. By the name God, I understand a substance infinite [eternal, immutable], independent, all-knowing, all-powerful, and by which I myself, and every other thing that exists, if any such there be, were created.[10] But these properties are so great and excellent, that the more attentively I consider them the less I feel persuaded that the idea I have of them owes its origin to myself alone. And thus it is absolutely necessary to conclude, from all that I have before said, that God exists : for though the idea of substance be in my mind owing to this, that I myself am a substance, I should not, however, have the idea of an infinite substance, seeing I am a finite being, unless it were given me by some substance in reality infinite.

And I must not imagine that I do not apprehend the infinite by a true idea, but only by the negation of the finite, in the same way that I comprehend repose and darkness by the negation of motion and light : since, on the contrary, I clearly perceive that there is more reality in the infinite substance than in the finite, and therefore that in some way I possess the perception (notion) of the infinite before that of the finite, that is, the perception of God before that of myself ; for how could I know that I doubt, desire, or that something is wanting to me, and that I am not wholly perfect, if I possessed no idea of a being more perfect than

interpreters press this, and, by reference to other places also, consider that Descartes was showing the way to explicit Idealism.

[10] In this definition of the Divine Being more is expressed than Descartes will make use of : in practice he uses the term Perfection to cover the whole attributes ; when he especially desires clearness he usually selects Infinity. He is not in sight of the problem of Personality : he is seeking the ultimate Reality in a more abstract way.

myself, by comparison of which I knew the deficiencies of my nature ?[11]

And it cannot be said that this idea of God is perhaps materially false, and consequently that it may have arisen from nothing [in other words, that it may exist in me from my imperfection], as I before said of the ideas of heat and cold, and the like; for, on the contrary, as this idea is very clear and distinct, and contains in itself more objective reality than any other, there can be no one of itself more true, or less open to the suspicion of falsity.

The idea, I say, of a being supremely perfect and infinite, is in the highest degree true, for although, perhaps, we may imagine that such a being does not exist, we cannot, nevertheless, suppose that his idea represents nothing real, as I have already said of the idea of cold. It is likewise clear and distinct in the highest degree, since whatever the mind clearly and distinctly conceives as real or true, and as implying any perfection, is contained entire in this idea. And this is true, nevertheless, although I do not comprehend the infinite, and although there may be in God an infinity of things that I cannot comprehend, nor perhaps even compass by thought in any way; for it is of the nature of the infinite that it should not be comprehended by the finite; and it is enough that I rightly understand this, and judge that all which I clearly perceive, and in which I know there is some perfection, and perhaps also an infinity of properties of which I am ignorant, are formally or eminently in God, in order that the idea I have of Him may become the most true, clear, and distinct of all the ideas in my mind.

But perhaps I am something more than I suppose myself

[11] This paragraph is important as showing that Descartes has always the notion of the *positive infinite* : there is no ambiguity in his mind between the infinite and the indefinite. It is the simple infinite that he regards as an innate idea, neither factitious nor adventitious.

to be, and it may be that all those perfections which I attribute to God, in some way exist potentially in me, although they do not yet show themselves, and are not reduced to act. Indeed, I am already conscious that my knowledge is being increased [and perfected] by degrees; and I see nothing to prevent it from thus gradually increasing to infinity, nor any reason why, after such increase and perfection, I should not be able thereby to acquire all the other perfections of the Divine nature; nor, in fine, why the power I possess of acquiring those perfections, if it really now exist in me, should not be sufficient to produce the ideas of them. Yet, on looking more closely into the matter, I discover that this cannot be; for, in the first place, although it were true that my knowledge daily acquired new degrees of perfection, and although there were potentially in my nature much that was not as yet actually in it, still all these excellences make not the slightest approach to the idea I have of the Deity, in whom there is no perfection merely potentially [but all actually] existent; for it is even an unmistakeable token of imperfection in my knowledge, that it is augmented by degrees. Further, although my knowledge increase more and more, nevertheless I am not therefore induced to think that it will ever be actually infinite, since it can never reach that point beyond which it shall be incapable of further increase. But I conceive God as actually infinite, so that nothing can be added to His perfection. And, in fine, I readily perceive that the objective being of an idea cannot be produced by a being that is merely potentially existent, which, properly speaking, is nothing, but only by a being existing formally or actually.[12]

[12] The last five paragraphs must be carefully studied. They contain the proof from the idea to the Cause of the idea ; and it will be found that Descartes is struggling to express a new and profound thought lying underneath an old and more superficial one. Superficially, the argument proceeds by using the principle of Causality in

And, truly, I see nothing in all that I have now said which it is not easy for anyone, who shall carefully consider it, to discern by the natural light; but when I allow my attention in some degree to relax, the vision of my mind being obscured, and, as it were, blinded by the images of sensible objects, I do not readily remember the reason why the idea of a being more perfect than myself, must of necessity have proceeded from a being in reality more perfect. On this account I am here desirous to inquire further, whether I, who possess this idea of God, could exist supposing there were no God. And I ask, from whom could I, in that case, derive my existence? Perhaps from myself, or from my parents, or from some other causes less perfect than God; for anything more perfect, or even equal to God, cannot be thought or imagined. But if I [were independent of every other existence, and] were myself the author of my being, I should doubt of nothing, I should desire nothing, and, in fine, no perfection would be awanting to me; for I should have bestowed upon myself every perfection of which I possess the idea, and I should thus be God. And it must not be imagined that what is now wanting to me is perhaps of more difficult acquisition than that of which I am already possessed; for, on the contrary, it is quite manifest that it was a matter of much higher difficulty

an external way, to construct a bridge from one thing (his idea) to another (a Perfect and Infinite Being as the Cause of that idea). It is his doctrine of representative perception that some ideas must have Causes. He then shows that the idea of perfection is one of these ; then by the method of exclusion, which he frequently employs, he concludes that the Cause must be a Perfect and Infinite Being. But underneath this he sees a relation between the "idea" and the "Object" which is of a more intimate kind, viz. that one is involved in the other by immanent and inherent necessity, the finite in the infinite, and the infinite in the finite. In this deeper view he is coming into the vein of thought in which later Idealism was to do its work.

that I, a thinking being, should arise from nothing, than it would be for me to acquire the knowledge of many things of which I am ignorant, and which are merely the accidents of a thinking substance; and certainly, if I possessed of myself the greater perfection of which I have now spoken [in other words, if I were the author of my own existence], I would not at least have denied to myself things that may be more easily obtained [as that infinite variety of knowledge of which I am at present destitute]. I could not, indeed, have denied to myself any property which I perceive is contained in the idea of God, because there is none of these that seems to me to be more difficult to make or acquire; and if there were any that should happen to be more difficult to acquire, they would certainly appear so to me (supposing that I myself were the source of the other things I possess), because I should discover in them a limit to my power. And though I were to suppose that I always was as I now am, I should not, on this ground, escape the force of these reasonings, since it would not follow, even on this supposition, that no author of my existence needed to be sought after. For the whole time of my life may be divided into an infinity of parts, each of which is in no way dependent on any other; and, accordingly, because I was in existence a short time ago, it does not follow that I must now exist, unless in this moment some cause create me anew as it were, —that is, conserve me. In truth, it is perfectly clear and evident to all who will attentively consider the nature of duration, that the conservation of a substance, in each moment of its duration, requires the same power and act that would be necessary to create it, supposing it were not yet in existence; so that it is manifestly a dictate of the natural light that conservation and creation differ merely in respect of our mode of thinking [and not in reality]. All that is here required, therefore, is that I interrogate myself to discover whether I possess any power by means of which

I can bring it about that I, who now am, shall exist a
moment afterwards : for, since I am merely a thinking thing
(or since, at least, the precise question in the meantime
is only of that part of myself), if such a power resided in me,
I should without doubt be conscious of it; but I am conscious
of no such power, and thereby I manifestly know that I am
dependent upon some being different from myself.[13]

But perhaps the being upon whom I am dependent is
not God, and I have been produced either by my parents,
or by some causes less perfect than Deity.   This cannot
be : for, as I before said, it is perfectly evident that there
must at least be as much reality in the cause as in its
effect; and accordingly, since I am a thinking thing, and
possess in myself an idea of God, whatever in the end be the
cause of my existence, it must of necessity be admitted that
it is likewise a thinking being, and that it possesses in itself
the idea and all the perfections I attribute to Deity.   Then it
may again be inquired whether this cause owes its origin and
existence to itself, or to some other cause.   For if it be
self-existent, it follows, from what I have before laid down,
that this cause is God; for, since it possesses the perfection
of self-existence, it must likewise, without doubt, have the
power of actually possessing every perfection of which it has
the idea,—in other words, all the perfections I conceive to
belong to God.   But if it owe its existence to another cause
than itself, we demand again, for a similar reason, whether
this second cause exists of itself or through some other,
until, from stage to stage, we at length arrive at an ultimate
cause, which will be God.   And it is quite manifest that in

[13] Here he has introduced the argument *à posteriori* as applied to
his own existence, both for creation and conservation.   His view of
conservation as repeated creation was afterwards formulated by
Geulinx as part of his Occasionalism.   It is important to notice that
conservation is in Descartes' mind, because in this way he avoids all
necessity of going back along a line of causes, possibly *ad infinitum.*

this matter there can be no infinite regress of causes, seeing that the question raised respects not so much the cause which once produced me, as that by which I am at this present moment conserved.

Nor can it be supposed that several causes concurred in my production, and that from one I received the idea of one of the perfections I attribute to Deity, and from another the idea of some other, and thus that all those perfections are indeed found somewhere in the universe, but do not all exist together in a single being who is God; for, on the contrary, the unity, the simplicity or inseparability of all the properties of Deity, is one of the chief perfections I conceive Him to possess; and the idea of this unity of all the perfections of Deity could certainly not be put into my mind by any cause from which I did not likewise receive the ideas of all the other perfections; for no power could enable me to embrace them in an inseparable unity, without at the same time giving me the knowledge of what they were [and of their existence in a particular mode].

Finally, with regard to my parents [from whom it appears I sprung], although all that I believed respecting them be true, it does not, nevertheless, follow that I am conserved by them, or even that I was produced by them, in so far as I am a thinking being. All that, at the most, they contributed to my origin was the giving of certain dispositions (modifications) to the matter in which I have hitherto judged that I or my mind, which is what alone I now consider to be myself, is enclosed; and thus there can here be no difficulty with respect to them, and it is absolutely necessary to conclude from this alone that I am, and possess the idea of a being absolutely perfect, that is, of God, that His existence is most clearly demonstrated.

There remains only the inquiry as to the way in which I received this idea from God; for I have not drawn it from the senses, nor is it even presented to me unexpectedly,

as is usual with the ideas of sensible objects, when these
are presented or appear to be presented to the external
organs of the senses; it is not even a pure production or
fiction of my mind, for it is not in my power to take from
or add to it; and consequently there but remains the alter-
native that it is innate, in the same way as is the idea of
myself. And, in truth, it is not to be wondered at that God,
at my creation, implanted this idea in me, that it might serve,
as it were, for the mark of the workman impressed on his
work; and it is not also necessary that the mark should
be something different from the work itself; but considering
only that God is my creator, it is highly probable that He in
some way fashioned me after His own image and likeness;
and that I perceive this likeness, in which is contained
the idea of God, by the same faculty by which I apprehend
myself,—in other words, when I make myself the object
of reflection, I not only find that I am an incomplete,
[imperfect], and dependent being, and one who unceasingly
aspires after something better and greater than he is; but,
at the same time, I am assured likewise that He upon whom
I am dependent possesses in Himself all the goods after
which I aspire [and the ideas of which I find in my mind],
and that not merely indefinitely and potentially, but
infinitely and actually, and that He is thus God. And
the whole force of the argument of which I have here
availed myself to establish the existence of God, consists
in this, that I perceive I could not possibly be of such a
nature as I am, and yet have in my mind the idea of
a God, if God did not in reality exist,—this same God,
I say, whose idea is in my mind—that is, a being who
possesses all those lofty perfections, of which the mind
may have some slight conception, without, however, being
able fully to comprehend them,—and who is wholly superior
to all defect [and has nothing that marks imperfection]:
whence it is sufficiently manifest that He cannot be a

deceiver, since it is a dictate of the natural light that all fraud and deception spring from some defect.

But before I examine this with more attention, and pass on to the consideration of other truths that may be evolved out of it, I think it proper to remain here for some time in the contemplation of God Himself—that I may ponder at leisure His marvellous attributes—and behold, admire, and adore the beauty of this light so unspeakably great, as far, at least, as the strength of my mind, which is to some degree dazzled by the sight, will permit. For just as we learn by faith that the supreme felicity of another life consists in the contemplation of the Divine majesty alone, so even now we learn from experience that a like meditation, though incomparably less perfect, is the source of the highest satisfaction of which we are susceptible in this life.[14]

In Meditation IV. Descartes is about to apply himself to the deduction of knowledge of the universe from the Supreme Being: "Now I am to discover a path that will conduct us from the contemplation of the true God, in whom are contained all the treasures of science and wisdom, to the knowledge of the other things in the universe." But immediately there presents itself to his mind the fact that in spite of our having access to this first principle we are immersed in many errors, and this needs explanation. It is plain that if all knowledge is deducible from the contemplation of the perfections of God, error cannot be anything more than privation of knowledge. This may arise from weakness and limitation in our faculties; the understanding cannot but be sound so far as it goes, but we may miss much through its limitation. But there is also another source of error even

---

[14] This outburst of sentiment is notable. Descartes is working as a metaphysician, but when he has secured his metaphysical conclusion he pauses to express the emotion which arises when he finds himself conducted by force of necessary thinking into the presence of Perfect Being. His conception may be impersonal, but to Descartes it is the Supreme Reality, and the contemplation of it touches the inmost fibre of his soul.

more serious, namely, our will, or power of choice, which may
lead us away from the indications of our understanding and
frustrate its light. (In this we see the ground for the claim
of Voluntarism for Descartes, referred to in Note 2.) In
this way error may be explained, Descartes thinks, without
derogating from the force of his proof of the existence of the
Perfect Being. With this possibility of error in his mind he
turns to inquire whether there are substances behind material
things, as we commonly suppose. He here comes upon
another group of clear and distinct ideas which "compel
assent," namely, the mathematical properties of bodies. He
perceives that in employing these we depend upon the content
of the ideas alone, by reason of their clearness and distinctness ; and with his mind full of desire to establish his supreme
metaphysical principle, it occurs to him that we may similarly
depend upon the idea we have of the Perfect Being ; and so
he comes to the statement of his Ontological argument, from
the content of the idea to belief in a reality corresponding
to it.

MEDITATION V.

On the Essence of Material Things : and, again, of God ; that He Exists.

Several other questions remain for consideration respecting
the attributes of God and my own nature or mind. I will,
however, on some other occasion perhaps resume the investigation of these. Meanwhile, as I have discovered what
must be done and what avoided to arrive at the knowledge of
truth, what I have chiefly to do is to essay to emerge from
the state of doubt in which I have for some time been, and
to discover whether anything can be known with certainty
regarding material objects. But before considering whether
such objects as I conceive exist without me, I must examine
their ideas in so far as these are to be found in my consciousness, and discover which of them are distinct and which
confused.

In the first place, I distinctly imagine that quantity which

the philosophers commonly call continuous, or the extension
in length, breadth, and depth that is in this quantity, or
rather in the object to which it is attributed. Further, I can
enumerate in it many diverse parts, and attribute to each of
these all sorts of sizes, figures, situations, and local motions;
and, in fine, I can assign to each of these motions all degrees
of duration. And I not only distinctly know these things
when I thus consider them in general; but besides, by a
little attention, I discover innumerable particulars respecting
figures, numbers, motion, and the like, which are so evidently
true, and so accordant with my nature, that when I now
discover them I do not so much appear to learn anything
new, as to call to remembrance what I before knew, or for
the first time to remark what was before in my mind, but to
which I had not hitherto directed my attention. And what
I here find of most importance is, that I discover in my mind
innumerable ideas of certain objects, which cannot be esteemed
pure negations, although perhaps they possess no reality
beyond my thought, and which are not framed by me, though
it may be in my power to think or not to think them, but
possess true and immutable natures of their own. As, for
example, when I imagine a triangle, although there is not
perhaps and never was in any place in the universe apart
from my thought one such figure, it remains true nevertheless
that this figure possesses a certain determinate nature, form,
or essence, which is immutable and eternal, and not framed
by me, nor in any degree dependent on my thought; as
appears from the circumstance, that diverse properties of the
triangle may be demonstrated, namely, that its three angles
are equal to two right, that its greatest side is subtended by
its greatest angle, and the like, which, whether I will or not, I
now clearly discern to belong to it, although before I did not
at all think of them, when, for the first time, I imagined a
triangle, and which accordingly cannot be said to have been
invented by me. Nor is it a valid objection to allege, that

perhaps this idea of a triangle came into my mind by the medium of the senses, through my having seen bodies of a triangular figure; for I am able to form in thought an innumerable variety of figures with regard to which it cannot be supposed that they were ever objects of sense, and I can nevertheless demonstrate diverse properties of their nature no less than of the triangle, all of which are assuredly true since I clearly conceive them : and they are therefore something, and not mere negations; for it is highly evident that all that is true is something [truth being identical with existence]; and I have already fully shown the truth of the principle, that whatever is clearly and distinctly known is true. And although this had not been demonstrated, yet the nature of my mind is such as to compel me to assent to what I clearly conceive while I so conceive it : and I recollect that even when I still strongly adhered to the objects of sense, I reckoned among the number of the most certain truths those I clearly conceived relating to figures, numbers, and other matters that pertain to arithmetic and geometry, and in general to the pure mathematics.

But now, if, because I can draw from my thought the idea of an object, it follows that all I clearly and distinctly apprehend to pertain to this object does in truth belong to it, may I not from this derive an argument for the existence of God? It is certain that I no less find the idea of a God in my consciousness, that is, the idea of a being supremely perfect, than that of any figure or number whatever : and I know with not less clearness and distinctness that an [actual and] eternal existence pertains to his nature than that all which is demonstrable of any figure or number really belongs to the nature of that figure or number; and, therefore, although all the conclusions of the preceding Meditations were false, the existence of God would pass with me for a truth at least as certain as I ever judged any truth of mathematics to be, although indeed such a doctrine may at

5

first sight appear to contain more sophistry than truth. For, as I have been accustomed in every other matter to distinguish between existence and essence, I easily believe that the existence can be separated from the essence of God, and that thus God may be conceived as not actually existing. But, nevertheless, when I think of it more attentively, it appears that the existence can no more be separated from the essence of God, than the idea of a mountain from that of a valley, or the equality of its three angles to two right angles, from the essence of a [rectilineal] triangle; so that it is not less impossible to conceive a God, that is, a being supremely perfect, to whom existence is awanting, or who is devoid of a certain perfection, than to conceive a mountain without a valley.[1]

---

[1] This is the Ontological argument which is specially associated with Descartes : it is the one which, with Anselm's, is criticised as "the Ontological argument" by Kant. But its late appearance in the order of the *Meditations* shows that it is not his principal argument.

For Descartes it is to be parallel with mathematical reasoning : as I can draw from thought (by Geometry) the knowledge of a triangle, and can depend upon it as truly representing properties of Space without needing to resort to any empirical tests ; so from my thought I can draw knowledge of God upon which I can depend with similar confidence without needing to look into the universe for any signs of His presence. It is like mathematical reasoning in its general character only : it is different in that it is the only case in which existence as contained in essence is the property to be deduced.

In the *Reply to the Second Objections*, Descartes sets out the argument in a more formal way :

Proposition I. The existence of God is known from the consideration of His nature alone.

Demonstration. To say that an attribute is contained in the nature or in the concept of a thing, is the same as to say that this attribute is true of this thing, and that it may be affirmed to be in it. (His Definition IX. had expressed this.)

But necessary existence is contained in the nature or in the concept of God. (His Axiom X. had asserted this.)

Hence it may with truth be said that necessary existence is in God, or that God exists,

But though, in truth, I cannot conceive a God unless as existing, any more than I can a mountain without a valley, yet, just as it does not follow that there is any mountain in the world merely because I conceive a mountain with a valley, so likewise, though I conceive God as existing, it does not seem to follow on that account that God exists; for my thought imposes no necessity on things; and as I may imagine a winged horse, though there be none such, so I could perhaps attribute existence to God though no God existed. But the cases are not analogous, and a fallacy lurks under the semblance of this objection: for because I cannot conceive a mountain without a valley, it does not follow that there is any mountain or valley in existence, but simply that the mountain or valley, whether they do or do not exist, are inseparable from each other; whereas, on the other hand, because I cannot conceive God unless as existing, it follows that existence is inseparable from Him, and therefore that He really exists; not that this is brought about by my thought, or that it imposes any necessity on things, but, on the contrary, the necessity which lies in the thing itself, that is, the necessity of the existence of God, determines me to think in this way: for it is not in my power to conceive a God

But he goes on to say that "this conclusion may be known without proof by those who are free from prejudice," and he only tries different ways because "it is not so easy to reach so great perspicacity of mind," and "there are certain truths which are manifest to some without proof which are not comprehended by others without a process of reasoning." From which it is fairly clear that the formal process is unnecessary, and that Descartes is really aware that he is asserting an intuitive judgment of an Ontological character, namely, that the necessary thought of a Perfect Being carries with it the thought of existence. As pointed out above, it is not Descartes' principal proof: and he does not resort to it as if it could stand alone. He associates it with the necessity of seeking some other cause than myself, for myself, imperfect as I am and yet possessing this innate idea of necessary perfection.

without existence, that is, a being supremely perfect, and yet devoid of an absolute perfection, as I am free to imagine a horse with or without wings.[2]

Nor must it be alleged here as an objection, that it is in truth necessary to admit that God exists, after having supposed Him to possess all perfections, since existence is one of them, but that my original supposition was not necessary; just as it is not necessary to think that all quadrilateral figures can be inscribed in the circle, since, if I supposed this, I should be constrained to admit that the rhombus, being a figure of four sides, can be therein inscribed, which, however, is manifestly false. This objection is, I say, incompetent; for although it may not be necessary that I shall at any time entertain the notion of Deity, yet each time I happen to think of a first and sovereign being, and to draw, so to speak,

[2] In this paragraph Descartes is grappling with the objection of Gassendi, as Anselm had done with that of Gaunilo, as to the legitimacy of passing from idea to existence. Descartes' reply is equivalent to that of Anselm; the Ontological assertion cannot be claimed for all ideas but only for necessary ones, and such the idea of God, of Perfection, of Infinity, is declared to be.

With Descartes' statement may be compared the vigorous expression of the Cambridge Platonist, Cudworth (*Intellectual System,* i. chap. v.):

"Our human soul cannot feign or create any new cogitation or conception that was not before, but only variously compound that which is; nor can it ever make a positive idea of an absolute non-entity—that is, such as hath neither actual nor possible existence: much less could our imperfect being create the entity of so vast a thought as that of an infinitely perfect Being out of nothing; this being indeed more than for God Almighty, or a perfect Being, to create a real world out of nothing; because there is no repugnancy at all in the latter, as there is in the former. We affirm, therefore, that was there no God, the idea of an absolutely or infinitely perfect Being could never have been made or feigned, neither by politicians, nor by poets, nor philosophers, nor any other. Which may be accounted another argument for Deity."

For general observations on the Ontological argument, see on Anselm, and on Kant.

the idea of Him from the storehouse of the mind, I am necessitated to attribute to Him all kinds of perfections, though I may not then enumerate them all, nor think of each of them in particular. And this necessity is sufficient, as soon as I discover that existence is a perfection, to cause me to infer the existence of this first and sovereign being : just as it is not necessary that I should ever imagine any triangle, but whenever I am desirous of considering a rectilineal figure composed of only three angles, it is absolutely necessary to attribute those properties to it from which it is correctly inferred that its three angles are not greater than two right angles, although perhaps I may not then advert to this relation in particular. But when I consider what figures are capable of being inscribed in the circle, it is by no means necessary to hold that all quadrilateral figures are of this number ; on the contrary, I cannot even imagine such to be the case, so long as I shall be unwilling to accept in thought aught that I do not clearly and distinctly conceive : and consequently there is a vast difference between false suppositions, as is the one in question, and the true ideas that were born with me, the first and chief of which is the idea of God. For indeed I discern on many grounds that this idea is not factitious, depending simply on my thought, but that it is the representation of a true and immutable nature : in the first place, because I can conceive no other being, except God, to whose essence existence [necessarily] pertains; in the second, because it is impossible to conceive two or more gods of this kind ; and it being supposed that one such God exists, I clearly see that He must have existed from all eternity, and will exist to all eternity ; and, finally, because I apprehend many other properties in God, none of which I can either diminish or change.

But, indeed, whatever mode of proof I in the end adopt, it always returns to this, that it is only the things I clearly and distinctly conceive which have the power of completely persuading me.   And although, of the objects I conceive in this manner, some, indeed, are obvious to every one, while others are only discovered after close and careful investigation; nevertheless, after they are once discovered, the latter are not esteemed less certain than the former.   Thus, for example, to take the case of a right-angled triangle, although it is not so manifest at first that the square of the base is equal to the squares of the other two sides, as that the base is opposite to the greatest angle; nevertheless, after it is once apprehended, we are as firmly persuaded of the truth of the former as of the latter.   And, with respect to God, if I were not preoccupied by prejudices, and my thought beset on all sides by the continual presence of the images of sensible objects, I should know nothing sooner or more easily than the fact of His being.   For is there any truth more clear than the existence of a Supreme Being, or of God, seeing it is to His essence alone that [necessary and eternal] existence pertains?   And although the right conception of this truth has cost me much close thinking, nevertheless at present I feel not only as assured of it as of what I deem most certain, but I remark further that the certitude of all other truths is so absolutely dependent on it, that without this knowledge it is impossible ever to know anything perfectly.

For although I am of such a nature as to be unable, while I possess a very clear and distinct apprehension of a matter, to resist the conviction of its truth, yet because my constitution is also such as to incapacitate me from keeping my mind continually fixed on the same object, and as I frequently recollect a past judgment without at the same time being able to recall the grounds of it, it may happen meanwhile that other reasons are presented to me which would readily cause me to change my opinion, if I did not know that God existed; and thus I should possess no true and certain knowledge, but merely vague and vacillating opinions. Thus, for example, when I consider the nature of the [rectilineal] triangle, it most clearly appears to me, who have been instructed in the principles of geometry, that its three angles are equal to two right angles, and I find it impossible to believe otherwise, while I apply my mind to the demonstration ; but as soon as I cease from attending to the process of proof, although I still remember that I had a clear comprehension of it, yet I may readily come to doubt of the truth demonstrated, if I do not know that there is a God : for I may persuade myself that I have been so constituted by nature as to be sometimes deceived, even in matters which I think I apprehend with the greatest evidence and certitude, especially when I recollect that I frequently considered many things to be true and certain which other reasons afterwards constrained me to reckon as wholly false.[3]

[3] In these two paragraphs we are brought into view of a confusion in Descartes' exposition which needs disentangling. We find him sometimes staking all knowledge simply on the clearness and distinctness of the deliverances of Reason in general (never on senses or imagination, of course) ; at other times on the clearness and distinctness of some particular deliverance, the *Cogito* or the existence of God. Hence a manifest circle sometimes appears—I trust to clear Reason, because it is from God, who, being perfect, cannot deceive ; and yet I believe in God solely because of the clearness and distinctness of the Reason by which I know Him. This wavering began early : it is in the *Discourse on Method* ; but at the close of Part IV. he takes his stand, as emphatically as words can enable him to do, on the belief in God as the ground for trusting clearness of Reason itself (and with God he conjoins the *Cogito*) ; and when he opens Part V. it is from the perfection of God. Elsewhere he seems to require Theistic belief only for another office, namely, to reassure him where clearness is in abeyance through failure of memory, or through other obstructions, or through necessity of having the whole universe of thought secured when only a part is present to the mind. The wavering recurs, however, in the *Meditations*, and is repeated in the *Principles*. It must therefore be acknowledged that Descartes had not cleared his own mind, and various explanations are offered as to why he had not done so. Our own interpretation is that it is the belief in the perfect Being which is for Descartes the ultimate ground of knowledge : this is the

But after I have discovered that God exists, seeing I also
at the same time observed that all things depend on Him, and
that He is no deceiver, and thence inferred that all which I
clearly and distinctly perceive is of necessity true : although
I no longer attend to the grounds of a judgment, no opposite
reason can be alleged sufficient to lead me to doubt of its
truth, provided only I remember that I once possessed a clear
and distinct comprehension of it.   My knowledge of it thus
becomes true and certain.   And this same knowledge extends
likewise to whatever I remember to have formerly demonstrated, as the truths of geometry and the like ; for what can
be alleged against them to lead me to doubt of them ?   Will
it be that my nature is such that I may be frequently
deceived ?   But I already know that I cannot be deceived in
judgments of the grounds of which I possess a clear knowledge.   Will it be that I formerly deemed things to be true
and certain which I afterwards discovered to be false ?   But
I had no clear and distinct knowledge of any of those things,

substantive belief.   Its clearness is *adjectival*, and admits of being
generalised into a criterion for universal use.   It is quite needless,
therefore, to separate them, and to use one as a ground for believing
in the other.   If we are to admit that the *Cogito* is another such
ultimate intuition, the same remark applies to that.

A circle also appears in another way.   Confidence in the veracity of
the perfect Being is necessary for the beginning of knowledge : when I
come to investigate knowledge, the most substantial content I find in
it is this very existence of perfect Being.   It is easy to call this a
fallacy of circular reasoning, but it is easy also to show that the
objection does not lie ; it is not reasoning in the sense of inference from
one thought to another at all, and so there is no objection to a circle.
It is the bringing into explicitness a movement of thought which does
not pass from one object to another, but is working within a circle.
From the perfect Being or presupposition I proceed to explore : in my
exploration I find also the perfect Being at the end.   But this is
really to say that I find Him everywhere : I am only making explicit
that to find Him everywhere means that He is both beginning and end,
and that between this beginning and end lies everything I know.

and, being as yet ignorant of the rule by which I am assured of the truth of a judgment, I was led to give my assent to them on grounds which I afterwards discovered were less strong than at the time I imagined them to be. What further objection, then, is there? Will it be said that perhaps I am dreaming (an objection I lately myself raised), or that all the thoughts of which I am now conscious have no more truth than the reveries of my dreams? But although, in truth, I should be dreaming, the rule still holds that all which is clearly presented to my intellect is indisputably true.

And thus I very clearly see that the certitude and truth of all science depends on the knowledge alone of the true God, insomuch that, before I knew Him, I could have no perfect knowledge of any other thing. And now that I know Him, I possess the means of acquiring a perfect knowledge respecting innumerable matters, as well relative to God Himself and other intellectual objects as to corporeal nature, in so far as it is the object of pure mathematics [which do not consider whether it exists or not].[4]

---

[4] This states Descartes' view, that from these first principles, which constitute Metaphysics, he can proceed to deduce all knowledge: they are "such that we can deduce from them the knowledge of whatever else is in the world" (*Principles*, Preface); and his tree of the sciences (*ibid.*) is, "Metaphysics the root, Physics the trunk, and the branches which grow out of this trunk, which are reduced to three principal, namely, Medicine, Mechanics, and Ethics." On this it should be observed that it is acknowledged by French philosophers that the "spirit of Cartesianism" has characterised too much of French thought, especially in the eighteenth century, by leading to an abstractness and a confidence in deductive method which prevented a true appreciation of the complexity of the universe and the need of historical method. The rich contributions of the French mind to historical work recently and in the present day represent a reaction from the Cartesian influence ; but to Englishmen there is still apparent in French historical work a fine sense of generalisation, which they regard with admiration, and value as an indispensable factor in European thought.

When Descartes came to work out the "little reality" he had candidly acknowledged to be left in *bodies* as not to be attributed to our ideas, he passed on to recognition of external substantiality to an extent which left Matter on a par with Mind.   This dualism, which he had had in his mind before he doubted, and which now recurred to him, might have been subordinated by him to the unity provided by his Metaphysical Theism ; but he left Matter very externally related to the perfect Being—much more so than Mind, in which he saw at times an immanent and inherent presence of Divinity.   Hence some of his followers became Deists for both Mind and Matter; by others the Theism was abandoned as providing a *Deus ex machinâ* ; and others even arose who, between the two substances, attributed superiority to Matter. But these were plainly reversals of Descartes' purpose : he stands out clearly himself for Metaphysical Theism.

In reference to other aspects of Theism.   Descartes made no use of the arguments *a contingentia mundi*, or from teleology, or from Morals ; nor does he touch the Idealism which starts from the subjective side of consciousness and regards the Divine Being as the all-comprehensive Subject.   Nor did he from his Theism deductively draw any system of Ethics or Politics or Religion, though he had indicated the possibility of all these.   He rested content with the doctrines of the Church for religious beliefs, and the prevalent opinions of French society for ethical and political life.   His interest passed from Metaphysics to the Physical Sciences ; and he followed up his deductions into Physics, and even into Anatomy and Physiology, with some reference to experimental observation.   But followers arose whose interest lay in the moral sphere, and the simple principles which served in the Physical Sciences were carried over by them without further criticism into the Moral Sciences and into Religion, and gave us Bayle, the Encyclopædists, and Voltaire.

The comparison of systems, for which it is a main purpose of this volume to furnish materials, may be assisted by the insertion here of the reasons why Descartes' Philosophy, Theistic as it was, was placed on the Index (1663) thirteen years after his death,—a prescription which was adopted by the Universities of Holland under Calvinist direction, and the University of Oxford under Anglican.   The opposition marks the differences between Cartesianism and Aquinism as both

were understood in Descartes' own age. The following are
the grounds assigned:—His principle of unreserved doubt
was opposed to the claim of religious Faith; his criterion
of clearness was subjective and individual; his *à priori*
reason left no scope for Revelation; his making thought the
essence of the Divine Being to the exclusion of spirit and
life; his attributing infinity to the universe instead of to God
only; the existence of uncreated matter; the mechanical
theory instead of teleological operation; and his attributing
error to the will instead of to will and intellect together. How
far these were true readings of Descartes is another matter:
these were the interpretations then current. As there are
factors in his system, *e.g.* the infinite, causality, representative
ideas, and the absolute difference between perceptions and
conceptions, in which Descartes retains leading points of
Scholasticism, we see how much he was a worker in an era of
transition.

References.—The translation in the text is that of the late John
Veitch, professor of Logic in the University of Glasgow : the volume
contains also translations of the *Method* and the *Principles*, and has an
introduction and notes by Veitch. New translations have been made
by Lowndes, London, 1878 ; H. A. P. Torrey, New York, 1892 ; and
by G. B. Rawlings (n. d., pub. W. Scott).

Recent monographs are : Wallace (in *Encycl. Brit.*) ; E. Caird,
"Cartesianism" (in *Encycl. Brit.*, reprinted in *Essays*, 1892) ;
Norman Smith, *Studies in the Cartesian Philosophy* (1902) ; Iverach,
Descartes and Spinoza, 1904 ; Mahaffy's, in Blackwood's Philosophical Classics, is mainly biographical. The chapter in Kuno
Fischer's *History of Philosophy* has been translated, and printed separately under the title *Descartes and his School*. But more attention
should be given by English students to French opinion : see especially
a memorial number of the *Revue de Métaphysique*, July 1896, by
thirteen writers ; and French histories of Philosophy, by Renouvier,
Weber, Fouillée, and Lévy Bruhl.

What is likely to be the standard account of Descartes for English
readers has been published in 1906—*Descartes, His Life and Times*
by Elizabeth S. Haldane.

IV.

GOD AS INFINITE SUBSTANCE

SPINOZA (1632–1677).

BY Spinoza we are invited to look at the world through God. The whole array of temporary, finite, contingent persons, events, and things are set in the Eternal, Infinite, Necessary Being. And, further, it is in this vision of Reality, and in it alone, that our Happiness lies: this is the true Religion.

We have seen Descartes start from *Cogito*, and soon arrive at the thought of God. Spinoza in his great systematic work omits all preliminaries, and commences with the *prius* of all knowledge and the substance of all reality: these he takes to be identical; he is Ontological. This should be kept clearly in mind. Spinoza has no scruples that he may be dealing with thoughts only: he is giving his view of Reality; and will find no after problem how to bring Reality under a scheme of thought which has been developed apart from it. The unity of Reality with Thought is in his conviction all along.

This settled, he adopts the method of Geometry for bringing Thought and Reality into explicitness: *Ethica, more geometrico demonstrata,* is his title. In this it is to be noticed that more is meant than the employment of geometrical method as a convenient method for Metaphysics as the study of ultimate Reality. There is an assumption of similarity in the subject-matter. To Spinoza, as to his contemporaries, it was not clear that the method of Geometry depended upon the specific subject-matter which was supplied to it to work upon, namely, Space. Spinoza took it that he could posit Reality as he could posit Space. In dealing with plurality in unity, attribute and substance, modes and

76

attributes, he finds Geometry, with its Figure and properties, an excellent illustration; going further, indeed, and finding in it the "standard of verity," to use his own expression. This Ontological presumption must be kept in mind when taking the system into account as a whole.

Spinoza in other writings gives some account of the genesis of his theory of knowing and being; and inquiry as to his intellectual ancestry leads along tracks of great interest in the history of religious and philosophical thought. Here we can print only his result as given in his chief work, the *Ethica*, written in Latin, and published immediately after his death.

CONCERNING GOD.

At the close of Part I., Spinoza sums up his result as follows: "I have unfolded the nature of God and His properties, namely, that He is that which exists of necessity; that He is one; that He exists and acts from the sole necessity of His own nature; that He is the free cause of all things, and how He is so. That all things are in God, and depend upon Him in such manner that without Him they cannot possibly either exist or be conceived. And, finally, that all things have been predetermined by God; not, indeed, from the freedom of a will, or from an absolutely arbitrary decree, but from the absolute nature or infinite power of God."

§ 1. God as Self-Existing Substance.

Definitions.

1. By a *cause of itself* (*causa sui*), I mean something of which the essence involves existence; or of which the nature is conceivable only as being in existence.[1]

---

[1] *Causa sui.*—The meaning of this much discussed expression seems fairly clear when it is looked at in the light of the purpose for which Spinoza required it. The action of cause and effect—or with him, more strictly, ground and consequent—implies two objects in relation. Could we not close the two up into one, and then we should have

2. A thing is called *finite in its kind* when it can be limited by another thing of the same nature. A body, for instance, is called finite because we always conceive another body greater than it. So also a thought can be limited by another thought. But a body is not limited by a thought, nor a thought by a body.

3. By *Substance*, I understand that which exists in itself, and is conceived through itself ; that is, something of which the conception needs for its formation the conception of no other thing.

4. By *Attribute*, I understand that which the intellect perceives in Substance as (*tanquam*) constituting its essence.

5. By *Mode*, I understand a modification of Substance ; or that which is in something other than itself, by means of which also it is conceived.

6. By *God*, I understand a Being which is absolutely infinite—that is, a Substance consisting of infinite attributes, each of which expresses eternal and infinite essence.

Explanations. I say infinite absolutely, not infinite in its kind. For an infinity of attributes may be denied to a thing which is infinite only in its own kind. But the absolutely infinite contains in its essence all that expresses reality, without any admission of negation whatever.[2]

---

something of which the existence depends only upon itself ? To Spinoza this self-existence was the starting-point of thought, it was the character of Reality as a whole. From this he thought he could unfold the universe. That the conception of Causation in the sense of dependence as between cause and effect is absent from Spinoza's fundamental method is agreed : with him the relation is a statical one of ground and consequent, the inherence of properties : and his constant parallel, as already pointed out, is geometrical properties in relation to their figures. Causation pushes its way in sometimes, no doubt, but it is alien to his main line of thought.

[2] The three moments seem to be X, *plus* extension and thought, *plus* modes of these (extended things and states of consciousness). And as all the modes are within the attributes, and the attributes are within X, all is within X, which is Reality itself. The difference

7. A thing is called *free* which exists solely by the necessity of its own nature, and acts solely as determined by itself. On the other hand, a thing is necessary, or, better constrained, which is determined by something other than itself to a fixed and definite way of existing or acting.

8. By *Eternity*, I mean existence itself, in so far as it is conceived as following solely from the definition of that which is eternal.

Explanation. Existence of this kind is conceived as eternal truth, like the essence of a thing. It cannot, therefore, be explained by reference to duration or time, even though duration may be conceived without beginning or ending.

Axioms.

1. Whatever exists, exists either in itself or in something else.[3]

2. Whatever cannot be conceived through anything else, must be conceived through itself.

3. From every definite cause an effect follows of necessity; and, on the other hand, if there is no definite cause, it is impossible for there to be any effect.

---

from Descartes appears in the removal of self-existing substantiality from both body and mind, and insisting on it being confined to the X of which they are the *attributes*. Of course it is open to ask, *what* the substance is? and if it is only the attributes over again, what purpose the conception serves? Spinoza meant it to serve the purpose of unification, at least.

[3] Axiom 1 must be looked at closely, for battle will be joined upon it by those who are keeping Pantheism at arm's length. They will say that we know of substances which are both *in se* and *in alio*, inherently substantial as regards their qualities yet dependent upon God, *e.g.* the world, and, possibly, each individual soul. Whereas Spinoza's statement is true only if confined to substance in his sense as wholly self-dependent. Much depends on this, as this Axiom enters into the structure of his chain of argument at several points, and so leads him to his one substance, because he started from it.

4. The knowledge of an effect depends upon the knowledge of a cause, and involves that knowledge.

5. Things which have nothing in common cannot be understood by means of one another; the conception of one does not involve the conception of the other.

6. An idea is true when it corresponds with its object.

7. If a thing can be conceived to be non-existent, existence is not involved in its essence.

Proposition I.   Substance is by nature prior to its modifications.

Proof.   This is clear from Defs. 3 and 5.

Proposition II.   Two substances with different attributes have nothing in common.

Proof.   This is evident from Def. 3.   For each substance must exist in itself and be conceived through itself; in other words, the conception of the one does not involve the conception of the other.

Proposition III.   Things which have nothing in common cannot be the cause of one another.

Proof.   If they have nothing in common, it follows that one cannot be conceived by means of the other (Ax. 5), and, therefore, one cannot be the cause of the other.

Proposition IV.   Two or more distinct things are distinguished from one another either by the difference of the attributes of the substances or by the difference of their modifications.

Proof.   Everything that exists, exists either in itself or in something else (by Ax. 1); that is (by Defs. 3 and 5), outside intellect there is nothing except substances and their modifications.   There is therefore nothing outside intellect by which a number of things can be distinguished among themselves except substances, or what is the same thing (by Def. 4), their attributes and their modifications.

Proposition V. In the nature of things there cannot be two or more substances of the same nature or attribute.

Proof. If several distinct substances were given, they must be distinguished from one another by the difference either of their attributes or of their modifications (Prop. IV.). If the difference is in their attributes it will be granted, therefore, that there is only one substance of the same attribute. But if the difference is in the modifications, since substance is by nature prior to its modifications (Prop. I.), then, setting aside the modifications and looking at substance in itself, *i.e.* (Defs. 3 and 6) truly, it cannot be conceived to be distinguished from another substance, *i.e.* (Prop. IV.) there cannot be several substances with the same attribute, but only one.

Proposition VI. One substance cannot be produced by another substance.

Proof. In the nature of things there cannot be two substances of the same attribute (by Prop. V.), *i.e.* (by Prop. II.), which have anything common to both. Therefore (by Prop. III.) one cannot be the cause of the other, nor be produced by the other.

Corollary. Hence it follows that a substance cannot be produced by something else. For in the nature of things there is nothing except substances and their modifications (Ax. 1 and Defs. 3 and 5). But it cannot be produced by another substance (by this Prop.). Therefore, absolutely, a substance cannot be produced by something else.

Another Proof. This is proved even more easily by reference to the law of contradiction. For if a substance could be produced by something else, the knowledge of it must depend upon the knowledge of that producing cause (Ax. 4); and therefore (Def. 3) it would not be substance.[4]

---

[4] In this chain (up to Prop. VI.) Propositions I. to III. only bring together some Definitions and incorporate Axioms 4 and 5 ; but Axiom 4 rests on Axiom 1, and Axiom 5 depends on Axiom 4 : while VI.

Proposition VII.   Existence belongs to the nature of substance.

Proof.   Substance cannot be produced by something else (by Prop. VI. Coroll.), it will therefore be its own cause (*causa sui*)—that is (by Def. 1), its essence necessarily involves existence, or existence belongs to its nature.[5]

Proposition VIII.   Every substance is necessarily infinite.

Proof.   A substance of one attribute must be a unique thing (Prop. V.), and existence belongs to its very nature (Prop. VII.).   From its nature, therefore, it must exist either as infinite or finite.   But not as finite, for (by Def. 2, a thing is finite in its class which can be limited by another thing of the same nature) it would have to be limited by another thing of the same nature, which also would have to exist by necessity (Prop. VII.).   And so there would be given two substances with the same attribute, which is absurd (by Prop. V.).   It exists therefore as infinite.

Scholium I.   Since to be finite is really in part a negation, and the infinite is the absolute affirmation of the existence of a nature, it follows, from Prop. VII. alone, that every substance must be infinite.

Scholium II. (referring to Prop. VII.).   I do not doubt that the demonstration of Prop. VII. will be comprehended with difficulty by all those who judge confusedly about things, and have not been accustomed to know things by means of their first causes ; for undoubtedly such persons do not make distinc-

and its Corollaries are on a similar footing.   And so to some the chain hangs in the air.   But Spinoza, with his conception of Substance, pursues his way.

[5] This demonstration illustrates Spinoza's way of taking for proof what is really the unfolding of previous assertions.   He means to prove existence for Substance ; and does it by drawing it out of the heart and meaning of Substance itself.   We noticed that he enclosed " Cause" (in his sense) in Substance, and now he has only to draw it out again : and Substance as necessarily causing and caused exists in the sense that everything exists of which the Cause exists.

tion between the modifications of substances and the substances themselves, nor do they know how things are produced. The consequence is that they attribute to substances a beginning such as they see belonging to things in nature. For those who are not acquainted with the real causes of things confuse all things together, and they find no intellectual repugnance in representing trees talking like men; or they imagine men originating sometimes from stones, sometimes from seed; and that forms of particular kinds are changed into forms of other kinds. So also those who confuse Divine nature with human nature easily attribute to the Deity human affections (*affectus*), especially so long as they are ignorant of the way in which affections are produced in the human mind. But if men would give attention to what the nature of a substance is, they would not have the smallest doubt of the truth of Prop. VII.; nay, this proposition would be accounted by all to be an axiom, and be ranked among common notions. For by " substance " they would understand that which is in itself and is conceived by means of itself; that is, that the knowledge of it needs the knowledge of nothing else : while by modifications, they would understand what are in something else, being conceived by means of the conception of the thing in which they are. So that we can have true ideas of modifications which do not exist : since, although they may not actually exist outside the intellect, yet their essence is so comprehended in something else, that by its means they can be conceived. But there is no truth of substances outside the intellect, except in themselves, because they are conceived through themselves. If anyone should say, therefore, that he has a clear and distinct—that is to say, a true idea of substance, and yet that he doubts whether such a substance exists, it would be the same thing, forsooth, as if he should say that he has a true idea, and yet is in doubt whether it is false (as becomes manifest to anyone who is sufficiently attentive); or, if anyone should affirm that a substance is created, he by doing so would be affirming that a false idea has become true, which is as great an absurdity as can be imagined. And so it must necessarily be acknowledged that the existence of substance, like its essence, is an eternal truth.

And hence we can conclude in another way, which I think worth adding here, that only one substance of any nature can be given.

But that I may do this in due order it is to be noted : (1) The true definition of each thing involves nothing, and expresses nothing, beyond the nature of the thing defined. From which it follows (2) that no definition involves or expresses a fixed number of individuals, seeing that it expresses nothing else than the nature of the thing defined. For example, the definition of a triangle expresses nothing else than the simple nature of a triangle, and certainly not any certain number of triangles. (3) It is to be noted that some certain cause is necessarily given for everything which exists, by virtue of which it comes into existence. (4) Lastly, it is to be noted that this cause, by virtue of which a thing comes into existence, must either be contained in the very nature and definition of the thing existing (simply because it pertains to the nature of the thing to exist), or must exist outside it. From these four points it follows that if in nature a certain number of individuals exists, a cause must necessarily be given why those individuals exist, and not fewer or more of them.

If, for instance, in the nature of things twenty men exist (whom, for the sake of simplicity, I suppose to exist at the same time, and that none existed in nature before), it will not be sufficient in giving a reason for the existence of the twenty to show the cause of human nature in general, but there will be an additional necessity to show the cause why neither more nor less than twenty exist, since by point 3 a cause must be shown for the existence of everything. But this cause (by the above points 2 and 3) cannot be contained within human nature itself, since the true definition of man does not involve the number twenty. And, therefore, by point 4, the cause why these twenty men exist, and consequently why any one of them exists, must necessarily be placed outside any one of them. And, therefore, we must absolutely conclude that everything of a nature which admits of the existence of several individuals must necessarily have an external cause in order that those individuals may exist. Now, since existence belongs to the nature of substance (as already proved in this Scholium), its definition must involve necessary existence, and consequently from its definition alone its existence must be inferred. But from its definition (as shown in the above points 2 and 3) the existence of several substances cannot follow. It follows, therefore, necessarily from that definition, that only a single thing of one nature exists, as was laid down.

Proposition IX. The more reality or being a thing has, the greater is the number of its attributes.

Proof. By Def. 4.

Proposition X. Each several attribute of the one substance must be conceived through itself only.

Proof. An attribute is that which the intellect perceives of substance as constituting its essence (Def. 4), and therefore it must be conceived through itself (Def. 3).

Scholium. It is thus evident that though the attributes are, in fact, conceived as distinct, that is, one without the help of the other, yet we cannot conclude from this that they constitute two beings or two different substances. For the nature of substance is such that each of its attributes is conceived through itself, as all its attributes have always existed together in it, and no one of them could be produced by any other of them, but each expresses the reality or being of substance. It is therefore by no means an absurdity to ascribe several attributes to one substance; for nothing in nature is more clear than that each and every being must be conceived under some attribute, and that its reality or being is in proportion to the number of its attributes expressing necessity or eternity or infinity. It is therefore abundantly clear that an absolutely infinite being must be defined as consisting of infinite attributes, every one of which expresses a certain eternal and infinite essence.

If it is now asked by what signs we may distinguish between different substances, let the following propositions be read, where it is shown that there is only one substance in the universe; and that that substance is absolutely infinite, and it will be seen that to search for any such distinguishing mark is futile : [6]—

Proposition XI. God, or Substance, consisting of infinite attributes, each of which expresses eternal and infinite essence, necessarily exists.

Proof. If you deny this, conceive (if possible) that God does not exist. Then (by Axiom 7) His essence does not involve existence. But this (by Prop. VII.) is absurd. Therefore God necessarily exists.

Another Proof. A cause or reason of everything should be assigned, either why it exists, or why it does not exist. For example, if a triangle exists, a reason or cause ought to be given why it exists; but if it does not exist, a reason or cause ought to be given which prevents it from existing, or

---

[6] An "attribute" is immediately cognisable through itself, or not at all ; while a mode requires reference to an attribute, *e.g.* motion and rest require reference to extension ; intellect and will, reference to thought.

Before we pass to consider Prop. XI., we notice that it speaks of an infinity of attributes ; but we also find all along that only two are known by us. Both these points must be kept constantly in view, namely, that there are two, the universe is dual ; but only two, so thought seems arrested abruptly. Spinoza insists that it cannot be arrested, but requires that we follow it up to infinity, and that only in that way are we in face of Reality.

which takes away its existence. But this reason or cause must be either contained in the nature of the thing, or lie outside that nature. For example, the reason why a square-circle does not exist is indicated in the very nature of it : simply because it involves a contradiction. But, on the other hand, why a substance exists follows from its nature alone, namely, because that nature involves existence (Prop. VII.). But the reason why a circle or a triangle exists, or why it does not exist, does not follow from the nature of those things, but from the order of corporeal nature in general. From which it must follow either that a triangle exists of necessity, or that it is impossible for it to exist. And these things are self-evident. Therefore it follows that a thing for which no reason or cause is given which prevents it from existing exists of necessity. If, therefore, neither reason nor cause can be given which prevents the Deity from existing, or which takes away His existence, the conclusion is certain that He exists of necessity. But if any such reason or cause should be given, it would require to be given either in the nature of God or outside that nature, that is, in another substance of another nature. For if it lay in a nature of the same kind, by that very fact it would be conceded that the existence of the Deity is given. But a substance of another nature could have nothing in common with the Deity (by Prop. II., two substances having different attributes have nothing in common with one another), and therefore could neither cause His existence nor remove it. Since, therefore, a reason or cause which can take away the Divine existence cannot possibly lie outside the Divine nature, it will have to lie of necessity, if He does not exist, within His own nature, which would therefore involve a contradiction. It is absurd to affirm this of an absolutely infinite and completely perfect being : therefore neither in God nor outside God is any cause or reason given which can take away His existence ; and therefore God exists of necessity.

Another Proof. To be able not to exist implies absence of power; and, on the other hand, to be able to exist is the presence of power, as is self-evident. So if there are now existing of necessity nothing but finite beings, there are therefore finite beings more powerful than a being absolutely infinite; and this is self-evidently absurd. Therefore, either nothing exists, or an absolutely infinite Being exists of necessity also. Now we ourselves exist, either in ourselves or in something else which exists of necessity (Axiom 1 : All things are either in themselves or in something else; and Prop. VII.). Therefore an absolutely infinite Being, that is (by Definition 6) God, exists of necessity.

Scholium. In this last proof I have desired to establish the existence of God *à posteriori*, as a demonstration more easily to be perceived, but not because from the same grounds the existence of God does not follow *à priori*. For since ability to exist is a power, it follows that the more reality belongs to the nature of anything, the more strength it has in itself for existing; and also that absolutely infinite Being, or God, has from Himself an absolutely infinite power of existing, and therefore exists absolutely. Yet many, perhaps, will not be able to see with ease the force of this demonstration, because they are accustomed to contemplate only those things which flow from causes external to the things; and, those things which come quickly into being, that is, which exist without difficulty, they see also perishing easily; and, on the other hand, they consider those things which they regard as more complex to be more difficult to bring about, that is, not so easily to be brought into existence. But that they may be liberated from these prejudices I have no need to show here how far the proverb, "Soon come, soon go," is true, nor even whether in respect of nature as a whole all things are equally easy, or otherwise; but this alone it is sufficient to observe, that I am not speaking now of things which come into being from external causes, but only of substances which (by Prop. **VI.** one substance cannot be produced by another substance) can be produced by no external cause. As to things which come into being from external causes, whether they are composed of many parts or of few, whatever perfection or reality they possess is all due to the virtue of their external causes, and so their existence has its origin from the perfection of these external causes alone, not from their own. On the other hand, whatever perfection substance has is due to no external cause: its existence therefore must follow from its own nature, which is nothing else than its essence. Therefore perfection does not annul the existence of a thing, but, on the contrary, establishes it; but imperfection, on the contrary, annuls existence, and so we cannot be more certain of the existence of anything than of the existence of a being absolutely infinite or perfect, that is, God. For, since His essence excludes every imperfection and involves absolute perfection, by that very fact every cause for doubting concerning His existence is removed, and the highest certitude of it is given. And this, I believe, will be clear to everyone who gives even a moderate amount of attention to it.[7]

[7] This Proposition, with its Scholium, contains four "Proofs" of the existence of the Divine Being. It would be quite futile for anyone to look here for support for proofs of existence of the Divine Being regarded in any other light than in that in which Spinoza has defined Him. They are variants of Ontological "argument"; if we have asserted that a being is *causa sui*, we have only to make explicit our belief that he exists. As nothing can prevent the equiangularity of a triangle, so nothing can prevent the operation of an infinite "Cause" which Spinoza has included in his conception of what Reality is. It must again be pointed out that he considered that in Geometry dealing with Space he had a proper analogue for Metaphysics dealing with Reality : his strength and his weakness both lie there.

In Proof 3, Spinoza seems to consider that he is holding out a hand to those who prefer *à posteriori* proof. For himself, he sets no store on it, but hastens at once to show that from the same premises *à priori* argument is available. In Proof 4, therefore, he simply leaves

Proposition XII. No attribute of a substance can be really conceived from which it may follow that substance can be divided.

Proof. For the parts into which substance, so conceived, would be divided, will either retain the nature of substance, or will not. Under the first supposition (by Prop. VIII.) each several part will have to be infinite, and (by Prop. VI.) be the cause of itself; and (by Prop. V.) it will have to consist of its own peculiar attribute, and thus from one substance many would be able to be constituted, which is absurd (by Prop. VI.). Further, that the parts (by Prop. II.) would have nothing in common with their whole, and the whole (by Def. 4 and Prop. X.) could both be and be conceived without its parts, is an absurdity about which no one can be in doubt. But under the second supposition, namely, that the parts will not retain the nature of substance; then, since the whole substance would be divided into parts of equal value, it would lose the nature of substance and cease to be, which (by Prop. VII.) is absurd.

Proposition XIII. Substance absolutely infinite is indivisible.

Proof. For if it were divisible, the parts into which it would be divided will either retain the nature of substance

---

out the empirical reference, and states the *à priori* in isolation again, namely, the power to exist is at the maximum in the Divine Substance by reason of His absolute perfection. It is tempting to agree with Mr. Joachim (*The Ethics of Spinoza*) in his excellent section on these proofs. This would imply that Spinoza discerned that connexion between *à priori* and *à posteriori* proofs which is shown by Kant (Selection VII.), adopted by Hegel, and now widely recognised. In his Proof 3 the combination of both is seen by him: there is a reference to fact, and a reference to thought, and to their combination. But the easy way in which he resumes reference to *à priori* thought makes it difficult to think that in the other three proofs he was making reference to finite substantiality in a suppressed premise.

absolutely infinite, or will not. If the former, there will be
several substances of the same nature, which (by Prop. V.) is
absurd. If the second, then (as above) an infinite substance
will be able to cease to be, which (by Prop. XI.) is also absurd.

Corollary. From these points it follows that no substance, and consequently no corporeal substance, in so far
as it is substance, is divisible.

Scholium. That substance is indivisible, is understood
more simply from this alone, that the nature of substance
cannot be conceived except as infinite, and that by part of
substance nothing else can be understood than finite substance, which (by Prop. VIII.) implies a manifest contradiction.

Proposition XIV. No substance can be granted or conceived except God.

Proof. Since God is Being absolutely infinite, of whom
no attribute expressing the essence of substance can be
denied (Def. 6), and He necessarily exists (Prop. XI.), if
any other substance than God were granted it must be
explained by reference to some attribute of God, and so
there would exist two substances with the same attribute,
which (by Prop. V.) is absurd. Thus no substance except
God can be given, and consequently no other can even be
conceived. For if any other could be conceived, it must
necessarily be conceived as existing; but this (by the first
part of this Demonstration) is absurd.

Corollary 1. Hence it follows in the clearest way that
God is one (*unicum*), *i.e.* (Def. 6) in the nature of things
only one substance is given, and that is absolutely infinite
(as proved in Prop. X. Schol.).

Corollary 2. Extension and thought are either attributes
of God, or (by Ax. 1) modifications of His attributes.[8]

[8] Having arrived at this link in the chain, some questions naturally
arise. The critical literature is indeed vast, but in referring to it
distinction should be made between criticisms from outside Spinoza's
scheme and criticisms from within it. It is one thing to oppose

§ 2. GOD ACTS NECESSARILY, IMMANENTLY, AND IS ETERNAL;
   THE WORLD IS CONTINGENT, BUT GOVERNED BY
   NECESSITY.

Proposition XVII. God acts by the laws of His own nature alone, without compulsion by any other being.

Proof. From the sole necessity of the Divine nature, or, what is the same thing, from the sole laws of that nature, infinite things proceed in an absolute manner, as we have shown in Prop. XVI.; and in Prop. XV. we demonstrated that nothing can exist or be conceived without God, but that all things are in Him. Nothing, therefore, can exist outside Him, by which He may be determined or compelled to act; and so God acts according to the laws of His own nature alone, compelled by no other being.

Corollary 1. Hence it follows that no cause is given which incites the Deity to action, either from without or from within, except the perfection of His own nature.

his conception of Substance altogether, and to continue a running fire of criticisms at each successive point of the advance : another to take up his intention, and raise questions as to whether he pursues a consistently and securely established line of march. Even from within, the process has met with varying receptions ; some think it irrefragable, others declare that it is replete with paralogisms. The principal points where conflict arises as to what Spinoza has accomplished are, the question whether the infinity of attributes is anything more than a conception, as it is plainly beyond all testing, and cannot be made use of when he comes to apply his conception to the universe ; the question whether "Substance," which is unknown and inconceivable, really unites the attributes, or only nominally—in other words, whether dualism is not carried out into ultimate Reality ; the incongruous character of the limitation of the attributes to two in an *à priori* system ; whether the attributes themselves (extension and thought) have sufficient character to be severally grounds for the two parallel series of modes which will have to be dealt with ; and, to name one more, the appearance sometimes given that thought is superior to the other attribute, inasmuch as both attributes are defined to be Substance in so far as it is thought about.

Corollary 2.   It follows also that God alone is a free cause, for He alone exists by necessity of His own nature (Props. XI. and XIV. Coroll. 1), and acts by necessity of His own nature (Prop. XVI.).   And so (by Def. 7, of freedom: A thing is free which acts from necessity of its own nature alone, and is determined to action by itself alone : a thing is necessitated, or rather compelled, which is determined by some other thing to action and operation, in some certain and determined way) He alone is a free cause.

Scholium.   . . . I will show,—without the aid of this Proposition,—that God acts by the laws of His own nature only, without compulsion by any one,—that neither intellect nor will belong to the nature of God.   There are many, I know, who think that they can demonstrate that supreme intelligence and free will belong to the nature of God ; for they say that they know of nothing more perfect to attribute to God than what is the highest perfection in us.

Now, although they conceive God in actuality as supreme intellect, yet they do not believe that He can cause everything to exist which is actually in His intellect ; for they think that in that way they are denying power to God.   If He had created, they say, everything which is in His intellect, He could then have created nothing further, and this they consider to be repugnant to His omnipotence ; therefore they have preferred to regard God as indifferent to all things, and not creating anything else than what He has decided upon by a certain absolute volition.   But I think that I have shown with sufficient clearness (Prop. XVI.) that there have flowed of necessity, or continue to flow by the same necessity, from the supreme power or infinite nature of God, infinite things in infinite ways ; in the same way as from the nature of a triangle it follows from eternity and to eternity that its three angles are equal to two right angles. Therefore the omnipotence of God has been actual from eternity, and will remain eternally in the same actuality. And in my judgment the omnipotence of God is established far more perfectly in this way than in theirs. Indeed, these opponents seem to me, if I may speak freely, to deny the omnipotence of God. For they are obliged to allow that God knows an infinity of things which might be created which He will never be able to create. For otherwise, if He were to create all the things that He knows, He would, according to them, exhaust His omnipotence and render Himself imperfect. In order, therefore, to establish the perfection of God, they are reduced to establishing at the same time an inability to effect all the things to which His power extends; and I do not see what can be imagined more absurd or more repugnant to His omnipotence.

Further,—to speak of both the intellect and the will, which we usually attribute to God,—I will also say this: If both intellect and will belong to the eternal essence of God, something else must be understood by each of them than men usually mean. For the intellect and will which would constitute the essence of God must totally differ from our intellect and will, and could coincide with them in nothing but their names: in precisely the same way as is the case with the constellation the Dog, and the dog, the animal which barks. I will prove it in this way. If intellect belongs to the Divine nature, it cannot, like our intellect, come into operation either later than the things understood (as most choose to think), or at the same time with them, since God is prior in causality to all things (Prop. XVI. Coroll. 1); but, on the other hand, the truth and formal essence of things is such as it is, because it exists as such objectively in the intellect of God. Therefore the intellect of God, in so far as it is conceived to constitute His essence, is really the cause of things both in their

essence and in their existence; which seems to have been
noticed by those who have asserted that the Divine intellect,
will, and power are all one and the same thing. Since,
therefore, the intellect of God is the only cause of things,
that is to say, (as we have shown), of their essence as well
as of their existence, it must of necessity differ from those
things with regard to both its essence and its existence.
For a thing caused differs from its cause precisely in that
which it has from the cause. For instance, a man is the
cause of the existence, but not of the essence, of another
man (for the essence is an eternal truth); and therefore as
to essence they are entirely similar, though they must differ
with regard to existence; and, therefore, if the existence of
one of them perishes, that of the other does not perish on
that account; but if the essence of one could be destroyed
and rendered false, the essence of the other would be
destroyed also. Therefore a thing which is the cause
both of the essence and of the existence of some effect,
must differ from such an effect both with regard to its
essence as well as with regard to its existence. But the
intellect of God is the cause both of the essence and the
existence of ours; therefore the intellect of God, in so far
as it is conceived to constitute Divine essence, differs from
our intellect both with regard to its essence and its existence; nor can it coincide with our intellect in anything
except in name. A similar proof applies to the will, as
everyone can easily see.

Proposition XVIII. God is the cause of all things,
immanently not transcendently (*transiens*).

Proof. All things that are, are in God, and must be
conceived through God (Prop. XV.), and therefore God is
the cause of the things which are in Himself. This is the
first point. Further, no substance can be granted outside
God (Prop. XIV.), that is (by Def. 3, of Substance), nothing
which is outside God exists in itself; which was the second

point.   Therefore God is the immanent, but not the transcendent, cause of all things.[9]

Proposition XIX.   God is eternal, that is, His attributes
are eternal.   For God (Def. 6) is substance, which (Prop. XI.)
exists of necessity, that is (Prop. VII.), it belongs to its nature
to exist; or, which is the same thing, He is substance from
the definition of which His existence follows; and, therefore
(Def. 8), He is eternal.   Further, we must understand by
attributes of God that which expresses the essence of Divine
substance (Def. 4), that is to say, that which belongs to
substance; for this, I say, is what attributes must themselves
involve.   But eternity belongs to the nature of substance
(Prop. VII.).   Therefore each of the attributes must involve
eternity, and therefore they are all of them eternal.

Scholium.   This proposition is as clear as possible from
the method in which I have proved the existence of God
(Prop. XI.).

Proposition XXIX.   In the nature of things there is
nothing contingent, but all things have been determined
from the necessity of the Divine nature to exist and operate
in a certain way.

Proof.   Whatever is, is in God (Prop. XV.).   But God

---

[9] The term *transiens* means, not temporary, of course, but passing
over from one thing to another, from agent to patient; and Spinoza
denies any such relation as between God and the world : the world is
in no way separated off from the Divine Being, but is within Him :
everything is in God.   If the world which we know had infinite
attributes, then we could also say that God is wholly in the world, and
Pantheism would be explicit in its complete form.   But as there is an
infinity of attributes unknown to us, Spinoza cannot be said to teach
that the Thought-Space world, though infinite in each of its two
aspects, is the totality of the Divine Being.   At least by his insisting
on the unknown attributes, he is obviously guarding himself from this.
Whether or not there is any value in this reference to an unknown
and, apparently, unknowable, is another question.   Spinoza here puts
the term "Cause" prominently; his real meaning has been indicated
in the Introduction and in note [1].

cannot be called a thing contingent; for (by Prop. XI.) He exists necessarily, and not contingently. The modes of the Divine nature have followed from that nature necessarily and not contingently (Prop. XVI.), and that, either considering the Divine nature as absolute or as in a certain way determined to action (Prop. XXVII.). Further, of these modes God is not only the cause in so far as they exist in simplicity (Prop. XXIV. Coroll.), but also (Prop. XXIV.) so far as they are considered as determined to some operation. But if they were not determined by God (by the same Proposition), it is impossible, and not contingent, that they should determine themselves; and, on the other hand, if they were determined by God, it is impossible, and not contingent, that they should render themselves indeterminate. All things, therefore, have been determined from the necessity of the Divine nature not only to exist, but also to exist and operate in a certain way, and nothing contingent is given.[10]

Scholium. Before I proceed further, I wish here to explain, or rather to recall to mind, what we should understand by *Natura naturans* and by *Natura naturata.* For I think that it now stands clear from what has preceded, that by *Natura naturans* we should understand what is in itself and is conceived through itself, or such attributes of substance as express eternal and infinite essence; that is (Prop. XIV. Coroll. 1, and Prop. XVII. Coroll. 2), God, in so far as He is considered as a free cause. By *Natura naturata* I mean everything which follows from the necessity of the nature of

---

[10] If every property flows from Attribute, *i.e.* from Essence, it is obvious that every property is necessary; and if the universe is the totality of such properties, it is plain that everything in it is wholly necessitated, there is no such thing as contingency ultimately; the opinion that there is, arises in human imagination only, which arrests our attention prematurely, and leaves us among imperfect and confused ideas. In this sense necessity and freedom are the same thing; a thing acts of necessity according to its own nature, and such a thing we also call free.

7

God or of any one of His attributes; that is, all the modes of
the attributes of God, in so far as they are considered as
things which are in God and without Him can neither exist
nor be conceived.[11]

Proposition XXXIII. Things could have been produced
by God in no other way and in no other order than the way
and order in which they have actually been produced.

Proof. For all things have followed necessarily from the
given nature of God (Prop. XVI.), and from the necessity of
His nature have been determined to existence and operation
of a particular kind (Prop. XXIX.). If, therefore, things
could have been of some other nature, or have been determined to operation in some other way, so that the order of
nature would be other than it is, then also the nature of God
could be other than it is now; and therefore (Prop. XI.)
that other nature must exist; and consequently there would be
two or more Divine Beings, which (by Prop. XIV. Coroll. 1)
is absurd.

Scholium 1. Since I have thus shown more clearly than
the light of noon that there is in things absolutely nothing
on account of which they may be called contingent, I desire
to explain in a few words what is meant by us by "contingent"; but, first, of "necessary" and "impossible." A
thing is called "necessary" either with reference to its
essence or its cause. For the existence of anything necessarily follows either from its essence and definition or from
some given efficient cause. Hence, similarly, a thing is

[11] *Natura naturans* and *natura naturata* : these famous phrases,
of Scholastic origin, call attention to the distinction between activity
and passivity (receptivity), and remind us of the necessity of regarding the infinite Substance as *actus purus*. How the receptive side of
nature arises is a crux on a par with that of accounting for the appearance of the modes at all. For Spinoza the distinction can be only of a
logical kind, as there is no nature or universe which is not in God, no
activity which is not His. Granted the distinction, it is easy to allow
that human intelligence may partake of both kinds, as Spinoza thinks.

called impossible; namely, either because its essence or
definition involves a contradiction, or because no external
cause is forthcoming determined for the production of such a
thing. But a thing is called contingent from no other cause
than in respect to the deficiency of our knowledge. For a
thing as to which we are ignorant whether its essence involves a contradiction or not, or as to which we are quite
sure that it involves no contradiction, while yet we are able to
make no certain affirmation of its existence because the order
of causes is concealed from us, can never appear to us either
necessary or impossible; and therefore we call it contingent
and possible.

Scholium 2 (part). From what has preceded, it clearly
follows that things have been produced in supreme perfection
by the Deity, since they have necessarily followed from the
given perfection of His nature. Nor does this argue any
imperfection in the Deity, for it is His perfection which has
compelled us to affirm this very thing. Indeed, from its
opposite it would clearly follow (as I lately showed) that the
Deity is not supremely perfect; namely, because, if things
had been produced in some other way, another nature would
have to be attributed to Him than the consideration of a most
perfect Being has compelled us to attribute.[12] . . .

Part II. Proposition XLIV. It is not in the nature of
Reason to regard things as contingent, but as necessary.

---

[12] This is quite different from Fatalism when used as an epithet
of opprobrium. Fatalism is obnoxious, because it signifies struggle
against an external power which may be sometimes favourable or
sometimes opposed in effect, but is always in itself completely indifferent
to our interests. The necessity of Spinozism is constancy of operation
within the system of Reality, and in things or persons as partakers of
that Reality, as against supposed power of things or persons to
originate wholly independent activities. From this issues Spinoza's
praise, not of optimism, but of cheerful contentment (*acquiescentia*).
In securing a foundation for this, his Metaphysics gives the basis for
his Ethics.

Proof. It is of the nature of Reason to perceive things truly (Part II. Prop. XLI., and Part I. Ax. 6) as they are, that is (Part I. Prop. XXIX.), not as contingent but as necessary.

Corollary 1. Hence it follows that it is solely due to our imagination that we regard things as contingent, whether in respect to the past or to the future.

Corollary 2. It is the nature of Reason to perceive things under a certain form of eternity (*sub quadam specie æternitatis*). For it is of the nature of Reason to regard things as necessary and not as contingent (by the present Proposition). It perceives this necessity of things truly (Prop. XLI.), that is (Part I. Ax. 6), as it is in itself. But (Part I. Prop. XVI.) this necessity of things is the very necessity of the eternal nature of God. Therefore it is of the nature of Reason to regard things under this form of eternity. Add that the foundations of Reason are notions which explain what is common to all things (Prop. XXXVIII.), and which (Prop. XXXVII.) do not explain the essence of single things : by it, therefore, things must be conceived apart from any temporal relation, but under a certain form of eternity.[13]

[13] In his view of the human soul, Spinoza disallows any permanent entity such as " soul" usually implies, though we shall find him, when his thought comes to its terminus, impelled to think of mind as eternal in its essence, as participatory in Reason and therefore in eternal truth and life. But at this stage he is concerned with the mind as psychology can take hold of it, so to speak, as willing, perceiving, imagining, feeling ; and here it is quite plain that there is nothing which can be accounted Divine. Spinoza's psychology is very interesting, and shows much acute discernment. But it has a markedly intellectualist cast : will, or rather volitions—for Spinoza is a nominalist in the sphere of phenomena, and believes in particular volitions, ideas, etc., not in general faculties or powers—are identical with ideas ; they are the ideas insisting on being what they are. Some recent writers endeavour to find more of the distinctive character of volition in his view, and lay stress on Part III., where striving effort (*conatus*) is brought in. But it is very doubtful whether he is

§ 3. GOD IS IMPERSONAL.

Part I. Proposition XXXI. The intellect in operation, whether the finite or the infinite, together with the will, desire, love, etc., must be referred to nature as passive not as active (to *natura naturata*, not to *natura naturans*).

Proof. For by intellect it is self-evident that we do not mean absolute thought, but only a certain mode of thinking, differing from other modes, such as desire, love, etc., and therefore (by Def. 5, of *Mode*) it must be conceived through absolute thought; that is to say, it must be conceived through some attribute of God (Prop. XV., whatever is, is in God, and nothing can either be or be conceived without God, and Def. 6, of God) which expresses the eternal and infinite essence of thought, in such a way that without that attribute it can neither exist nor be conceived. It must therefore (Prop. XXIX. Schol. on contingency and necessity) be referred to passive nature (*naturata*) and not to operative nature (*naturans*); as must also the other modes of thought.

§ 4. *Emotions (Affectus).*

Part III. Def. 3. By emotion, I mean affections of the body, by which the active power of the body is increased or diminished, or assisted or restrained; and also the ideas of these affections.

General Definition appended to Part III. Emotion, which is called *animi pathema*, is a confused idea, by which the mind affirms of its body or of any part of it a greater

referring to anything more than the thing, the idea, being what it is, continuing so to be. It is quite likely that so comprehensive a mind as Spinoza's could not be confined within the limits he had formulated, and that he had occasional penetrative glances over the boundary towards what we now call Voluntarism.

or a less force of existence than there was before; on the appearance of which increase the mind is determined to one mode of consciousness (*cogitandi*) rather than to another.[14]

Part V. Proposition XVII. God is free from passion, and is not affected by any emotions of either joy or sorrow.

Proof. All ideas are true in so far as they are referred to God, *i.e.* (Part II. Prop. XXXII.) are adequate, and therefore God is free from passions (which, by their general definition, are inadequate ideas). Further, God can pass to neither a greater nor a less perfection, and therefore He is affected by no emotion of either joy or sorrow; and (Corollary), properly speaking, He neither loves nor hates anyone.

Part IV., in Preface. As for the terms *good* and *bad*, they indicate nothing positive in things considered in themselves; and, indeed, are nothing more than modes of thought or notions which we form when we compare things amongst themselves. For one and the same thing can be good and bad at the same time, and also indifferent. Music, for instance, is good for a man in a melancholy mood, and bad for

---

[14] In spite of all the attention he gave, it seems very doubtful whether Spinoza allows to the properly *æsthetic* quality of emotion any value at all. This general definition is quite wide of the mark, it defines feeling by reference to its *effects*. And in the special treatment it is the effects or the conditions which give the basis of classification and treatment. Yet he saw with singular clearness that emotion can enter into conflict only with emotion ; and this psychological principle he kept as a clue when looking for the final state of salvation for man, and finding it necessary to allow intellect to be associated with love. But there again he shrinks from really admitting genuine feeling ; and we find that the blessed state is rest and quietude from all that could be called emotion, and intellectual contemplation remains alone. Feeling if thus identified with its conditions and its functions is, of course, wholly inapplicable to the essence of the Divine Being, as is stated in the next Proposition.

one in mourning, while for a deaf man it is neither the one nor the other. Nevertheless, we must retain these two terms; for as we desire to form an idea of a man as an example of human nature, it will be of service for us to retain the terms in the sense I here give.

Part IV. Definitions 1 *and* 2. By Good, I mean that which we certainly know to be useful to us; by Evil, I mean that which we certainly know to prevent our being competent to attain any goodness.

Proposition VIII. The knowledge of good and evil is nothing else than an emotion of joy or of sadness in so far as we are conscious of it.[15]

[15] Goodness and Evil, being qualities relative to the human mind in its lower ranges, have no applicability to the Divine Nature. This is not to deny their significance for man, but the locating them in the lower side of his nature gives the clue to deliverance from human bondage. Salvation and Peace are to be looked for in the possibility of our transcending the sphere when good and evil have significance, and rising to the sphere when their distinction has disappeared. To God everything is good, and we should think so if we would only think with Him. It is quite parallel with the solution of the problem of error and falsity : all ideas are true if looked at as God looks at them : the error, untruth, falsity, is due to the confusions and one-sided views of human intelligence in its lower ranges. A glance over the eliminations from Divine Essence made in the Propositions given in this section makes it clear that Spinoza was bound to be opposed in his day, and for many days. At the opposition or neglect which befell him for a century after his death there need be no surprise. Bayle and Voltaire were as outspoken as Malebranche and Clarke ; the defenders of Personal Theism joined with the guardians of historical Religion in opposing the substitution of an impersonal *Deus sive Natura sive Substantia* for a Personal Creator of the world and Ruler of mankind. And, on the other hand, when in the nineteenth century Goethe and Schleiermacher and Coleridge raised him to a high pedestal among the wise men of our race, it was for the characters of eternity, infinity, necessity, and rationality that they brushed aside the abstract and utilitarian eighteenth century to listen to Spinoza on the Divine Essence and the universe which flows from Him. See especially Bradley, *op. cit.* c. xxv.

§ 5. MAN'S BLESSEDNESS IS IN THE INTELLECTUAL LOVE OF GOD.

Part V. Proposition XXVII.   In this third and ultimate kind of knowledge lies the source of tranquillity for the mind.

Proof. The highest virtue of the mind is to know God (Part IV. Prop. XXVIII.), or to understand things by the third kind of knowledge; and this virtue is the greater as the mind knows more of things by knowledge of this kind. Whoever, therefore, knows things by this kind of knowledge, passes to the summit of human perfection, and consequently is affected (Part III. Def. 2) by the highest pleasure, with the accompaniment of an idea of himself and of his own virtue; and therefore (Part III. Def. 25) tranquillity of the mind arises in this highest kind of knowledge.[16]

Proposition XXX.   Our mind, in so far as it knows itself and its body under the form of eternity, necessarily knows God, and is aware that it is in God and is conceived through God.

---

[16] The three orders of knowledge recognised by Spinoza are, first, knowledge derived from the particulars of sense-experience : these are confused ideas, opinions, imaginations ; the second kind, which he calls "reason" in a lower sense, the notions as to laws and properties collected by discursive reasoning ; and, third, *scientia intuitiva*, intuitive knowledge of the essences of things, and ultimately of the Divine Essence.   This latter Mr. Bradley illustrates by supposing that we might rise from looking out through this, that, or the other window-frame and seeing the world as a succession of vignettes, to looking out upon it as a whole with all the frames removed.   No thinker has ever made a bolder claim than Spinoza's for the presence in man of the intuitive Reason which sees things as they are, *i.e.* as in God.   In the early treatise, *De Deo*, c. xix., Spinoza makes an interesting parallel between the stages of knowledge and the stages of progress as marked by Christian theologians ; Sin is parallel with false opinion ; perception of the Law with reasoned opinion ; and appreciation of Grace with intuitive knowledge.

Proof. Eternity is the very essence of God, in so far as this essence involves necessary existence (Part I. Def. 8). Therefore, to conceive things under the form of eternity is to conceive them in so far as they are conceived through the essence of God as being real entities, or in so far as through the essence of God they involve existence.[17]

Proposition XXXII. Whatever we understand by the third kind of knowledge we delight in; and this is accompanied by the idea of God as cause.

Proof. From this kind of knowledge arises the highest possible peace of mind, that is (Def. of Emotions, 2), pleasure arises; and this is accompanied by the idea of itself (Prop. XXVII.), and consequently (Prop. XXX.) it is accompanied by the idea of God as cause.

Corollary. From this third kind of knowledge arises necessarily the intellectual love of God. For from this kind of knowledge arises (by this Proposition) pleasure, with the accompanying idea of God as cause, that is (by Def. of Emotions, 6), the love of God; not in so far as we imagine Him to be present now, but in so far as we understand Him to be eternal: and this is what I call the intellectual love of God.

Proposition XXXVI. The intellectual love of the mind towards God is that very love of God with which God loves Himself, not in so far as He is infinite, but in so far as He can be explained through the essence of the human mind considered under the form of eternity; that is to say, the intellectual love of the mind towards God is a part of the infinite love with which God loves Himself.

---

[17] The mind is now treated as participating in Divine knowledge: we can think *sub quadam specie æternitatis*. Our body as a mode of extension has no permanence, and our mental life in lower ranges comes and goes with it: in intuitive knowledge coming and going cease. And, further, there is no need to wait for this until after the dissolution of the lower range of our nature: we can attain eternal life *now*.

Proof. This love of the mind must be referred to the actions of the mind (Prop. XXXII. Coroll. above, and Part III. Prop. III., Actions of the mind arise only from adequate ideas, but Emotions depend upon inadequate ideas); and it is, therefore, an action in which the mind contemplates itself with the accompanying idea of God as cause (Prop. XXXII.); that is (Part I. Prop. XXV., and Part II. Prop. XI. Coroll.), an action by which God, so far as He can be explained by the human mind, contemplates Himself, with the accompanying idea of Himself. And so (Prop. XXXV., God loves Himself with an infinite intellectual love) this intellectual love of the mind towards God is part of the infinite love with which God loves Himself.

Corollary. Hence it follows that God, in so far as He loves Himself, loves men; and, consequently, that the love of God towards men and the intellectual love of the mind towards God, is one and the same thing.

Scholium. From this we clearly understand in what our salvation (*salus*) or blessedness (*beatitudo*) or freedom consists, namely, in our permanent and eternal love towards God, or in the love of God towards us. In the Holy Scriptures this love or blessedness is called Glory; and not undeservedly. For, whether this love be referred to God or to the mind, it can rightly be called Peace of mind, which is really not different from glory. (Def. of Emotions, 25 : *Peace* within one's self is pleasure arising when a man contemplates himself and his power of action; and 30, *Glory* is a pleasure with an accompanying idea of some action of ours which we imagine other men to be praising.) For, in so far as it is referred to God, it is (by Prop. XXXV., God loves Himself with an infinite love) a pleasure—if I may still use this term—with the accompanying idea of Himself; and similarly as it is referred to the mind (Prop. XXVII.). Again, because the essence of our mind consists solely in knowledge (*cognitione*), and God is the first principle and the foundation of

knowledge (by Part I. Prop. XV., and Part II. Prop. XLVII.
Schol.), it is clear to us how and in what way our mind, in its
essence and its existence, follows from the Divine nature, and
is permanently dependent upon God. I have considered it
important to draw attention to this here, that I might show
by this example what is the value of the knowledge of
single things which I have called intuitive or of the third
kind (Part II. Prop. XL. Schol. 2), and how it excels that
universal knowledge which I have called knowledge of the
second kind. For, although I showed in a general way in
Part I. that all things, and with them the mind of man,
depend upon God both for essence and existence, yet that
first demonstration, though legitimate and placed beyond
reach of doubt, does not affect our mind so much as when the
same inference is made from the very essence of each single
thing which we affirm to depend upon God.

Proposition XXXVII. There is nothing in nature which
is opposed to this intellectual love, or which can take it
away.

Proof. This intellectual love follows necessarily from the
nature of mind, in so far as it is considered, through the
nature of God, as an eternal truth (Props. XXXIII. and
XXIX.). If, therefore, anything were given which were
opposed to this love, it would be opposed to what is true;
and, consequently, whatever could take away this love would
cause what is true to be false, which is self-evidently
absurd.[18]

[18] The "intellectual love of God" seems to be designed to
include more than "contemplation of God" would do. In the *Ethics*
Spinoza had become more intellectualist than in earlier stages of his
thought. Yet we find him as the close approaches reluctant to leave
the emotional side of our nature entirely in the lower and transitory
region of our life. His psychological provision for control of the
"passions" by means of some influence akin to them had included a
reference to emotion of an elevated kind involved with the activity of
the highest intellect. His "intellectual love" aims at being some-

Social Life of the Rational Man.

Part IV. Appendix VII.　It is not possible to exclude man from being a part of nature and following its general order; but if a man be situated among such individuals as accord with his own nature, his power of action will be helped and fostered.　But if, on the other hand, he is among such individuals as are in very slight accord with his own nature, he will scarcely be able to accommodate himself to them without a great change in himself.

Appendix IX.　Nothing can be more in accord with the nature of anything than other individuals of the same species. And so (by App. VII.) there is nothing given to man more useful for his preservation and his enjoyment of rational life than another man who lives by Reason.　Further, as we know of nothing among particular things better than a man who is led by reason, therefore in no way can anyone better show what he is worth in skill and character than in training other men towards the attainment of life under the government of Reason.[19]

thing more than Aristotle's θεωρία ; it anticipates Kant's doctrine of Reason operating by means of the Reverence specifically arising when Reason speaks.　But, in any case, Spinoza does not consider that this highest form of the soul's life includes what we call ethical regards ; he does not raise love of justice, for example, to this highest region : the intellectual love of God is love of God alone.　And, after all, his praise of tranquillity and repose of soul seems to exclude the æsthetic side of our mental life.

[19] Spinoza provides for the social sentiments in his psychology of the emotions.　He worked out a theory of Society in his *Tractatus Theologico-Politicus*, where Society is regarded as indispensable and advantageous as coming from the surrender by individuals of conflicting rights in favour of the State.　In a perfect Society of wise men no such surrender would be necessary, as interference would have no place.　Meanwhile the range of rights surrendered is wide as to externals, but must not include the inner life.

Peace of Mind obtained through following the Order of Nature.

Part IV. Appendix XXXII. Human power is very limited, and is infinitely surpassed by the power of external things; so that we are not in possession of absolute power to adapt external things to our own convenience. And yet whatever things happen to us in opposition to the requirements of our own convenience, we shall bear them with tranquillity of mind if we are conscious that we have discharged our duty, and that the power with which we are endowed could not extend to the avoiding such opposition; and that we are a part of universal nature, and follow its general order. If we clearly and distinctly understand this, that better part of ourselves which is defined as *intelligence* will be entirely at peace in this status, and will strive to stand fast in its tranquillity. For, in so far as we are intelligent, we can desire nothing save what is necessary, nor absolutely rest in anything save what is true. In so far, therefore, as we rightly understand these things, the effort of the better part of ourselves is in accord with the order of nature as a whole.

Eternity of Mind.

Part V. Proposition XXIII. The human mind cannot be absolutely destroyed with the body, but there remains something of it which is eternal. (Proved from various propositions in Part II. dealing with the relation of mind and body.)

Proposition XXX. (see p. 104) on the mind's conception of itself and of the body under the form of eternity.

Proposition XXXIV. It is only while the body endures that the mind is susceptible to those emotions which are referred to passion.

Proof. Imagination is an idea by which the mind con-

templates something as present (Part II. Prop. XVII.
Schol.); though it indicates the present constitution of the
human body rather than the nature of the external thing.
Emotion therefore (Def. of Emotion) is imagination in so far
as it indicates the present constitution of the body; and
therefore it is only, etc.

Corollary. Hence it follows that no love is eternal except
intellectual love.

Scholium. If we refer to the common opinion of men, we
shall find that they are conscious of the eternity of their
mind, but confuse eternity with duration, and refer it to imagination or memory, which they believe to persist after death.

Proposition XXXVIII. In proportion as the mind
understands more things by the second and third kind of
knowledge, it suffers less from those emotions which are evil,
and has the less fear of death.

Proposition XXXIX. He who possesses the most adapt-
able body has the greatest part of his mind eternal.[20]

Blessedness is Virtue and Freedom.

Proposition XLII. (closing the *Ethics*). Blessedness
(*beatitudo*) is not the reward of virtue, but it is itself virtue:
and we do not rejoice in it because we restrain our lusts,
but, on the contrary, we are able to restrain them because we
rejoice in blessedness.

[20] This eternity of mind is not equivalent to "immortality," if
by this we mean persistence of the lower ranges of mind. It is an
assertion that a participant in Divine reason is in a sphere where
beginning and ending has no place: it is life in the eternal present.
In the earlier treatise, *On God, Man, and Happiness*, Spinoza had
expounded this view as between one man and another, the man of the
sensuous type and the spiritual man; he now applies it within each
man, indicating a part which is perishable and a part which is eternal.
The position to which Spinoza has worked is that of Aristotle, with
the νοῦς παθητικός perishable and the νοῦς ποιητικός imperishable; and
the bearing on "personal" immortality is the same.

Proof. Blessedness consists in love towards God (Prop. XXXVI.), and this arises from knowledge of the third kind (Prop. XXXII.). This love, therefore (Prop. LIX., and Part III. Prop. III.), must be referred to the mind as active, and therefore (Part IV. Def. 8) it is virtue itself; which was the first point. Again, in proportion as the mind rejoices in this Divine love or blessedness it has understanding (Prop. XXXII.); that is, it has the more power over emotions (Prop. III. Coroll.), and suffers the less from such as are evil. And thus the mind has the more power of controlling lusts the more it rejoices in this Divine love or blessedness. And, since human power of controlling emotions rests solely with the intellect, no one rejoices in blessedness because he has controlled his emotions; but, on the contrary, the power of controlling the lusts arises from this blessedness itself.[21]

Scholium. I have now completed all that I wished to show concerning the power of the mind over emotions, and concerning the liberty of the mind. From what has been shown, we see the power of the wise man and his superiority over the ignorant man, who is moved by lust alone. For the ignorant man is agitated by external causes in many ways, and never obtains true peace of soul; he lives, as it were, ignorant of himself and of God and of things, and as soon as he ceases to suffer he ceases also to exist. Whereas the wise man, in so far as he is considered wise, is scarcely ever moved in his soul; conscious, by a kind of eternal necessity both of himself and of God and of things, he never ceases to exist, but is always in possession of true contentment of soul.

[21] Here is a true touch of transcendental method. We do not attain the heights, he says, by a succession of victories in lower stages: no single victory would be possible if we were not already occupants of the higher position: the successive stages of control to which we win are themselves evidences that we have had power from above all the while. "Born from above" is in Spinoza's philosophy as it is in the Gospel.

The way I have shown may seem very arduous, yet it can be found. And it must indeed be arduous, for its discovery is so rare. If salvation lay at our hand, and could be discovered without any great toil, how could it be neglected by nearly all men? But all things excellent are as difficult as they are rare.[22]

[22] The elevation ot Mind to eternity is either a mystical absorption into union with God, or it amounts to a replacement of the one Eternal by a plurality of eternal beings. Some authorities (*e.g.* Erdmann, *History of Philosophy*, ii. § 273) consider that Spinoza did really pass from the one Substance of his Part I. to the admission of many "Substances," from Monism to Pluralism. Sir F. Pollock agrees that this is the issue, but considers that Spinoza was unaware of it, and refers the situation to his having started with a predominantly Theological interest, but having been led into Metaphysics, with this result. He was consistent, Erdmann thinks, not in keeping to his starting-point, but in being faithful to principles which led him away from it. This amounts to admitting, if we take the Theism of Part I. to be what is usually meant by his "system," that Spinoza himself passed out of Spinozism. It is a significant fact that a Cambridge expounder and critic of Hegel, Mr. McTaggart, has come to the conclusion that Hegel either came to see, or might be shown to involve, the Pluralism of the Absolute (*Studies in Hegelian Cosmology*, 1901); and that Pluralism enters largely into the speculations of Professors Royce and Howison, and is the express doctrine of Mr. Schiller.

This high debate as to the issue of Spinozism brings up the other great problem as to its real significance. The union of the soul with God at the end brings us back to the starting-point, and we have to ask, What really is the Divine Substance of Spinoza? Is it X behind the Attributes which are behind the modes? or is it the Attributes and therefore also the modes? Is it Nothing or Everything? the Void or Absolute Fulness? Advocates appear for each side of the contention: "A dark abyss," says Hegel; "the negative gulf of Substance," Schwegler; "refunds all into undifferentiated and featureless unity," Fraser; either "an indeterminate abstract or the sum of all possible reality," Adamson; "a positive, concrete, most real being," Weber; "Divine Substance is the Attributes, therefore the modes, therefore everything," Pollock; "the most concrete being, the fullest and richest nature," Joachim. We have endeavoured to present

References.—Our translation is from the text of Bruder (Tauchnitz' edition), compared with the standard text of Van Vloten and Land ; and we have consulted the translations of Elwes (Bohn's Library) and White (Trübner). In English we have five recent Monographs— J. Caird (1888), Martineau (3rd ed. 1895), Sir F. Pollock (2nd ed. 1899), Mr. H. H. Joachim (1901), Mr. Duff (1902) on the Ethical and Political Philosophy, and E. E. Kellett (in *Encyclopædia of Religion and Ethics* (1920)). In every History of philosophy Spinoza finds prominent treatment—" all the authorities make a primate of Spinoza," says Stirling ; and no one enters upon philosophy of religion without reference to him. E. Caird, in his Essays, treats Spinoza as more closely dependent on Descartes than is now usual, as does Professor Iverach, *Descartes and Spinoza,* 1904. The treatment in the late Professor Adamson's *Development of Modern Philosophy* should also be studied. Professor Sorley's article in *Mind* (1880) should be read for a critical study of the reference to Jewish influences, with an adverse decision. In this reference a beginning could be made with Maimonides' *Guide to the Perplexed* (Trübner's Foreign Translation Library). For the treatment in Continental literature, if the reader commences with J. P. N. Land's Essay, with its notes, printed by Professor Knight along with Kuno Fischer's, Renan's, and Van Vloten's memorial panegyrics (Williams & Norgate, 1882), he will have a starting-point for the investigations he may desire to pursue. In the *Critical Review* for January 1903 is an admirable article on the present position of the philosophy of Spinoza, by the late Professor Johnston, the scholar referred to in our Preface. For different modes of treating of God as immanent, see Illingworth's *Divine Immanence* and Fairbairn's *Philosophy of the Christian Religion.*

material upon which the reader may form at least a provisional judgment for himself.

For "Religion" in other ranges of life than knowledge and what knowledge can do for us, Spinoza made an offer of a simple character, set forth at large in his treatise *Theologico-Politicus.* He remitted it to a lower region than philosophy, the region of imagination and lower reason and emotion ; to piety, in short. There the multitudes dwell with their Prophets and Priests and the historical religions ; and for it, with his fine sympathies and strong social feeling, he felt the greatest consideration and respect. He did even better, in his own character and life he combined a grave and kindly regard for religious feelings and observances in others, with a peace of mind nearly as philosophic as his own ideal.

8

V.

MYSTICISM.

THE CAMBRIDGE PLATONISTS (SEVENTEENTH CENTURY).

THIS short discourse is printed as an example of Mystical Theism. The Neo-Platonism of Alexandria never wholly failed to have its votaries in succeeding centuries, although there was a long period of partial eclipse when the more intellectualist method which was regarded as Aristotelian was in vogue. The triumph of Aquinas marked the ebb of Neo-Platonic influence, but there was always a current in Germany, France, and England, and when the Renaissance and the Reformation had made some way its tide returned. In the seventeenth century a group of Cambridge divines were drawn together towards Plato, and are known by the name of the Cambridge Platonists. But they did not go back all the way to Plato; they halted at Alexandria, finding there a vein of thought that suited them. They were regarded as the Broad Churchmen of their day, and their influence ran over into many small channels besides its main stream, although it was again to wane in the eighteenth century, until revived by Coleridge. The chief men of the group were Whichcote, Culverwell, Cudworth, Henry More, and John Smith.

It might have been expected that these theologians—these five were clerical fellows of colleges, two of them heads of houses—would have resorted to the Christian Platonists of Alexandria, Clement and Origen, or the later pseudo-Dionysius; but they preferred to go to the philosophers Plotinus, Iamblichus, and Simplicius, and to re-read Christian theology for themselves. They varied in the degree of their attachment to Neo-Platonism, from Cudworth who had least of it and most of Intellectualism, to Henry More in his

114

later stage, who from a Cartesian gradually became a rhapsodist in his Alexandrianism. A central position was occupied by John Smith, who died at the age of thirty-six (1652).

In the discourse here printed John Smith gives in a few broad strokes the general method of this group; the paper was designed by him as "a necessary introduction" to his other discourses, his friend John Worthington says. As this looks at religion from the point of view of how man is to know God, we add the chapter from his fine discourse on the *Excellency and Nobleness of True Religion*, in which he speaks of knowledge as given by God to man. We have not printed the references for the very numerous quotations; they will be found in the Cambridge edition mentioned in our reference paragraph.

A PREFATORY DISCOURSE CONCERNING THE TRUE WAY OR METHOD OF ATTAINING DIVINE KNOWLEDGE.

It hath been long since well observed, that every art and science hath some certain principles upon which the whole frame and body of it must depend; and he that will fully acquaint himself with the mysteries thereof, must come furnished with some *præcognita*, or προλήψεις, that I may speak in the language of the Stoics. Were I indeed to define divinity, I should rather call it a *Divine life* than a *Divine science*; it being something rather to be understood by a spiritual sensation, than by any verbal description, as all things of sense and life are best known by sentient and vital faculties; γνῶσις ἑκάστων δι᾽ ὁμοιότητος γίνεται, as the Greek philosopher hath well observed — everything is best known by that which bears a just resemblance and analogy with it; and therefore the Scripture is wont to set forth a good life as the prolepsis and fundamental principle of Divine science; "Wisdom hath builded her house, and hewn out her seven pillars"; but "the fear of

the Lord is the beginning of wisdom,"—the foundation of
the whole fabric.[1]

We shall therefore, as a prolegomenon or preface to what
we shall afterward discourse upon the heads of divinity,
speak something of this *true method of knowing*, which is
not so much by notions as actions; as religion itself consists
not so much in words as in things.   They are not always
the best skilled in divinity that are the most studied in
those pandects, into which it is sometimes digested, or that
have erected the greatest monopolies of art and science.
He that is most practical in Divine things hath the purest
and sincerest knowledge of them, and not he that is most
dogmatical.   Divinity, indeed, is a true efflux from the eternal
light, which, like the sunbeams, does not only enlighten, but
heat and enliven ; and therefore our Saviour hath, in His
beatitudes, connected purity of heart with the beatifical
vision.   And as the eye cannot behold the sun, ἡλιοειδὴς μὴ
γινόμενος,—unless it be sunlike, and hath the form and
resemblance of the sun drawn in it; so neither can the
soul of man behold God, θεοειδὴς μὴ γινομένη,—unless it
be Godlike, hath God formed in it, and be made partaker
of the Divine nature.   And the Apostle St. Paul, when he
would lay open the right way of attaining to Divine truth,
saith that "knowledge puffeth up," but it is "love that
edifieth."   The knowledge of divinity that appears in systems
and models is but a poor wan light; but the powerful energy
of Divine knowledge displays itself in purified souls : here
we shall find the true πεδίον ἀληθείας, as the ancient philosophy speaks—"the land of truth."

[1] This paragraph strikes the keynote : the "Way" is not to be
won by intellect alone ; the nature of the Divine Being is too full for
that.   It is not a Metaphysical principle, nor a Substance with some
definite Attributes, however far-reaching, but the living God, of
whom Smith is to speak.   The searcher must come with his whole
personality.   A comparison with Spinoza, both as to the nature of
God and the nature of the believer, is full of suggestion.

To seek our divinity merely in books and writings, is to seek the living among the dead : we do but in vain seek God many times in these, where His truth too often is not so much enshrined as entombed :—no ; *intra te quære Deum*, seek for God within thine own soul; He is best discerned νοερᾷ ἐπαφῇ, as Plotinus phraseth it, — by an intellectual touch of Him—we must " see with our eyes, and hear with our ears, and our hands must handle the word of life," that I may express it in St. John's words. Ἔστι καὶ ψυχῆς αἴσθησίς τις—the soul itself hath its sense, as well as the body ; and therefore David, when he would teach us how to know what the Divine goodness is, calls not for speculation but sensation : " Taste and see how good the Lord is." That is not the best and truest knowledge of God which is wrought out by the labour and sweat of the brain, but that which is kindled within us by a heavenly warmth in our hearts. As, in the natural body, it is the heart that sends up good blood and warm spirits into the head, whereby it is best enabled to perform its several functions ; so that which enables us to know and understand aright in the things of God, must be a living principle of holiness within us. When the tree of knowledge is not planted by the tree of life, and sucks not up sap from thence, it may as well be fruitful with evil as with good, and bring forth bitter fruit as well as sweet. If we would indeed have our knowledge thrive and flourish, we must water the tender plants of it with holiness. When Zoroaster's scholars asked him what they should do to get winged souls, such as might soar aloft in the bright beams of Divine truth, he bids them bathe themselves in the waters of life : they asking what they were, he tells them, the four cardinal virtues, which are the four rivers of Paradise. It is but a thin, airy knowledge that is got by mere speculation, which is ushered in by syllogisms and demonstrations ; but that which springs forth from true

goodness is θειότερόν τι πάσης ἀποδείξεως, as Origen speaks—
it brings such a Divine light into the soul, as is more clear
and convincing than any demonstration. The reason why,
notwithstanding all our acute reasons and subtile disputes,
truth prevails no more in the world, is, we so often disjoin
truth and true goodness, which in themselves can never
be disunited; they grow both from the same root, and
live in one another. We may, like those in Plato's deep
pit, with their faces bended downwards, converse with
sounds and shadows, but not with the life and substance
of truth, while our souls remained defiled with any vice or
lusts. These are the black Lethe lake which drench the
souls of men: he that wants true virtue, in heaven's logic,
"is blind, and cannot see afar off." Those filthy mists that
arise from impure and terrene minds, like an atmosphere,
perpetually encompass them, that they cannot see that
sun of Divine truth that shines about them, but never
shines into any unpurged souls; the darkness comprehends
it not, the foolish man understands it not. All the light
and knowledge that may seem sometimes to rise up in
unhallowed minds, is but like those fuliginous flames that
rise up from our culinary fire, that are soon quenched in
their own smoke; or like those foolish fires that fetch
their birth from terrene exudations, that do but hop up
and down, and flit to and fro upon the surface of this
earth, where they were first brought forth; and serve not
so much to enlighten, as to delude us; not to direct the
wandering traveller into his way, but to lead him farther
out of it. While we lodge any filthy vice in us, this will
be perpetually twisting up itself into the thread of our
finest-spun speculations; it will be continually climbing up
into the τὸ Ἡγεμονικόν—the hegemonical powers of the
soul, into the bed of reason, and defile it: like the wanton
ivy twisting itself about the oak, it will twine about
our judgments and understandings, till it hath sucked

out the life and spirit of them. I cannot think such black oblivion should possess the minds of some, as to make them question that truth which to good men shines as bright as the sun at noonday, had they not foully defiled their own souls with some hellish vice or other, how fairly soever it may be they may dissemble it. There is a benumbing spirit, a congealing vapour that ariseth from sin and vice, that will stupefy the senses of the soul; as the naturalists say there is from the torpedo, that smites the senses of those that approach it. This is that venomous *solanum*—that deadly nightshade that infuses its cold poison into the understandings of men.

Such as men themselves are, such will God Himself seem to be. It is the maxim of most wicked men, that the Deity is some way or other like themselves; their souls do more than whisper it, though their lips speak it not; and though their tongues be silent, yet their lives cry it upon the house-tops and in the public streets. That idea which men generally have of God is nothing else but the picture of their own complexion: that archetypal notion of Him which hath the supremacy in their minds, is none else but such a one as hath been shaped out according to some pattern of themselves; though they may so clothe and disguise this idol of their own, when they carry it about in a pompous procession to expose it to the view of the world, that it may seem very beautiful, and indeed anything else rather than what it is. Most men (though it may be they themselves take no great notice of it), like that dissembling monk—*aliter sentire in scholis, aliter in musæis,*—are of a different judgment in the schools from what they are in the retirements of their private closets. There is a double head as well as a double heart. Men's corrupt hearts will not suffer their notions and conceptions of Divine things to be cast into that form into which a higher reason, which may sometimes work within them, would put them.[2]

I would not be thought, all this while, to banish the belief of all innate notions of Divine truth; but these are too often smothered, or tainted with a deep dye of men's filthy lusts. It is but *lux sepulta in opaca materia*—light buried and stifled in some dark body, from whence all those coloured, or rather discoloured, notions and apprehensions of Divine things are begotten. Though these common notions may be very busy sometimes in the vegetation of Divine knowledge, yet the corrupt vices of men may so clog, disturb, and overrule them (as the naturalists say this unruly and masterless matter doth the natural forms in the formation of living creatures), that they may produce nothing but monsters, miserably distorted and misshapen. This kind of science, as Plotinus speaks, "associating too familiarly with matter, and receiving and imbibing it into itself, changeth its shape by this incestuous

[2] The place of search is the seeker's own soul : this also is a cardinal maxim with the Platonists. Not by reference to external nature, nor to the abstractions of being in general, but in the depths and heights of the soul's own life, man must look for a reflection of Divinity. Smith has a discourse on "the Existence and Nature of God," in which he expounds this, claiming to be with Plato and Plotinus. In that discourse he finds in the soul (1) reason, but deficient reason, so he must look away to infinite reason ; (2) the exercise of power, but very limited, so he must look from that to omnipotence ; (3) love, so he must look to infinite love ; (4) and (5), limitation in place and time, so he must look to eternity and infinity ; (6) a limited freedom, so he must look to perfect freedom ; and (7) ideals (imperfect and unrealised) of goodness, so he must look away to eternal goodness and perfect beauty. He closes with a preference for this last reflection. The affirmative aspect of mysticism is thus very marked in Smith ; he and his Cambridge associates found nothing congenial in the *via negativa* to which Neo-Platonism resorted in its later phase. For historical evidence that it is Love, and not Fear, which has predominated in Religion, see Dr. Jevons, *Introduction to the History of Religion.*

mixture." At best, while any inward lust is harboured in the minds of men, it will so weaken them, that they can never bring forth any masculine or generous knowledge; as Ælian observes of the stork, that if the night-owl chanceth to sit upon her eggs, they become presently as it were ὑπηνέμια, and all incubation is rendered impotent and ineffectual. Sin and lust are always of a hungry nature, and suck up all those vital affections of men's souls which should feed and nourish their understandings.

What are all our most sublime speculations of the Deity, that are not impregnated with true goodness, but insipid things that have no taste nor life in them, that do but swell, like empty froth, in the souls of men! They do not feed men's souls, but only puff them up, and fill them with pride, arrogance, contempt, and tyranny towards those that cannot well understand their subtile curiosities: as those philosophers that Cicero complains of in his times, *qui disciplinam suam ostentationem scientiæ, non legem vitæ, putabant*—who made their knowledge only matter of ostentation, to vindicate and set off themselves, but never caring to square and govern their lives by it. Such as these do but, spider-like, take a great deal of pains to spin a worthless web out of their own bowels, which will not keep them warm. These, indeed, are those silly souls that are "ever learning, but never come to the knowledge of the truth." They may, with Pharaoh's lean kine, eat up and devour all tongues and sciences, and yet, when they have done, still remain lean and ill-favoured as they were at first. Jejune and barren speculations may be hovering and fluttering up and down about divinity, but they cannot settle or fix themselves upon it: they unfold the plicatures of truth's garment, but they cannot behold the lovely face of it. There are hidden mysteries in Divine truth, wrapt up one within another, which cannot be discerned but by Divine "Epoptists."

We must not think we have then attained to the right

knowledge of truth, when we have broken through the outward shell of words and phrases that house it up; or when, by a logical analysis, we have found out the dependencies and coherencies of them one with another; or when, like stout champions of it, having well guarded it with the invincible strength of our demonstration, we dare stand out in the face of the world, and challenge the field of all those that would pretend to be our rivals.[3]

We have many grave and reverend idolaters that worship truth only in the image of their own wits; that could never adore it so much as they may seem to do, were it anything else but such a form of belief as their own wandering speculations had at last met together in; were it not that they find their own image and superscription upon it.

There is a knowing of "the truth as it is in Jesus"—as it is in a Christlike nature, as it is in that sweet, mild, humble, and loving spirit of Jesus, which spreads itself, like a morning sun, upon the souls of good men, full of light and life. It profits little to know Christ Himself after the flesh; but He gives His Spirit to good men, that searcheth the deep things of God. There is an inward beauty, life, and loveliness in Divine truth, which cannot be known but then when it is digested into life and practice. The Greek philosopher could tell those high-soaring Gnostics that thought themselves no less than *Jovis alites*; that could (as he speaks in the Comedy) ἀεροβατεῖν καὶ περιφρονεῖν τὸν ἥλιον, and cried out so much, "look upon God," that "without virtue and real goodness God is but a name," a dry and empty notion. The profane sort of men, like those old Gentile Greeks, may make many ruptures in the walls of God's temple, and break into the holy ground, but yet may find God no more there than they did.

Divine truth is better understood, as it unfolds itself in the

[3] These protests against intellectualism are repeated throughout; Cudworth would not have endorsed them all, and called his own chief work, *The True Intellectual System of the Universe.*

purity of men's hearts and lives, than in all those subtile niceties into which curious wits may lay it forth. And therefore our Saviour, who is the great master of it, would not, while He was here on earth, draw it up into any system or body, nor would His disciples after Him ; He would not lay it out to us in any canons or articles of belief, not being, indeed, so careful to stock and enrich the world with opinions and notions, as with true piety, and a Godlike pattern of purity, as the best way to thrive in all spiritual understanding. His main scope was to promote a holy life, as the best and most compendious way to a right belief. He hangs all true acquaintance with divinity upon the doing God's will : " If any man will do His will, he shall know of the doctrine, whether it be of God." This is that alone which will make us, as St. Peter tells us, " that we shall not be barren nor unfruitful in the knowledge of our Lord and Saviour." There is an inward sweetness and deliciousness in Divine truth, which no sensual mind can taste or relish : this is that ψυχικὸς ἀνήρ—that natural man that savours not the things of God. Corrupt passions and terrene affections are apt, of their own nature, to disturb all serene thoughts, to precipitate our judgments, and warp our understandings. It was a good maxim of the old Jewish writers : " The Holy Spirit dwells not in terrene and earthly passions." Divinity is not so well perceived by a subtile wit, ὥσπερ αἰσθήσει κεκαθαρμένῃ, " as by a purified sense,"—as Plotinus phraseth it.

Neither was the ancient philosophy unacquainted with this way and method of attaining to the knowledge of Divine things ; and therefore Aristotle himself thought a young man unfit to meddle with the grave precepts of morality till the heat and violent precipitancy of his youthful affections were cooled and moderated. And it is observed of Pythagoras, that he had several ways to try the capacity of his scholars, and to prove the sedateness and moral temper of their minds, before he would entrust them with the sublimer mysteries of his philosophy. The Platonists were herein so wary and solicitous, that they thought the minds of men could never be purged enough from those earthly dregs of sense and passion, in which they were so much steeped, before they could be capable of their Divine metaphysics : and therefore they so much solicit a χωρισμὸς ἀπὸ τοῦ σώματος, as they are wont to phrase it—"a separation from the body," in all those that would καθαρῶς φιλοσοφεῖν, as Socrates speaks, that is indeed, "sincerely understand Divine truth"; ·for that was the scope of their philosophy. This was also intimated by them in their defining philosophy to be μελέτη θανάτου—"a meditation of death"; aiming herein at only a moral way of dying, by loosening the soul from the body and this sensitive life, which they thought was necessary to a right contemplation of intelligible things; and therefore, besides those ἀρεταὶ καθαρτικαί by which the souls of men were to be separated from sensuality and purged from fleshly filth, they devised a further way of separation more accommodated to the condition of philosophers, which was their *mathemata*, or mathematical contemplations, whereby the souls of men might further shake off their dependency upon sense, and learn to go as it were alone, without the crutch of any sensible or material thing to support them ; and so be a little inured, being once got up above the body, to converse freely with immaterial natures, without looking down again and falling back into sense. Besides, many other ways they had, whereby to rise out of this dark body,—ἀναβάσεις ἐκ τοῦ σπηλαίου, as they are wont to call them,—several steps and ascents out of this miry cave of mortality, before they could set any sure footing with their intellectual part in the land of light and immortal being.

And thus we should pass from this topic of our discourse, upon which we have dwelt too long already, but that before we quite let it go, I hope we may fairly make this use of it further (besides what we have openly aimed at all this while), which is to learn not to devote or give up ourselves to any private opinions or dictates of men in matters of religion, nor too zealously to propugn the dogmas of any sect. As we should not, like rigid censurers, arraign and condemn the creeds of other men which we comply not with, before a full and mature understanding of them, ripened not only by the natural sagacity of our own reason, but by the benign influence of holy and mortified affection ; so neither should we over hastily *credere in fidem alienam*—subscribe to the symbols and articles of other men. They are not always the best men that blot most paper ; truth is not, I fear, so voluminous, nor swells into such a mighty bulk as our books do. Those minds are not always the most chaste that are most parturient with these learned discourses, which too often bear upon them a foul stain of their unlawful propagation. A bitter juice of corrupt affections may sometimes be strained into the ink of our greatest scholars ; their doctrines may taste too sour of the cask they come through. We are not always happy in meeting with that wholesome food (as some are wont to call the doctrinal part of religion) which hath been dressed out by the cleanest hands. Some men have too bad hearts to have good heads : they cannot be good at theory who have been so bad at the practice, as we may justly fear too many of those from whom we are apt to take the articles of our belief have been. Whilst we plead so much our right to the patrimony of our fathers, we may take too fast a possession of their errors, as well as of their sober opinions. There are *idola specûs*—innate prejudices, and deceitful hypotheses, that many times wander up and down in the minds of good men, that may fly out from them with their graver determinations. We can never be well assured what our traditional divinity is ; nor can we securely enough addict ourselves to any sect of men. That which was the philosopher's motto, Ἐλεύθερον εἶναι δεῖ τῇ γνώμῃ τὸν μέλλοντα φιλοσοφεῖν, we may a little enlarge, and so fit it for an

ingenuous pursuer after Divine truth: "he that will find
truth, must seek it with a free judgment and a sanctified
mind ": he that thus seeks shall find ; he shall live in truth,
and that shall live in him ; it shall be like a stream of living
waters issuing out of his own soul; he shall drink of the
waters of his own cistern, and be satisfied; he shall every
morning find this heavenly manna lying upon the top of his
own soul, and be fed with it to eternal life ; he will find
satisfaction within, feeling himself in conjunction with truth,
though all the world should dispute against him.[4]

And thus I should again leave this argument, but that
perhaps we may, all this while, have seemed to undermine
what we intend to build up.   For if Divine truth spring up
only from the root of true goodness, how shall we endeavour
to be good, before we know what it is to be so ? or how shall
we convince the gainsaying world of truth, unless we could
also inspire virtue into it ?

To both which we shall make this reply : that there are
some radical principles of knowledge that are so deeply sunk
in the souls of men, as that the impression cannot easily be
obliterated, though it may be much darkened.   Sensual base-
ness doth not so grossly sully and bemire the souls of all
wicked men at first, as to make them, with Diagoras, deny
the Deity, or, with Protagoras, doubt of, or, with Diodorus,
to question the immortality of rational souls.   Neither are
the common principles of virtue so pulled up by the roots in
all, as to make them so dubious in stating the bounds of
virtue and vice as Epicurus was, though he could not but

---

[4] Divine knowledge cannot be acquired at second hand ; neither
ecclesiastical tradition nor social opinion can be substitutes for first-
hand knowledge.   The insistence on this when the Church of England
was passing through the turmoil of the Stuart period, and ecclesiastical order was the prominent interest in the minds of so many
religious men, led to the designation of Latitudinarian being applied
by the controversialists to this group of men who endeavoured to rise
to a serener plane.

sometimes take notice of them. Neither is the retentive power of truth so weak and loose in all sceptics, as it was in him, who, being well scourged in the streets till the blood ran about him, questioned, when he came home, whether he had been beaten or not. Arrian hath well observed, that the common notions of God and virtue impressed upon the souls of men, are more clear and perspicuous than any else; and that if they have not more *certainty*, yet they have more *evidence*, and display themselves with less difficulty to our reflective faculty than any geometrical demonstrations : and these are both available to prescribe out ways of virtue to men's own souls, and to force an acknowledgment of truth from those that oppose, when they are well guided by a skilful hand. Truth needs not at any time fly from reason, there being an eternal amity between them. They are only some private dogmas, that may well be suspected as spurious and adulterate, that dare not abide the trial thereof. And this reason is not everywhere so extinguished, as that we may not, by that, enter into the souls of men. What the magnetical virtue is in these earthly bodies, that reason is in men's minds, which, when it is put forth, draws them one to another. Besides, in wicked men there are sometimes distastes of vice, and flashes of love to virtue; which are the motions which spring from a true intellect, and the faint strugglings of a higher life within them, which they crucify again by their wicked sensuality. As truth doth not always act in good men, so neither doth sense always act in wicked men ; they may sometimes have their *lucida intervalla*— their sober fits ; and a Divine Spirit blowing and breathing upon them, may then blow up some live sparks of true understanding within them ; though they may soon endeavour to quench them again, and to rake them up in the ashes of their own earthly thoughts.

All this, and more that might be said upon this argument, may serve to point out the way of virtue. We want not so much means of knowing what we ought to do, as wills to do that which we may know. But yet all that knowledge which is separated from an inward acquaintance with virtue and goodness is of a far different nature from that which ariseth out of a true living sense of them, which is the best discerner thereof, and by which alone we know the true perfection, sweetness, energy, and loveliness of them, and all that which is οὔτε ῥητόν, οὔτε γραπτόν—that which can no more be known by a naked demonstration than colours can be perceived by a blind man, by any definition or description which he can hear of them.

And, further, the clearest and most distinct notions of truth that shine in the souls of the common sort of men may be extremely clouded if they be not accompanied with that answerable practice that might preserve their integrity: these tender plants may soon be spoiled by the continual droppings of our corrupt affections upon them; they are but of a weak and feminine nature, and so may be sooner deceived by that wily serpent of sensuality that harbours within us.

While the soul is πλήρης τοῦ σώματος—"full of the body" —while we suffer those notions and common principles of religion to lie asleep within us; that γενεσιουργὸς δύναμις— "the power of an animal life" will be apt to incorporate and mingle itself with them; and that reason that is within us, as Plotinus hath well expressed it, becomes more and more σύμφυτος κακαῖς ταῖς ἐπιγινομέναις δόξαις—it will be infected with those evil opinions that arise from our corporeal life. The more deeply our souls dive into our bodies, the more will reason and sensuality run one into another, and make up a most dilute, unsavoury, and muddy kind of knowledge. We must therefore endeavour more and more to withdraw ourselves from these bodily things, to set our soul as free as may be from its miserable slavery to this base flesh: we must shut the eyes of sense, and open that brighter eye of our understandings, that other eye of the soul (as the philosopher calls our intellectual faculty), ἣν ἔχει μὲν πᾶς, χρῶνται δὲ ὀλίγοι—"which indeed all have, but few make use of." This is the way to see clearly; the light of the Divine world will then begin to fall upon us, and those sacred ἐλλάμψεις—those pure coruscations of immortal and everliving truth will shine into us, and in God's own light shall we behold Him. The fruit of this knowledge will be sweet to our taste, and pleasant to our palates, "sweeter than honey or the honeycomb." The priests of Mercury, as Plutarch tells us, in the eating of their holy things, were wont to cry out γλυκὺ ἡ ἀλήθεια—"sweet is truth." But how sweet and delicious that truth is, which holy and heaven-born souls feed upon in their mysterious converse with the Deity, who can tell but they that taste it? When reason once is raised, by the mighty force of the Divine Spirit, into a converse with God, it is turned into sense: that which before was only faith well built upon sure principles (for such our science may be) now becomes vision. We shall then converse with God τῷ νῷ, whereas before, we conversed with Him only τῇ διανοίᾳ—with our discursive faculty—as the Platonists were wont to distinguish. Before, we laid hold on Him only λόγῳ ἀποδεικτικῷ—with a struggling, agonistical, and contentious reason, hotly combating with difficulties and sharp contests of diverse opinions, and labour-ing in itself, in its deductions of one thing from another; we shall then fasten our minds upon Him λόγῳ ἀποφαντικῷ, with such a "serene understanding," γαλήνη νοερᾷ, such an intellectual calmness and serenity as will present us with a blissful, steady, and invariable sight of Him.[5]

[5] Here is raised the intellectualist's question : Surely we must know an object before we can have respect for it? Surely we must learn what goodness is before we can attempt to aim at it? This is the question which, in the opinion of all thoroughgoing intuitivists, has slain many souls; as Bunyan, for example, was for months

And now, if you please, setting aside the Epicurean herd of brutish men, who have drowned all their own sober reason in the deepest Lethe of sensuality, we shall divide the rest of men into these four ranks, according to that method which Simplicius upon Epictetus hath already laid out to us, with respect to a fourfold kind of knowledge, which we have all this while glanced at.[6]

The first whereof is ἄνθρωπος συμπεφυρμένος τῇ γενέσει, or, if you will, ἄνθρωπος ὁ πολύς—"That complex and multifarious man that is made up of soul and body," as it were by a just equality and arithmetical proportion of parts and powers in each of them. The knowledge of these men

entirely perplexed with the suggestion that he must prove Christ before he accepted Him. The Intuitivists' answer is peremptory—such knowledge as the knowledge of God must arise deeper down in the soul than where such a division could take effect ; below where knowing and loving divide, lies the soul, with its own simple vision. The impulses of our superficial nature and the notions of our superficial understanding come in to disguise and cloak and confuse the deeper presentments. This is the constantly-expressed answer of the Mystic to the assertions that not all men can see what they see, and therefore love what they love : "You are clogged with superficial influences," they reply ; "let your inner soul be opened, and you will see what we see, and find that love issues from that vision."

[6] In his discourse on the *Excellency of Religion*, Smith is content with the older Platonists' graduated scheme of *three* orders of knowledge. Here he adopts the more elaborated forms given by Simplicius of Cilicia, one of the last of those Neo-Platonists who had to leave Athens when Justinian closed its School of Philosophy (A.D. 529). It is by reference to such methods of graduating human nature that the sane Mystics keep in touch with actual experiences. This formulates the ideal character of their knowledge also, for they do not claim that they actually occupy the highest stage. The praise of "ecstasy," which has proved the snare of many, did not ensnare these Cambridge men, at their best. It is their firm hold upon an ideal, while acknowledging the presence of an actual which includes even error and confusion, that is the source of that balance between humility and boldness, modesty and insatiable aspiration, which most readers will acknowledge to be present in John Smith.

I should call ἀμυδρὸν δόξαν in Plutarch's phrase; "a knowledge wherein sense and reason are so twisted up together," that it cannot easily be unravelled and laid out into its first principles. Their highest reason is ὁμόδοξος ταῖς αἰσθήσεσι,— "complying with their senses,"—and both conspire together in vulgar opinion. To these that motto which the Stoics have made for them may very well agree, βίος ὑπόληψις, their life being steered by nothing else but opinion and imagination. Their higher notions of God and religion are so entangled with the birdlime of fleshy passions and mundane vanity that they cannot rise up above the surface of this dark earth, or easily entertain any but earthly conceptions of heavenly things. Such souls as are here lodged, as Plato speaks, are ὀπισθοβαρεῖς, "heavy behind," and are continually pressing down to this world's centre; and though, like the spider, they may appear sometime moving up and down aloft in the air, yet they do but sit in the loom, and move in that web of their own gross fancies, which they fasten and pin to some earthly thing or other.

The second is ἄνθρωπος κατὰ τὴν λογικὴν ζωὴν οὐσιωμένος —the man that looks at himself as being what he is rather by his soul than by his body; that thinks not fit to view his own face in any other glass but that of reason and understanding; that reckons upon his soul as that which was made to rule, his body as that which was born to obey, and, like a handmaid, perpetually to wait upon his higher and nobler part. And in such a one the *communes notitiæ*, or common principles of virtue and goodness, are more clear and steady. To such a one we may allow τρανεστέραν καὶ ἐμφανεστέραν δόξαν—"more clear and distinct opinions," as being already ἐν καθάρσει—"in a method or course of purgation," or, at least, fit to be initiated into the *mysteria minora*—"the lesser mysteries of religion." For, though these innate notions of truth may be but poor, empty, and hungry things of themselves, before they be fed and filled with the practice of true virtue; yet they are capable of being impregnated and exalted with the rules and precepts of it. And therefore the Stoics supposed ὅτι τοιούτῳ προσήκουσιν αἱ ἠθικαὶ καὶ πολιτικαὶ ἀρεταί—that the doctrine of political and moral virtues was fit to be delivered to such as these; and though they may not be so well prepared for Divine virtue (which is of a higher emanation), yet they are not immature for human, as, having the seeds of it already within themselves, which, being watered by answerable practice, may sprout up within them.

The third is ἄνθρωπος ἤδη κεκαθαρμένος—he whose soul is already purged by this lower sort of virtue, and so is continually flying off from the body and bodily passion, and returning into himself. Such, in St. Peter's language, are those "who have escaped the pollutions which are in the world through lust." To these we may attribute a νόθη ἐπιστήμη,—a lower degree of science,—their inward sense of virtue and moral goodness being far transcendent to all mere speculative opinions of it. But, if this knowledge settle here, it may be quickly apt to corrupt. Many of our most refined moralists may be, in a worse sense than Plotinus means, πληρωθέντες τῇ ἑαυτῶν φύσει—"full with their own pregnancy"; their souls may have too much heave and swell with the sense of their own virtue and knowledge; there may be an ill ferment of self-love lying at the bottom, which may puff it up the more with pride, arrogance, and self-conceit. These forces with which the Divine bounty supplies us to keep a stronger guard against the evil spirit, may be abused by our own rebellious pride, enticing them from their allegiance to God, to strengthen itself in our souls, and fortify them against heaven: like that supercilious Stoic, who, when he thought his mind well armed and appointed with wisdom and virtue, cried out, *Sapiens contendet cum ipso Jove de felicitate.* They may make an airy heaven of these, and wall it about with their own self-flattery, and then sit in it as gods, as Cosroes, the Persian king, was sometimes laughed at for enshrining himself in a temple of his own. And therefore, if this knowledge be not attended with humility and a deep sense of self-penury and self-emptiness, we may easily fall short of that true knowledge of God after which we seem to aspire. We may carry such an image and species of ourselves constantly before us as will make us lose the clear sight of the Divinity, and be too apt to rest in a mere "logical life" (an expression of Simplicius) without any true participation of the Divine life, if we do not (as many do, if not all, who rise no higher) relapse and slide back by vainglory, popularity, or such like vices, into some mundane and external vanity or other.

The fourth is ἄνθρωπος θεωρητικός—the true metaphysical and contemplative man, ὃς τὴν ἑαυτοῦ λογικὴν ζωὴν ὑπερτρέχων, ὅλως εἶναι βούλεται τῶν κρειττόνων—who, running and shooting up above his own logical or self-rational life, pierceth into the highest life; such a one, who, by universal love and holy affection, abstracting himself from himself, endeavours to attain the nearest union with the Divine essence that may be, κέντρον κέντρῳ συνάψας, as Plotinus speaks; knitting his own centre, if he have any, unto the centre of Divine being. To such a one the Platonists are wont to attribute θείαν ἐπιστήμην—"a true Divine wisdom," powerfully displaying itself ἐν νοερᾷ ζωῇ— "in an intellectual life," as they phrase it. Such a knowledge, they say, is always pregnant with Divine virtue, which ariseth out of a happy union of souls with God, and is nothing else but a living imitation of a Godlike perfection drawn out by a strong fervent love of it. This Divine knowledge καλοὺς καὶ ἐραστοὺς ποιεῖ, etc., as Plotinus speaks, makes us more amorous of Divine beauty, beautiful and lovely; and this Divine love and purity reciprocally exalts Divine knowledge; both of them growing up together, like that Ἔρως and Ἀντέρως that Pausanias sometimes speaks of. Though, by the Platonists' leave, such a life and knowledge as this is, peculiarly belongs to the true and sober Christian, who lives in Him who is life itself, and is enlightened by Him who is the truth itself, and is made partaker of the Divine unction, "and knoweth all things," as St. John speaks. This life is nothing else but God's own breath within him, and an *infant-Christ* (if I may use the expression) formed in his soul, who is, in a sense, ἀπαύγασμα τῆς δόξης, the shining forth of the Father's glory.[7] But yet we must not mistake; this knowledge is but here in its infancy; there is a higher knowledge, or a higher degree of this knowledge, that doth not, that cannot, descend upon us in these earthly habitations. We cannot here see *in speculo lucido*; here we can see but in a glass, and that darkly too. Our own imaginative powers, which are perpetually attending the highest acts of our souls, will be breathing a gross dew upon the pure glass of our understandings, and so sully and besmear it that we cannot see the image of the Divinity sincerely in it. But yet this knowledge, being a true, heavenly fire, kindled from God's own altar, begets an undaunted courage in the souls of good men, and enables them to cast a holy scorn upon the poor, petty trash of this life, in comparison with Divine things, and to pity these poor, brutish Epicureans that have nothing but the mere husks of fleshly pleasure to feed themselves with. This sight of God makes pious souls breathe after that blessed time when mortality shall be swallowed up of life, when they shall no more behold the Divinity through the dark mediums that eclipse the blessed sight of it.

As this introductory discourse looks at Divine knowledge from the point of view of human nature, we print Chapter I.

[7] This expression represents the way in which the school applied their method to Christian religion.

of the *Excellency and Nobleness of True Religion*, where the
point of view is rather that of revelation, from the nature
of God to the excellency of the knowledge and enjoyment of
Him which is open to man.

THE EXCELLENCY AND NOBLENESS OF TRUE RELIGION.

*True religion is a noble thing in its rise and original, and
in regard of its descent.* True religion derives its pedigree
from heaven, — is βλάστημα τοῦ οὐρανοῦ, — it comes from
heaven, and constantly moves toward heaven again ; it is a
beam from God,[1] as "every good gift and every perfect
gift is from above, and cometh down from the Father of
lights, with whom is no variableness, neither shadow of
turning," as St. James speaks. God is the first truth and
primitive goodness : true religion is a vigorous efflux and
emanation of both upon the spirits of men, and, therefore,
is called "a participation of the Divine nature.[2] Indeed,
God hath copied out Himself in all created being, having
no other pattern to frame anything by, than His own
essence ; so that all created being is *umbratilis similitudo
entis increati*, and is, by some stamp or other of God upon
it, at least remotely allied to Him ; but true religion is such
a communication of the Divinity, as none but the highest
of created beings are capable of. On the other side, sin
and wickedness is of the basest and lowest original, as being

[1] The metaphors in this short chapter alone express very vividly
the revelational character of religion, that it comes by operation of
the Divine Spirit. It is "a beam from God"; "a vigorous efflux
and emanation"; "a seed of God"; truths are "inscribed"; God
has "stamped a copy"; "imprinted as with the point of a diamond";
He "communicates Divinity."

[2] The combination of Truth and Goodness is asserted. Any
separation between them is neither in the depths of man's soul nor
in the height of the Divine Nature.

nothing else but a perfect degeneration from God, and those eternal rules of goodness which are derived from Him. Religion is a heaven-born thing, the seed of God in the spirits of men, whereby they are formed to a similitude and likeness of Himself. A true Christian is every way of a most noble extraction, of a heavenly and Divine pedigree, being born ἄνωθεν, "from above," as St. John expresseth it. The line of all earthly nobility, if it were followed to the beginning, would lead to Adam, where all the lines of descent meet in one; and the root of all extractions would be found planted in nothing else but Adamah, "red earth"; but a Christian derives his line from Christ, who is the only-begotten Son of God, "the shining forth of His glory, and the character of His person," as He is styled. We may truly say of Christ and Christians, as Zebah and Zalmunna said of Gideon's brethren, "As he is, so are they (according to their capacity), each one resembling the children of a king." Titles of worldly honour in heaven's heraldry are only *tituli nominales*; but titles of Divine dignity signify some real thing, some real and Divine communications to the spirits and minds of men. All perfections and excellences, in any kind, are to be measured by their approach to that primitive Perfection of all, God Himself; and, therefore, participation of the Divine nature cannot but entitle a Christian to the highest degree of dignity—"Behold what manner of love the Father hath bestowed upon us, that we should be called the sons of God."

Thus much for a more general discovery of the nobleness of religion, as to its fountain and original; we may further, and more particularly, take notice of this in reference to that twofold fountain in God, from whence all true religion flows and issues forth, namely—(1) *His immutable nature*, (2) *His will.*

1. *The immutable nature of God.*—From thence arise all

those eternal rules of truth and goodness,[3] which are the
foundation of all religion, and which God, at the first
creation, folded up in the soul of man.[4]   These we may
call the truths of natural inscription ; understanding, hereby,
either those fundamental principles of truth which reason, by
a naked intuition, may behold in God, or those necessary
corollaries and deductions that may be drawn from thence. I
cannot think it as proper to say, that God ought infinitely
to be loved because He commands it, as because He is,
indeed, an infinite and unchangeable goodness.   God hath
stamped a copy of His own archetypal loveliness upon the
soul, that man, by reflecting into himself, might behold there
the glory of God—*intra se videre Deum*,—see within his soul
all those ideas of truth which concern the nature and
essence of God, by reason of its own resemblance to God ;
and so beget within himself the most free and generous
motions of love to God. Reason in man being *lumen de
lumine*—a light flowing from the Fountain and Father of
lights—and being, as Cicero phraseth it, *participata similitudo rationis æternæ* (as the law of nature—the νόμος
γραπτός—the law written in man's heart is *participatio legis
æternæ in rationali creatura*), it was to enable man to work
out of himself all those notions of God which are the true

[3] Truth and Goodness are both asserted again. The Beautiful
is not separately set out, but in general tone and by frequent
expressions John Smith makes it manifest that this sentiment was
highly developed in him. In this respect the influence of the Neo-
Platonists, especially of Plotinus, was marked. It would not be very
venturesome to regard the sentiment for Beauty and Nobleness and
Excellency as one of the traits which drew these Cambridge men,
undergraduates of the same decade as Milton, towards the Platonic
tradition.

[4] The phrase "folded up" reminds us of the answer of Descartes when supposed to mean by innate ideas that we always
have the full idea before us. As Smith says, lower down in this
paragraph, the notions must be "worked out of himself " by man,
the Spirit itself enabling him to do this.

groundwork of love and obedience to God, and conformity
to Him, and in moulding the inward man into the greatest
conformity to the nature of God was the perfection and
efficacy of the religion of nature.	But since man's fall from
God,[5] the inward virtue and vigour of reason is much
abated, the soul having suffered a πτεροῤῥύησις, as Plato
speaks—a *defluvium pennarum*; those principles of Divine
truth, which were first engraved upon man's heart with the
finger of God, are now, as the characters of some ancient
monument, less clear and legible than at first.	And, there-
fore, besides the truth of natural inscription—

2. God hath provided the truth of Divine revelation,
which issues forth from His own free will, and clearly
discovers the way of our return to God, from whom we are
fallen.	And this truth, with the effects and productions of
it in the minds of men, the Scripture is wont to set forth
under the name of *grace*, as proceeding merely from the free
bounty and overflowings of the Divine love.	Of this revealed
will is that of the apostle to be understood—τὰ τοῦ Θεοῦ
οὐδεὶς οἶδεν—" The things of God knoweth no man";
" οὐδείς," none, neither angel nor man, could know the mind
of God, could unlock the breast of God, or search out the
counsels of His will.	But God, out of the infinite riches
of His compassions toward mankind, is pleased to un-
bosom His secrets, and most clearly to manifest " the way
into the holiest of all," and " bring to light life and immortality," and, in these last ages, to send His Son, who
lay in His bosom from all eternity, to teach us His will, and
declare His mind to us.	When we " look unto the earth,
then behold darkness and dimness of anguish," that I may
use those words of the prophet Isaiah.	But when we look
towards heaven, then behold light breaking forth upon us,
like the eyelids of the morning, and spreading its wings

[5] The doctrine of the Fall is accepted, and Plato invoked to
endorse it.	Upon it is based the need for extraordinary revelation.

over the horizon of mankind, sitting in darkness and the shadow of death, "to guide our feet into the way of peace."

But, besides this outward revelation of God's will to men, there is also an inward impression of it on their minds and spirits, which is, in a more special manner, attributed to God.[6] We cannot see Divine things but in a Divine light : God only, who is the true light, and in whom there is no darkness at all, can so shine out of Himself upon our glassy understandings, as to beget in them a picture of Himself, His own will and pleasure, and turn the soul, as the phrase is, like wax or "clay to the seal" of His own light and love. He that made our souls in His own image and likeness, can easily find a way into them. The word that God speaks, having found a way into the soul, imprints itself there, as with the point of a diamond, and becomes λόγος ἐγγεγραμμένος ἐν τῇ τοῦ μανθάνοντος ψυχῇ, that I may borrow Plato's expression. Men may teach the grammar and rhetoric, but God teaches the divinity. Thus it is God alone that acquaints the soul with the truths of revelation ; and He it is also that does strengthen and raise the soul to better apprehensions even of natural truth ; "God being that in the intellectual world which the sun is in the sensible,"—ὅπερ ἐν τοῖς αἰσθητοῖς ὁ ἥλιος, τοῦτο ἐν τοῖς νοητοῖς ὁ Θεός,—as some of the ancient Fathers love to speak, and the ancient philosophers too, who meant God by their *intellectus agens*, whose proper work they

[6] The phrase "in a more special manner" is significant. So thoroughgoing is the confidence of Smith in the Natural Light, that the special revelation of Christianity — or rather Christianity in so far as it is special, differential — has something of an "outward" character. After indicating its place, he falls back again to the general fact of the Natural Light. We can see how it was that the School was regarded as more philosophical than Christian. The affinity with Schleiermacher and the contrast with Mansel should be studied.

supposed to be, not so much to enlighten the object as the faculty.[7]

References.—For Smith's *Select Discourses*, edition of H. G. Williams (Camb. Univ. Press, 1859). For Neo-Platonism : the Christian Platonists of Alexandria, Bigg's *Bampton Lectures* ; the Cambridge School, Tulloch's *Rational Theology in England* ; Campagnac, *The Cambridge Platonists* (1901). For all of these Dean Inge's Bampton lectures, *Christian Mysticism* (1899), and his Gifford lectures on Plotinus (1917). For Mysticism generally, Evelyn Underhill, *Mysticism* (1910), *The Mystic Way* (1913), and other writings ; F. von Hügel, *The Mystical Element of Religion* ; W. James, in *Varieties of Religious Experience* ; Rufus M. Jones, various writings ; Pratt, *The Religious Consciousness* (1921) ; Caroline M. Spurgeon, *Mysticism in English Literature* (1913).

---

[7] This phrase suggests the use of " Inspiration " as in some ways more accurate for Smith's view than " Revelation." God is always there, and always showing Himself ; it is man's power of vision which needs the operation of the Spirit in order that religious knowledge may arise.

VI.

GOD AS ETERNAL MIND.

BERKELEY, BISHOP GEORGE (1685–1753).

The Third Dialogue between Hylas and Philonous.

In this Dialogue we shall find Berkeley's demonstration of the existence of Eternal Mind ; his Idealism in the sense that we can know the ultimate reality, and that it is spiritual. It is a polemic against our being called upon to believe in a dead, senseless, inert something called " Matter." It aims at showing that there is no such thing, whether as superior to mind, as Materialists were urging, or as of equal rank with it, as Descartes and Spinoza had, more or less consistently, maintained. Of course, the crude notion of Matter as the congeries of all the qualities we perceive when we are in contact with the external world, was not what was put forward ; the conception had been refined, and indeed reduced to a thin residuum, being, in fact, only extension in length and breadth and depth for some, with inclusion of unknown force for others. But Berkeley thought that extension was amenable to explanation as quality perceived, and should be so regarded, and not set up as if independent. And then to suppose that there was behind that a something altogether unperceived and unperceivable he held to be not what common sense meant, nor what philosophy justified ; and the opinion that there was, was inimical to the cause of Religion ; was Atheistic, in short.

There is only one substance known to us directly, he thought, our conscious, perceiving, thinking mind ; and his Theism consisted in proving from this that we ought to infer the existence of an Eternal Mind. This inference was resistless, he held, and by reference to it the problems of philosophy and of religion were to be solved.

Berkeley commenced his philosophical works with his *Essay towards a New Theory of Vision* (æt. 24); in this an original psychological analysis was given of our perception of *distance*, showing that the perception is acquired by means of a systematic way of interpreting certain quite arbitrary signs. This was followed by his *Principles of Knowledge* (æt. 25), in which he expounded more comprehensively his doctrine of Perception. Three years later he followed these up by *Three Dialogues*, in which his views were expressed in a free and animated manner. Written when his theory was in full possession of his mind, and when his powers of forcible and attractive expression were in somewhat precocious maturity, these Dialogues attained a high pitch of excellence,—"the gem of British metaphysical literature," Professor Fraser admiringly calls them; and certainly no one has ventured to set up a rival claim for any other single work.

In Dialogues I. and II. he has worked up to his demonstration of the inconsistency and the uselessness of supposing that there was any substance, known as Matter, giving reality to the phenomena of external nature. He has reasserted his analysis of visual extension, as in the *Essay on Vision*, and the extension of analysis to dissolve the supposed substantiality evinced by tactual reality as resistance in extended body, as in the *Principles*. So that what we have in knowledge is factors of perception, and their synthesis by the mind. Hylas, the unsophisticated representative of ordinary men, has been led along so far by Philonous, the spokesman for philosophy. At the opening of Dialogue III. Hylas presents himself as one who has been convinced of the unreality of Matter, and is at present of the opinion that there is no reality at all. Philonous is now to lead him forward.

THE THIRD DIALOGUE.

Philonous. Tell me, *Hylas*, what are the fruits of yesterday's meditation? Hath it confirmed you in the same mind you were in at parting, or have you since seen cause to change your opinion?

Hylas. Truly, my opinion is that all our opinions are alike vain and uncertain. What we approve to-day, we condemn to-morrow. We keep a stir about knowledge, and spend our lives in the pursuit of it, when, alas! we know nothing all the while: nor do I think it possible for us ever to know anything in this life. Our faculties are too narrow and too few. Nature certainly never intended us for Speculation.

Phil. What! say you we can know nothing, *Hylas*?

Hyl. There is not that single thing in the world whereof we can know the real nature, or what it is in itself.

Phil. Will you tell me I do not really know what fire or water is?

Hyl. You may indeed know that fire appears hot, and water fluid; but this is no more than knowing what sensations are produced in your own mind, upon the application of fire and water to your organs of sense. Their internal constitution, their true and real nature, you are utterly in the dark as to *that*.

Phil. Do I not know this to be a real stone that I stand on, and that which I see before my eyes to be a real tree?

Hyl. Know? No, it is impossible you or any man alive should know it. All you know is, that you have such a certain idea or appearance in your own mind. But what is this to the real tree or stone? I tell you that colour, figure, and hardness, which you perceive, are not the real natures of those things, or in the least like them. The same may be said of all other real things or corporeal substances which compose the world. They have none of them anything of themselves, like those sensible qualities by us perceived. We should not therefore pretend to affirm or know anything of them, as they are in their own nature.

Phil. But surely, *Hylas*, I can distinguish gold, for example, from iron: and how could this be if I knew not what either truly was?

Hyl. Believe me, *Philonous*, you can only distinguish between your own ideas. That yellowness, that weight, and other sensible qualities, think you they are really in the gold? They are only relative to the senses, and have no absolute existence in nature. And in pretending to distinguish the species of real things, by the appearances in your mind, you may perhaps act as wisely as he that should conclude two men were of a different species, because their clothes were not of the same colour.

Phil. It seems, then, we are altogether put off with the appearances of things, and those false ones too. The very meat I eat, and the cloth I wear, have nothing in them like what I see and feel.

Hyl. Even so.

Phil. But is it not strange the whole world should be thus imposed on, and so foolish as to believe their senses? And yet I know not how it is, but men eat, and drink, and sleep, and perform all the offices of life, as comfortably and conveniently as if they really knew the things they are conversant about.

Hyl. They do so : but you know ordinary practice does not require a nicety of speculative knowledge. Hence the vulgar retain their mistakes, and for all that make a shift to bustle through the affairs of life. But philosophers know better things.

Phil. You mean, they know that they *know nothing*.

Hyl. That is the very top and perfection of human knowledge.

Phil. But are you all this while in earnest, *Hylas*; and are you seriously persuaded that you know nothing real in the world? Suppose you are going to write, would you not call for pen, ink, and paper, like another man; and do you not know what it is you call for?

Hyl. How often must I tell you that I know not the real nature of any one thing in the universe? I may indeed upon occasion make use of pen, ink, and paper. But, what any one of them is in its own true nature, I declare positively I know not. And the same is true with regard to every other corporeal thing. And, what is more, we are not only ignorant of the true and real nature of things, but even of their existence. It cannot be denied that we perceive such certain appearances or ideas; but it cannot be concluded from thence that bodies really exist. Nay, now I think on it, I must, agreeably to my former concessions, further declare that it is impossible any real corporeal thing should exist in nature.

Phil. You amaze me. Was ever anything more wild and extravagant than the notions you now maintain; and is it not evident you are led into all these extravagances by the belief of *material substance*? This makes you dream of those unknown natures in everything. It is this occasions your distinguishing between the reality and sensible appearances of things. It is to this you are indebted for being ignorant of what everybody else knows perfectly well. Nor is this all: you are not only ignorant of the true nature of everything, but you know not whether any thing really exists, or whether there are any true natures at all; forasmuch as you attribute to your material beings an absolute or external existence, wherein you suppose their reality consists. And, as you are forced in the end to acknowledge such an existence means either a direct repugnancy, or nothing at all, it follows that you are obliged to pull down your own hypothesis of material Substance, and positively to deny the real existence of any part of the universe. And so you are plunged into the deepest and most deplorable *Scepticism* that ever man was. Tell me, *Hylas*, is it not as I say?

Hyl. I agree with you. *Material substance* was no more than an hypothesis, and a false and groundless one too. I will no longer spend my breath in defence of it. But, whatever hypothesis you advance, or whatsoever scheme of things you introduce in its stead, I doubt not it will appear every whit as false : let me but be allowed to question you upon it. That is, suffer me to serve you in your own kind, and I warrant it shall conduct you through as many perplexities and contradictions, to the very same state of Scepticism that I myself am in at present.

Phil. I assure you, *Hylas,* I do not pretend to frame any hypothesis at all. I am of a vulgar cast, simple enough to believe my senses, and leave things as I find them. To be plain, it is my opinion that the real things are those very things I see and feel, and perceive by my senses. These I know, and, finding they answer all the necessities and purposes of life, have no reason to be solicitous about any other unknown beings. A piece of sensible bread, for instance, would stay my stomach better than ten thousand times as much of that insensible, unintelligible, real bread you speak of. It is likewise my opinion that colours and other sensible qualities are on the objects. I cannot for my life help thinking that snow is white, and fire hot. You, indeed, who by *snow* and *fire* mean certain external, unperceived, unperceiving substances, are in the right to deny whiteness or heat to be affections inherent in them. But I, who understand by those words the things I see and feel, am obliged to think like other folks. And, as I am no sceptic with regard to the nature of things, so neither am I as to their existence. That a thing should be really perceived by my senses, and at the same time not really exist, is to me a plain contradiction ; since I cannot prescind or abstract, even in thought, the existence of a sensible thing from its being perceived. Wood, stones, fire, water, flesh, iron, and the like things, which I name and discourse of, are things that I know. And I should not have known them but that I perceived them by my senses ; and things perceived by the senses are immediately perceived ; and things immediately perceived are ideas ; and ideas cannot exist without the mind; their existence therefore consists in being perceived; when, therefore, they are actually perceived, there can be no doubt of their existence. Away then with all that Scepticism, all those ridiculous philosophical doubts. What a jest is it for a philosopher to question the existence of sensible things, till he hath it proved to him from the veracity of God; [1] or to pretend our knowledge in this point falls short of intuition or demonstration ! I might as well doubt of my own being, as of the being of those things I actually see and feel.

Hyl. Not so fast, *Philonous*; you say you cannot conceive how sensible things should exist without the mind. Do you not?

Phil. I do.

Hyl. Supposing you were annihilated, cannot you conceive it possible that things perceivable by sense may still exist?

Phil. I can; but then it must be in another mind. When I deny sensible things an existence out of the mind, I do not mean my mind in particular, but all minds. Now, it is plain they have an existence exterior to my mind; since I find them by experience to be independent of it. There is therefore some other mind wherein they exist, during the intervals between the times of my perceiving them : as likewise they did before my birth, and would do after my supposed annihilation. And, as the same is true with regard to all other finite created spirits, it necessarily follows there is an *omnipresent eternal Mind*, which knows and comprehends all things, and exhibits them to our view in such a manner, and according to such rules, as He

---

[1] Cf. Selection from Descartes, p. 43. Philonous is assuring Hylas that it is not "sensible things" on which doubt has been thrown, but "Matter" supposed to be behind them or within them : he cannot agree that it is wise to go so far in "doubting" as he professes to suppose that Descartes had done, and hold belief in sensible things wholly in suspense. His point is that he is going to give an account of them as they exist, in all their orderly arrangement.

Himself hath ordained, and are by us termed the *laws of nature*.[2]

Hyl. Answer me, *Philonous.* Are all our ideas perfectly inert beings? Or have they any agency included in them?

Phil. They are altogether passive and inert.

Hyl. And is not God an agent, a being purely active?

Phil. I acknowledge it.

Hyl. No idea therefore can be like unto, or represent the nature of God?

Phil. It cannot.

Hyl. Since, therefore, you have no idea of the mind of God, how can you conceive it possible that things should exist in His mind? Or, if you can conceive the mind of God, without having an idea of it, why may not I be allowed to conceive the existence of Matter, notwithstanding I have no idea of it?

Phil. As to your first question : I own I have properly no *idea*, either of God or any other spirit; for these being active, cannot be represented by things perfectly inert, as our ideas are. I do nevertheless know that I, who am a spirit or thinking substance, exist as certainly as I know my ideas exist. Further, I know what I mean by the terms *I* and *myself*; and I know this immediately or intuitively, though I do not perceive it as I perceive a triangle, a colour, or a sound. The Mind, Spirit, or Soul is that indivisible unextended thing which thinks, acts, and perceives. I say

[2] Here we have Berkeley's Theism in a paragraph : every word tells. The Materialists—*e.g.* some of those who took up the substantiality allowed to Matter by Descartes, and set it up by itself— ask, what becomes of, say, Mont Blanc when no human being is near it, or looking at it. Berkeley gives his answer. He shows that he is not for " subjective idealism " or " solipsism " or " pan-egoism "; true, his own percipience was his starting-point for knowledge, but he moves out to the inference to an Eternal Mind, and holds this inference to be valid in itself, and adequate to account for the existence of Mont Blanc, and of all else.

indivisible, because unextended; and *unextended,* because extended, figured, movable things are ideas; and that which perceives ideas, which thinks and wills,. is plainly itself no idea, nor like an idea. Ideas are things inactive and perceived. And Spirits a sort of beings altogether different from them. I do not therefore say my soul is an idea, or like an idea. However, taking the word *idea* in a large sense, my soul may be said to furnish me with an idea, that is, an image or likeness of God—though indeed extremely inadequate. For, all the notion I have of God is obtained by reflecting on my own soul, heightening its powers, and removing its imperfections. I have, therefore, though not an inactive idea, yet in *myself* some sort of an active thinking image of the Deity. And though I perceive Him not by sense, yet I have a notion of Him, or know Him by reflection and reasoning. My own mind and my own ideas I have an immediate knowledge of; and, by the help of these, do mediately apprehend the possibility of the existence of other spirits and ideas. Further, from my own being, and from the dependency I find in myself and my ideas, I do, by an act of reason, necessarily infer the existence of a God, and of all created things in the mind of God. So much for your first question. For the second: I suppose by this time you can answer it yourself. For you neither perceive Matter objectively, as you do an inactive being or idea; nor know it, as you do yourself, by a reflex act; neither do you mediately apprehend it by similitude of the one or the other; nor yet collect it by reasoning from that which you know immediately. All which makes the case of *Matter* widely different from that of the *Deity.*[3]

[3] The ideas we derive from perception Berkeley unreservedly regards as "passive and inert." Hume, Brown, Comte, the Mills, followed on this line, but a different view culminated in recent treatment of them as activities of the mind: as to some extent in the "presentative activities" of Herbartian psychology, the *idées-forces*

[*Hyl.* You say your own soul supplies you with some sort of an idea or image of God. But, at the same time, you acknowledge you have, properly speaking, no *idea* of your own soul. You even affirm that spirits are a sort of beings altogether different from ideas. Consequently that no idea can be like a spirit. We have therefore no idea of any spirit. You admit nevertheless that there is spiritual Substance, although you have no idea of it; while you deny there can be such a thing as material Substance, because you have no notion or idea of it. Is this fair dealing? To act consistently, you must either admit Matter or reject Spirit. What say you to this?[4]

of Fouillée, and the description of mind by Professor James as a seething mass of living yeast, or an ant-heap. For Berkeley they are passive; he will therefore need some active cause for their appearance. He declines the reference to Matter; and as they are not due to activity of the percipient's mind, the only course is to refer them directly to the Mind which pervades the universe. But he is far from allowing that the passive ideas cover the whole range of knowledge, and in this paragraph he is recognising "a sort of beings altogether different from ideas." For these he brings up the term "notion." Of myself as an activity, "perceiving, knowing, willing, and operating about ideas," I have a "notion"; by inference, I form a similar "notion" of similar spiritual activities on a par with myself; and a further ultimate "notion" of Divine Mind arises by inference, by "act of reason." Whenever he comes into view of any ideas, or order among ideas, which he cannot assign to operations of his own mind, he refers to the agency of the Divine Mind. For Hegelian objection to this procedure, see Stirling's Note on Berkeley, in *Schwegler*, p. 419; and Green's *Introduction to Hume*, p. 153.

[4] The reader must be uncompromisingly severe with our author here. Berkeley has given an admirable specimen of philosophical criticism in his polemic against Materialism: he must be subjected to every test that can be applied when he comes forward to offer Mind as the universal substitute. He is himself aware that all depends upon his establishing the validity of the "notions" he has just brought in. This and the next three paragraphs were added in his third edition, and Professor Fraser accounts them to be "perhaps the most important passages in the Dialogues." It was by refusing to admit such

Phil. I say, in the first place, that I do not deny the existence of material substance, merely because I have no notion of it, but because the notion of it is inconsistent; or, in other words, because it is repugnant that there should be a notion of it. Many things, for aught I know, may exist, whereof neither I nor any other man hath or can have any idea or notion whatsoever. But then those things must be possible, that is, nothing inconsistent must be included in their definition. I say, secondly, that, although we believe things to exist which we do not perceive, yet we may not believe that any particular thing exists, without some reason for such belief; but I have no reason for believing the exist-ence of Matter. I have no immediate intuition thereof; neither can I immediately from my sensations, ideas, notions, actions, or passions infer an unthinking, unperceiving, in-active Substance—either by probable deduction, or necessary consequence. Whereas the being of my Self, that is, my own soul, mind, or thinking principle, I evidently know by reflection. You will forgive me if I repeat the same things in answer to the same objections. In the very notion or definition of *material Substance*, there is included a manifest repugnance and inconsistency. But this cannot be said of the notion of Spirit. That ideas should exist in what doth not perceive, or be produced by what doth not act, is

"notions" that Hume carried the perceptive theory of knowledge to Scepticism as to our knowing Self or Deity, or any "substance" at all. As it was Hume who awoke Kant from slumberous acceptance of such "substances," it is plain that these paragraphs, as containing such constructive effort as Berkeley had exerted, require the closest scrutiny.

We should ask especially—(1) Does Berkeley justify his Idealism as a broad, simple, principle? and (2) does he contribute anything to the detailed construction of Idealism as an illuminative system of philosophy? That he was personally conscious of inability (in some way) to achieve the latter purpose is evidenced by his own resort in his later life to a Platonic Mysticism.

repugnant. But, it is no repugnancy to say that a perceiving thing should be the subject of ideas, or an active thing the cause of them. It is granted we have neither an immediate evidence nor a demonstrative knowledge of the existence of other finite spirits; but it will not thence follow that such spirits are on a foot with material substances: if to suppose the one be inconsistent, and it be not inconsistent to suppose the other; if the one can be inferred by no argument, and there is a probability for the other; if we see signs and effects indicating distinct finite agents like ourselves, and see no sign or symptom whatever that leads to a rational belief of Matter. I say, lastly, that I have a notion of Spirit, though I have not, strictly speaking, an idea of it. I do not perceive it as an idea, or by means of an idea, but know it by reflection.

Hyl. Notwithstanding all you have said, to me it seems that, according to your own way of thinking, and in consequence of your own principles, it should follow that *you* are only a system of floating ideas, without any substance to support them. Words are not to be used without a meaning. And, as there is no more meaning in *spiritual Substance* than in *material Substance*, the one is to be exploded as well as the other.

Phil. How often must I repeat, that I know or am conscious of my own being; and that *I myself* am not my ideas, but somewhat else, a thinking, active principle that perceives, knows, wills, and operates about ideas. I know that I, one and the same self, perceive both colours and sounds: that a colour cannot perceive a sound, nor a sound a colour: that I am therefore one individual principle, distinct from colour and sound; and, for the same reason, from all other sensible things and inert ideas. But, I am not in like manner conscious either of the existence or essence of matter. On the contrary, I know that nothing inconsistent can exist, and that the existence of matter implies an inconsistency. Further, I know what I mean when I affirm that there is a spiritual substance or support of ideas, that is, that a spirit knows and perceives ideas. But, I do not know what is meant when it is said that an unperceiving substance hath inherent in it and supports either ideas or the archetypes of ideas. There is therefore upon the whole no parity of case between Spirit and Matter.]

Hyl. I own myself satisfied in this point. But, do you in earnest think the real existence of sensible things consists in their being actually perceived? If so; how comes it that all mankind distinguish between them? Ask the first man you meet, and he shall tell you, *to be perceived* is one thing, and *to exist* is another.[5]

Phil. I am content, *Hylas*, to appeal to the common sense of the world for the truth of my notion. Ask the gardener why he thinks yonder cherry-tree exists in the garden, and he shall tell you, because he sees and feels it; in a word, because he perceives it by his senses. Ask him why he thinks an orange-tree not to be there, and he shall tell you, because he does not perceive it. What he perceives by sense, that he terms a real being, and saith it *is* or *exists*; but, that which is not perceivable, the same, he saith, hath no being.

Hyl. Yes, *Philonous*, I grant the existence of a sensible thing consists in being perceivable, but not in being actually perceived.

Phil. And what is perceivable but an idea? And can

---

[5] In the following paragraphs Berkeley strives once more to make fast his position : " existence " is " being perceived," and the perceiver of the universe is Mind, active Spiritual Intelligence. Berkeley's Idealism, it may here be noted, applies not only to Matter behind obvious concrete objects, it applies to such remote constituents as our modern *atoms* and *cells*. The nature of mathematical, physical, and biological elements is not different in this respect from the subject-matter of morals or æsthetics : the existence of all of them involves their being " perceived " in some way or other.

an idea exist without being actually perceived? These are points long since agreed between us.

Hyl. But, be your opinion never so true, yet surely you will not deny it is shocking, and contrary to the common sense of men. Ask the fellow whether yonder tree hath an existence out of his mind: what answer think you he would make?

Phil. The same that I should myself, to wit, that it doth exist out of his mind. But then to a Christian it cannot surely be shocking to say, the real tree, existing without his mind, is truly known and comprehended by (that is *exists in*) the infinite mind of God. Probably he may not at first glance be aware of the direct and immediate proof there is of this; inasmuch as the very being of a tree, or any other sensible thing, implies a mind wherein it is. But the point itself he cannot deny. The question between the Materialists and me is not, whether things have a *real* existence out of the mind of this or that person, but, whether they have an *absolute* existence, distinct from being perceived by God, and exterior to all minds. This indeed some heathens and philosophers have affirmed, but whoever entertains notions of the Deity suitable to the Holy Scriptures will be of another opinion.

Hyl. But, according to your notions, what difference is there between real things, and chimeras formed by the imagination, or the visions of a dream—since they are all equally in the mind?

Phil. The ideas formed by the imagination are faint and indistinct; they have, besides, an entire dependence on the will. But the ideas perceived by sense, that is, real things, are more vivid and clear; and, being imprinted on the mind by a spirit distinct from us, have not the like dependence on our will. There is therefore no danger of confounding these with the foregoing: and there is as little of confounding them with the visions of a dream, which are dim, irregular, and confused. And, though they should happen to be never so lively and natural, yet, by their not being connected, and of a piece with the preceding and subsequent transactions of our lives, they might easily be distinguished from realities. In short, by whatever method you distinguish *things* from *chimeras* on your scheme, the same, it is evident, will hold also upon mine. For it must be, I presume, by some perceived difference; and I am not for depriving you of any one thing that you perceive.

Hyl. But still, *Philonous*, you hold there is nothing in the world but spirits and ideas. And this, you must needs acknowledge, sounds very oddly.

Phil. I own the word *idea*, not being commonly used for *thing*, sounds something out of the way. My reason for using it was, because a necessary relation to the mind is understood to be implied by that term; and it is now commonly used by philosophers to denote the immediate objects of the understanding. But, however oddly the proposition may sound in words, yet it includes nothing so very strange or shocking in its sense; which in effect amounts to no more than this, to wit, that there are only things perceiving, and things perceived; or that every unthinking being is necessarily, and from the very nature of its existence, perceived by some mind; if not by a finite created mind, yet certainly by the infinite mind of God, in whom "we live, and move, and have our being," Is this as strange as to say, the sensible qualities are not on the objects: or that we cannot be sure of the existence of things, or know anything of their real natures—though we both see and feel them, and perceive them by all our senses?

Hyl. And, in consequence of this, must we not think there are no such things as physical or corporeal causes; but that a Spirit is the immediate cause of all the phenomena in nature? Can there be anything more extravagant than this?

Phil. Yes, it is infinitely more extravagant to say—a thing

which is inert operates on the mind, and which is unperceiving is the cause of our perceptions, [without any regard either
to consistency, or the old known axiom, *Nothing can give to
another that which it hath not itself*].* Besides, that which
to you, I know not for what reason, seems so extravagant is
no more than the Holy Scriptures assert in a hundred places.
In them God is represented as the sole and immediate Author
of all those effects which some heathens and philosophers are
wont to ascribe to Nature, Matter, Fate, or the like unthinking principle. This is so much the constant language of
Scripture that it were needless to confirm it by citations.

Hyl. You are not aware, *Philonous*, that, in making God
the immediate Author of all the motions in nature, you make
Him the Author of murder, sacrilege, adultery, and the like
heinous sins.[6]

Phil. In answer to that, I observe, first, that the imputa-
tion of guilt is the same, whether a person commits an action
with or without an instrument. In case, therefore, you
suppose God to act by the mediation of an instrument, or
occasion, called *Matter*, you as truly make Him the author of
sin as I, who think Him the immediate agent in all those
operations vulgarly ascribed to Nature. I further observe
that sin or moral turpitude doth not consist in the outward
physical action or motion, but in the internal deviation of the
will from the laws of reason and religion. This is plain, in
that the killing an enemy in a battle, or putting a criminal
legally to death, is not thought sinful ; though the outward
act be the very same with that in the case of murder. Since,

---

* The words within brackets were omitted in the third edition.

[6] The questions of Moral responsibility and of Evil come up if the
Divine Mind is to be an all-pervading agency. Matter had for ages
served as an intermediate substance, or even an independent substance, to which the possibility of Evil could be referred : what will
Berkeley do if this intermediary disappears ? He does not pause here
to give any elaborate answer, it will be seen ; but to what is urged in
this paragraph must be added the treatment of Pain later (p. 161).

therefore, sin doth not consist in the physical action, the making God an immediate cause of all such actions is not making Him the Author of sin. Lastly, I have nowhere said that God is the only agent who produces all the motions in bodies. It is true I have denied there are any other agents besides spirits; but this is very consistent with allowing to thinking rational beings, in the production of motions, the use of limited powers, ultimately indeed derived from God, but immediately under the direction of their own wills, which is sufficient to entitle them to all the guilt of their actions.

Hyl. But the denying Matter, *Philonous*, or corporeal Substance; there is the point. You can never persuade me that this is not repugnant to the universal sense of mankind. Were our dispute to be determined by most voices, I am confident you would give up the point, without gathering the votes.

Phil. I wish both our opinions were fairly stated and submitted to the judgment of men who had plain common sense, without the prejudices of a learned education. Let me be represented as one who trusts his senses, who thinks he knows the things he sees and feels, and entertains no doubts of their existence; and you fairly set forth with all your doubts, your paradoxes, and your scepticism about you, and I shall willingly acquiesce in the determination of any indifferent person. That there is no substance wherein ideas can exist beside spirit is to me evident. And that the objects immediately perceived are ideas, is on all hands agreed. And that sensible qualities are objects immediately perceived no one can deny. It is therefore evident there can be no *substratum* of those qualities but spirit; in which they exist, not by way of mode or property, but as a thing perceived in that which perceives it. I deny, therefore, that there is any unthinking *substratum* of the objects of sense, and in that acceptation that there is any material substance. But if by *material substance* is meant only sensible body, that which is seen and felt (and the unphilosophical part of the world, I dare say, mean no more), then I am more certain of Matter's existence than you or any other philosopher pretend to be. If there be anything which makes the generality of mankind averse from the notions I espouse, it is a misapprehension that I deny the reality of sensible things; but, as it is you who are guilty of that and not I, it follows that in truth their aversion is against your notions and not mine. I do therefore assert that I am as certain as of my own being, that there are bodies or corporeal substances (meaning the things I perceive by my senses); and that, granting this, the bulk of mankind will take no thought about, nor think themselves at all concerned in the fate of those unknown natures and philosophical quiddities which some men are so fond of.[7]

Hyl. What say you to this? Since, according to you, men judge of the reality of things by their senses, how can a man be mistaken in thinking the moon a plain lucid surface about

[7] He returns to the question of Matter as substance, in order to show that his philosophy is perfectly congruous with what common sense means when it is cleared up. When Dr. Johnson, as a representative of Common Sense, kicked a stone as a silent but sufficient refutation of Berkeleianism, it is obvious that he was supposing Berkeley to deny the existence of the stone, and that he appealed to the sensation of muscular resistance as a fact of experience which could not be gainsaid. But Berkeley had in no way denied that sensation : it was one of those "passive ideas" which he has all along recognised in our experience. And the fact that Dr. Johnson would experience that particular sensation, in connexion with the visual sensations present to him when he was looking at the stone, was also fully recognised by Berkeley. What he did deny was the reference of the sensations and of their connexion to some supposed substance within the stone, quite occult and in no way perceived by Dr. Johnson, but supposed by him as a cause for the sensations and their connexion. Such a supposition, Berkeley keeps saying, is a fiction ; and worse, it is an intrusion perniciously obscuring the true inference, namely, to a Mind which is the ultimate source of all ideas, and of all those connexions between them which we call "laws of nature."

a foot in diameter; or a square tower, seen at a distance, round; or an oar, with one end in the water, crooked?

Phil. He is not mistaken with regard to the ideas he actually perceives, but in the inferences he makes from his present perceptions. Thus, in the case of the oar, what he immediately perceives by sight is certainly crooked; and so far he is in the right. But if he thence conclude that upon taking the oar out of the water he shall perceive the same crookedness; or that it would affect his touch as crooked things are wont to do: in that he is mistaken. In like manner, if he shall conclude from what he perceives in one station, that, in case he advances towards the moon or tower, he should still be affected with the like ideas, he is mistaken. But his mistake lies not in what he perceives immediately and at present (it being a manifest contradiction to suppose he should err in respect of that), but in the wrong judgment he makes concerning the ideas he apprehends to be connected with those immediately perceived: or, concerning the ideas that, from what he perceives at present, he imagines would be perceived in other circumstances. The case is the same with regard to the Copernican system. We do not here perceive any motion of the earth: but it were erroneous thence to conclude that, in case we were placed at as great a distance from that as we are now from the other planets, we should not then perceive its motion.

Hyl. I understand you; and must needs own you say things plausible enough: but, give me leave to put you in mind of one thing. Pray, *Philonous*, were you not formerly as positive that Matter existed, as you are now that it does not?

Phil. I was. But here lies the difference. Before, my positiveness was founded, without examination, upon prejudice; but now, after inquiry, upon evidence.

Hyl. After all, it seems our dispute is rather about words than things. We agree in the thing, but differ in the name.

That we are affected with ideas from without is evident; and it is no less evident that there must be (I will not say archetypes, but) powers without the mind, corresponding to those ideas. And as these powers cannot subsist by themselves, there is some subject of them necessarily to be admitted, which I call *Matter* and you call *Spirit*. This is all the difference.[8]

Phil. Pray, *Hylas*, is that powerful being, or subject of powers, extended?

Hyl. It hath not extension; but it hath the power to raise in you the idea of extension.

Phil. It is therefore itself unextended?

Hyl. I grant it.

Phil. Is it not also active?

Hyl. Without doubt: otherwise, how could we attribute powers to it?

Phil. Now let me ask you two questions: *first*, Whether it be agreeable to the usage either of philosophers or others to give the name *Matter* to an unextended active being? And, *secondly*, Whether it be not ridiculously absurd to misapply names contrary to the common use of language?

Hyl. Well then, let it not be called Matter, since you will have it so, but some *third nature* distinct from Matter and Spirit.[9] For what reason is there why you should call it spirit? Does not the notion of spirit imply that it is thinking as well as active and unextended?

Phil. My reason is this: because I have a mind to have some notion of meaning in what I say: but I have no notion of any action distinct from volition, neither can I conceive volition to be anywhere but in a spirit; therefore, when I speak of an active being, I am obliged to mean a spirit.

[8] He reverts to the considerations in favour of reference to Mind rather than to a supposed "Matter."

[9] He will not accept such an intermediary substance as the Plastic Nature of Cudworth.

physical affection

Beside, what can be plainer than that a thing which hath no ideas in itself cannot impart them to me; and, if it hath ideas, surely it must be a spirit. To make you comprehend the point still more clearly if it be possible—I assert as well as you that, since we are affected from without, we must allow powers to be without, in a being distinct from ourselves. So far we are agreed. But then we differ as to the kind of this powerful being. I will have it to be spirit, you Matter, or I know not what (I may add too, you know not what) third nature. Thus, I prove it to be spirit. From the effects I see produced I conclude there are actions; and, because actions, volitions; and, because there are volitions, there must be a will. Again, the things I perceive must have an existence, they or their archetypes, out of my mind : but, being ideas, neither they nor their archetypes can exist otherwise than in an understanding; there is therefore an understanding. But will and understanding constitute, in the strictest sense, a mind or spirit. The powerful cause, therefore, of my ideas is, in strict propriety of speech, a *spirit*.

Hyl. And now I warrant you think you have made the point very clear, little suspecting that what you advance leads directly to a contradiction. Is it not an absurdity to imagine any imperfection in God?

Phil. Without a doubt.

Hyl. To suffer pain is an imperfection?

Phil. It is.

Hyl. Are we not sometimes affected with pain and uneasiness by some other being?

Phil. We are.

Hyl. And have you not said that being is a spirit, and is not that spirit God?

Phil. I grant it.

Hyl. But you have asserted that whatever ideas we perceive from without are in the mind which affects us. The

11

ideas, therefore, of pain and uneasiness are in God; or, in other words, God suffers pain: that is to say, there is an imperfection in the Divine nature, which, you acknowledge, was absurd. So you are caught in a plain contradiction.

Phil. That God knows or understands all things, and that He knows, among other things, what pain is, even every sort of painful sensation, and what it is for His creatures to suffer pain, I make no question. But that God, though He knows and sometimes causes painful sensations in us, can Himself suffer pain, I positively deny. We, who are limited and dependent spirits, are liable to impressions of sense, the effects of an external agent, which, being produced against our wills, are sometimes painful and uneasy. But God, whom no external being can affect, who perceives nothing by sense as we do, whose will is absolute and independent, causing all things, and liable to be thwarted or resisted by nothing; it is evident such a Being as this can suffer nothing, nor be affected with any painful sensation, or indeed any sensation at all. We are chained to a body, that is to say, our perceptions are connected with corporeal motions. By the law of our nature we are affected upon every altera- tion in the nervous parts of our sensible body; which sensible body, rightly considered, is nothing but a complexion of such qualities or ideas as have no existence distinct from being perceived by a mind: so that this connection of sensations with corporeal motions means no more than a correspondence in the order of nature between two sets of ideas, or things immediately perceivable. But God is a pure spirit, dis- engaged from all such sympathy or natural ties. No cor- poreal motions are attended with the sensations of pain or pleasure in His mind. To know everything knowable is certainly a perfection; but to endure, or suffer, or feel any- thing by sense, is an imperfection. The former, I say, agrees to God, but not the latter. God knows or hath ideas; but His ideas are not conveyed to Him by sense, as ours are.

Your not distinguishing, where there is so manifest a difference, makes you fancy you see an absurdity where there is none.[10]

. . . .

Phil. It is your opinion the ideas we perceive by our senses are not real things, but images or copies of them.[11] Our knowledge, therefore, is no farther real than as our ideas are the true representations of those originals. But as these supposed originals are in themselves unknown, it is impossible to know how far our ideas resemble them; or whether they resemble them at all. We cannot, therefore, be sure we have any real knowledge. Farther, as our ideas are perpetually varied, without any change in the supposed real things, it necessarily follows they cannot all be true copies of them; or, if some are and others are not, it is impossible to distinguish the former from the latter. And this plunges us yet deeper in uncertainty. Again, when we consider the point, we cannot conceive how any idea, or anything like an idea, should have an absolute existence out of a mind; nor consequently, according to you, how there should be any real thing in nature. The result of all which is that we are thrown into the most hopeless and abandoned Scepticism. Now, give me leave to ask you, First, whether your referring ideas to certain absolutely existing unperceived substances as their originals be not the source of all this Scepticism?

[10] We omit six pages here: they contain a brief refutation of a suggestion that Matter is required to explain gravitation, and a defence against the charge of novelty in dispensing with "Matter," as to which sufficient is said in other parts of the Dialogue to show Berkeley's determination to insist on common opinion being really on his side, sometimes expressing himself with Socratic irony, but often with the direct earnestness of the advocate of a very serious cause.

[11] Here Berkeley shows that he has shaken himself free from the doctrine of Representative perception—that our ideas are copies of things — which we saw Descartes retaining from Scholasticism (see p. 43).

Secondly, whether you are informed, either by sense or reason, of the existence of those unknown originals? And, in case you are not, whether it be not absurd to suppose them? Thirdly, whether, upon inquiry, you find there is anything distinctly conceived or meant by the *absolute or external existence of unperceiving substances*? Lastly, whether, the premises considered, it be not the wisest way to follow nature, trust your senses, and, laying aside all anxious thought about unknown natures or substances, admit with the vulgar those for real things which are perceived by the senses?

Hyl. For the present I have no inclination to the answering part. I would much rather see how you can get over what follows. Pray, are not the objects perceived by the senses of one likewise perceivable to others present? If there were a hundred more here, they would all see the garden, the trees, and flowers, as I see them. But they are not in the same manner affected with the ideas I frame in my imagination. Does not this make a difference between the former sort of objects and the latter? [12]

Phil. I grant it does. Nor have I ever denied a difference between the objects of sense and those of imagination. But what would you infer from thence? You cannot say that sensible objects exist unperceived, because they are perceived by many.

Hyl. I own I can make nothing of that objection; but it hath led me into another. Is it not your opinion that by our senses we perceive only the ideas existing in our minds?

---

[12] This is the question raised by asking what is the real sun, if the perceptions of it by, say, ten men are diverse, with the presumption that no one of them is more correct than the others. This carries us into a region where higher Idealism takes up its stand: agreeing with Berkeley that the supposition of "Matter" has no special claim for a hearing there; that, on the contrary, it is Mind which alone touches the problem raised. (See Ward, *Naturalism and Agnosticism.*)

Phil. It is.

Hyl. But the same idea which is in my mind cannot be in yours, or in any other mind. Doth it not therefore follow, from your principles, that no two can see the same thing? And is not this highly absurd?

Phil. If the term *same* be taken in the vulgar acceptation, it is certain (and not at all repugnant to the principles I maintain) that different persons may perceive the same thing; or the same thing or idea exist in different minds. Words are of arbitrary imposition; and, since men are used to apply the word *same* where no distinction or variety is perceived, and I do not pretend to alter their perceptions, it follows that, as men have said before, *several saw the same thing*, so they may, upon like occasions, still continue to use the same phrase, without any deviation either from propriety of language or the truth of things. But if the term *same* be used in the acceptation of philosophers who pretend to an abstracted notion of identity, then according to their sundry definitions of this notion (for it is not yet agreed wherein that philosophic identity consists), it may or may not be possible for divers persons to perceive the same thing. But whether philosophers shall think fit to call a thing the *same* or no, is, I conceive, of small importance. Let us suppose several men together, all endued with the same faculties, and consequently affected in like sort by their senses, and who have yet never known the use of language; they would, without question, agree in their perceptions. Though perhaps, when they came to the use of speech, some regarding the uniformness of what was perceived, might call it the *same* thing; others, especially regarding the diversity of persons who perceived, might choose the denomination of *different* things. But who sees not that all the dispute is about a word? to wit, whether what is perceived by different persons may yet have the term *same* applied to it? Or, suppose a house, whose walls or outward shell remained unaltered, the chambers are all pulled down and new ones built in their place; and that you should call this the *same*, and I should say it was not the *same* house;—would we not, for all this, perfectly agree in our thoughts of the house, considered in itself? And would not all the difference consist in a sound? If you should say, We differ in our notions; for that you superadded to your idea of the house the simple abstracted idea of identity, whereas I did not; I would tell you I know not what you mean by the *abstracted idea of identity*, and should desire you to look into your own thoughts and be sure you understood yourself.—Why so silent, *Hylas*? Are you not yet satisfied men may dispute about identity and diversity without any real difference in their thoughts and opinions, abstracted from names? Take this further reflection with you—that whether Matter be allowed to exist or no, the case is exactly the same as to the point in hand. For the Materialists themselves acknowledge what we immediately perceive by our senses to be our own ideas. Your difficulty, therefore, that no two see the same thing, makes equally against the Materialists and me.

Hyl. [**Ay,** *Philonous,*] But they suppose an external archetype to which referring their several ideas they may truly be said to perceive the same thing.

Phil. And (not to mention your having discarded those archetypes) so may you suppose an external archetype on my principles;—*external*, I mean, to your own mind; though indeed it must be supposed to exist in that mind which comprehends all things; but then, this serves all the ends of *identity*, as well as if it existed out of a mind. And I am sure you yourself will not say it is less intelligible.

Hyl. You have indeed clearly satisfied me—either that there is no difficulty at bottom in this point, or, if there be, that it makes equally against both opinions.

Phil. But that which makes equally against two contradictory opinions can be a proof against neither.

Hyl. I acknowledge it. But, after all, *Philonous*, when I consider the substance of what you advance against *Scepticism*, it amounts to no more than this :—We are sure that we really see, hear, feel ; in a word, that we are affected with sensible impressions.

Phil. And how are we concerned any further ? I see this *cherry*, I feel it, I taste it : and I am sure *nothing* cannot be seen, or felt, or tasted ; it is therefore *real*. Take away the sensations of softness, moisture, redness, tartness, and you take away the *cherry*. Since it is not a being distinct from sensations ; a *cherry*, I say, is nothing but a congeries of sensible impressions, or ideas perceived by various senses ; which ideas are united into one thing (or have one name given them) by the mind ;—because they are observed to attend each other. Thus, when the palate is affected with such a particular taste, the sight is affected with a red colour, the touch with roundness, softness, etc. Hence, when I see, and feel, and taste, in sundry certain manners, I am sure the *cherry* exists, or is real ; its reality being in my opinion nothing abstracted from those sensations. But if, by the word *cherry*, you mean an unknown nature, distinct from all those sensible qualities, and by its *existence* something distinct from its being perceived ; then, indeed, I own, neither you nor I, nor anyone else, can be sure it exists.

Hyl. But what would you say, *Philonous*, if I should bring the very same reasons against the existence of sensible things in a mind, which you have offered against their existing in a material *substratum* ?

Phil. When I see your reasons, you shall hear what I have to say to them.

Hyl. Is the mind extended or unextended ?

Phil. Unextended, without doubt.

Hyl. Do you say the things you perceive are in your mind ?

Phil. They are.

Hyl. Again, have I not heard you speak of sensible impressions.

Phil. I believe you may.

Hyl. Explain to me now, O *Philonous*! how it is possible there should be room for all those trees and houses to exist in your mind. Can extended things be contained in that which is unextended? Or are we to imagine impressions made on a thing void of all solidity? You cannot say objects are in your mind, as books in your study; or that things are imprinted on it, as the figure of a seal upon wax. In what sense, therefore, are we to understand those expressions? Explain me this if you can: and I shall then be able to answer all those queries you formerly put to me about my *substratum*.

Phil. Look you, *Hylas*, when I speak of objects as existing in the mind, or imprinted on the senses, I would not be understood in the gross literal sense—as when bodies are said to exist in a place, or a seal to make an impression upon wax. My meaning is only that the mind comprehends or perceives them; and that it is affected from without, or by some being distinct from itself. This is my explication of your difficulty, and how it can serve to make your tenet of an unperceiving material *substratum* intelligible, I would fain know.

Hyl. Nay, if that be all, I confess I do not see what use can be made of it. But are you not guilty of some abuse of language in this?

Phil. None at all. It is no more than common custom, which, you know, is the rule of language, hath authorised; nothing being more usual than for philosophers to speak of the immediate objects of the understanding as things existing in the mind. Nor is there anything in this but what is conformable to the general analogy of language, most part of the mental operations being signified by words borrowed from sensible things, as is plain in the terms *comprehend*, *reflect, discourse*, etc., which, being applied to the mind, must not be taken in their gross original sense.

Hyl. You have, I own, satisfied me in this point.[13] . . .

Phil. Then as to *absolute existence* ;—was there ever known a more jejune notion than that? Something it is so abstracted and unintelligible that you have frankly owned you could not conceive it, much less explain anything by it. But, allowing matter to exist, and the notion of absolute existence to be as clear as light, yet, was this ever known to make the creation more credible? Nay, hath it not furnished the atheists and infidels of all ages with the most plausible arguments against a creation? That a corporeal substance, which hath an absolute existence without the minds of spirits, should be produced out of nothing, by the mere will of a Spirit, hath been looked upon as a thing so contrary to all reason, so impossible and absurd, that not only the most celebrated among the ancients, but even divers modern and Christian philosophers have thought Matter coeternal with the Deity. Lay these things together, and then judge you whether Materialism disposes men to believe the creation of things.

Hyl. I own, *Philonous*, I think it does not. This of the *creation* is the last objection I can think of ; and I must needs own it hath been sufficiently answered as well as the rest. Nothing now remains to be overcome but a sort of unaccountable backwardness that I find in myself towards your notions.[14]

Phil. When a man is swayed, he knows not why, to one side of the question, can this, think you, be anything else

[13] Six pages are omitted in which Berkeley refutes the objection that the Mosaic account of Creation is concerned to retain the supposition of "Matter." We resume with what is briefly urged as to the difficulty which Matter raises to the belief in "creation" at all.

[14] We are now to hear of the advantages to be gained by the replacement of Matter by Mind, both for human learning in general and for Religion.

but the effect of prejudice, which never fails to attend old and rooted notions? And indeed in this respect I cannot deny the belief of Matter to have very much the advantage over the contrary opinion, with men of a learned education.

Hyl. I confess it seems to be as you say.

Phil. As a balance, therefore, to this weight of prejudice, let us throw into the scale the great advantages that arise from the belief of Immaterialism, both in regard to religion and human learning.—The being of a God, and incorruptibility of the soul, those great articles of religion, are they not proved with the clearest and most immediate evidence? When I say the being of a *God*, I do not mean an obscure general cause of things, whereof we have no conception, but *God*, in the strict and proper sense of the word; a Being whose spirituality, omnipresence, providence, omniscience, infinite power and goodness, are as conspicuous as the existence of sensible things, of which (notwithstanding the fallacious pretences and affected scruples of Sceptics) there is no more reason to doubt than that of our own being.— Then, with relation to human sciences: in Natural Philosophy, what intricacies, what obscurities, what contradictions hath the belief of Matter led men into! To say nothing of the numberless disputes about its extent, continuity, homogeneity, gravity, divisibility, etc.,—do they not pretend to explain all things by bodies operating on bodies, according to the law of motion? and yet, are they able to comprehend how one body should move another? Nay, admitting there was no difficulty in reconciling the notion of an inert being with a cause, or in conceiving how an accident might pass from one body to another; yet, by all their strained thoughts and extravagant suppositions, have they been able to reach the mechanical production of any one animal or vegetable body? Can they account, by the laws of motion, for sounds, tastes, smells, or colours, or for the regular course of things? Have they accounted, by physical principles, for the aptitude and contrivance even of the most inconsiderable parts of the universe? But laying aside Matter and corporeal causes, and admitting only the efficiency of an All-perfect Mind, are not all the effects of nature easy and intelligible? If the *phenomena* are nothing else but *ideas*; God is a *spirit*, but Matter an unintelligent, unperceiving being. If they demonstrate an unlimited power in their cause; God is active and omnipotent, but Matter an inert mass. If the order, regularity, and usefulness of them can never be sufficiently admired; God is infinitely wise and provident, but Matter destitute of all contrivance and design. These surely are great advantages in *physics*. Not to mention that the apprehension of a distant Deity naturally disposes men to a negligence in their moral actions, which they would be more cautious of, in case they thought Him immediately present, and acting on their minds, without the interposition of Matter, or unthinking second causes.— Then in *metaphysics*: what difficulties concerning entity in abstract, substantial forms, hylarchic principles, plastic natures, substance and accident, principle of individuation, possibility of Matter's thinking, origin of ideas, the manner how two independent substances so widely different as *Spirit* and *Matter*, should mutually operate on each other? what difficulties, I say, and endless disquisitions, concerning these and innumerable other the like points, do we escape, by supposing only Spirits and ideas?—Even the *mathematics* themselves, if we take away the absolute existence of extended things, become much more clear and easy; the most shocking paradoxes and intricate speculations in those sciences depending on the infinite divisibility of finite extension, which depends on that supposition.—But what need is there to insist on the particular sciences? Is not that opposition to all science whatsoever, that frenzy of the ancient and modern Sceptics, built on the same foundation? Or can you produce so much as one argument against the

reality of corporeal things, or in behalf of that avowed utter
ignorance of their natures, which doth not suppose their
reality to consist in an external absolute existence? Upon
this supposition, indeed, the objections from the change of
colours in a pigeon's neck, or the appearance of the broken
oar in the water, must be allowed to have weight. But
these and the like objections vanish, if we do not maintain
the being of absolute external originals, but place the reality
of things in ideas, fleeting indeed, and changeable;—however, not changed at random, but according to the fixed
order of nature. For, herein consists that constancy and
truth of things which secures all the concerns of life, and
distinguishes that which is *real* from the irregular visions
of the fancy.[15]

Hyl. I agree to all you have now said, and must own
that nothing can incline me to embrace your opinion more
than the advantages I see it is attended with. I am by
nature lazy; and this would be a mighty abridgment in
knowledge. What doubts, what hypotheses, what labyrinths
of amusement, what fields of disputation, what an ocean
of false learning may be avoided by that single notion of
Immaterialism !

[15] To elucidate his view of how the constancy and regularity and
order we find in the Universe are explained by reference to a Divine
Mind, Berkeley conceived the Supreme Intelligence as communicating
with us by a system of signs. The conception takes its root in his early
Theory of Visual Signs, and is by him generalised in an impressive
manner by referring to our study of the Universe as reading a Divine
Language. Two passages from the Fourth Dialogue of his *Alciphron*
(1732) illustrate his position. In the latter passage the reference to the
constancy and order involved in the Language being for our guidance,
suggests, if it does not establish, a profounder Theism than some are
disposed to credit to Berkeley's philosophy.

"I propound it fairly to your own conscience" (says Alciphron)
"whether you really think that God speaks Himself every day and
in every place to the eyes of all men." "That is really and in
truth my opinion" (replies Euphranor), "and it should be yours

Phil. After all, is there anything further remaining to be done? You may remember you promised to embrace that opinion which upon examination should appear most agreeable to Common Sense and remote from Scepticism. This, by your own confession, is that which denies Matter, or the absolute existence of corporeal things. Nor is this all; the same notion has been proved several ways, viewed in different lights, pursued in its consequences, and all objections against it cleared. Can there be a greater evidence of its truth? or is it possible it should have all the marks of a true opinion and yet be false?

Hyl. I own myself entirely satisfied for the present in all respects. But, what security can I have that I shall

too, if you are consistent with yourself, and abide by your own definition of language. Since you cannot deny that the great Mover and Author of nature constantly explaineth Himself to the eyes of men by the sensible intervention of arbitrary signs, which have no similitude or connection with the things signified ; so as, by compounding and disposing them, to suggest and exhibit an endless variety of objects, differing in nature, time, and place ; thereby informing and directing men how to act with regard to things distant and future, as well as near and present. In consequence, I say, of your own sentiments and concessions, you have as much reason to think the Universal Agent or God speaks to your eyes, as you have for thinking any particular person speaks to your ears."

(Crito) "Some philosophers being convinced of the wisdom and power of the Creator, from the make and contrivance of organised bodies and orderly system of the world, did nevertheless imagine that he left this system with all its parts well adjusted and put in motion, as an artist leaves a clock, to go thenceforward of itself for a certain period. But this Visual Language proves, not a Creator merely, but a provident Governor, actually and intimately present, and attentive to all our interests and motions, who watches over our conduct, and takes care of our minutest actions and designs throughout the whole course of our lives, informing, admonishing, and directing incessantly, in a most evident and sensible manner. This is truly wonderful." "And is it not so" (subjoins Euphranor), "that men should be encompassed by such a wonder without reflecting on it?"

still continue the same full assent to your opinion, and that no unthought-of objection or difficulty will occur hereafter?

Phil. Pray, Hylas, do you in other cases, when a point is once evidently proved, withhold your consent on account of objections or difficulties it may be liable to? Are the difficulties that attend the doctrine of incommensurable quantities, of the angle of contact, of the asymptotes to curves, or the like, sufficient to make you hold out against mathematical demonstration? Or will you disbelieve the Providence of God, because there may be some particular things which you know not how to reconcile with it? If there are difficulties attending *Immaterialism*, there are at the same time direct and evident proofs of it. But for the existence of Matter there is not one proof, and far more numerous and insurmountable objections lie against it. But where are those mighty difficulties you insist on? Alas! you know not where or what they are; something which may possibly occur hereafter. If this be a sufficient pretence for withholding your full assent, you should never yield it to any proposition, how free soever from exceptions, how clearly and solidly soever demonstrated.

Hyl. You have satisfied me, Philonous.

Phil. But, to arm you against all future objections, do but consider—that which bears equally hard on two contradictory opinions can be proof against neither. Whenever, therefore, any difficulty occurs, try if you can find a solution for it on the hypothesis of the *Materialists*. Be not deceived by words; but sound your own thoughts. And in case you cannot conceive it easier by the help of *Materialism*, it is plain it can be no objection against *Immaterialism*. Had you proceeded all along by this rule, you would probably have spared yourself abundance of trouble in objecting; since of all your difficulties I challenge you to show one that is explained by Matter: nay, which is not more unintelligible with than without that supposition, and consequently makes rather *against* than *for* it. You should consider, in each particular, whether the difficulty arises from the *non-existence of Matter*. If it doth not, you might as well argue from the infinite divisibility of extension against the Divine prescience, as from such a difficulty against *Immaterialism*. And yet, upon recollection, I believe you will find this to have been often if not always the case. You should likewise take heed not to argue on a *petitio principii*. One is apt to say, the unknown substances ought to be esteemed real things, rather than the ideas in our minds: and who can tell but the unthinking external substance may concur as a cause or instrument in the productions of our ideas? But is not this proceeding on a supposition that there are such external substances? And to suppose this, is it not begging the question? But, above all things, you should beware of imposing on yourself by that vulgar sophism which is called *ignoratio elenchi*. You talked often as if you thought I maintained the non-existence of Sensible Things:—whereas in truth no one can be more thoroughly assured of their existence than I am: and it is you who doubt; I should have said, positively deny it. Everything that is seen, felt, heard, or any way perceived by the senses, is, on the principles I embrace, a real being, but not on yours. Remember, the Matter you contend for is an unknown somewhat (if indeed it may be termed *somewhat*), which is quite stripped of all sensible qualities, and can neither be perceived by sense, nor apprehended by the mind. Remember, I say, that it is not any object which is hard or soft, hot or cold, blue or white, round or square, etc.;—for all these things I affirm do exist. Though indeed I deny they have an existence distinct from being perceived; or that they exist out of all minds whatsoever. Think on these points; let them be attentively considered and still kept in view. Otherwise you will not comprehend the state of the question; without which your objections will always be wide of the mark, **and,** instead of mine, may possibly be directed (as more than once they have been) against your own notions.

Hyl. I must needs own, Philonous, nothing seems to have kept me from agreeing with you more than this same *mistaking the question.* In denying Matter, at first glimpse I am tempted to imagine you deny the things we see and feel; but, upon reflection, find there is no ground for it. What think you, therefore, of retaining the name *Matter,* and applying it to *sensible things?* This may be done without any change in your sentiments; and, believe me, it would be a means of reconciling them to some persons who may be more shocked at an innovation in words than in opinion.

Phil. With all my heart: retain the word *Matter,* and apply it to the objects of sense, if you please; provided you do not attribute to them any subsistence distinct from their being perceived. I shall never quarrel with you for an expression. *Matter,* or *material substance,* are terms introduced by philosophers; and, as used by them, imply a sort of independency, or a subsistence distinct from being perceived by a mind: but are never used by common people; or, if ever, it is to signify the immediate objects of sense. One would think, therefore, so long as the names of all particular things, with the terms *sensible, substance, body, stuff,* and the like, are retained, the word *Matter* should be never missed in common talk. And in philosophical discourses it seems the best way to leave it quite out: since there is not, perhaps, any one thing that hath more favoured and strengthened the depraved bent of the mind towards Atheism than the use of that general confused term.

Hyl. Well but, Philonous, since I am content to give up the notion of an unthinking substance exterior to the mind, I think you ought not to deny me the privilege of using the word *Matter* as I please, and annexing it to a collection of sensible qualities subsisting only in the mind. I freely own there is no other substance, in a strict sense, than *Spirit*. But I have been so long accustomed to the term *Matter* that I know not how to part with it. To say, there is no *Matter* in the world, is still shocking to me. Whereas to say—There is no *Matter*, if by that term be meant an unthinking substance existing without the mind; but if by *Matter* is meant some sensible thing, whose existence consists in being perceived, then there is *Matter* :—this distinction gives it quite another turn; and men will come into your notions with small difficulty, when they are proposed in that manner. For, after all, the controversy about *Matter* in the strict acceptation of it, lies altogether between you and the philosophers; whose principles, I acknowledge, are not near so natural, or so agreeable to the common sense of mankind, and Holy Scripture, as yours. There is nothing we either desire or shun but as it makes, or is apprehended to make, some part of our happiness or misery. But what hath happiness or misery, joy or grief, pleasure or pain, tc do with Absolute Existence; or with unknown entities, abstracted from all relation to us? It is evident, things regard us only as they are pleasing or displeasing; and they can please or displease only so far forth as they are perceived. Farther, therefore, we are not concerned; and thus far you leave things as you found them. Yet still there is something new in this doctrine. It is plain, I do not now think with the philosophers, nor yet altogether with the vulgar. I would know how the case stands in that respect; precisely, what you have added to, or altered in my former notions.

Phil. I do not pretend to be a setter-up of new notions. My endeavours tend only to unite and place in a clearer light that truth which was before shared between the vulgar and the philosophers :—the former being of opinion, that *those things they immediately perceive are the real things* ; and the latter, that *the things immediately perceived are*

12

ideas which exist only in the mind. Which two notions put
together, do, in effect, constitute the substance of what I
advance.

Hyl. I have been a long time distrusting my senses;
methought I saw things by a dim light and through false
glasses. Now the glasses are removed and a new light
breaks in upon my understanding. I am clearly convinced
that I see things in their native forms, and am no longer
in pain about their *unknown natures* or *absolute existence.*
This is the state I find myself in at present; though, indeed,
the course that brought me to it I do not yet thoroughly
comprehend. You set out upon the same principles that
Academics, Cartesians, and the like sects usually do, and
for a long time it looked as if you were advancing their
Philosophical Scepticism; but, in the end, your conclusions
are directly opposite to theirs.

Phil. You see, Hylas, the water of yonder fountain, how
it is forced upwards, in a round column, to a certain height;
at which it breaks, and falls back into the basin from
whence it rose; its ascent as well as descent proceeding
from the same uniform law or principle of *gravitation.*
Just so, the same principles which, at first view, lead to
Scepticism, pursued to a certain point, bring men back to
Common Sense.

References.—Fraser's edition of Berkeley's Works, with revised
Text, prefaces, and annotations; his volume of *Selections,* and his
monograph in Blackwood's *Philosophical Classics.* For critical
analysis of Berkeley's main position, Pringle-Pattison in *Scottish
Philosophy,* and G. A. Johnston, *The Development of Berkeley's
Philosophy* (1923). Perhaps Ferrier in *Institutes of Metaphysics,* and
Rashdall in *Contentio Veritatis,* come nearest to being Berkeleians.

VII

RELIGION IN THE CRITICAL PHILOSOPHY.

KANT (1724–1804).

IMMANUEL KANT, from whom dates the modern era of philosophy, gave an impulse to metaphysical thought in every department, which has lasted for more than a century, and is still very far from spent. His influence has been all-pervasive, and to-day no philosophical work is studied so widely, or with such minute care, as the epoch-making *Critique of Pure Reason.* Not only idealists like Fichte, Schelling, and Hegel, but realists like Herbart and Lotze, have largely drawn their inspiration from his original method and results, and in various ways have contributed to develop the fruitful germs of profound philosophic truth in which his system is so rich. And now the modern Neo-Kantian school, both in philosophy and theology (represented by such men as Lange, Dühring, and Paulsen on the one side, Herrmann and Reischle on the other), proclaims its theoretical Agnosticism or Positivism as the consistent outcome of the authentic Kantian principles. As Dr. Stirling has aptly said, "Whatever metal of speculation is anywhere turned now, the ore of it is Kant's."

There are four works from Kant's pen which the student of Theism should have steadily in view—the three great Critiques of *Pure Reason,* of *Practical Reason,* and of *Judgment,* while to these may be added the *Religion within the bounds of mere Reason.* The *Critique of Pure Reason,* the ultimate and fontal source of most modern speculative thinking, was published in 1781. It had for its occasion the desire with which Kant had been fired to vindicate for the principle of causality that objective and apodictic necessity which Hume had analysed and explained away as the deposit of mere non-rational custom.   In Kant's own words, " It was reflection on David Hume that several years ago first broke my dogmatic slumber, and gave a completely new direction to my inquiries in the field of speculative philosophy." The question about causality gradually shaped itself for his mind into the larger one, how propositions which are based, not on experience but on pure thought, can nevertheless possess validity for the world of objects.   His solution, in brief, consisted in reversing the relation which had been supposed to obtain between the mind and its objects, a revolution which in a well-known passage he compares to that effected by Copernicus in astronomy.   Previously it had been assumed that our knowledge must adapt itself to the objects. "Suppose we try now," said Kant, " whether better success may not attend us in the problems of metaphysics if we assume objects to be under a necessity of adapting themselves to the nature of our cognition."   It will be observed that these words are a deliberate enunciation of the principle of subjective idealism.   We can know nature *à priori*, because it is in reality the work of our own mind, or, in other words, because what we know is, after all, not things in themselves, but appearances.   This, on the whole, is the outcome of Kant's argument, despite the undoubted realistic elements which his system retains.

The problem which he has before him, therefore, in the *Critique of Pure Reason*, may be stated thus : In realising an act of perception, how much do we contribute from within ? And the answer is to the effect that our *sensibility*, the receptive factor in cognition, contributes space and time, as the *à priori* pure forms of perceptive sense, innate networks of sensuous intuition, as they may be called, which are cast around, and embrace, the manifold of sense-elements ; while *understanding*, the active or spontaneous factor, supplies the categories, or intellectual forms of synthesis,—such as unity, substance, and cause,—by which perceptive experience as a whole is clothed upon with rational order, and objects, which apart from them would be mere blurs of blind sensation, are shot through with intelligibility.   These categories, then, are constitutive in character and function, "they actually enter into the composition and constitution of things as these present themselves for the perception of sense."   But for that very reason we are forbidden to make of them any other than an empirical use. They are valid for objects *in* experience, where a manifold of sense has been given which they can precipitate into intelligibility; they are not valid for objects *apart from* experience, or for things as they are in themselves, for they cannot work in a vacuum from which all sense-elements have been withdrawn. In an atmosphere so rarefied they are powerless. Still, the human mind has always been prone to forget that, owing to the very make of our faculties, experience of phenomena is our sole domain of knowledge. There are certain notions which pretend to pass beyond experiential limits, and to rise to a science of the unconditioned. These speculative Ideas of Reason are the objects of rational psychology, cosmology, and theology, or the ideas of the soul as a real subject, of the world as a single system, and of God as a supreme being. There is nothing which Kant repeats more frequently or more unambiguously than the statement that these are *mere* ideas, yielding no cognition proper, but entangling the mind in metaphysical paralogisms and antinomies. Their real use is to furnish hints by which we may better arrange what we know, and bring it under certain supreme working conceptions. The best way to simplify and systematise our multiplex experiences is to proceed as though those ideas were objectively valid. They have regulative but not constitutive truth. We may put them as Postulates, and wonderful order will follow, but we are not entitled to state them as Dogmas.

Kant's treatment of Rational Theology consists mainly in his criticism of the three proofs which it was usual, since Wolf, to bring forward in dogmatic form as demonstrative of the existence of God. The passages in question are classical in importance, and we have given them below.

So far the *Critique of Pure Reason*. But the *Critique of Practical Reason* (1788) strikes another note. If knowledge has been removed, room has been made for belief, and what has been lost in the theoretical domain is now to be amply recovered. Laying what he never ceased to regard as an absolutely immovable basis in the categorical moral imperative of duty, by which the practical Ego determines its own will, Kant argues, with what is manifestly unclouded conviction, that we are justified in affirming the objective reality of freedom, immortality, and God. The man to whom the moral law is the supreme principle of the inner life, he implies, cannot but believe in personal immortality and the existence of a Personal and Moral Ruler of the universe. Yet even so we are repeatedly warned that the reality we thus ascribe to these objects is not such that it can be confirmed by the theoretical reason. Here again we have quoted the relevant passages.

Finally, in the *Critique of Judgment* (1798), the subject of which may be described broadly as the philosophy of Feeling, and of Art as its expression, Kant examines the ideas of Beauty, Sublimity, and Design. Even here, though we can see that he is reaching out to a deeper view which might reconcile and embrace the sharp distinctions (*e.g.* between phenomena and noumena, empirical world and intelligible self) by which alone his previous results had been rendered possible, Kant is unable quite to get rid of the radical dualism characteristic of his system, which seems eternally fated to forbid intelligence and reality to come to terms with one another. Still, in this work we meet with two cognate, and, in a sense, equivalent conceptions, which are of the very highest moment for a constructive Theism. One is the idea of an *intuitive understanding*, for which the whole and the parts mutually and organically involve each other; and this may be said to be Kant's conception of God in its profoundest form. The other is the idea of *immanent adaptation*, in which mechanism and teleology are fused together; and this is plainly the same conception, looked at from the side of the world. These speculative suggestions have yielded much richer results to later thought than Kant himself succeeded in educing from them. They must be pronounced inalienable elements in the edifice of modern Theism.

The world is Kant's debtor for the infinitely fruitful seed of speculative truth in which his philosophy abounds; and not for these only, but for the pure and noble morality enshrined in his ethics. And if it must be held that a Deistic flavour still clings about his Theism, this is but to say that the greatest minds are themselves in part creatures of their time. His strong individualism may have impoverished his capacity for the work of philosophical construction; his criticism laid the foundation on which all later thought has built.

§ 1. CRITICISM OF RATIONAL THEOLOGY.

Critique of Pure Reason: Transcendental Dialectic, Bk. II.
c. iii. §§ 3, 4, 5, 6.

OF THE ARGUMENTS EMPLOYED BY SPECULATIVE REASON IN PROOF OF THE EXISTENCE OF A SUPREME BEING.[1]

Notwithstanding the pressing necessity which reason feels to form some presupposition that shall serve the understanding as a proper basis for the complete determination of its conceptions, the idealistic and factitious nature of such a presupposition is too evident to allow reason for a moment to

---

[1] In the foregoing sections Kant had criticised Rational Psychology, or the doctrine of the Soul, and Rational Cosmology, or the doctrine of the World, with the view of showing how in those supposed sciences reason attempts to apply the categories to the unconditioned, and thus simply entangles itself in deception. He now proceeds to examine Rational Theology, or the doctrine of God, in precisely the same fashion, with the object of proving that here reason, in its speculative aspect, is once more operating with an empty ideal, which never can elicit a content adequate to it from the only experience capable of yielding knowledge proper, namely, the experience of sense.

Let it be noted that when Kant uses the word "sense," he means by it something more than the special sensations which come through the bodily organs ; he means the whole mental susceptibility or sensibility on its outward side as well. Passivity is the signature of sense, as spontaneity is of understanding. It is obvious how the term "sense" naturally, and almost inevitably, suggests "bodily sensation" alone ; and thus for Kant the problem of knowledge tends to be, How do we know the external world? rather than the deeper and more universal question, How do we know *reality* (which may be described in terms *either* of Spirit *or* Nature)? This is but one aspect of the truth that Kant's philosophy, after all, belongs to the eighteenth century, though it was his to set the problems on which nineteenth century thought, from first to last, was engaged. Once for all, the student is here referred to Dr. E. Caird's *The Critical Philosophy of Kant* (Maclehose, 1889, 2 vols.) as the standard English work on the Kantian system. Cf. also Paulsen, *Immanuel Kant : His Life and Doctrine* (Nimmo, 1902).

persuade itself into a belief of the objective existence of a mere creation of its own thought. But there are other considerations which compel reason to seek out some resting-place in the regress from the conditioned to the unconditioned, which is not given as an actual existence from the mere conception of it, although it alone can give completeness to the series of conditions. And this is the natural course of every human reason, even of the most uneducated, although the path at first entered it does not always continue to follow. It does not begin from conceptions, but from common experience, and requires a basis in actual existence. But this basis is insecure, unless it rests upon the immovable rock of the absolutely necessary. And this foundation is itself unworthy of trust, if it leave under and above it empty space, if it do not fill all, and leave no room for a *why* or a *wherefore*, if it be not, in one word, infinite in its reality.[2]

If we admit the existence of some one thing, whatever it may be, we must also admit that there is something which exists *necessarily*.[3] For what is contingent exists only under the condition of some other thing which is its cause; and from this we must go on to conclude the existence of a cause which is not contingent, and which consequently exists necessarily and unconditionally. Such is the argument by which reason justifies its advances towards a primal being.

Now reason looks round for the conception of a being that may be admitted, without inconsistency, to be worthy of the attribute of absolute necessity, not for the purpose of inferring

[2] "In general we may say that [the different supposed proofs of the Being of God] are all based on the connexion which is supposed to exist between two conceptions, the conception of an *Ens realissimum*, and the conception of a necessary Being. A necessary Being is the presupposition to which we are led by a natural and inevitable tendency of our reason" (Caird, *The Philosophy of Kant*, 1877, p. 628).

[3] For an example of this form of the Theistic argument, see Locke, *Essay*, Bk. IV. chap. x., a passage which, of course, was familiar to Kant.

à priori, from the conception of such a being, its objective existence (for if reason allowed itself to take this course, it would not require a basis in given and actual existence, but merely the support of pure conceptions), but for the purpose of discovering, among all our conceptions of possible things, that conception which possesses no element inconsistent with the idea of absolute necessity. For that there must be some absolutely necessary existence, it regards as a truth already established. Now, if it can remove every existence incapable of supporting the attribute of absolute necessity, excepting one,—this must be the absolutely necessary being, whether its necessity is comprehensible by us, that is, deducible from the conception of it alone, or not.

Now that, the conception of which contains a *therefore* to every *wherefore*, which is not defective in any respect whatever, which is all-sufficient as a condition, seems to be the being of which we can justly predicate absolute necessity— for this reason, that, possessing the conditions of all that is possible, it does not and cannot itself require any condition. And thus it satisfies, in one respect at least, the requirements of the conception of absolute necessity. In this view it is superior to all other conceptions, which, as deficient and incomplete, do not possess the characteristic of independence of all higher conditions. It is true that we cannot infer from this that what does not contain in itself the supreme and complete condition—the condition of all other things, must possess only a conditioned existence; but as little can we assert the contrary, for this supposed being does not possess the only characteristic which can enable reason to cognize by means of an *à priori* conception the unconditioned and necessary nature of its existence.[4]

[4] That is to say, while there is no logical inconsistency in supposing a limited or conditioned being to be necessary, the *ens realissimum* (best defined as "a Being which contains all reality in itself") alone is transparently necessary from its very idea.

The conception of the *ens realissimum* is that which best agrees with the conception of an unconditioned and necessary being.[5] The former conception does not satisfy all the requirements of the latter ; but we have no choice, we are obliged to adhere to it, for we find that we cannot do without the existence of a necessary being ; and even although we admit it, we find it out of our power to discover in the whole sphere of possibility any being that can advance well-grounded claims to such a distinction.

The following is therefore the natural course of human reason. It begins by persuading itself of the existence of some necessary being. In this being it recognises the characteristics of unconditioned existence. It then seeks the conception of that which is independent of all conditions, and finds it in that which is itself the sufficient condition of all other things—in other words, in that which contains all reality. But the unlimited all is an absolute unity, and is conceived by the mind as a being one and supreme ; and thus reason concludes that the Supreme Being, as the primal basis of all things, possesses an existence which is absolutely necessary.

This conception must be regarded as in some degree satisfactory, if we admit the existence of a necessary being, and consider that there exists a necessity for a definite and final answer to these questions. In such a case, we cannot make

[5] Confusion is introduced into Kant's argument all through by the fact that his idea of the *ens realissimum* hovers between two extremes : (*a*) *the sum of all possible positive predicates*, without a shadow of negation (this is sheerly impossible as a conception, and leads to an Absolute which is a mere featureless blank) ; and (*b*) *a perceptive or intuitive understanding, i.e.* an intellectual Being whose objects come into existence by the mere fact of its representing them to itself, and which requires neither space nor time to conceive them. The first is an inheritance from the previous abstract Wolfian philosophy ; the second is taken up as vital and central in the post-Kantian idealistic systems. Cf. *infra*, note, p. 223.

a better choice, or rather we have no choice at all, but feel ourselves obliged to declare in favour of the absolute unity of complete reality, as the highest source of the possibility of things. But if there exists no motive for coming to a definite conclusion, and we may leave the question unanswered till we have fully weighed both sides,—in other words, when we are merely called upon to decide how much we happen to know about the question, and how much we merely flatter ourselves that we know,—the above conclusion does not appear to so great advantage, but, on the contrary, seems defective in the grounds upon which it is supported.

For, admitting the truth of all that has been said, that, namely, the inference from a given existence (my own, for example) to the existence of an unconditioned and necessary being is valid and unassailable ; that, in the second place, we must consider a being which contains all reality, and consequently all the conditions of other things, to be absolutely unconditioned ; and admitting, too, that we have thus discovered the conception of a thing to which may be attributed, without inconsistency, absolute necessity,—it does not follow from all this that the conception of a limited being, in which the supreme reality does not reside, is therefore incompatible with the idea of absolute necessity.[6] For although I do not discover the element of the unconditioned in the conception of such a being,—an element which is manifestly existent in the sum total of all conditions,—I am not entitled to conclude that its existence is therefore conditioned ; just as I am not entitled to affirm, in a hypothetical syllogism, that where a certain condition does not exist (in the present, completeness, as far as pure conceptions are concerned), the conditioned does not exist either. On the contrary, we are free to consider all limited beings as likewise unconditionally necessary, although we are unable to infer this from the general conception which we have of them. Thus conducted,

[6] Cf. note [4].

this argument is incapable of giving us the least notion of the properties of a necessary being, and must be in every respect without result.

This argument continues, however, to possess a weight and an authority which, in spite of its objective insufficiency, it has never been divested of. For, granting that certain responsibilities lie upon us, which, as based on the ideas of reason, deserve to be respected and submitted to, although they are incapable of a real or practical application to our nature, or, in other words, would be responsibilities without motives, except upon the supposition of a Supreme Being to give effect and influence to the practical laws : in such a case we should be bound to obey our conceptions, which, although objectively insufficient, do, according to the standard of reason, preponderate over and are superior to any claims that may be advanced from any other quarter.[7]   The equilibrium of doubt would in this case be destroyed by a practical addition ; indeed, Reason would be compelled to condemn herself, if she refused to comply with the demands of the judgment, no superior to which we know—however defective her understanding of the grounds of these demands might be.

This argument, although in fact transcendental, inasmuch as it rests upon the intrinsic insufficiency of the contingent, is so simple and natural, that the commonest understanding can appreciate its value.   We see things around us change, arise, and pass away ; they, or their condition, must therefore have a cause.   The same demand must again be made of the cause itself—as a datum of experience.   Now it is natural that we should place the *highest* causality just where we place *supreme* causality, in that being, which contains the conditions of all possible effects, and the conception of which is

---

[7] This points forward to a line of thought which is developed at length in Kant's practical philosophy, and is his positive counter-stroke to the negative conclusions forced upon reason in its purely speculative capacity.

so simple as that of an all-embracing reality.[8] This highest cause, then, we regard as absolutely necessary, because we find it absolutely necessary to rise to it, and do not discover any reason for proceeding beyond it. Thus, among all nations, through the darkest polytheism glimmer some faint sparks of monotheism, to which these idolaters have been led, not from reflection and profound thought, but by the study and natural progress of the common understanding.

There are only three modes of proving the existence of a Deity on the grounds of speculative reason.

All the paths conducting to this end begin either from determinate experience and the peculiar constitution of the world of sense, and rise, according to the laws of causality, from it to the highest cause existing apart from the world,— or from a purely indeterminate experience, that is, some empirical existence,—or abstraction is made of all experience, and the existence of a supreme cause is concluded from *à priori* conceptions alone. The first is the *physico-theological* argument, the second the *cosmological*, the third the *ontological*. More there are not, and more there cannot be.

I shall show that it is as unsuccessful on the one path— the empirical, as on the other—the transcendental, and that it stretches its wings in vain, to soar beyond the world of sense by the mere might of speculative thought.[9] As regards

[8] This is just one form of the problem Kant is discussing all along, namely, Can we raise to the absolute sphere, *over and beyond* experience, that which, after all, is only the supreme existence as manifested *in* experience ?

[9] The exact significance of Kant's terminology is to be carefully observed. An *Idea* of reason is *transcendent* in so far as it suggests an object which has no existence in the reality known to us ; it is *transcendental* in so far as it serves to bring systematic unity and totality into the manifold of experience as a whole. The one, *i.e.*, is a term of blame, the other of praise, from Kant's point of view ; for a transcendent idea is useless and illusory, one that is transcendental has a real function in knowledge.

the order in which we must discuss those arguments, it will be exactly the reverse of that in which reason, in the progress of its development, attains to them—the order in which they are placed above. For it will be made manifest to the reader that, although experience presents the occasion and the starting-point, it is the *transcendental idea* of reason which guides it in its pilgrimage, and is the goal of all its struggles. I shall therefore begin with an examination of the transcendental argument, and afterwards inquire what additional strength has accrued to this mode of proof from the addition of the empirical element.

OF THE IMPOSSIBILITY OF AN ONTOLOGICAL PROOF OF THE EXISTENCE OF GOD.[10]

It is evident from what has been said, that the conception of an absolutely necessary being is a mere idea, the objective

---

[10] Kant took this argument, and criticised it, in the shape in which it had been handed down to him by Wolf. But we ought to note that it can be stated in terms far more worthy of its real import, which disarm most of Kant's objections. The real question is whether we are not obliged to declare valid an ideal which is bound up organically with the very conception of knowledge. Further, a modern idealist would point to the agreement between the ideal laws of our thought and the real laws of being, and would argue that the only way in which this fundamental correspondence can be made intelligible is by presupposing a common ground of both, in which thought and being are radically one, and which as Absolute Spirit manifests itself alike in objective existence and subjective thinking. Cf. Pfleiderer, *The Philosophy of Religion* (Eng. trans.), iii. p. 272 ff. ; Orr, *The Christian View of God and the World*, p. 124 ff. But in the form in which Kant is handling it here it has never been stated better than by Hume, in a few simple words : "The idea of infinite perfection implies that of actual existence." As formulated by Kant the argument runs thus : God, being the *ens realissimum*, which includes all possible positive predicates, must include the predicate of existence, *i.e.* He exists *per se*, or necessarily.

reality of which is far from being established by the mere fact that it is a need of reason. On the contrary, this idea serves merely to indicate a certain unattainable perfection, and rather limits the operations than, by the presentation of new objects, extends the sphere of the understanding. But a strange anomaly meets us at the very threshold ; for the inference from a given existence in general to an absolutely necessary existence, seems to be correct and unavoidable, while the conditions of the *understanding* refuse to aid us in forming any conception of such a being.

Philosophers have always talked of an *absolutely necessary* being, and have nevertheless declined to take the trouble of conceiving whether—and how—a being of this nature is even cogitable, not to mention whether its existence is actually demonstrable. A verbal definition of the conception is certainly easy enough : it is something, the non-existence of which is impossible. But does this definition throw any light upon the conditions which render it impossible to cogitate the non-existence of a thing—conditions which we wish to ascertain, that we may discover whether we think anything in the conception of such a being or not? For the mere fact that I throw away, by means of the word *Unconditioned*, all the conditions which the understanding habitually requires in order to regard anything as necessary, is very far from making clear whether by means of the conception of the unconditionally necessary I think of something, or really of nothing at all.

Nay, more, this chance-conception, now become so current, many have endeavoured to explain by examples, which seemed to render any inquiries regarding its intelligibility quite needless. Every geometrical proposition,—a triangle has three angles,—it was said, is absolutely necessary ; and thus people talked of an object which lay out of the sphere of our understanding as if it were perfectly plain what the conception of such a being meant.

All the examples adduced have been drawn, without exception, from *judgments*, and not from *things*. But the unconditioned necessity of a judgment does not form the absolute necessity of a thing. On the contrary, the absolute necessity of a judgment is only a conditioned necessity of a thing, or of the predicate in a judgment. The proposition above mentioned does not enounce that three angles necessarily exist, but, upon condition that a triangle exists, three angles must necessarily exist—in it. And thus this logical necessity has been the source of the greatest delusions. Having formed an *à priori* conception of a thing, the content of which was made to embrace existence, we believed ourselves safe in concluding that, because existence belongs necessarily to the object of the conception (that is, under the condition of my positing this thing as given), the existence of the thing is also posited necessarily, and that it is therefore absolutely necessary—merely because its existence has been cogitated in the conception.

If, in an identical judgment, I annihilate the predicate in thought, and retain the subject, a contradiction is the result; and hence I say, the former belongs necessarily to the latter. But if I suppress both subject and predicate in thought, no contradiction arises; for there *is nothing* at all, and therefore no means of forming a contradiction. To suppose the existence of a triangle and not that of its three angles, is self-contradictory; but to suppose the non-existence of both triangle and angles is perfectly admissible. And so is it with the conception of an absolutely necessary being. Annihilate its existence in thought, and you annihilate the thing itself, with all its predicates; how, then, can there be any room for contradiction? Externally, there is nothing to give rise to a contradiction, for a thing cannot be necessary externally; nor internally, for, by the annihilation or suppression of the thing itself, its internal properties are also annihilated. God is omnipotent—that is a necessary judgment. His omnipotence cannot be denied, if the existence of a Deity is posited—the existence, that is, of an infinite being, the two conceptions being identical. But when you say, *God does not exist*, neither omnipotence nor any other predicate is affirmed; they must all disappear with the subject, and in this judgment there cannot exist the least self-contradiction.[11]

You have thus seen, that when the predicate of a judgment is annihilated in thought along with the subject, no internal contradiction can arise, be the predicate what it may. There is no possibility of evading the conclusion—you find yourselves compelled to declare : There are certain subjects which cannot be annihilated in thought. But this is nothing more than saying : There exist subjects which are absolutely necessary—the very hypothesis which you are called upon to establish. For I find myself unable to form the slightest conception of a thing which, when annihilated in thought with all its predicates, leaves behind a contradiction;[12] and contradiction is the only criterion of impossibility, in the sphere of pure *à priori* conceptions.

Against these general considerations, the justice of which no one can dispute, one argument is adduced, which is regarded as furnishing a satisfactory demonstration from the

[11] The gist of this paragraph may be put shortly as follows :— We may think away such a thing as a triangle, and so escape all contradiction by supposing both subject and predicates non-existent; why may we not, in like manner, think away such a Being as God ?

[12] This is exactly the point that Hume would have urged, drawing his famous distinction between *relations of ideas* and *matters of fact*, which was merely an emphasised rendering of Berkeley's view of the arbitrariness of natural connexions. (Cf. Hume's *Inquiry* sects. 4 and 7 ; *Treatise*, vol. i. p. 436 of Green and Grose's edition.) Necessity is attributable to judgments only, as deduced from valid premises, but not to things. Or as Hume puts it, "the contrary of every matter of fact is possible." There is no contradiction in supposing the non-existence of the object represented in any idea.

fact. It is affirmed that there is one, and only one, conception in which the non-being or annihilation of the object is self-contradictory, and this is the conception of an *ens realissimum*. It possesses, you say, all reality, and you feel yourselves justified in admitting the possibility of such a being. (This I am willing to grant for the present, although the existence of a conception which is not self-contradictory is far from being sufficient to prove the possibility of an object.*) Now the notion of all reality embraces in it that of existence; the notion of existence lies, therefore, in the conception of this possible thing. If this thing is annihilated in thought, the internal possibility of the thing is also annihilated, which is self-contradictory.

I answer: It is absurd to introduce—under whatever term disguised—into the conception of a thing, which is to be cogitated solely in reference to its possibility, the conception of its existence. If this is admitted, you will have apparently gained the day, but in reality have enounced nothing but a mere tautology. I ask, Is the proposition, *this or that thing* (which I am admitting to be possible) *exists*, an analytical or a synthetical proposition? If the former, there is no addition made to the subject of your thought by the affirmation of its existence; but then the conception in your minds is identical with the thing itself, or you have supposed the existence of a thing to be possible, and then inferred its existence from its internal possibility—which is

* A conception is always possible, if it is not self-contradictory. This is the logical criterion of possibility, distinguishing the object of such a conception from the *nihil negativum*. But it may be, notwithstanding, an empty conception, unless the objective reality of this synthesis, by which it it is generated, is demonstrated; and a proof of this kind must be based upon principles of possible experience, and not upon the principle of analysis or contradiction. This remark may be serviceable as a warning against concluding, from the possibility of a conception—which is logical, the possibility of a thing—which is real. (*Note by Kant.*)

but a miserable tautology. The word *reality* in the conception of the thing, and the word *existence* in the conception of the predicate, will not help you out of the difficulty. For, supposing you were to term all positing of a thing, reality, you have thereby posited the thing with all its predicates in the conception of the subject and assumed its actual existence, and this you merely repeat in the predicate. But if you confess, as every reasonable person must, that every existential proposition is synthetical, how can it be maintained that the predicate of existence cannot be denied without contradiction—a property which is the characteristic of analytical propositions alone.[13]

I should have a reasonable hope of putting an end for ever to this sophistical mode of argumentation, by a strict definition of the conception of existence, did not my own experience teach me that the illusion arising from our confounding a logical with a real predicate (a predicate which aids in the determination of a thing) resists almost all the endeavours of explanation and illustration. A *logical predicate* may be what you please, even the subject may be predicated of itself ; for logic pays no regard to the content of a judgment. But the determination of a conception is a predicate, which adds to and enlarges the conception. It must not therefore be contained in the conception.

Being is evidently not a real predicate, that is, a conception of something which is added to the conception of some other thing. It is merely the positing of a thing, or of certain determinations in it.[14] Logically, it is merely the copula

[13] Or in other words, to affirm existence is not to affirm a quality like other qualities ; it is the positing of a thing with all its qualities.

[14] *Existence* expresses a relation not *in* our thought, but *to* our thought, and implies that something is *given*, towards which we are receptive. Kant's real objection is that for him our sensibility is the only means by which an object can be given to the mind, and, since God is not given so, we are cut off from affirming His existence.

of a judgment. The proposition, *God is omnipotent*, contains two conceptions, which have a certain object or content ; the word *is*, is no additional predicate—it merely indicates the relation of the predicate to the subject. Now, if I take the subject (God) with all its predicates (omnipotence being one), and say, *God is*, or *There is a God*, I add no new predicate to the conception of God, I merely posit or affirm the existence of the subject with all its predicates—I posit the *object* in relation to my *conception*. The content of both is the same ; and there is no addition made to the conception, which expresses merely the possibility of the object, by my cogitating the object—in the expression, it *is*—as absolutely given or existing. Thus the real contains no more than the possible. A hundred real dollars contain no more than a possible hundred dollars.[15] For, as the latter indicate the conception, and the former the object, on the supposition that the content of the former was greater than that of the latter, my conception would not be an expression of the whole object, and would consequently be an inadequate conception of it. But in reckoning my wealth there may be said to be more in a hundred real dollars than in a hundred possible dollars—that is, in the mere conception of them. For the real object—the dollars—is not analytically contained in my conception, but forms a synthetical addition to my conception (which is merely a determination of my mental state), although this objective reality—this existence—apart

[15] Are we to consent to say that God is thus upon a level with *things* like a hundred dollars ? Are we to conceive Him as a particular being ? Does not the fact that God is infinite, the ground of the unity of the intelligible world, lift the conception of His being away from this unworthy comparison with things, and compel us to affirm that "the very thought of God is of that *which is, and cannot not-be*" ? (Stirling). It is strange that Kant, of all people, should sometimes appear to argue as though it were a positive defect in the nature of God that His being cannot be presented as an object of sense.

from my conception, does not in the least degree increase the aforesaid hundred dollars.[16]

By whatever and by whatever number of predicates—even to the complete determination of it—I may cogitate a thing, I do not in the least augment the object of my conception by the addition of the statement, this thing exists. Otherwise, not exactly the same, but something more than what was cogitated in my conception, would exist, and I could not affirm that the exact object of my conception had real existence. If I cogitate a thing as containing all modes of reality except one, the mode of reality which is absent is not added to the conception of the thing by the affirmation that the thing exists; on the contrary, the thing exists—if it exist at all—with the same defect as that cogitated in its conception; otherwise not that which was cogitated, but something different, exists. Now, if I cogitate a being as the highest reality, without defect or imperfection, the question still remains — whether this being exists or not? For although no element is wanting in the possible real content of my conception, there is a defect in its relation to my mental state, that is, I am ignorant whether the cognition of the object indicated by the conception is possible *à posteriori*.[17] And here the cause of the present difficulty becomes

[16] An existential judgment, *i.e.* a judgment affirming existence, is, says Kant, always *synthetic* (in contrast to *analytic*). That is, though nothing is added to the *content* of the idea of the subject, the predication of existence adds something which the idea of the subject, as such, does not include, and which, consequently, cannot be deduced from it by simple analysis. A modern logician would say that what takes place in an existential proposition is not an internal modification of the subject; but rather the subject, as an ideal complex, is referred or attributed to objective reality. In other words, the contents of the subject are not modified, but it has a new relation predicated of it. Cf. Bradley, *Principles of Logic*, Bk. I. ; Bosanquet, *The Essentials of Logic*, p. 66 ff.

[17] *À priori* means prior to all experience, and in harmony with its general conditions ; *à posteriori*, in the light of experience as we

apparent. If the question regarded an object of sense merely, it would be impossible for me to confound the conception with the existence of a thing. For the conception merely enables me to cogitate an object as according with the general conditions of experience; while the existence of the object permits me to cogitate it as contained in the sphere of actual experience. At the same time, this connexion with the world of experience does not in the least augment the conception, although a possible perception has been added to the experience of the mind. But if we cogitate existence by the pure category alone, it is not to be wondered at that we should find ourselves unable to present any criterion sufficient to distinguish it from mere possibility.

Whatever be the content of our conception of an object, it is necessary to go beyond it, if we wish to predicate existence of the object. In the case of sensuous objects, this is attained by their connexion according to empirical laws with some one of my perceptions; but there is no means of cognising the existence of objects of pure thought, because it must be cognised completely *à priori*. But all our knowledge of existence (be it immediately by perception, or by inferences connecting some object with a perception) belongs entirely to the sphere of experience—which is in perfect unity with itself; and although an existence out of this sphere cannot be absolutely declared to be impossible, it is a hypothesis the truth of which we have no means of ascertaining.[18]

find it to be. Thus, for Kant, space and time are the *à priori* principles of sense; the categories, such as substance and cause, are the *à priori* forms of understanding. The *Critique of Pure Reason*, in short, is meant to give a complete outline of all that we can know *à priori*, in systematic arrangement; for there are notions embedded *in* experience, which experience cannot justify or explain, and which turn out to be provided *for* experience antecedently in the mind. For a general treatment of Reason as giving only Postulates, see **F. C. S.** Schiller, *Humanism*, 1903.

[18] In this one sentence we have the principle succinctly formulated

The notion of a Supreme Being is in many respects a highly useful idea; but for the very reason that it is an idea, it is incapable of enlarging our cognition with regard to the existence of things. It is not even sufficient to instruct us as to the possibility of a being which we do not know to exist. The analytical criterion of possibility, which consists in the absence of contradiction in propositions, cannot be denied it. But the connexion of real properties in a thing is a synthesis of the possibility of which an *à priori* judgment cannot be formed, because these realities are not presented to us specifically; and even if this were to happen, a judgment would still be impossible, because the criterion of the possibility of synthetical cognitions must be sought for in the world of experience, to which the object of an idea cannot belong. And thus the celebrated Leibnitz has utterly failed in his attempt to establish upon *à priori* grounds the possibility of this sublime ideal being.[19]

The celebrated ontological or Cartesian argument for the existence of a Supreme Being is therefore insufficient;[20]

from which spring all Kant's objections to the validity of the Theistic proofs. If knowledge is indissolubly wedded to sense, of course it is vain to speak of our "knowing" God.

[19] In his *Meditationes de Cognitione Veritate et Ideis* (1684), and his *Noveaux Essais*, Leibnitz had adopted and amended the Cartesian form of the Ontological argument. He argued that God's existence can be inferred from His definition, only if it is proved that His existence is *possible, i.e.* involves no real contradiction. This he endeavoured to prove by showing that it is an idea which contains nothing but realities. In rejecting here the *à priori* criterion of possibility, Kant has Liebnitz' addition to the Cartesian argument specially in view.

[20] It is to be noticed carefully at this point, as Professor Orr has pointed out (*Christian View*, p. 478), that while Kant rejects every kind of inference from the idea of God to His reality, he yet assigns no little importance to this "Ideal of Pure Reason" as an element in Natural Theology. His own words are, "A Supreme Being is, therefore, for the speculative reason, a mere ideal, though a

and we may as well hope to increase our stock of knowledge by the aid of mere ideas, as the merchant to augment his wealth by the addition of noughts to his cash account.

OF THE IMPOSSIBILITY OF A COSMOLOGICAL PROOF OF THE EXISTENCE OF GOD.

It was by no means a natural course of proceeding, but, on the contrary, an invention entirely due to the subtlety of the schools, to attempt to draw from a mere idea a proof of the existence of an object corresponding to it. Such a course would never have been pursued, were it not for that need of reason which requires it to suppose the existence of a necessary being as a basis for the empirical regress, and that, as this necessity must be unconditioned and *à priori*, reason is bound to discover a conception which shall satisfy, if possible, this requirement, and enable us to attain to the *à priori* cognition of such a being. This conception was thought to be found in the idea of an *ens realissimum*, and thus this idea was employed for the attainment of a better defined knowledge of a necessary being of the existence of which we

faultless one,—a conception which crowns and perfects the system of cognition, but the objective reality of which can neither be proved nor disproved by pure reason " (*Critique of Pure Reason*, Meiklejohn's trans., pp. 392–393). We shall see, when we pass to his Moral Theology, how persistently he holds the speculative reason to this neutral point of view.

While the Ontological argument fares so badly at the hands of Kant, we note with interest that in Hegel's opinion it stands highest of the three. " Of the proofs," he goes so far as to say, " it alone is the true one." Once reaffirm, as Hegel did, the objective validity of thought, and an ideal which is inseparable from the very existence of intelligence forces us to recognise its intrinsic reality. Of course, this is to transform the notion of God with which Kant was working, and to lift it clear of the Deism which still infected his theology. Cf. the Selections from Anselm and Descartes.

were convinced, or persuaded, on other grounds. Thus Reason was seduced from her natural course; and, instead of concluding with the conception of an *ens realissimum*, an attempt was made to begin with it, for the purpose of inferring from it that idea of a necessary existence which it was in fact called in to complete. Thus arose that unfortunate ontological argument, which neither satisfies the healthy common sense of humanity, nor sustains the scientific examination of the philosopher.

The *cosmological proof*, which we are about to examine, retains the connexion between absolute necessity and the highest reality; but, instead of reasoning from this highest reality to a necessary existence, like the preceding argument, it concludes from the given unconditioned necessity of some being its unlimited reality.[21] The track it pursues, whether rational or sophistical, is at least natural, and not only goes far to persuade the common understanding, but shows itself deserving of respect from the speculative intellect; while it contains, at the same time, the outlines of all the arguments employed in natural theology—arguments which always have been, and still will be, in use and authority. These, however adorned, and hid under whatever embellishments of rhetoric and sentiment, are at bottom identical with the arguments we are at present to discuss. This proof, termed by Leibnitz the *argumentum a contingentiâ mundi*, I shall now lay before the reader, and subject to a strict examination.[22]

[21] This argument moves in a direction opposite to that of the Ontological. As stated by Kant, it runs thus : (*a*) contingent things exist, therefore a necessary Being must exist; (*b*) but, further, this necessary Being must be the *ens realissimum*, which includes all reality, for no other has the conditions of its existence in itself. This second step (*b*), says Kant, can be taken only if the two conceptions, necessary being and *ens realissimum*, are convertible—in other words, if the Ontological argument is valid.

[22] By *contingency* is here meant the quality of not being self-contained, self-explanatory, and self-sufficient. Things are contingent

It is framed in the following manner :—If something exists, an absolutely necessary being must likewise exist. Now I, at least, exist. Consequently, there exists an absolutely necessary being. The minor contains an experience, the major reasons from a general experience to the existence of a necessary being.* [23]   Thus this argument really begins at experience, and is not completely *à priori*, or ontological. The object of all possible experience being the world, it is called the *cosmological* proof. It contains no reference to any peculiar property of sensuous objects, by which this world of sense might be distinguished from other possible worlds; and in this respect it differs from the physico-theological proof, which is based upon the consideration of the peculiar constitution of our sensuous world.

The proof proceeds thus :—A necessary being can be determined only in one way, that is, it can be determined by only one of all possible opposed predicates; consequently, it must be *completely* determined in and by its conception. But there is only a single conception of a thing possible, which completely determines the thing *à priori*; that is, the conception of the *ens realissimum*. It follows that the conception of the *ens realissimum* is the only conception by and in which we can cogitate a necessary

when they require support from something else, and depend on that which is outside of themselves.

* This inference is too well known to require more detailed discussion. It is based upon the spurious transcendental law of causality, that everything which is *contingent* has a cause, which, if itself contingent, must also have a cause ; and so on, till the series of subordinated causes must end with an absolutely necessary cause, without which it would not possess completeness. (*Note by Kant.*)

[23] The cosmological argument, so far, yields no more than *some* necessary being. This, however, is less than we require, which is God as *perfect* Being. Accordingly, for this further contribution, we are thrown back on the Ontological argument.

being.[24]   Consequently, a Supreme Being necessarily exists.

In this cosmological argument are assembled so many sophistical propositions, that speculative Reason seems to have exerted in it all her dialectical skill to produce a transcendental illusion of the most extreme character. We shall postpone an investigation of this argument for the present, and confine ourselves to exposing the stratagem by which it imposes upon us an old argument in a new dress, and appeals to the agreement of two witnesses, the one with the credentials of pure Reason, and the other with those of Empiricism; while, in fact, it is only the former who has changed his dress and voice, for the purpose of passing himself off for an additional witness.[25] That it may possess a secure foundation, it bases its conclusions upon experience, and thus appears to be completely distinct from the ontological argument, which places its confidence entirely in pure *à priori* conceptions. But this experience merely aids reason in making one step—to the existence of a necessary being. What the properties of this being are, cannot be learned from experience; and therefore Reason abandons it altogether, and pursues its inquiries in the sphere of pure conceptions, for the purpose of discovering what the properties of an absolutely necessary being ought to be, that is, what among all possible things contain the conditions (*requisita*) of absolute necessity. Reason believes that it

[24] The necessary Being of the first part, *i.e.*, is converted into the perfect Being of the second. Hume has stated the process of thought thus: "There is something necessarily existent, and what is so is infinitely perfect." Kant protests that such a conversion is a logical fallacy; but is this so certain? May we not legitimately argue—a necessary being must have all reality within itself, otherwise it would be partially dependent for its reality on something else, *i.e.* it is supremely, perfectly real?

[25] The causality argument proper, in the first place; the ontological argument, in the second.

has discovered these requisites in the conception of an *ens realissimum*—and in it alone, and hence concludes : The *ens realissimum* is an absolutely necessary being. But it is evident that Reason has here presupposed that the conception of an *ens realissimum* is perfectly adequate to the conception of a being of absolute necessity, that is, that we may infer the existence of the latter from that of the former—a proposition which formed the basis of the ontological argument, and which is now employed in the support of the cosmological argument, contrary to the wish and professions of its inventors. For the existence of an absolutely necessary being is given in conceptions alone. But if I say—the conception of the *ens realissimum* is a conception of this kind, and in fact the only conception which is adequate to our idea of a necessary being, I am obliged to admit that the latter may be inferred from the former. Thus it is properly the ontological argument which figures in the cosmological, and constitutes the whole strength of the latter ; while the spurious basis of experience has been of no further use than to conduct us to the conception of absolute necessity, being utterly insufficient to demonstrate the presence of this attribute in any determinate existence or thing.[26] For when we propose to ourselves an aim of this character, we must abandon the sphere of experience, and rise to that of pure conceptions, which we examine with the purpose of discovering whether any one contains the conditions of the possibility of an absolutely necessary being. But if the possibility of such a being is thus demonstrated, its existence is also proved ; for we may then assert that, of all possible beings there is one which possesses the attribute of necessity—in other words, this being possesses an absolutely necessary existence.

[26] It is certainly odd that Kant, whose philosophy is nothing if not experiential, should here appear to be dissatisfied with this argument, on the ground that it is not wholly a thing of conceptions, but claims to have a basis in experience.

All illusions in an argument are more easily detected when they are presented in the formal manner employed by the schools, which we now proceed to do.

If the proposition, Every absolutely necessary being is likewise an *ens realissimum*, is correct (and it is this which constitutes the *nervus probandi* of the cosmological argument), it must, like all affirmative judgments, be capable of conversion—the *conversio per accidens*, at least. It follows, then, that some *entia realissima* are absolutely necessary beings. But no *ens realissimum* is in any respect different from another, and what is valid of some is valid of all. In this present case, therefore, I may employ simple conversion, and say, Every *ens realissimum* is a necessary being. But as this proposition is determined *à priori* by the conceptions contained in it, the mere conception of an *ens realissimum* must possess the additional attribute of absolute necessity. But this is exactly what was maintained in the ontological argument, and not recognised by the cosmological, although it formed the real ground of its disguised and illusory reasoning.[27]

Thus the second mode employed by speculative reason of demonstrating the existence of a Supreme Being, is not only, like the first, illusory and inadequate, but possesses the additional blemish of an *ignoratio elenchi*—professing to conduct us by a new road to the desired goal, but bringing us back, after a short circuit, to the old path which we had deserted at its call.[28]

[27] See note [21].

[28] It is of extreme importance to note that the cosmological argument, in the form of it criticised by Kant, does exhibit defects which leave it open to damaging assault. Its tendency is to treat God merely as " an unbeginning Something," to which we reason back from the present ; and this is simply to launch us upon the infinite regress from phenomenon to phenomenon, which can never end. Modern Theism would state the argument in a different and more philosophical form. The true cause of the world cannot be something that belongs to the past, but rather " the supernatural sustaining

I mentioned above, that this cosmological argument contains a perfect nest of dialectical assumptions, which transcendental criticism does not find it difficult to expose and to dissipate.[29] I shall merely enumerate these, leaving it to the reader, who must by this time be well practised in such matters, to investigate the fallacies residing therein.

The following fallacies, for example, are discoverable in this mode of proof :—1. The transcendental principle, Everything that is contingent must have a cause—a principle without significance, except in the sensuous world.   For the purely intellectual conception of the contingent cannot produce any synthetical proposition, like that of causality, which is itself without significance or distinguishing characteristic except in the phenomenal world.   But in the present case it is employed to help us beyond the limits of its sphere.   2. From the impossibility of an infinite ascending series of causes in the world of sense a first cause is inferred ;—a conclusion which the principles of the employment of reason do not justify even in the sphere of experience, and still less when an attempt is made to pass the limits of this sphere.   3. Reason allows itself to be satisfied upon insufficient grounds, with regard to the completion of this series.   It removes all conditions (without which, however, no conception of Necessity

Power immanent in all existence and operative in all change," and the proof is thus seen to yield an ever-present Energy as the source and ground of all cosmical change and happening.   In this shape the cosmological argument has been developed with great impressiveness by Lotze.   Cf. *Lotze's Theistic Philosophy*, by Professor H. N. Gardiner.

[29] On this Dr. Stirling well remarks, "the entire 'nest' may be said to be a construction of Kant's peculiar system" (*Philosophy and Theology*, p. 315).   For if we repudiate the agnostic relativism of the Kantian theory of knowledge, refusing to believe that we can know nothing save phenomena, or that to apply the idea of cause except within the phenomenal world is essentially invalid and illusory, the "nest" disappears, to trouble us no more.

can take place); and, as after this it is beyond our power to form any other conception, it accepts this as a completion of the conception it wishes to form of the series. 4. The logical possibility of a conception of the total of reality (the criterion of this possibility being the absence of contradiction) is confounded with the transcendental, which requires a principle of the practicability of such a synthesis—a principle which again refers us to the world of experience. . .

Detection and Explanation of the Dialectical Illusion in all Transcendental Arguments for the Existence of a Necessary Being.

Both of the above arguments are transcendental; in other words, they do not proceed upon empirical principles. For, although the cosmological argument professed to lay a basis of experience for its edifice of reasoning, it did not ground its procedure upon the peculiar constitution of experience, but upon pure principles of reason — in relation to an existence given by empirical consciousness; utterly abandoning its guidance, however, for the purpose of supporting its assertions entirely upon pure conceptions.[30] Now what is the cause, in these transcendental arguments, of the dialectical, but natural, illusion, which connects the conceptions of necessity and supreme reality, and hypostatises that which cannot be anything but an idea? What is the cause of this unavoidable step on the part of reason, of admitting that some one among all existing things must be necessary, while it falls back from the assertion of the existence of such a being as from an abyss? And how does reason proceed to explain this anomaly to itself, and from the wavering condition of a

---

[30] That is to say, it does not argue from the fact that the constitution of experience is of a peculiar or specific kind, *purposive* to wit, but purely from the contingency of experience as such to its producing cause.

timid and reluctant approbation—always again withdrawn—arrive at a calm and settled insight into its cause?

It is something very remarkable that, on the supposition that something exists, I cannot avoid the inference that something exists necessarily.[31] Upon this perfectly natural —but not on that account reliable — inference does the cosmological argument rest. But, let me form any conception whatever of a thing, I find that I cannot cogitate the existence of the thing as absolutely necessary, and that nothing prevents me—be the thing or being what it may— from cogitating its non-existence. I may thus be obliged to admit that all existing things have a necessary basis, while I cannot cogitate any single or individual thing as necessary. In other words, I can never *complete* the regress through the conditions of existence, without admitting the existence of a necessary being; but, on the other hand, I cannot make a *commencement* from this being.

If I must cogitate something as existing necessarily as the basis of existing things, and yet am not permitted to cogitate any individual thing as in itself necessary, the inevitable inference is, that necessity and contingency are not properties of things themselves — otherwise an internal contradiction would result; that consequently neither of these principles are objective, but merely subjective principles of reason—the one requiring us to seek for a necessary ground for every thing that exists, that is, to be satisfied with no other explanation than that which is complete *à priori*, the other forbidding us ever to hope for the attainment of this completeness, that is, to regard no member of the empirical world as unconditioned. In this mode of viewing them, both principles, in their purely heuristic and regulative character, and as concerning merely the formal interest of reason, are quite consistent with each other. The one says—

---

[31] This naïve remark, if pressed against Kant, really has the effect so far of rehabilitating the cosmological argument.

you must philosophise upon nature, as if there existed a necessary primal basis of all existing things, solely for the purpose of introducing systematic unity into your knowledge, by pursuing an idea of this character,—a foundation which is arbitrarily admitted to be ultimate; while the other warns you to consider no individual determination, concerning the existence of things, as such an ultimate foundation, that is, as absolutely necessary, but to keep the way always open for further progress in the deduction, and to treat every determination as determined by some other.[32]   But if all that we perceive must be regarded as conditionally necessary, it is impossible that anything which is empirically given should be absolutely necessary.

It follows from this, that you must accept the absolutely necessary as *out of* and beyond the world, inasmuch as it is useful only as a principle of the highest possible unity in experience, and you cannot discover any such necessary existence in the *world*, the second rule requiring you to regard all empirical causes of unity as themselves deduced. . . . These remarks will have made it evident to the reader that the ideal of the Supreme Being, far from being an enouncement of the existence of a being in itself necessary, is nothing more than a *regulative principle* of reason, requiring us to regard all connexion existing between phenomena as if [33]

---

[32] No better passage than this paragraph could be found to illustrate what Kant means by a *regulative* principle of knowledge, as distinct from one that is *constitutive*, and necessarily enters into the texture of (sensible) cognition as such.   The idea of God, it appears, simply because incapable of being actually experienced, is strictly for Kant no more than a convenient notion whereby our knowledge is given final unity and arrangement.   Indeed we may say that the Idea of God is condemned before examination begins, for Kant has already laid down the definition, "I understand by Idea a necessary notion of reason, to which there can be given no congruent sensuous object."

[33] The whole virtue of the word *regulative* lies in this phrase "as if."

it had its origin from an all-sufficient necessary cause, and basing upon this the rule of a systematic and necessary unity in the explanation of phenomena. We cannot, at the same time, avoid regarding, by a transcendental *subreptio*, this formal principle as constitutive, and hypostatising this unity. Precisely similar is the case with our notion of space. Space is the primal condition of all forms, which are properly just so many different limitations of it; and thus, although it is merely a principle of sensibility, we cannot help regarding it as an absolutely necessary and self-subsistent thing—as an object given *à priori* in itself. In the same way, it is quite natural that, as the systematic unity of nature cannot be established as a principle for the empirical employment of reason, unless it is based upon the idea of an *ens realissimum*, as the supreme cause, we should regard this idea as a real object, and this object, in its character of supreme condition, as absolutely necessary, and that in this way a *regulative* should be transformed into a *constitutive* principle. This interchange becomes evident when I regard this Supreme Being, which, relatively to the world, was absolutely (unconditionally) necessary, as a thing *per se*. In this case I find it impossible to represent this necessity in or by any conception, and it exists merely in my own mind, as the formal condition of thought, but not as a material and hypostatic condition of existence.

Of the Impossibility of a Physico-Theological Proof.

If, then, neither a pure conception nor the general experience of an existing being can provide a sufficient basis for the proof of the existence of the Deity, we can make the attempt by the only other mode—that of grounding our argument upon a *determinate experience* of the phenomena of the present world, their constitution and disposition, and discover whether we can thus attain to a sound conviction of the existence of a Supreme Being.[34] This argument we shall term the *physico-theological* argument. If it is shown to be insufficient, speculative reason cannot present us with any satisfactory proof of the existence of a being corresponding to our transcendental idea.

It is evident from the remarks that have been made in the preceding sections, that an answer to this question will be far from being difficult or unconvincing. For how can any experience be adequate with an idea? The very essence of an idea consists in the fact that no experience can ever be discovered congruent or adequate with it.[35] The transcendental idea of a necessary and all-sufficient Being is so immeasurably great, so high above all that is empirical, which is always conditioned, that we hope in vain to find materials in the sphere of experience sufficiently ample for our conception, and in vain seek the unconditioned among things that are conditioned, while examples, nay, even guidance, is denied us by the laws of empirical synthesis.

If the Supreme Being forms a link in the chain of empirical conditions, it must be a member of the empirical series, and, like the lower members which it precedes, have its origin in some higher member of the series. If, on the other hand, we disengage it from the chain, and cogitate it as an intelligible being, apart from the series of natural causes—how shall reason bridge the abyss that separates the latter from the former?[36] All laws respecting the regress from effects to causes, all synthetical additions to our knowledge, relate

[34] The teleological argument, as we may more conveniently name it, starts from empirical data, but data of a particular and determinate kind, such, namely, as exhibit marks of order and purpose.

[35] From this unequivocal statement it is clear that, on Kantian principles, the proofs are implicitly non-suited ere the trial has begun. The presupposition that an Idea is invalid which cannot be presented in sense, is fatal to their claims from the first.

[36] For considerations which turn the flank of this dilemma, see note [28].

solely to possible experience and the objects of the sensuous world, and, apart from them, are without significance.

The world around us opens before our view so magnificent a spectacle of order, variety, beauty, and conformity to ends, that whether we pursue our observations into the infinity of space in the one direction, or into its illimitable divisions on the other, whether we regard the world in its greatest or its least manifestations,—even after we have attained to the highest summit of knowledge which our weak minds can reach, we find that language in the presence of wonders so inconceivable has lost its force, and number its power to reckon, nay, even thought fails to conceive adequately, and our conception of the whole dissolves into an astonishment without the power of expression—all the more eloquent that it is dumb.[37] Everywhere around us we observe a chain of causes and effects, of means and ends, of death and birth; and, as nothing has entered of itself into the condition in which we find it, we are constantly referred to some other thing, which itself suggests the same inquiry regarding its cause, and thus the universe must sink into the abyss of nothingness, unless we admit that, besides this infinite chain of contingencies, there exists something that is primal and self-subsistent— something which, as the cause of this

[37] These expressions of respect for the argument from design are made still more emphatic in the *Critique of Judgment*, written some years later; it is true, however, that there even more stress is laid on the regulative, non-constitutive nature and validity of the idea of design. In order to ensure a complete view of Kant's conclusions, the student should read carefully Professor Orr's note entitled "Kant on the Teleological Argument" (*Christian View*, p. 475), especially the following valuable suggestion :—" It is not always noticed that, intermediate between full theoretic demonstration and mere opinion, Kant has a form of conviction which he calls 'doctrinal faith,'—distinct from 'moral faith,'—the characteristic of which is that it is an expression of modesty from the objective point of view, but of assured confidence from the subjective."

phenomenal world, secures its continuance and preservation.

This highest cause—what magnitude shall we attribute to it? Of the content of the world we are ignorant; still less can we estimate its magnitude by comparison with the sphere of the possible. But this supreme cause being a necessity of the human mind, what is there to prevent us from attributing to it such a degree of perfection as to place it above the sphere of *all that* is possible? This we can easily do, although only by the aid of the faint outline of an abstract conception, by representing this being to ourselves as containing in itself, as an individual substance, all possible perfection,—a conception which satisfies that requirement of reason which demands parsimony in principles,[38] which is free from self-contradiction, which even contributes to the extension of the employment of reason in experience, by means of the guidance afforded by this idea to order and system, and which in no respect conflicts with any law of experience.

This argument always deserves to be mentioned with respect. It is the oldest, the clearest, and that most in conformity with the common reason of humanity. It animates the study of nature, as it itself derives its existence and draws ever new strength from that source. It introduces aims and ends into a sphere in which our observation could not of itself have discovered them, and extends our knowledge of nature by directing our attention to a unity, the principle of which lies beyond nature. This knowledge of nature again reacts upon this idea—its cause; and thus our belief in a Divine author of the universe rises to the power of an irresistible conviction.

For these reasons it would be utterly hopeless to attempt

[38] Meiklejohn adds here the note:—"A reference to the metaphysical dogma: *Entia præter necessitatem non sunt multiplicanda*, which may also be applied to logic, by the substitution of *principia* for *entia*."

to rob this argument of the authority it has always enjoyed. The mind, unceasingly elevated by these considerations, which, although empirical, are so remarkably
powerful and continually adding to their force, will not
suffer itself to be depressed by the doubts suggested by
subtle speculation; it tears itself out of this state of uncertainty the moment it casts a look upon the wondrous
forms of nature and the majesty of the universe, and
rises from height to height, from condition to condition,
till it has elevated itself to the supreme and unconditioned
author of all.

But although we have nothing to object to the reasonable-
ness and utility of this procedure,[39] but have rather to
commend and encourage it, we cannot approve of the claims
which this argument advances to demonstrative certainty, and
to a reception upon its own merits, apart from favour or
support by other arguments. Nor can it injure the cause of
morality to endeavour to lower the tone of the arrogant
sophist, and to teach him that modesty and moderation,
which are the properties of a belief that brings calm and
content into the mind, without prescribing to it an unworthy
subjection. I maintain, then, that the physico-theological
argument is insufficient of itself to prove the existence of a
Supreme Being, that it must intrust this to the ontological
argument—to which it serves merely as an introduction, and
that, consequently, this argument contains the *only possible*

[39] The service rendered by the idea of final end (teleology) to the
empirical investigation of living structures, its utility, that is, as a
heuristic principle, is more fully elaborated in the *Critique of Judgment.* See Bernard's translation (1892), p. 257 ff. It is sometimes forgotten, too, that Kant rendered Theism no little service by demonstrating so conclusively the utter insufficiency of materialism to explain
the order and purpose in nature. Cf. his emphatic statement, "It is
quite certain that we cannot adequately cognise, much less explain,
organised beings and their internal possibility, according to mere
mechanical principles of nature" (*ibid.* p. 312).

ground of proof (possessed by speculative reason) for the existence of this being.

The chief momenta in the physico-theological argument are as follow:[40]—1. We observe in the world manifest signs of an arrangement full of purpose, executed with great wisdom, and existing in a whole of a content indescribably various, and of an extent without limits. 2. This arrangement of means and ends is entirely foreign to the things existing in the world — it belongs to them merely as a contingent attribute; in other words, the nature of different things could not of itself, whatever means were employed, harmoniously tend towards certain purposes, were they not chosen and directed for these purposes by a rational and disposing principle, in accordance with certain fundamental ideas.[41] 3. There exists, therefore, a sublime and wise cause (or several), which is not merely a blind, all-powerful nature,

[40] Kant's formulation of the argument, as he had it before him, must be allowed to be eminently just.

[41] This element in the proof is a decided weakness; as it has been put, "it seems to make God the author of a difficulty in order that He may show His skill in overcoming it." The very existence of the cosmological argument should have prevented men from conceiving the material on which Omnipotence had to work as unsuitable or recalcitrant, and the order and purpose of the world, so far as the material is concerned, as a pure accident. The material itself is the product of the organising Intelligence to which all is referred. Further, the conception of teleology required to be widened, as is done in recent philosophy, to denote not so much particular cases of adaptation, as rather the presence of adaptive thought in nature as a whole, making ultimately for the evolution of "persons." It is interesting to observe that in his early work (1755), *The Universal Natural History and Theory of the Heavens*, Kant gives a quite general, modern, and scientific form of the argument from design. Insisting upon the fact that matter, when left to its own laws, "must necessarily bring forth beautiful combinations," he proceeds, "*There is a God, just because nature even in chaos cannot proceed otherwise than regularly and according to order.*" See Kant's *Cosmology*, translated by Hastie, p. 26.

producing the beings and events which fill the world in unconscious *fecundity*, but a *free* and intelligent cause of the world. 4. The unity of this cause may be inferred from the unity of the reciprocal relation existing between the parts of the world, as portions of an artistic edifice—an inference which all our observation favours, and all principles of analogy support.

In the above argument, it is inferred from the analogy of certain products of nature with those of human art, when it compels Nature to bend herself to its purposes, as in the case of a house, a ship, or a watch, that the same kind of causality —namely, understanding and will—resides in nature. It is also declared that the internal possibility of this freely-acting nature (which is the source of all art, and perhaps also of human reason) [42] is derivable from another and superhuman art,—a conclusion which would perhaps be found incapable of standing the test of subtle transcendental criticism. But to neither of these opinions shall we at present object. We shall only remark that it must be confessed that, if we are to discuss the subject of cause at all, we cannot proceed more securely than with the guidance of the analogy subsisting between nature and such products of design—these being the only products whose causes and modes of origination are completely known to us. Reason would be unable to satisfy her own requirements if she passed from a causality which she does know, to obscure and indemonstrable principles of explanation which she does not know.

According to the physico-theological argument, the connexion and harmony existing in the world evidence the contingency of the form merely, but not of the matter, that

[42] This line of thought, which, general as it is, Kant does not follow out, may have been suggested to him by Hume's *Dialogues on Natural Religion*, where the idea is thrown out that possibly, in our search for the origin of artistic powers and qualities, we need not go beyond nature, or even matter.

is, of the substance of the world.[43] To establish the truth
of the latter opinion, it would be necessary to prove that all
things would be in themselves incapable of this harmony and
order, unless they were, even as regards their *substance*, the
product of a supreme wisdom. But this would require very
different grounds of proof from those presented by the
analogy with human art. This proof can at most, therefore,
demonstrate the existence of an *architect of the world*, whose
efforts are limited by the capabilities of the material with
which he works, but not of a *creator of the world*, to whom
all things are subject. Thus this argument is utterly
insufficient for the task before us—a demonstration of the
existence of an all-sufficient being. If we wish to prove the
contingency of matter, we must have recourse to a transcendental argument, which the physico-theological was constructed expressly to avoid.

We infer, from the order and design visible in the universe,
as a disposition of a thoroughly contingent character, the
existence of a cause *proportionate thereto*. The conception
of this cause must contain certain *determinate* qualities, and
it must therefore be regarded as the conception of a being
which possesses all power, wisdom, and so on, in one word,
all perfection—the conception, that is, of an all-sufficient

[43] Cf. note [41]. Kant has two main objections to urge. First,
that since the form is taken to be purely external to the matter and
substance of the universe, the argument proves no more than a World-
Architect who works upon a given material from without. To this
the reply might surely be made that the teleological argument does
not stand alone, and that, in proving an Architect, it achieves all
that is claimed for it.

The second objection is, that from a limited effect you can
infer only a limited cause ; and as no one knows the world in its
infinitude, to affirm a perfect Being as its author is to put more into
the conclusion than the premises contain. Accordingly we are once
more thrown back on the Ontological argument, which alone can
bridge the gulf between the relative and the absolute.

being.   For the predicates of *very great*, astonishing, or immeasurable power and excellence, give us no determinate conception of the thing, nor do they inform us what the thing may be in itself.   They merely indicate the relation existing between the magnitude of the object and the observer, who compares it with himself and with his own power of comprehension, and are mere expressions of praise and reverence, by which the object is either magnified, or the observing subject depreciated in relation to the object. Where we have to do with the magnitude (of the perfection) of a thing, we can discover no determinate conception, except that which comprehends all possible perfection or completeness, and it is only the total (*omnitudo*) of reality which is completely determined in and through its conception alone.

Now it cannot be expected that anyone will be bold enough to declare that he has a perfect insight into the relation which the magnitude of the world he contemplates bears (in its extent as well as in its content) to omnipotence, into that of the order and design in the world to the highest wisdom, and that of the unity of the world to the absolute unity of a Supreme Being.*   Physico-theology is therefore incapable of presenting a determinate conception of a supreme cause of the world, and is therefore insufficient as a principle of theology,—a theology which is itself to be the basis of religion.

The attainment of absolute totality is completely impossible on the path of empiricism.   And yet this is the path pursued in the physico-theological argument.   What means shall we employ to bridge the abyss ?

After elevating ourselves to admiration of the magnitude of

---

* Kant's meaning is, that no one will be bold enough to declare that he is certain that the world could not have existed without an *omnipotent* author ; that none but the *highest* wisdom could have produced the harmony and order we observe in it ; and that its unity is possible only under the condition of an absolute unity.—Tr.

the power, wisdom, and other attributes of the author of
the world, and finding we can advance no further, we leave
the argument on empirical grounds, and proceed to infer the
contingency of the world from the order and conformity to
aims that are observable in it. From this contingency we
infer, by the help of transcendental conceptions alone, the
existence of something absolutely necessary; and, still
advancing, proceed from the conception of the absolute
necessity of the first cause to the completely determined or
determining conception thereof—the conception of an all-
embracing reality. Thus the physico-theological, failing in its
undertaking, recurs in its embarrassment to the cosmological
argument; and, as this is merely the ontological argument in
disguise,[44] it executes its design solely by the aid of pure
reason, although it at first professed to have no connexion
with this faculty, and to base its entire procedure upon
experience alone.

The physico-theologians have therefore no reason to regard
with such contempt the transcendental mode of argument,
and to look down upon it with the conceit of clear-sighted
observers of nature, as the brain-cobweb of obscure speculatists.
For if they reflect upon and examine their own arguments,
they will find that, after following for some time the path of
nature and experience, and discovering themselves no nearer
their object, they suddenly leave this path and pass into the
region of pure possibility, where they hope to reach upon the
wings of ideas, what had eluded all their empirical investigations. Gaining, as they think, a firm footing after this
immense leap, they extend their determinate conception—
into the possession of which they have come, they know not
how—over the whole sphere of creation, and explain their

[44] The other two arguments, Kant maintains, have to be called
in to help out the teleological argument. The cosmological proof
supplies the notion of Creator, which the teleological had failed to
reach, while the ontological raises all to the absolute plane.

ideal, which is entirely a product of pure Reason, by illustrations drawn from experience—though in a degree miserably unworthy of the grandeur of the object, while they refuse to acknowledge that they have arrived at this cognition or hypothesis by a very different road from that of experience.

Thus the physico-theological is based upon the cosmological, and this upon the ontological proof of the existence of a Supreme Being; and as besides these three there is no other path open to speculative Reason, the ontological proof, on the ground of pure conceptions of Reason, is the only possible one, if any proof of a proposition so far transcending the empirical exercise of the understanding is possible at all.[45]

§ 2. KANT'S ETHICAL THEISM.

Critique of Practical Reason, Bk. II. c. 2, §§ 3, 4, 5, 8

OF THE PRIMACY OF PURE PRACTICAL REASON IN ITS
UNION WITH THE SPECULATIVE REASON.[1]

By primacy between two or more things connected by reason, I understand the prerogative belonging to one, of

[45] Hegel took precisely the same view; with this difference, that he regarded as uniquely valid what Kant rejects as illegitimate. Cf. note [20].

[1] On the relation between the speculative and practical parts of Kant's philosophy, cf. the remark : "The unbiassed reader of his *Critique of Practical Reason* and of his *Metaphysic of Ethics* will hardly gather that he is in the company of a defeated general trying another method of assault : there is rather, I think, the tone of one who has dislodged a pretender, and is now engaged in making good the claims of the sovereign " (Caldecott, *Philosophy of Religion*, p. 49). One noteworthy distinction between Kant and Butler, who may both be called Ethical Theists, is that Kant's speculative views are sceptical, or at least agnostic, while Butler in the main held to the positive rationalism of his day, using the Cosmological and Teleological proofs as well as the Moral (cf. *ibid*. p. 207 f.). Coleridge was the first to give currency to the Kantian ideas in English.

being the first determining principle in the connexion with all the rest. In a narrower, practical sense it means the prerogative of the interest [2] of one in so far as the interest of the other is subordinated to it, while it is not postponed to any other. To every faculty of the mind we can attribute an interest, that is, a principle that contains the condition on which alone the former is called into exercise. Reason, as the faculty of principles, determines the interest of all the powers of the mind, and is determined by its own. The interest of its speculative employment consists in the *cognition* of the object pushed to the highest *à priori* principles, that of its practical employment in the determination of the *will* in respect of the final and complete end. As to what is necessary for the possibility of any employment of reason at all, namely, that its principles and affirmations should not contradict one another, this constitutes no part of its interest, but is the condition of having reason at all; it is only its development, not mere consistency with itself, that is reckoned as its interest.

If practical reason could not assume or think as given, anything further than what speculative reason of itself could offer it from its own insight, the latter would have the primacy. But supposing that it had of itself original *à priori* principles with which certain theoretical positions were inseparably connected, while these were withdrawn from any possible insight of speculative reason (which, however, they must not contradict [3]); then the question is, which interest

[2] In a note to the *Metaphysic of Morals* (Abbott, p. 30), Kant gives the following definition: "The dependence of a contingently determinable will on principles of reason is called an *interest*." This is further elucidated in the paragraph below.

[3] One of the chief problems in the Kantian philosophy is to decide whether, consistently with its principles, speculative reason is to be viewed as sceptical or agnostic (cf. Professor Seth Pringle-Pattison, *Scottish Philosophy*, p. 181). In the former case, it might be contended that an insoluble antinomy obtains between Kant's speculative

is the superior (not which must give way, for they are not necessarily conflicting),—whether speculative reason, which knows nothing of all that the practical offers for its acceptance, should take up these propositions, and (although they transcend it) try to unite them with its own concepts as a foreign possession handed over to it, or whether it is justified in obstinately following its own separate interest, and, according to the canonic [4] of Epicurus, rejecting as vain subtlety everything that cannot accredit its objective reality by manifest examples to be shown in experience, even though it should be never so much interwoven with the interest of the practical (pure) use of reason, and in itself not contradictory to the theoretical, merely because it infringes on the interest of the speculative reason to this extent, that it removes the bounds which this latter had set to itself, and gives it up to every nonsense or delusion of imagination?

In fact, so far as practical reason is taken as dependent on pathological [5] conditions, that is, as merely regulating the inclinations under the sensible principle of happiness, we could not require speculative reason to take its principles

and his ethical theology ; in the latter, practical reason might be regarded as yielding theistic results to which the only attitude that metaphysics can take up is one of neutrality.   The latter thought is certainly indicated here.   Cf. *infra*, p. 224.   The student should read the important note on this point by Dr. Hutchison Stirling, *Schwegler*, p. 424.

[4] Epicurus termed logic Canonic, as furnishing the Canons, or rules, of cognition.

[5] Any faculty or action which is moved by desire or inclination, and not solely by reverence for the pure principles of reason, is named by Kant *pathological*.   This rigorism is the defect of his merit in securing at all costs the unconditional character of obligation, a merit which is too often ungratefully forgotten.   On Kant's ethical stringency, see Mackenzie, *Manual of Ethics*, 3rd ed. p. 192 ff.   English writers who follow Kant and Butler in this line are Newman, Mozley, Martineau, M'Cosh, and, in the main, Professors Fraser and Flint.

from such a source. *Mohammed's* paradise, or the absorption into the Deity of the *theosophists* and *mystics*, would press their monstrosities on the reason according to the taste of each, and one might as well have no reason as surrender it in such fashion to all sorts of dreams. But if pure reason of itself can be practical, and is actually so, as the consciousness of the moral law proves, then it is still only one and the same reason [6] which, whether in a theoretical or a practical point of view, judges according to *à priori* principles; and then it is clear that, although it is in the first point of view incompetent to establish certain propositions positively, which, however, do not contradict it, then as soon as these propositions are *inseparably* attached *to the practical interest* of pure reason, then it must accept them, though it be as something offered to it from a foreign source, something that has not grown on its own ground, but yet is sufficiently authenticated; and it must try to compare and connect them with everything that it has in its power as speculative reason. It must remember, however, that these are not additions to its insight, but yet are extensions of its employment in another, namely, a practical

[6] This identification of the theoretical and practical reason, if pressed, would go far to undermine the dualism between thought and being which runs through so much of Kant's philosophy. But the philosopher's statements are ambiguous, and force us to ask whether the identification here is as genuine as the differentiation in other passages, or whether it rests merely upon the use in both references of the word "reason." Still, we may at least say that what reason as practical is certain of, cannot be doubtful for reason as speculative, if they are really "one and the same reason." This haunting dualism between thought and being, freedom and nature, might have been overcome had Kant worked out the implications of the great idea to which he recurs again and again—that of God as an archetypal Intelligence, not limited by sense, but creative, and working by an apprehension which is direct, like perception, and whose notions constitute things as they are in themselves. Cf. *supra*, pp. 182, 186 n. (*Vide* Pfleiderer, *Philosophy of Religion*, vol. i. pp. 154, 172.)

aspect; and this is not in the least opposed to its interest, which consists in the restriction of wild speculation.

Thus when pure speculative and pure practical reason are combined in one cognition, the latter has the *primacy,* provided, namely, that this combination is not *contingent* and arbitrary, but founded *à priori* on reason itself, and therefore *necessary.* For without this subordination there would arise a conflict of reason with itself; since if they were merely co-ordinate, the former would close its boundaries strictly and admit nothing from the latter into its domain, while the latter would extend its bounds over everything, and when its needs required would seek to embrace the former within them. Nor could we reverse the order, and require pure practical reason to be subordinate to the speculative, since all interest is ultimately practical, and even that of speculative reason is conditional, and it is only in the practical employment of reason that it is complete.

The Immortality of the Soul as a Postulate of Pure Practical Reason.[7]

The realisation of the *summum bonum* in the world is the necessary object of a will determinable by the moral law.

[7] What follows is based upon the prior postulate of *moral freedom,* which Kant had deduced as an objective certainty from the fact of the moral law.

The argument in this and the subsequent section may be briefly summarised thus :—The *summum bonum* (for its definition see Abbott, p. 206) or supreme good is composed of two elements : (1) perfect virtue, (2) perfect felicity. For the realisation of the first, we have to postulate *the immortality of the soul* ; for the second, *the existence of God.*

The three postulates, as Kant repeatedly claims, are the " practical" equivalents of the three speculative Ideas, to which, he had argued in the earlier *Critique,* it is impossible for pure theoretical reason to attribute objective reality. It is an interesting problem whether he has succeeded in proving the equivalence.

But in this will the *perfect accordance* of the mind with
the moral law is the supreme condition of the *summum
bonum*. This then must be possible, as well as its object,
since it is contained in the command to promote the latter.
Now the perfect accordance of the will with the moral law
is *holiness*, a perfection of which no rational being of the
sensible world is capable at any moment of his existence.
Since, nevertheless, it is required as practically necessary,
it can only be found in a *progressus in infinitum* towards that
perfect accordance, and on the principles of pure practical
reason it is necessary to assume such a practical progress as
the real object of our will.

Now this endless progress is only possible on the supposition of an *endless* duration of the *existence* and personality
of the same rational being (which is called the immortality
of the soul).[8] The *summum bonum*, then, practically is
only possible on the supposition of the immortality of the

[8] In the earlier work the principles of critical idealism appear to
have led Kant to the hypothesis that immortality may consistently
involve the unbeginning pre-existence of the soul as well as its endless
existence after death (*Critique of Pure Reason*, p. 473). Here, however, immortality is meant as the continuance of a moral development
which has taken its rise in this life.

It may be noted at this point that Kant's moral Theism is of an
exclusively individual type : he has in view always the single rational
being, rather than man as essentially formed and developed in a
social environment. So far he was but the representative of the
eighteenth century, with its curious insensibility to the meaning of
history, and its tendency to theorise about man as though he were an
isolated unit. The deeper and more universal relations of the individual to the life of Spirit in history and in society have been
elaborated with the richest and most illuminating results by later
thinkers, especially by Hegel and Hegelians. At the same time, we do
find in Kant the idea of a Kingdom of Ends, a community of rational
beings, viewed as subject to universal objective laws, and determined
by universal objective ends. This notion, while not made prominent
in his system, has proved extremely suggestive for later philosophy.

soul; consequently this immortality, being inseparably connected with the moral law, is a postulate of pure practical reason (by which I mean a *theoretical* proposition, not demonstrable as such, but which is an inseparable result of an unconditional *à priori practical* law).

This principle of the moral destination of our nature, namely, that it is only in an endless progress that we can attain perfect accordance with the moral law, is of the greatest use, not merely for the present purpose of supplementing the impotence of speculative reason, but also with respect to religion. In default of it, either the moral law is quite degraded from its *holiness*, being made out to be *indulgent*, and conformable to our convenience, or else men strain their notions of their vocation and their expectation to an unattainable goal, hoping to acquire complete holiness of will, and so they lose themselves in fanatical *theosophic* dreams, which wholly contradict self-knowledge. In both cases the unceasing *effort* to obey punctually and thoroughly a strict and inflexible command of reason, which yet is not ideal, but real, is only hindered. For a rational, but finite being, the only thing possible is an endless progress from the lower to higher degrees of moral perfection. The *Infinite* Being, to whom the condition of time is nothing, sees in this to us endless succession a whole of accordance with the moral law; and the holiness which His command inexorably requires, in order to be true to His justice in the share which He assigns to each in the *summum bonum*, is to be found in a single intellectual intuition of the whole existence of rational beings.[9] All that can be expected of

[9] This is Kant's way of putting the Pauline doctrine of justification by faith. We are accounted righteous or holy because God views our infinite moral progress in a single intuition, and thus reckons us holy in the light of the end. The existence of God, it is plain, is already postulated here, in order that holiness may be predicable of any human being, for to none other than God is so far-reaching an intuition possible.

the creature in respect of the hope of this participation would be the consciousness of his tried character, by which, from the progress he has hitherto made from the worse to the morally better, and the immutability of purpose which has thus become known to him, he may hope for a further unbroken continuance of the same, however long his existence may last, even beyond this life ; * and thus he may hope, not indeed here, nor at any imaginable point of his future existence, but only in the endlessness of his duration (which God alone can survey) to be perfectly adequate to his will (without judgment or excuse, which do not harmonise with justice).[10]

* It seems, nevertheless, impossible for a creature to have the *conviction* of his unwavering firmness of mind in the progress towards goodness. On this account the Christian religion makes it come only from the same Spirit that works sanctification, that is, this firm purpose, and with it the consciousness of steadfastness in the moral progress. But naturally one who is conscious that he has persevered through a long portion of his life up to the end in the progress to the better, and this from genuine moral motives, may well have the comforting hope, though not the certainty, that even in an existence prolonged beyond this life he will continue steadfast in these principles ; and although he is never justified here in his own eyes, nor can ever hope to be so in the increased perfection of his nature, to which he looks forward, together with an increase of duties, nevertheless in this progress which, though it is directed to a goal infinitely remote, yet is in God's sight regarded as equivalent to possession, he may have a prospect of a *blessed* future ; for this is the word that reason employs to designate perfect *well-being* independent on all contingent causes of the world, and which, like *holiness*, is an idea that can be contained only in an endless progress and its totality, and consequently is never fully attained by a creature. (*Note by Kant.*)

[10] It should be carefully observed that Kant elsewhere admits what he calls a *doctrinal faith* in immortality. " In the wisdom of a Supreme Being, and in the shortness of life, so inadequate to the development of the glorious powers of human nature, we may find equally sufficient grounds for a doctrinal belief in the future life of the human soul " (*Critique of Pure Reason*, pp. 500, 501). But this is neither a theoretical demonstration nor a *moral* belief, and is thus wanting in stability. Cf. Orr, *Christian View*, p. 187.

THE EXISTENCE OF GOD AS A POSTULATE OF PURE PRACTICAL REASON.[11]

In the foregoing analysis the moral law led to a practical problem which is prescribed by pure reason alone, without the aid of any sensible motives, namely, that of the necessary completeness of the first and principal element of the *summum bonum*, namely, Morality; and as this can be perfectly solved only in eternity, to the postulate of *immortality*. The same law must also lead us to affirm the possibility of the second element of the *summum bonum*, namely, Happiness, proportioned to that morality,[12] and this on grounds as disinterested as before, and solely from impartial reason; that is, it must lead to the supposition of the existence of a cause adequate to this effect; in other words, it must postulate the *existence of God*, as the necessary condition of the possibility of the *summum bonum* (an object of the will which is

[11] With this should be compared the section of the *Critique of Pure Reason* (pp. 487–496), entitled "On the Ideal of the *Summum Bonum* as a Determining Ground of the Ultimate End of Pure Reason." A little further down we find Kant facing the thorny question whether the idea of God belongs to metaphysics or to morals, and giving the reply, "the conception is one that belongs not to physics, *i.e.* to speculative reason, but to morals" (Abbott, pp. 236–238).

[12] One can hardly avoid charging Kant with inconsistency at this point. We have noted above his ethical rigorism, in the stringency of which he rejects every reference to happiness as a permissible motive. But now, at the next stage in the argument, happiness, as an element in the supreme good, becomes an object of the moral will. It is an illustration of the maxim that "nature will out." The very introduction of happiness here as *an* ethical end, though, of course, not *the* ethical end, goes to prove the unnatural severity of the original view.

The arguments which Kant used to prove that it is our duty to promote the happiness of others are stated and criticised by Sidgwick *Methods of Ethics*, Bk. III. c. xiii. note.

necessarily connected with the moral legislation of pure reason). We proceed to exhibit this connexion in a convincing manner.

Happiness is the condition of a rational being in the world with whom *everything goes according to his wish and will*; it rests, therefore, on the harmony of physical nature with his whole end, and likewise with the essential determining principle of his will. Now the moral law as a law of freedom commands by determining principles, which ought to be quite independent on nature and on its harmony with our faculty of desire (as springs). But the acting rational being in the world is not the cause of the world and of nature itself. There is not the least ground, therefore, in the moral law for a necessary connexion between morality and proportionate happiness in a being that belongs to the world as part of it, and therefore dependent on it, and which for that reason cannot by his will be a cause of this nature, nor by his own power make it thoroughly harmonise, so far as his happiness is concerned, with his practical principles. Nevertheless, in the practical problem of pure reason, *i.e.* the necessary pursuit of the *summum bonum*, such a connexion is postulated as necessary; we ought to endeavour to promote the *summum bonum*, which, therefore, must be possible. Accordingly, the existence of a cause [13] of all nature, distinct from nature itself and containing the principle of this connexion, namely, of the exact harmony of happiness with morality, is also *postulated*. Now, this supreme cause must contain the principle of the harmony of nature, not merely with a law of the will of rational beings, but with the conception of this *law*, in so far as they make it the *supreme determining principle of*

[13] This use of the category of cause simply annuls what was said with such emphatic repetition, in the earlier *Critique*, as to the necessary limitation of the categories to the spatial and temporal world of phenomena. For the application of the term *cause* to God, cf. *supra*, p. 205, note.

the will,[14] and consequently not merely with the form of morals, but with their morality as their motive, that is, with their moral character. Therefore, the *summum bonum* is possible in the world only on the supposition of a supreme Being having a causality corresponding to moral character. Now a being that is capable of acting on the conception of laws is an *intelligence* (a rational being), and the causality of such a being according to this conception of laws is his *will;* therefore the supreme cause of nature, which must be pre-supposed as a condition of the *summum bonum,* is a being which is the cause of nature by *intelligence* and *will,*[15] consequently its author, that is, God. It follows that the postulate of the possibility of the *highest derived good* (the best world) is likewise the postulate of the reality of a *highest original good,* that is to say, of the existence of God. Now it was seen to be a duty for us to promote the *summum bonum;* consequently it is not merely allowable, but it is a necessity connected with duty as a requisite, that we should presuppose the possibility of this *summum bonum;* and as this is possible only on condition of the existence of God, it inseparably connects the supposition of this with duty; that is, it is morally necessary to assume the existence of God.[16]

[14] The first might be unconscious, the second must be conscious. Cf. Kant's famous utterance (*Metaphysic of Morals,* Abbott, p. 29): "Everything in nature works according to laws. Rational beings alone have the faculty of acting according *to the conception* of laws, that is, according to principles."

[15] This seems as plain and unequivocal an assertion of the *personality* of God as could well be desired.

[16] We see from this passage what is meant by charging Kant with Deism. He introduces belief in a God externally related to experience, in order to effect a reconciliation between happiness and duty—a reconciliation which cannot be more than mechanical and adventitious, "a nail to hold together a morality which was falling to pieces," in Herder's happy phrase. It has been remarked by various writers, and the point is of interest, that Kant, as a practical philosopher desirous of reconciling the moral law and nature, here

It must be remarked here that this moral necessity is *sub jective*, that is, it is a want, and not *objective*, that is, itself a duty, for there cannot be a duty to suppose the existence of anything (since this concerns only the theoretical employment of reason).[17] Moreover, it is not meant by this that it is necessary to suppose the existence of God *as a basis of all obligation in general* (for this rests, as has been sufficiently proved, simply on the autonomy of reason itself). What belongs to duty here is only the endeavour to realise and promote the *summum bonum* in the world, the possibility of which can therefore be postulated ; and as our reason finds it not conceivable except on the supposition of a supreme intelligence, the admission of this existence is therefore connected with the consciousness of our duty, although the admission itself belongs to the domain of speculative reason. Considered in respect of this alone, as a principle of explanation, it may be called a *hypothesis*, but in reference to the intelligibility of an object given us by the moral law (the

accepts without demur the very hypothesis which he had rejected when brought forward, in theoretical philosophy, to explain the correspondence between knowledge and reality.

Modern theistic philosophy, it may be observed, would throw Kant's argument into the deeper form that the presence of a Moral Reason within us, charged with its categorical imperatives of duty, and the existence in nature and history of what, in general terms, we name "the moral order," are parallel and organically united manifestations of an Absolute Moral Reason, or God. And this is essentially the idea to which we are guided by the profoundest suggestions of the *Critique of Judgment.* Cf. Fairbairn, *Philosophy of the Christian Religion,* Bk. I. c. 2.

[17] As already remarked (p. 223, note [6]), it is one great problem of the Kantian philosophy to reconcile dicta of this kind with the principle, enunciated ever and anon, that the speculative and the practical Reason are one and the same. And it is at this point, where the dualism between scientific and moral or religious knowledge is dwelt upon, that we can best see with what justice the theology of Ritschl and his followers (especially, perhaps, Herrmann) claims lineal descent from Kant.

summum bonum), and consequently of a requirement for practical purposes, it may be called *faith*, that is to say, a pure *rational faith*, since pure reason (both in its theoretical and its practical use) is the sole source from which it springs.[18]

.   .   .   .

In this manner the moral laws lead through the conception of the *summum bonum* as the object and final end of pure practical reason to *religion*, that is, to the *recognition of all duties as Divine commands*,[19] *not as sanctions,* that is to say, arbitrary ordinances of a foreign will and contingent in themselves*, but as essential *laws* of every free will in itself, which, nevertheless, must be regarded as commands of the Supreme Being, because it is only from a morally perfect (holy and good) and at the same time all-powerful will, and consequently only through harmony with this will, that we can hope to attain the *summum bonum* which the moral law makes it our duty to take as the object of our endeavours. Here again, then, all remains disinterested, and founded merely on duty; neither fear nor hope being made the fundamental springs, which, if taken as principles, would destroy the whole moral worth of actions. The moral law commands me to make the highest possible good in a world the ultimate object of all my conduct. But I cannot hope to effect this otherwise than by the harmony of my will with

[18] A modern representative of the same temper is Professor Fraser. Cf. his Gifford Lectures, *The Philosophy of Theism*.

[19] Kant develops this definition further in his *Religion within the bounds of mere Reason*. It is clear that religion is here all but swallowed up in morality, and the sense of personal fellowship between God and the soul completely ignored. This has been justly censured as the Moralism of Kant. For a somewhat similar position see the Selection from Martineau.

* The word "sanction" is here used in the technical German sense, which is familiar to students of history in connexion with the "Pragmatic Sanction." (*Note by Translator.*)

that of a holy and good Author of the world ; and although
the conception of the *summum bonum* as a whole, in which
the greatest happiness is conceived as combined in the most
exact proportion with the highest degree of moral perfection
(possible in creatures), includes *my own happiness*, yet it is
not this that is the determining principle of the will which is
enjoined to promote the *summum bonum*, but the moral law,
which, on the contrary, limits by strict conditions my unbounded desire of happiness.

Hence also morality is not properly the doctrine how we
should *make* ourselves happy, but how we should become
worthy of happiness. It is only when religion is added that
there also comes in the hope of participating some day in
happiness in proportion as we have endeavoured to be not
unworthy of it.

.   .   .   .

OF BELIEF FROM A REQUIREMENT OF PURE REASON.

A want or requirement of pure reason in its speculative use
leads only to a hypothesis ; that of pure practical reason to a
postulate ; for in the former case I ascend from the result as
high as I please in the series of causes, not in order to give
objective reality to the result (*e.g.* the causal connexion of
things and changes in the world), but in order thoroughly to
satisfy my inquiring reason in respect of it. Thus I see
before me order and design in nature, and need not resort to
speculation to assure myself of their *reality*, but to *explain*
them I have *to presuppose a Deity* as their cause ; and then
since the inference from an effect to a definite cause is always
uncertain and doubtful, especially to a cause so precise and so
perfectly defined as we have to conceive in God, hence the
highest degree of certainty to which this presupposition can
be brought is, that it is the most rational opinion for us

men.* On the other hand, a requirement of pure *practical* reason is based on a *duty*, that of making something (the *summum bonum*) the object of my will so as to promote it with all my powers; in which case I must suppose its possibility, and consequently also the conditions necessary thereto, namely, God, freedom, and immortality; since I cannot prove these by my speculative reason, although neither can I refute them. This duty is founded on something that is indeed quite independent on these suppositions, and is of itself apodictically certain, namely, the moral law; and so far it needs no further support by theoretical views as to the inner constitution of things, the secret final aim of the order of the world, or a presiding ruler thereof, in order to bind me in the most perfect manner to act in unconditional conformity to the law. But the subjective effect of this law, namely, the mental *disposition* conformed to it, and made necessary by it, to promote the practically possible *summum bonum*, this presupposes at least that the latter is *possible*, for it would be practically impossible to strive after the object of a conception which at bottom was empty, and had no object.[20]   Now the

* But even here we should not be able to allege a requirement *of reason*, if we had not before our eyes a problematical, but yet inevitable, conception of reason, namely, that of an absolutely necessary being. This conception now seeks to be defined, and this, in addition to the tendency to extend itself, is the objective ground of a requirement of speculative reason, namely, to have a more precise definition of the conception of a necessary being which is to serve as the first cause of other beings, so as to make these latter knowable by some means. Without such antecedent necessary problems there are no *requirements* —at least not of *pure reason*—the rest are requirements of *inclination*. (*Note by Kant.*)

[20] This is parallel to Kant's argument on behalf of freedom. The moral law declares, "Thou canst, for thou oughtest," and thus I am assured that freedom is a fact. So, to use his own words, "the moral law commands me to make the highest possible good the ultimate object of all my conduct," and thus assures me of the objective possibility that the *summum bonum* may be realised.

above-mentioned postulates concern only the physical or metaphysical conditions of the *possibility* of the *summum bonum*; in a word, those which lie in the nature of things; not, however, for the sake of an arbitrary speculative purpose, but of a practically necessary end of a pure rational will, which in this case does not *choose*, but *obeys* an inexorable command of reason, the foundation of which is *objective*, in the constitution of things as they must be universally judged by pure reason, and is not based on *inclination*; for we are in nowise justified in assuming, on account of what we *wish* on merely *subjective* grounds, that the means thereto are possible or that its object is real.[21] This then is an absolutely necessary requirement, and what it presupposes is not merely justified as an allowable hypothesis, but as a postulate in a practical point of view; and admitting that the pure moral law inexorably binds every man as a command (not as a rule of prudence), the righteous man may say : I *will* that there be a God, that my existence in this world be also an existence outside the chain of physical causes, and in a pure world of the understanding, and, lastly, that my duration be endless; I firmly abide by this, and will not let this faith be taken from me ; for in this instance alone my interest, because I *must* not relax anything of it, inevitably determines my judgment, without regarding sophistries, how-ever unable I may be to answer them or to oppose them with others more plausible.

*   *   *   *   *   *

In order to prevent misconception in the use of a notion as yet so unusual as that of a faith of pure practical reason, let me be permitted to add one more remark. It might almost

---

[21] Such words show how studiously Kant would guard against the intrusion of a subjective *hedonistic* influence in our religious judgments. We may postulate only what is inseparably bound up with the thought of duty. So that Kant's subjectivity is that of personal and ethical conviction, not of arbitrary taste.

seem as if this rational faith were here announced as itself a *command*, namely, that we should assume the *summum bonum* as possible. But a faith that is commanded is nonsense. Let the preceding analysis, however, be remembered of what is required to be supposed in the conception of the *summum bonum*, and it will be seen that it cannot be commanded to assume this possibility, and no practical disposition of mind is required to *admit* it; but that speculative reason must concede it without being asked, for no one can affirm that it is *impossible* in itself that rational beings in the world should at the same time be worthy of happiness in conformity with the moral law, and also possess this happiness proportionately. Now in respect of the first element of the *summum bonum*, namely, that which concerns morality, the moral law gives merely a command, and to doubt the possibility of that element would be the same as to call in question the moral law itself.   But as regards the second element of that object, namely, happiness perfectly proportioned to that worthiness, it is true that there is no need of a command to admit its possibility in general, for theoretical reason has nothing to say against it; but *the manner* in which we have to conceive this harmony of the laws of nature with those of freedom has in it something in respect of which we have a *choice*, because theoretical reason decides nothing with apodictic certainty about it, and in respect of this there may be a moral interest which turns the scale.[22]

[22] Cf. the saying of Lotze that "faith is an act." A modernised statement of the same position is James' *The Will to Believe*; and the same view is defended by the school of Voluntarism now rising into prominence, and represented in the volume of Oxford essays entitled *Personal Idealism* (1902). Cf. the Selection from Descartes, *supra*, p. 42, note [2]. This belief is described by Kant a few lines further down as "a voluntary determination of our judgment." This is vitally connected with the later Ritschlian doctrine that the apprehension of moral and spiritual reality is morally and spiritually conditioned, and hence that the only valid apologetic must move

I had said above that in a mere course of nature in the world an accurate correspondence between happiness and moral worth is not to be expected, and must be regarded as impossible, and that therefore the possibility of the *summum bonum* cannot be admitted from this side except on the supposition of a moral Author of the world. I purposely reserved the restriction of this judgment to the *subjective* conditions of our reason, in order not to make use of it until the manner of this belief should be defined more precisely. The fact is that the impossibility referred to is *merely subjective*, that is, our reason finds it *impossible for it* to render conceivable in the way of a mere course of nature a connexion so exactly proportioned and so thoroughly adapted to an end, between two sets of events happening according to such distinct laws ; although, as with everything else in nature that is adapted to an end, it cannot prove, that is, show by sufficient objective reasons, that it is not possible by universal laws of nature.

Now, however, a deciding principle of a different kind comes into play to turn the scale in this uncertainty of speculative reason. The command to promote the *summum bonum* is established on an objective basis (in practical reason); the possibility of the same in general is likewise established on an objective basis (in theoretical reason, which has nothing to say against it). But reason cannot decide objectively in what way we are to conceive this possibility ; whether by universal laws of nature without a wise Author presiding over nature, or only on supposition of such an Author. Now here there comes in a *subjective* condition of reason ; the only way theoretically possible for it, of conceiv-

on the lines of St. John vii. 17, "If any man willeth to do His will, he shall know of the teaching."

The whole passage may very well be taken as suggesting the supreme example adducible by Kant of the power of the practical Reason to decide problems which the speculative reason has left open.

ing the exact harmony of the kingdom of nature with the kingdom of morals, which is the condition of the possibility of the *summum bonum*; and at the same time the only one conducive to morality (which depends on an objective law of reason).[23] Now, since the promotion of this *summum bonum*, and therefore the supposition of its possibility, are *objectively* necessary (though only as a result of practical reason), while at the same time the manner in which we would conceive it rests with our own choice, and in this choice a free interest of pure practical reason decides for the assumption of a wise Author of the world; it is clear that the principle that herein determines our judgment, though as a want it is *subjective*, yet at the same time being the means of promoting what is *objectively* (practically) necessary, is the foundation of a *maxim* of belief in a moral point of view, that is, a *faith of pure practical reason*. This, then, is not commanded, but being a voluntary determination of our judgment, conducive to the moral (commanded) purpose, and, moreover, harmonising with the theoretical requirement of reason, to assume that existence and to make it the foundation of our further employment of reason, it has itself sprung from the moral disposition of mind; it may therefore at times waver even in the well-disposed, but can never be reduced to unbelief.

[23] Kant's meaning seems to be that, in the interests of morality, we need to be assured not only of the possibility of the *summum bonum* (*i.e.* the ultimate combination of happiness and morality in perfect degree and exact proportions), but of its *reality*. Now theoretical Reason cannot disprove the possibility of a Moral Author of the universe who will realise the *summum bonum*; consequently, practical Reason is entitled to postulate His existence. At the same time, only those who are profoundly convinced of the infinite worth of duty can win it from themselves to grant the right of practical Reason to make this assumption. There remains, therefore, an inevitable element of choice which cannot possibly be eliminated. The affinities of the later Ritschlianism with this are obvious; see Selection XV.

§ 3. GENERAL REMARK ON TELEOLOGY.[1]

Critique of Judgment, Part II. Appendix, § 91.

If the question is, what rank the moral argument, which proves the Being of God only as a thing of faith for the practical pure Reason, maintains among the other arguments in philosophy, it is easy to count up the whole possessions of this last; by which it appears that there is here no choice, but that our theoretical faculty must give up all its pretensions before an impartial Kritik.[2]

[1] The following extract, which forms the concluding part of the last section of the *Critique of Judgment*, is one of the clearest statements of his general Theistic attitude ever penned by Kant. It is eminently worthy of note, and significant of much, that it was this *Critique* that Kant's successors, Fichte, Schelling, and Hegel, took as the point of departure in constructing their speculative systems. The problem with which it is occupied may be briefly stated as the possibility of identifying the ultimate basis of the world of nature with the world of freedom. Thus " the Critique of Judgment completes the whole undertaking of criticism ; its endeavour is to show that there are *à priori* principles at the basis of Judgment just as there are in the case of Understanding and of Reason ; that these principles, like the principles of Reason, are not constitutive but only regulative of experience, *i.e.* that they do not teach us anything positive about the characteristics of objects, but only indicate the conditions under which we find it necessary to view them" (Bernard in Introduction to Trans. of *Critique of Judgment*, p. xvi). The work has two main divisions, first the philosophy of Taste—the Beautiful and Sublime in nature ; second, the Teleology of Nature's operations. In the course of the latter discussion Kant recurs to the problems of his religious philosophy, and closes with the section we have given here.

[2] At various points in this extract, as will be observed, Kant's inveterate caution in regard to Theistic affirmation comes out very clearly. He is prepared to say that Theism is not only demanded by the practical needs of morality, but is an hypothesis indispensable for the guidance of scientific research, yet to the last he hesitates to claim for it objective truth. We must not say dogmatically—God exists . but we may say, it is impossible for our judgment to view nature save as

All belief must in the first place be grounded upon facts, if it is not to be completely groundless; and therefore the only distinction in proofs that there can be is that belief in the consequence derived therefrom can either be grounded on this fact as *knowledge* for theoretical cognition, or merely as *faith* for practical. All facts belong either to the *natural concept* which proves its reality in the objects of sense, given (or which may possibly be given) before all natural concepts; or to the *concept of freedom*, which sufficiently establishes its reality through the causality of Reason in regard of certain effects in the world of sense, possible through it, which it incontrovertibly postulates in the moral law. The natural concept (merely belonging to theoretical cognition) is now either metaphysical and thinkable completely *à priori*, or physical, *i.e.* thinkable *à posteriori*, and only necessary through determinate experience. The metaphysical natural concept (which presupposes no determinate experience) is therefore ontological.

The *ontological* proof of the being of God from the concept of an original Being is either that which from ontological predicates, by which alone it can be thought as completely determined, infers absolutely necessary being; or that which, from the absolute necessity of the being somewhere of some thing, whatever it be, infers the predicates of the original

implying design which has been put there by an intelligent Cause—*i.e.* God. In other words, teleology is a regulative, not a constitutive, principle; it holds good for the reflective, but not for the determinant, judgment (cf. p. 209, note [32], and p. 212, note [37]). But why, we may ask, this antinomy between the necessities of thought and the realities of being? The reason, plainly, is to be found in the subjective idealism, or agnostic relativism, of Kant's doctrine of cognition. We have no real knowledge of things themselves, still less, of course, of the design or beauty which God may have put into them. It was by sweeping away this limitation of knowledge to the subjective that Hegel opened a path for those who aimed at advancing philosophy further.

Being. For there belongs to the concept of an original Being, inasmuch as it is not derived from anything, the unconditioned necessity of its presence, and (in order to represent this) its complete determination by its (mere *) concept. It was believed that both requirements were found in the concept of the ontological Idea of a *Being the most real of all*; and thus two metaphysical proofs originated.

The proof (properly called ontological) resting upon a merely metaphysical natural concept concludes from the concept of the Being the most real of all, its absolutely necessary existence; for (it is said), if it did not exist, a reality would be wanting to it, namely, existence. The other (which is also called the metaphysico-*cosmological* proof) concludes from the necessity of the existence somewhere of a thing (which must be conceded, for a being is given to us in self-consciousness), its complete determination as that of a Being the most real of all; for everything existing must be completely determined, but the absolutely necessary (*i.e.* that which *we* ought to cognise as such and consequently *à priori*) must be completely determined *by means of its own concept*. But this is only the case with the concept of a thing the most real of all. It is not needful to expose here the sophistry in both arguments, which has been already done elsewhere; † it is only needful to remark that neither proof, even if they could be defended by all manner of dialectical subtlety, could ever pass from the schools into the world, or have the slightest influence on the mere sound Understanding.[3]

The proof, which rests on a natural concept that can only be empirical and yet is to lead us beyond the bounds of nature regarded as the complex of the objects of sense, can be no other than that derived from the *purposes* of nature. The concept of these cannot, it is true, be given *à priori*

---

* *First edition.* † In the *Critique of Pure Reason.*

[3] Cf. *supra*, pp. 190–207.

but only through experience; but yet it promises such a concept of the original ground of nature as alone, among all those which we can conceive, is suited to the supersensible, namely, that of a highest Understanding as Cause of the world.   This, in fact, it completely performs in accordance with principles of the reflective Judgment, *i.e.* in accordance with the constitution of our (human) faculty of cognition.   But whether or not it is in a position to supply from the same data this concept of a *supreme*, *i.e.* independent intelligent Being, in short of a God or Author of a world under moral laws, and consequently as sufficiently determined for the Idea of a final purpose of the being of the world — this is the question upon which everything depends, whether we desire a theoretically adequate concept of the Original Being on behalf of our whole knowledge of nature, or a practical concept for religion.

This argument, derived from physical Teleology, is worthy of respect.[4]   It produces a similar effect in the way of conviction upon the common Understanding as upon the subtlest thinker; and a *Reimarus*[5] has acquired immortal honour in his work (not yet superseded), in which he abundantly develops this ground of proof with his peculiar thoroughness and lucidity.   But how does this proof acquire such mighty influence upon the mind, especially in a judgment by cold reason (for we might refer to persuasion the emotion and elevation of reason produced by the wonders

[4] Nothing is clearer, from repeated expressions, than that Kant always cherished the most friendly and respectful consideration for the argument from design, both for its own sake, and on Aristotle's ground of respect for common opinion.   Cf. *supra*, p. 212.

[5] Hermann Samuel Reimarus (1694–1768), a professor in Hamburg, was the author of the *Wolfenbüttel Fragments*, a work which created a sensation by its bold denial of the supernatural origin of Christianity, and was first published by Lessing in 1777.   Another work of the same type was his *Vornehmste Wahrheiten der natürlichen Religion*, and it is possible that this is the book to which Kant refers.

of nature) upon a calm and resigned assent? It is not the
physical purposes, which all indicate in the World Cause
an unfathomable intelligence; these are inadequate thereto,
because they do not content the want of the inquiring Reason.
For, wherefore (it asks) are all those natural things that
exhibit art? Wherefore is man himself, whom we must
regard as the ultimate purpose of nature thinkable by us?
Wherefore is this collective Nature here, and what is the
final purpose of such great and manifold art? Reason cannot
be contented with enjoyment or with contemplation, observation, and admiration (which, if it stops there, is only
enjoyment of a particular kind) as the ultimate final purpose
for the creation of the world and of man himself; for this
presupposes a personal worth, which man alone can give
himself, as the condition under which alone he and his
being can be the final purpose.[6] Failing this (which alone
is susceptible of a definite concept), the purposes of
nature do not satisfactorily answer our questions; especially because they cannot furnish any *determinate* concept
of the highest Being[7] as an all-sufficient (and therefore

[6] In such a statement as this, of which there are many scattered
through Kant's writings, we may find one of the main sources (through
Lotze) of the Ritschlian theology. Kant drew a fundamental distinction between relative value or *price*, and inner value or *worthiness*, and
declares that "that which constitutes the condition under which alone
anything can be an end in itself, has not merely a relative worth, *i.e.*
value, but an intrinsic worth, that is, *dignity*" (*Metaphysic of Morals*,
Abbott's trans. p. 53). Although he did not employ the term
"value-judgment," we find the term "taste-judgment" in his pages.
For the conception of the worth of personality as a religious motive,
see passage from Ritschl, *infra*, p. 432.

[7] This is an important vein of criticism to which Kant returns again
and again. As he says a few paragraphs later (p. 247), "you arrive in
this way at no definite concept of an original Being available for a
Theology; for this can only be found in the concept of the totality of
perfections compatible with intelligence, and you cannot help yourself
to this by merely *empirical* data." On the other hand, however, we

unique and so properly called *highest*) being, and of the laws according to which an Understanding is Cause of the world.

Hence that the physico-teleological proof convinces, just as if it were a theological proof, does not arise from our availing ourselves of the Ideas of purposes of nature as so many empirical grounds of proof of a *highest* Understanding. But it mingles itself unnoticed with that moral ground of proof, which dwells in every man and influences him secretly, in the conclusion by which we ascribe to the Being, which manifests itself with such incomprehensible art in the purposes of nature, a final purpose and consequently wisdom (without, however, being justified in doing so by the perception of the former) ; and by which therefore we arbitrarily fill up the lacunas of the (design) argument.[8] In fact, it is only the moral ground of proof which produces conviction, and that only in a moral reference with which every man feels inwardly his agreement. But the physico-teleological proof has only the merit of leading the mind in its consideration of the world by the way of purposes, and through them to an *intelligent* Author of the world ; for the moral reference to purposes and the Idea of a moral legislator and Author of the world, as a theological concept, seem to be

should note the service which Kant has done to Theism by his reasoned and emphatic repudiation of *any other* theory (*e.g.* materialism) as an explanation of what we find in nature. Cf. *Critique of Judgment*, §§ 72, 73.

    [8] Compare and contrast the way in which in the first *Critique* the cosmological argument is charged with bringing in the Ontological argument to supply its own deficiencies.   Earlier in this treatise Kant had argued that whereas the teleological argument allows us to infer at most only very great wisdom and power, these qualities in an infinite degree can be justly inferred from the Moral argument (§ 88).   Does it not suggest the essential unity of the mind's response to the thought of God that the various proofs thus turn out to be dependent on one another ? Cf. J. H. Kennedy, *Natural Theology and Modern Science*, p. 240 ff.

developed of themselves out of that ground of proof, although they are in truth pure additions.

From this on we may allow the customary statement to stand. For it is generally difficult (if the distinction requires much reflection) for ordinary sound Understanding to distinguish from one another as heterogeneous the different principles which it confuses, and from one of which alone it actually draws conclusions with correctness. The moral ground of proof of the Being of God, properly speaking, does not merely *complete* and render perfect the physico-teleological proof, but it is a special proof that *supplies* the conviction which is wanting in the latter. This latter in fact can do nothing more than guide Reason, in its judgment upon the ground of nature and that contingent but admirable order of nature only known to us by experience, to the causality of a Cause containing the ground of the same in accordance with purposes (which we by the constitution of our cognitive faculties must think as an intelligent cause); and thus by arresting the attention of Reason it makes it more susceptible of the moral proof. For what is requisite to the latter concept is so essentially different from everything which natural concepts contain and can teach, that there is need of a particular ground of proof quite independent of the former, in order to supply the concept of the original Being adequately for Theology and to infer its existence. The moral proof (which, it is true, only proves the Being of God in a practical though indispensable aspect of Reason) would preserve all its force, if we found in the world no material, or only that which is doubtful, for physical Teleology. It is possible to conceive rational beings surrounded by a nature which displayed no clear trace of organisation, but only the effects of a mere mechanism of crude matter; on behalf of which, and amid the changeability of some merely contingent purposive forms and relations, there would appear to be no ground for inferring an intelligent Author. In such case there would be no occasion for a physical Teleology ; and yet Reason, which here gets no guidance from natural concepts, would find in the concept of freedom and in the moral Ideas founded thereon a practically sufficient ground for postulating the concept of the original Being in conformity with these, *i.e.* as a Deity, and for postulating nature (even the nature of our own being) as a final purpose in accordance with freedom and its laws—and all this in reference to the indispensable command of practical Reason. However, the fact that there is in the actual world for the rational beings in it abundant material for physical Teleology (even though this is not necessary) serves as a desirable confirmation of the moral argument, as far as nature can exhibit anything analogous to the (moral) rational ideas. For the concept of a supreme Cause possessing intelligence (though not reaching far enough for a Theology) thus acquires sufficient reality for the reflective Judgment, but it is not required as the basis of the moral proof ; nor does this latter serve to complete as a proof the former, which does not by itself point to morality at all, by means of an argument developed according to a single principle. Two such heterogeneous principles as nature and freedom can only furnish two different kinds of proof ; and the attempt to derive one from the other is found unavailing as regards that which is to be proved.

If the physico-teleological ground of proof sufficed for the proof which is sought, it would be very satisfactory for the speculative Reason ; for it would furnish the hope of founding a Theosophy (for so we must call the theoretical cognition of the Divine nature and its existence, which would suffice at once for the explanation of the constitution of the world and for the determination of moral laws). In the same way, if Psychology enabled us to arrive at a cognition of the immortality of the soul it would make Pneumatology possible, which would be just as welcome to the speculative

Reason. But neither, agreeable as they would be to the arrogance of our curiosity, would satisfy the wish of Reason in respect of a theory which must be based on a cognition of the nature of things. Whether the first, as Theology, and the second, as Anthropology, when founded on the moral principle, *i.e.* the principle of freedom, and consequently in accordance with the practical use (of Reason) do not better fulfil their objective final design, is another question which we need not here pursue.

The physico-teleological ground of proof does not reach to Theology, because it does not, and cannot, give any determinate concept, sufficient for this design, of the original Being ; but we must derive this from quite another quarter, or must supply its lacuna by an arbitrary addition. You infer, from the great purposiveness of natural forms and their relations, an intelligent Cause of the world ; but what is the degree of this intelligence (*Verstand*)? Without doubt you cannot assume that it is the highest possible intelligence ; because for that it would be requisite that you should see that a greater intelligence than that of which you perceive proofs in the world, is not thinkable ; and this would be to ascribe omniscience to yourself.[9] In the same way, if you infer from the magnitude of the world the very great might of its Author, you must be content with this having only a comparative significance for your faculty of comprehension ; for since you do not know all that is possible, so as to compare it with the magnitude of the world as far as you know it, you cannot infer the almightiness of its Author from so small a standard, and so on. Now you arrive in this way at no definite concept of an original Being available for a Theology ; for this can only be found in the concept of the totality of perfections compatible with intelligence, and you cannot help yourself to this by merely

[9] Kant had these arguments before him, it is probable, in the form in which they are given in Hume's *Inquiry*, § vii. Cf. *supra*, p. 193.

empirical data. But without such a definite concept you cannot infer a *unique*, intelligent, original Being ; you can only assume it (with whatever motive). Now it may certainly be conceded that you should arbitrarily add (for Reason has nothing fundamental to say to the contrary) : Where so much perfection is found, we may well assume that all perfection is united in a unique Cause of the world, because Reason succeeds better both theoretically and practically with a principle thus definite. But then you cannot regard this concept of the original Being as proved by you, for you have only assumed it on behalf of a better employment of Reason. Hence all lamentation or impotent anger on account of the alleged mischief of rendering doubtful the coherency of your chain of reasoning, is vain pretentiousness, which would fain have us believe that the doubt here freely expressed as to your argument is a doubting of sacred truth, in order that under this cover the shallowness of your argument may pass unnoticed.

Moral Teleology, on the other hand, which is not less firmly based than physical,—which, indeed, rather deserves the preference, because it rests *à priori* on principles inseparable from our Reason, — leads to that which is requisite for the possibility of a Theology, namely, to a determinate *concept* of the supreme Cause, as Cause of the world according to moral laws, and, consequently, to the concept of such a cause as satisfies our moral final purpose. For this are required, as natural properties belonging to it, nothing less than Omniscience, Omnipotence, Omnipresence, and the like, which must be thought as bound up with the moral final purpose which is infinite and thus as adequate to it. Hence moral Teleology alone can furnish the concept of a *unique* Author of the world which is available for a Theology.

In this way Theology leads immediately to *Religion*, i.e. *the recognition of our duties as Divine commands* ; * because it

* Cf. Kritik of *Practical Reason*, Dialectic, c. ii. § v.

is only the recognition of our duty and of the final purpose
enjoined upon us by Reason which brings out with definiteness the concept of God.[10]   This concept, therefore, is inseparable in its origin from obligation to that Being.   On
the other hand, even if the concept of the original Being
could be also found determinately by the merely theoretical
path (namely, the concept of it as mere Cause of nature),
it would afterwards be very difficult—perhaps impossible,
without arbitrary interpolation (of elements)—to ascribe to
this Being by well-grounded proofs a causality in accordance
with moral laws ; and yet without this that quasi-theological
concept could furnish no foundation for religion.   Even if a
religion could be established by this theoretical path, it
would actually, as regards sentiment (wherein its essence
lies), be different from that in which the concept of God and
the (practical) conviction of His Being originate from the
fundamental Ideas of morality.   For if we must suppose the
Omnipotence, Omniscience, etc., of an Author of the world

[10] Cf. *supra*, p. 232, for a previous statement of this definition of
religion.   This passage shows more clearly than any other, perhaps,
that in Kant's view religion is possible only when the conception of
God as Ruler of the World is from the first essentially bound up with
the conception of God as Moral Legislator.   Moral Theology in the
first place, teleology in the second, are the fundamental motives to
Theistic belief by which Kant's mind was influenced and his judgment
decided.   Perhaps his most positive statement on the subject is the
following : " For the theoretical reflective Judgment physical Teleology sufficiently proves from the purposes of Nature an intelligent
world-cause ; for the practical Judgment moral Teleology establishes
it by the concept of a final purpose, which it is forced to ascribe to
creation " (*Critique of Judgment*, § 88).   Yet on this there never fails to
follow the agnostic counterstroke that this is a matter of faith, not a
fact of knowledge.   In order, however, that we may be fully persuaded
of the complete independence of faith and knowledge we should need
to ask the further question—Can practical faith in God be combined
with *positive theoretical disbelief* in Him ?   Kant's reply, in our judgment, would probably have been in the negative.

as concepts given to us from another quarter, in order afterwards only to apply our concepts of duties to our relation to Him, then these latter concepts must bear very markedly the appearance of compulsion and forced submission. If, instead of this, the respect for the moral law, quite freely, in virtue of the precept of our own Reason, represents to us the final purpose of our destination, we admit among our moral views a Cause harmonising with this and with its accomplishment, with the sincerest reverence, which is quite distinct from pathological fear; and we willingly submit ourselves thereto.*

If it be asked why it is incumbent upon us to have any Theology at all, it appears clear that it is not needed for the extension or correction of our cognition of nature or, in general, for any theory, but simply in a subjective point of view for Religion, *i.e.* the practical or moral use of our Reason. If it is found that the only argument which leads to a definite concept of the object of Theology is itself moral, it is not only not strange, but we miss nothing in respect of its final purpose as regards the sufficiency of belief from this ground of proof, provided that it be admitted that such an argument only establishes the Being of God sufficiently for our moral destination, *i.e.* in a practical point of view, and that here speculation neither shows its strength in any way, nor extends by means of it the sphere of its domain. Our surprise, and the alleged contradiction between

---

* The admiration for beauty, and also the emotion aroused by the manifold purposes of nature, which a reflective mind is able to feel, even prior to a clear representation of a rational Author of the world, have something in themselves like *religious* feeling. They seem, in the first place, by a method of judging analogous to moral, to produce an effect upon the moral feeling (gratitude to, and veneration for, the unknown Cause); and thus, by exciting moral Ideas, to produce an effect upon the mind, when they inspire that admiration which is bound up with far more interest than mere theoretical observation can bring about. (*Note by Kant.*)

the here asserted possibility of a Theology and that which
the Kritik of Speculative Reason said of the Categories,
namely, that they can only produce knowledge when applied
to objects of sense, but in no way when applied to the
supersensible—vanish, if we see that they are here used for
a cognition of God, not in a theoretical point of view (in
accordance with what His own nature, which is inscrutable
by us, may be), but simply in a practical. In order, then,
at this opportunity to make an end of the misinterpretation
of that very necessary doctrine of the Kritik, which, to the
chagrin of the blind dogmatist, refers Reason to its bounds,
I add here the following elucidation.

If I ascribe to a body *motive force* and thus think it by
means of the category of *causality*, then I at the same time
cognise it by that (category) ; *i.e.* I determine the concept of
it, as of an Object in general, by means of what belongs to
it by itself (as the condition of the possibility of that
relation) as an object of sense. If the motive force ascribed
to it is repulsive, then there belongs to it (although I do
not place near it any other body upon which it may exert
force) a place in space, and, moreover, extension, *i.e.* space
in itself, besides the filling up of this by means of the
repulsive forces of its parts. In addition, there is the law of
this filling up (that the ground of the repulsion of the parts
must decrease in the same proportion as the extension of the
body increases, and as the space, which it fills with the same
parts by means of this force, is augmented). On the contrary,
if I think a supersensible Being as the first *mover*, and thus
by the category of causality as regards its determination of
the world (motion of matter), I must not think it as existing
in any place in space, nor as extended; I must not even
think it as existing in time or simultaneously with other
beings. Hence I have no determinations whatever, which
could make intelligible to me the condition of the possibility of motion by means of this Being as its

ground.[11]   Consequently, I do not in the very least cognise it by means of the predicate of Cause (as first mover), for itself; but I have only the representation of a something containing the ground of the motions in the world;[12] and the relation of the latter to it as their cause, since it does not besides furnish me with anything belonging to the constitution of the thing which is cause, leaves its concept quite empty.   The reason of this is, that by predicates which only find their Object in the world of sense I can indeed proceed to the being of something which must contain their ground, but not to the determination of its concept as a supersensible being, which excludes all those predicates.   By the category of causality, then, if I determine it by the concept of a *first mover*, I do not in the very least cognise what God is. Perhaps, however, I shall have better success if I start from the order of the world, not merely to *think* its causality as that of a supreme *Understanding*, but to *cognise* it by means of this determination of the said concept; because here the troublesome condition of space and of extension disappears. At all events the great purposiveness in the world compels us to *think* a supreme cause of it, and to *think* its causality as that of an Understanding; but we are not therefore entitled to *ascribe* this to it.   (*E.g.* we think of the eternity of God as presence in all time, because we can form no other concept of mere being as a quantum, *i.e.* as duration; or we think of the Divine omnipresence as presence in all places, in

[11] As Dr. Stirling remarks (*Gifford Lectures*), in another context, it would almost seem as though it were a matter of disappointment to Kant that the sensible determination of God is *ex hypothesi* impossible.

[12] The conception of God as "the ground of the motions of the world" is surely an immense advance, philosophically, on the conception of Him as "first mover."   It is just by substituting the one for the other, and filling the term "ground" with sufficiently deep and rich content, that the weakness of the old cosmological argument can be transcended.   Cf. Professor Pringle-Pattison, *Man's Place in the Cosmos*, p. 235.   Cf. the Selection from Aquinas, *supra*, p. 23.

order to make comprehensible to ourselves His immediate
presence in things which are external to one another, without
daring to ascribe to God any of these determinations as
something cognised in Him.) If I determine the causality
of a man, in respect of certain products which are only
explicable by designed purposiveness, by thinking it as that
of Understanding, I need not stop here, but I can ascribe to
him this predicate as a well-known property, and cognise
him accordingly. For I know that intuitions are given to
the senses of men, and are brought by the Understanding
under a concept, and thus under a rule; that this concept
only contains the common characteristic (with omission of
the particular ones), and is thus discursive; and that the
rules for bringing given representations under a consciousness,
in general, are given by Understanding before those intuitions, etc. I therefore ascribe this property to man as a
property by means of which I *cognise* him. However, if I
wish to *think* a supersensible Being (God) as an intelligence,
this is not only permissible in a certain aspect of my employment of Reason—it is unavoidable; but to ascribe to Him
Understanding, and to flatter ourselves that we can *cognise*
Him by means of it as a property of His, is in no way
permissible. For I must omit all those conditions under
which alone I know an Understanding, and thus the
predicate which only serves for determining man cannot be
applied at all to a supersensible Object; and therefore by a
causality thus determined, I cannot cognise what God is.[13]

[13] If the objection to applying the categories (even the most adequate categories at our disposal) to the Divine existence means that
the sensible data to which alone the categories are applicable, are in
this case lacking, may not the same objection be levelled at the
ascription of self-conscious reason to our fellow-men? And if this
ascription is but an explanatory hypothesis which we accept as true,
because it enables us synthetically to interpret the facts, may we not,
by parity of reasoning, use the corresponding category to affirm a
Theistic interpretation of the world? That the mind inferred is *finite*

And so it is with all Categories, which can have no significance for cognition in a theoretical aspect, if they are not applied to objects of possible experience. However, according to the analogy of an Understanding, I can in a certain other aspect think a supersensible Being, without at the same time meaning thereby to cognise it theoretically, namely, if this determination of its causality concerns an effect in the world, which contains a design morally necessary, but unattainable by a sensible being. For then a cognition of God and of His Being (Theology) is possible by means of properties and determinations of His causality merely thought in Him according to analogy, which has all requisite reality in a practical reference, though *only in respect of this* (as moral). An Ethical Theology is therefore possible; for though morality can subsist without theology as regards its rule, it cannot do so as regards the final design which this proposes, unless Reason in respect of it is to be renounced. But a Theological Ethic (of pure Reason) is impossible; for laws which Reason itself does not give, and whose observance it does not bring about as a pure practical faculty, cannot be moral.[14]   In the same way, a Theological Physic would be a nonentity, for it would propose no laws of nature, but ordinances of a Highest Will; while, on the other hand, a physical (properly speaking, a physico-teleological) Theology can serve at least as a propædeutic to Theology proper, by giving occasion for the Idea of a final purpose, which nature cannot present by the observation of natural purposes, of which it offers abundant material. It thus makes felt the need of a Theology which shall determine the concept of

in the one case and *infinite* in the other, implies no essential difference of principle.   " All that the Design argument undertakes to prove is that mind lies at the basis of nature " (Bernard).

[14] That is, Ethics furnish Kant with his *punctum stans* ; he feels that he can use moral principles as presuppositions in Theology.   But he consistently declines to reverse the relation, and make theological principles the basis of Ethics.

God adequately for the highest practical use of Reason, but it cannot develop this and base it satisfactorily on its proofs.

References.—Dr. E. Caird, *The Critical Philosophy of Kant*, 2nd ed. 1889 ; Paulsen, *Immanuel Kant, His Life and Doctrine* (Eng. trans.) ; Dr. J. H. Stirling, *Philosophy and Theology* (Gifford Lectures) ; Pfleiderer, *The Philosophy of Religion*, vol. i. ; Adamson, *The Philosophy of Kant* ; Professor (Seth) Pringle-Pattison, *Scottish Philosophy*, and especially *Theism*, two lectures, 1897 ; Professor John Watson, *Kant and His English Critics*, and *The Philosophy of Kant explained* (1908) ; Dr. Abbott, Introduction to his edition of the *Ethics* ; Wallace's *Kant* in Blackwood's "Philosophical Classics " ; and the various histories of philosophy. More recent works are, C. C. J. Webb, *Kant's Philosophy of Religion* (1926), and F. E. England, *Kant's Conception of God* (1929). In the second edition of his *Commentary to Kant's Critique of Pure Reason* (1923), pp. 636–641, Professor Kemp Smith gives an account of Kant's discussion, in his *Opus Posthumum*, of the nature and validity of the Idea of God. He there writes that " Kant now rejects as being untenable, and as being illegitimately theoretical, the proof of God's existence upon which he has relied in the *Critique of Practical Reason*, namely, by reference to the *Summum Bonum.* . . . The whole tenor of his argument is towards substituting a proof of a more strictly moral character, all the emphasis being laid upon the direct relation in which the Idea of God stands to the moral imperative. . . . God is no longer viewed as a Being who must be postulated in order to make possible the coincidence of virtue with happiness. He speaks with the voice of the categorical imperative, and thereby reveals Himself in a direct manner." For Kant's use of terms, see Professor Royce's elaborate article, " Kant's Terminology," in Baldwin's *Dictionary of Philosophy* (1901).

An important series of idealistic writers on Theism have recurred to Kant after Hegel's great contribution. They include John and Edward Caird, T. H. Green, J. Illingworth, A. S. Pringle-Pattison, H. Jones, John Watson, Archbishop D'Arcy, C. C. J. Webb, G. Galloway, R. G. Collingwood.

VIII.

ROMANTICISM, OR RELIGION AS FEELING.

SCHLEIERMACHER (1768–1834).

FRIEDRICH Schleiermacher, whose influence in modern theology has been as creative as that of Kant in philosophy, furnishes a type of thought which may broadly be named mystico-romantic. In the *Addresses on Religion*, from which our extracts are taken, he stands forth as the prophet of the abiding value of religion, and we can see now that he was the herald of a new era in theology, offering many points of resemblance to the new poetical epoch inaugurated by Coleridge and Wordsworth in England. Faith had sunk to a very low ebb when those speeches were written. In the arid Deism of the Eighteenth Century religion had been reduced to a collection of rational doctrines about God and the world, while even in the impressive statement of Kant it had too much been identified with a mere aspect of morality, and that of an extremely rigorous, if lofty, type. The age needed to be recalled to the fact that religion is experience, to be enjoyed rather than explained, and with its home in man's emotional life. It was to such an audience, be it remembered, that those speeches were addressed. They were published for the first time in 1799, and a second edition, altered in many respects, appeared in 1806.

In this book Schleiermacher comes before us as the spokesman of Romanticism. That movement, in which eclectic and æsthetic elements were strangely mingled, owed its vogue chiefly to Goethe, and was a protest in every domain of life against the tyranny of abstract ideas and meagrely rational formulas. It sought to return to nature, to what is real and immediate, to feeling and fancy and impression. Accordingly, the misconceptions of religion with which Schleiermacher deals are mainly two—that which views it as consisting essentially in knowledge, and that which makes it purely a means to morality. The one was the sin of the Eighteenth Century, and was being perpetuated in a different form by the idealistic school of Schleiermacher's own day, especially by Schelling; the other was traceable to Kant. The historical importance of Schleiermacher's work, indeed, is in great measure due to the success with which he vindicated the independent reality of religion as distinct from knowledge and morals. Its seat, he argues passionately, is neither in reason, conscience, nor will; religion is feeling,—the feeling of absolute dependence. It is the immediate consciousness of all that is finite as existing in and through the Infinite, of all that is temporal as existing in and through the Eternal; it is to feel, amid all becoming and change, all action and suffering, that life is life only as it is in and through God. "Schleiermacher never abandoned the conviction that the innermost life of men must be lived in feeling, and that this, and this alone, can bring men into immediate relation to the Highest" (Höffding). His view has obvious affinities with both the mystic and the artistic temper. Indeed "the Universe" (in his first edition a favourite name for the object of the religious sentiment) is conceived as forming, by its endless multiplicity of finite manifestations, an internally harmonious work of art.

The second and third editions of the *Reden* betray a steady advance towards more definitely Theistic conclusions. Previously there had been a tendency to place Pantheism by the side of Theism, as a form of religious impressionism which can plead equal justification with the other. We are even told that the idea of God is irrelevant for religion, and that genuine faith can exist without it. But later this is changed. The distinction between God and our feeling of Him is drawn ever more sharply. It is made quite clear that "God" denotes, not "the Universe" (a term more and more discarded), but the transcendent unity which is the ground of the whole of things and of each separate existence. Nature and history are now construed as a Divine revelation. But while this is true, it cannot be denied that Schleiermacher always leant to the view that religious feeling has no primary concern with the nature of God; and some have argued, not without a colour of reason, that he never did more than approximate to a clear statement of the Divine personality.

We present here the most important parts of the *Second Address*, as given in the admirable rendering by Mr. Oman (*Schleiermacher on Religion : Speeches to its cultured despisers*, translated by the Rev. J. Oman, B.D. ; Kegan Paul, London, 1893). The subject of the address is religion, not, however, as a concrete or historical phenomenon, but rather in its universal essence. As thus defined, analysed, and expounded, it is only an abstraction, the generalised product of reflection Schleiermacher does not aim at describing religion exhaustively. He is rather bent on persuading his contemporaries, orthodox and rationalist alike, to visit with him the profound depths in the being of man where religion takes its rise, for when once its origin has been unveiled it will be impossible to think of it as other than an integral element in human life, indissolubly linked to all that is highest and noblest in experience. And therefore, for the time, such things as conduct, culture, and social environment are put aside. What Schleiermacher examines and reports upon is religion, so to speak, in movement—the definite, momentary, pious frame or experience as it arises in the soul of the religious individual, a purely inward and spiritual process, chiefly characterised by immediacy and passivity. Here he finds the moving force which produces and sustains religion as a human, social fact. For though primarily an individual thing, exhibiting an endless variety of forms and modes, religion is also a social affair, because a human affair, and communicates itself through contact and tradition.

The influence of Schleiermacher in religious philosophy rests upon the fact that he was the first to undertake a critical analysis of religion, in order to discover and to vindicate that in it which is originally and authentically derived from the inmost life of the human soul, and may therefore be distinguished from accretions which are derivate and secondary. And the problem at which he wrought ceaselessly, and which he has done more, perhaps, than any other modern thinker to solve, is that of mediating between experience and history, between the conscience of the individual and the conscience of the religious society of which he forms a part.

THE NATURE OF RELIGION.

. . . .

In order to make quite clear to you what is the original and characteristic possession of religion, it resigns at once all claims on anything that belongs either to science or morality. Whether it has been borrowed or bestowed, it is now returned. What then does your science of being, your natural science, all your theoretical philosophy, in so far as it has to do with the actual world, have for its aim? To know things, I suppose, as they really are; to show the peculiar relations by which each is what it is; to determine for each its place in the Whole, and to distinguish it rightly from all else; to present the whole real world in its mutually conditioned necessity; and to exhibit the oneness of all phenomena with their eternal laws. This is truly beautiful and excellent, and I am not disposed to depreciate. Rather, if this description of mine, so slightly sketched, does not suffice, I will grant the highest and most exhaustive you are able to give.

And yet, however high you go, though you pass from the laws to the Universal Lawgiver, in whom is the unity of all things; though you allege that nature cannot be comprehended without God, I would still maintain that religion has nothing to do with this knowledge, and that, quite apart from it, its nature can be known. Quantity of knowledge is not quantity of piety. Piety can gloriously display itself, both with originality and individuality, in those to whom this kind of knowledge is not original. They may only know it as everybody does, as isolated results known in connexion with other things. The pious man must, in a sense, be a wise man, but he will readily admit, even though you somewhat proudly look down upon him, that, in so far as he is pious, he does not hold his knowledge in the same way as you. Let me interpret in clear words what most pious persons only guess at and never know how to express. Were you to set God at the apex of your science as the foundation of all knowing as well as of all knowledge, they would accord praise and honour, but it would not be their way of having and knowing God. From their way, as they would readily grant, and as is easy enough to see, knowledge and science do not proceed.

It is true that religion is essentially contemplative. You would never call anyone pious who went about in impervious stupidity, whose sense is not open for the life of the world. But this contemplation is not turned, as your knowledge of nature is, to the existence of a finite thing, combined with and opposed to another finite thing.[1] It has not even, like your knowledge of God—if for once I might use an old expression—to do with the nature of the first cause, in itself and in its relation to every other cause and operation. The contemplation of the pious is the immediate consciousness of the universal existence of all finite things, in and through the Infinite, and of all temporal things in and through the Eternal.[2] Religion is to seek this and find it in all that lives and moves, in all growth and change, in all doing and suffering. It is to have life and to know life in immediate feeling, only as such an existence in the Infinite

[1] The single or finite thing stirs feeling or religious emotion, not *quâ* finite, but only in so far as it is a revelation of the Infinite.

[2] In the first edition the terms most commonly employed to denote the object of religion are such as "the Universe," "the Infinite," "the World-All." Here the close affinity between certain aspects of Schleiermacher's theory and Spinozism is obvious, for what he designates thus is simply Spinoza's *natura naturans*. But in the later texts, while these earlier terms do not wholly disappear, "God," "Godhead," and "the Divine" more and more take their place. For Schleiermacher had in the interval come to draw a growingly clear distinction between God and the totality of the world —God had become for him the highest unity whereby all things are constituted a whole,

and Eternal.[3] Where this is found religion is satisfied, where it hides itself there is for her unrest and anguish, extremity and death. Wherefore it is a life in the infinite nature of the Whole, in the One and in the All, in God, having and possessing all things in God, and God in all. Yet religion is not knowledge and science, either of the world or of God. Without being knowledge, it recognises knowledge and science. In itself it is an affection, a revelation of the Infinite in the finite, God being seen in it and it in God.

Similarly, what is the object of your ethics, of your science of action? [4] Does it not seek to distinguish precisely each part of human doing and producing, and at the same time to combine them into a whole, according to actual relations? But the pious man confesses that, as pious, he knows nothing about it. He does, indeed, contemplate human action, but it is not the kind of contemplation from which an ethical

[3] Schleiermacher's purpose in laying so marked a stress on the element of *immediacy* in religious feeling was to secure the independence of piety as distinct from science and morality. The question later thinkers have discussed is whether he has not made feeling so exclusively "immediate" as to shut religion up in the dungeon of subjectivity. Might it not be held that the life of feeling develops beyond itself, mediated by thought and action, and so returns to feeling again, but clarified and intensified by the process?

[4] Throughout this address Schleiermacher has in view the Kantian ethics as developed by Fichte. Kant had practically absorbed religion in morality by his definition of it—a definition meant to be exhaustive—as the recognition of all our duties as Divine commands. To Schleiermacher, on the other hand, the separate self-sufficiency of both piety and morality is an intense conviction. Piety is not a cause, it is a concomitant, of moral action; still, not only must every one who is religious be moral, but no one can be moral without being religious. The relations of piety and science are analogous. Religion is "an indispensable third" to science and moral action, and without it the spiritual nature of man is incomplete. Their common roots spring from the unity of the subject; while knowing, acting, and feeling correspond respectively to science, morals, and religion.

system takes its rise.   Only one thing he seeks out and detects, action from God, God's activity among men.   If your ethics are right, and his piety as well, he will not, it is true, acknowledge any action as excellent which is not embraced in your system.   But to know and to construct this system is your business, ye learned, not his.   If you will not believe, regard the case of women.   You ascribe to them religion, not only as an adornment, but you demand of them the finest feeling for distinguishing the things that excel : do you equally expect them to know your ethics as a science ?

It is the same, let me say at once, with action itself.   The artist fashions what is given him to fashion, by virtue of his special talent.   These talents are so different that the one he possesses another lacks ; unless someone, against heaven's will, would possess all.   But when anyone is praised to you as pious, you are not accustomed to ask which of these gifts dwell in him by virtue of his piety The citizen—taking the word in the sense of the ancients, not in its present meagre significance—regulates, leads, and influences in virtue of his morality.   But this is something different from piety.   Piety has also a passive side.   While morality always shows itself as manipulating, as self-controlling, piety appears as a surrender, a submission to be moved by the Whole that stands over against man.[5] Morality depends, therefore, entirely on the consciousness of freedom, within the sphere of which all that it produces

[5] This is an early adumbration of the theory, elaborated in Schleiermacher's great work on Systematic Theology, *Der christliche Glaube* (1821, § 4 ff.), that religion is at bottom the feeling of absolute dependence.   (It is perhaps in reaction from the exaggerated emphasis placed on this dependence, that we find Ritschl, Schleiermacher's greatest successor in constructive theology, laying so marked stress on the fact that religion confers on man true freedom.)   But as this later work or *Glaubenslehre* was dogmatic in character, while the *Reden* were essentially apologetic, it is not surprising that the expressions used in 1821 should be much more consistently Theistic.

falls. Piety, on the contrary, is not at all bound to this side of life. In the opposite sphere of necessity, where there is no properly individual action, it is quite as active. Wherefore the two are different. Piety does, indeed, linger with satisfaction on every action that is from God, and every activity that reveals the Infinite in the finite, and yet it is not itself this activity. Only by keeping quite outside the range both of science and of practice can it maintain its proper sphere and character. Only when piety takes its place alongside of science and practice, as a necessary, an indispensable third, as their natural counterpart, not less in worth and splendour than either, will the common field be altogether occupied, and human nature on this side complete.

But pray understand me fairly. I do not mean that one could exist without the other, that, for example, a man might have religion and be pious, and at the same time be immoral. That is impossible. But, in my opinion, it is just as impossible to be moral or scientific without being religious. But have I not said that religion can be had without science? Wherefore, I have myself begun the separation. But remember, I only said piety is not the measure of science. Just as one cannot truly be scientific without being pious, the pious man may not know at all, but he cannot know falsely.[6] His proper nature is not of that subordinate kind, which, according to the old adage that like is only known to like, knows nothing except semblance of reality.

His nature is reality which knows reality, and where it encounters nothing it does not suppose it sees something. And what a precious jewel of science, in my view, is ignorance, for those who are captive to semblance. If you have

[6] For, in so far as he is pious, he has no concern with the reciprocal relations of finite phenomena, but views each separate object as a partial representation of the infinite whole.

not learned it from my Speeches or discovered it for your selves, go and learn it from your Socrates. Grant me consistency at least. With ignorance your knowledge will ever be mixed, but the true and proper opposite of knowledge is presumption of knowledge. By piety this presumption is most certainly removed, for with it piety cannot exist.

Such a separation of knowledge and piety, and of action and piety, do not accuse me of making.[7] You are only ascribing to me, without my deserving it, your own view and the very confusion, as common as it is unavoidable, which it has been my chief endeavour to show you in the mirror of my Speech. Just because you do not acknowledge religion as the third, knowledge and action are so much apart that you can discover no unity, but believe that right knowing can be had without right acting, and *vice versâ*. I hold that it is only in contemplation that there is division. There, where it is necessary, you despise it, and instead transfer it to life, as if in life itself objects could be found independent one of the other. Consequently you have no living insight into any of these activities. Each is for you a part, a fragment. Because you do not deal with life in a living way, your conception bears the stamp of perishableness, and is altogether meagre. True science is complete vision; |

---

[7] Knowledge and action are divergent manifestations of consciousness; in the one case the object imposes itself on us, in the other we impose ourselves on the object. Their unity in one experience despite this difference Schleiermacher traces back to the fact that both spring from the original identity of the Ego and the world, the "mystic moment" in which sense and object are one, and out of which knowledge and action are born. This immediate unity of subjective and objective consciousness, however, is simply feeling in its primordial form. So that feeling is seen to be the higher and more comprehensive bond between knowledge and action, *i.e.* they are related to one another, not directly, but mediately, through their common relation to this basal experience of the subject. For a description of this "inmost sanctuary of life," see p. 267.

true practice is culture and art self-produced; true religion is sense and taste [8] for the infinite. To wish to have true science or true practice without religion, or to imagine it is possessed, is obstinate, arrogant delusion, and culpable error It issues from the unholy sense that would rather have a show of possession by cowardly purloining than have secure possession by demanding and waiting. What can man accomplish that is worth speaking of, either in life or in art, that does not arise in his own self from the influence of this sense for the Infinite? Without it, how can anyone wish to comprehend the world scientifically, or if, in some distinct talent, the knowledge is thrust upon him, how should he wish to exercise it? What is all science, if not the existence of things in you, in your reason? what is all art and culture if not your existence in the things to which you give measure, form, and order? And how can both come to life in you except in so far as there lives immediately in you the eternal unity of Reason and Nature, the universal existence of all finite things in the Infinite?

Wherefore, you will find every truly learned man devout and pious. Where you see science without religion, be sure it is transferred, learned up from another. It is sickly, if indeed it is not that empty appearance which serves neces-

[8] "Sense" (*Sinn*), or, as we should say, "inward sensibility," is the specific organ of religion, and may be viewed either as a faculty which *uses* intuition (*Anschauung*) and feeling (*Gefühl*) as its instruments, or as their combination. In regard to "taste" (*Geschmack*) the following explanation is given by Schleiermacher, in a note to the third edition : "Taste includes liking, as well as mere faculty, and it is by this liking, this desire to find not merely the finite thing, but to be conscious through it of the Infinite, that the pious person finds that the existence of the finite in the infinite is universal." This thought, that a love and desire for the Divine must pre-exist ere it will reveal itself to us, may perhaps be regarded as an element in Schleiermacher's system which receives fuller development in the Ritschlian doctrine of the value-judgments of religion. See Selection XV.

sity and is no knowledge at all. And what else do you take this deduction and weaving together of ideas to be, which neither live nor correspond to any living thing? Or in ethics, what else is this wretched uniformity that thinks it can grasp the highest human life in a single dead formula? The former arises because there is no fundamental feeling of that living nature which everywhere presents variety and individuality, and the latter because the sense fails to give infinity to the finite by determining its nature and boundaries only from the Infinite. Hence the dominion of the mere notion; hence the mechanical erections of your systems instead of an organic structure; hence the vain juggling with analytical formulas, in which, whether categorical or hypothetical, life will not be fettered. Science is not your calling, if you despise religion and fear to surrender yourself to reverence and aspiration for the primordial. Either science must become as low as your life, or it must be separated and stand alone, a division that precludes success. If man is not one with the Eternal, in the unity of intuition and feeling which is immediate, he remains, in the unity of consciousness which is derived, for ever apart.

What, then, shall become of the highest utterance of the speculation of our days, complete rounded idealism, if it do not again sink itself in this unity, if the humility of religion do not suggest to its pride another realism than that which it so boldly, and with such perfect right, subordinates to itself? It annihilates the Universe, while it seems to aim at constructing it. It would degrade it to a mere allegory, to a mere phantom of the one-sided limitation of its own empty consciousness. Offer with me reverently a tribute to the manes of the holy, rejected Spinoza. The high World-Spirit pervaded him; the Infinite was his beginning and his end; the Universe was his only and his everlasting love. In holy innocence and in deep humility he beheld himself mirrored in the eternal world, and perceived how he also was its most worthy mirror. He was full of religion, full of the Holy Spirit. Wherefore, he stands there alone and unequalled; master in his art, yet without disciples and without citizenship, sublime above the profane tribe.

Why should I need to show that the same applies to art? Because, from the same causes, you have here also a thousand phantoms, delusions, and mistakes. In place of all else I would point to another example which should be as well known to you all. I would point in silence—for pain that is new and deep has no words. It is that superb youth, who has too early fallen asleep, with whom everything his spirit touched became art. His whole contemplation of the world was forthwith a great poem. Though he had scarce more than struck the first chords, you must associate him with the most opulent poets, with those select spirits who are as profound as they are clear and vivacious. See in him the power of the enthusiasm and the caution of a pious spirit, and acknowledge that when the philosophers shall become religious and seek God like Spinoza, and the artists be pious and love Christ like Novalis, the great resurrection shall be celebrated for both worlds.

But, in order that you may understand what I mean by this unity and difference of religion, science, and art, we shall endeavour to descend into the inmost sanctuary of life. There, perhaps, we may find ourselves agreed. There alone you discover the original relation of intuition and feeling from which alone this identity and difference is to be understood.[9] But I must direct you to your own selves.

[9] This paragraph is supremely important for the understanding of Schleiermacher's terminology. The description he gives of the actual process through which the soul passes in a complete experience of religious feeling, is evidently modelled on what he supposes to take place at the awakening of human consciousness. In this "mysterious" and "indescribable" moment, the mind and the object, not yet being clearly differentiated, must be conceived as merged in each other. Out of this fusion of both there arise (1) a representation of the

You must apprehend a living movement. You must know how to listen to yourselves before your own consciousness. At least you must be able to reconstruct from your consciousness your own state. What you are to notice is the rise of your consciousness, and not to reflect upon something already there. Your thought can only embrace what is sundered. Wherefore, as soon as you have made any given definite activity of your soul an object of communication or of contemplation, you have already begun to separate. It is impossible, therefore, to adduce any definite example; for, as soon as anything is an example, what I wish to indicate is already past. Only the faintest trace of the original unity could then be shown. Such as it is, however, I will not despise it, as a preliminary.

Consider how you delineate an object. Is there not both a stimulation and a determination by the object, at one and the same time, which for one particular moment forms your existence? The more definite your image, the more, in this way, you become the object, and the more you lose yourselves. But just because you can trace the growing

object working on the mind, *i.e.* an _intuition_ ; (2) a change in the inner state of the subject, *i.e.* a _feeling_. Similarly, each religious act has as its basis a moment of immediate contact and fusion between the self and the Divine, out of which arise an *intuition* of the Divine as acting upon the self (through some particular object or event), and a consequent excitation of the inner life of the soul, or *feeling*. Of this feeling the Divine is the cause, but what is felt is the inner state of the subject. Schleiermacher's mysticism finds its most concentrated expression here. It ought to be noted that the psychological hypothesis just set forth has its roots in Schelling's Philosophy of Identity, which taught the essential oneness and homogeneity of spirit and nature. In the first edition "intuition" had rather predominated over "feeling" in importance; later, in order still more strongly to underline the radical distinction between philosophy and religion, Schleiermacher threw all the emphasis upon feeling, as the less intellectual of the two, and the better fitted to express the *immediacy* of piety.

preponderance of one side over the other, both must have been one and equal in the first, the original moment that has escaped you. Or sunk in yourselves, you find all that you formerly regarded as a disconnected manifold compacted now indivisibly into the one peculiar content of your being. Yet when you give heed, can you not see, as it disappears, the image of an object, from whose influence, from whose magical contact, this definite consciousness has proceeded? The more your own state sways you the paler and more unrecognisable your image becomes. The greater your emotion, the more you are absorbed in it, the more your whole nature is concerned to retain for the memory an imperishable trace of what is necessarily fleeting, to carry over to what you may engage in, its colour and impress, and so unite two moments into a duration, the less you observe the object that caused it. But just because it grows pale and vanishes, it must before have been nearer and clearer. Originally it must have been one and the same with your feeling. But, as was said, these are mere traces. Unless you will go back on the first beginning of this consciousness, you can scarcely understand them.

And suppose you cannot? Then say, weighing it quite generally and originally, what is every act of your life in itself and without distinction from other acts? What is it merely as act, as movement? Is it not the coming into being of something for itself, and at the same time in the Whole? It is an endeavour to return into the Whole, and to exist for oneself at the same time. These are the links from which the whole chain is made. Your whole life is such an existence for self in the Whole. How now are you in the Whole? By your senses. And how are you for yourselves? By the unity of your self-consciousness, which is given chiefly in the possibility of comparing the varying degrees of sensation. How both can only rise together, if both together fashion every act of life, is easy to see.

You become sense and the Whole becomes object. Sense and object mingle and unite, then each returns to its place, and the object rent from sense is a perception, and you rent from the object are, for yourselves, a feeling. It is this earlier moment I mean, which you always experience yet never experience. The phenomenon of your life is just the result of its constant departure and return. It is scarcely in time at all, so swiftly it passes; it can scarcely be described, so little does it properly exist. Would that I could hold it fast and refer to it your commonest as well as your highest activities.[10]

Did I venture to compare it, seeing I cannot describe it, I would say it is fleeting and transparent as the vapour which the dew breathes on blossom and fruit, it is bashful and tender as a maiden's kiss, it is holy and fruitful as a bridal embrace. Nor is it merely like, it is all this. It is the first contact of the universal life with an individual. It fills no time and fashions nothing palpable. It is the holy wedlock of the Universe with the incarnated Reason for a creative, productive embrace. It is immediate, raised above all error and misunderstanding. You lie directly on the bosom of the infinite world. In that moment you are its soul. Through one part of your nature you feel, as your own, all its powers and its endless life. In that moment it is your body; you pervade, as your own, its muscles and members, and your thinking and forecasting set its inmost nerves in motion. In this way every living, original movement in your life is first received. Among the rest it is the source of every religious emotion. But

---

[10] A vivid, almost passionate, description of an immediate experience of the Eternal. What Schleiermacher means is no ecstatic rapture, but the emotional consciousness of the Infinite as awakened through the finite, *i.e.* a warm and intimate awareness of an eternal essence and significance in all being and becoming around us. A classical passage for the mysticism of these *Addresses*,

it is not, as I said, even a moment. The incoming of
existence to us, by this immediate union, at once stops as
soon as it reaches consciousness. Either the intuition displays itself more vividly and clearly, like the figure of the
vanishing mistress to the eyes of her lover; or feeling issues
from your heart and overspreads your whole being, as the
blush of shame and love over the face of the maiden. At
length your consciousness is finally determined as one or
other, as intuition or feeling. Then, even though you have
not quite surrendered to this division and lost consciousness
of your life as a unity, there remains nothing but the
knowledge that they were originally one, that they issued
simultaneously from the fundamental relation of your nature.
Wherefore, it is in this sense true what an ancient sage
has taught you, that all knowledge is recollection.[11] It is
recollection of what is outside of all time, and is therefore
justly to be placed at the head of all temporal things.

And as it is with intuition and feeling on the one hand, so
it is with knowledge, which includes both, and with activity
on the other. Through the constant play and mutual
influence of these opposites, your life expands and has its
place in time. Both knowledge and activity are a desire
to be identified with the Universe through an object. If
the power of the objects preponderates; if, as intuition or
feeling, it enters and seeks to draw you into the circle of
their existence, it is always a knowledge. If the preponder-
ating power is on your side, so that you give the impress
and reflect yourselves in the objects, it is activity in the
narrower sense, external working. Yet it is only as you
are stimulated and determined that you can communicate
yourselves to things. In founding or establishing anything
in the world you are only giving back what that original

[11] An allusion to Plato's doctrine of ἀνάμνησις : cf. *Meno,* 82 ;
Phœdo, 73. See Wordsworth's "Ode," with prefatory note ; and
Tennyson's "The Two Voices."

act of fellowship has wrought in you, and similarly everything the world fashions in you must be by the same act.
One must mutually stimulate the other. Only in an interchange of knowing and activity can your life consist. A
peaceful existence, wherein one side did not stimulate the
other, would not be your life. It would be that from which
it first developed, and into which it will again disappear.

There then you have the three things about which my
Speech has so far turned—perception, feeling, and activity,
and you now understand what I mean when I say they
are not identical and yet are inseparable. Take what belongs
to each class and consider it by itself. You will find that
those moments in which you exercise power over things and
impress yourselves upon them, form what you call your
practical, or, in the narrower sense, your moral life; again
the contemplative moments, be they few or many, in which
things produce themselves in you as intuition, you will
doubtless call your scientific life. Now, can either series
alone form a human life? Would it not be death? If each
activity were not stimulated and renewed by the other,
would it not be self-consumed? Yet they are not identical.
If you would understand your life and speak comprehensibly
of it, they must be distinguished. As it stands with these
two in respect of one another, it must stand with the third
in respect of both. How then are you to name this third,
which is the series of feeling? What life will it form? The
religious as I think, and as you will not be able to deny,
when you have considered it more closely.

The chief point in my Speech is now uttered. This is
the peculiar sphere which I would assign to religion—the
whole of it, and nothing more. Unless you grant it, you
must either prefer the old confusion to clear analysis, or
produce something else, I know not what, new and quite
wonderful. Your feeling is piety, in so far as it expresses,
in the manner described, the being and life common to you

and to the All. Your feeling is piety in so far as it is the result of the operation of God in you by means of the operation of the world upon you. This series is not made up either of perceptions or of objects of perception, either of works or operations or of different spheres of operation, but purely of sensations and the influence of all that lives and moves around, which accompanies them and conditions them. These feelings are exclusively the elements of religion, and none are excluded. There is no sensation that is not pious,[12] except it indicate some diseased and impaired state of the life, the influence of which will not be confined to religion. Wherefore, it follows that ideas and principles are all foreign to religion.[13] This truth we here come upon for the second time. If ideas and principles are to be anything, they must belong to knowledge, which is a different department of life from religion.

.   .   .   .

RELIGION AND KNOWLEDGE.

From within, in their original, characteristic form, the emotions of piety must issue. They must be indubitably your own feelings, and not mere stale descriptions of the feelings of others, which could at best issue in a wretched imitation.

Now the religious ideas which form those systems can and

[12] By this is meant, as Schleiermacher explains in a note, that no natural and moral feeling, *e.g.* wedded love, can be inconsistent with piety.

[13] Here is raised in an acute form the question whether, if ideas are foreign to religion, there can be any real meaning in the words "religious *truth.*" Is it sufficient to reply, as Schleiermacher does, that religion as such must be rigidly distinguished from what merely belongs to it, but that while ideas are not in themselves an element in the religious act, they are yet required to propagate religion in other minds? See p. 129 n., and cf. James, *op. cit.* Lect. xviii.

18

ought to be nothing else than such a description, for religion cannot and will not originate in the pure impulse to know.[14] What we feel and are conscious of in religious emotions is not the nature of things, but their operation upon us. What you may know or believe about the nature of things is far beneath the sphere of religion. The Universe is ceaselessly active and at every moment is revealing itself to us. Every form it has produced, everything to which, from the fulness of its life, it has given a separate existence, every occurrence scattered from its fertile bosom is an operation of the Universe upon us. Now religion is to take up into our lives and to submit to be swayed by them, each of these influences and their consequent emotions, not by themselves but as a part of the Whole, not as limited and in opposition to other things, but as an exhibition of the Infinite in our life. Anything beyond this, any effort to penetrate into the nature and substance of things, is no longer religion, but seeks to be a science of some sort.

On the other hand, to take what are meant as descriptions of our feelings for a science of the object, in some way the revealed product of religion, or to regard it as science and religion at the same time, necessarily leads to mysticism [15] and vain mythology. For example, it was religion when the Ancients, abolishing the limitations of time and space, regarded every special form of life throughout the whole

[14] A protest against both the older Dogmatism and the newer intellectual Idealism. Ritschl also maintains the secondary and derivative place of knowledge in religion. For him religion springs, not from subjective feeling, but from the practical necessities of man ; the absolute worth of personality demands such a supernatural government of the world as shall preserve and develop personal life.

[15] The mysticism which Schleiermacher rejects is that which Harnack has defined as " rationalism applied to a sphere above reason." But that his own view is in another, and a true, sense mystical, we have seen above.

world as the work and as the kingdom of a being who in
this sphere was omnipresent and omnipotent, because one
peculiar way in which the Universe operates was present as
a definite feeling, and they described it after this fashion.
It was religion when they assigned a peculiar name and
built a temple to the god to whom they ascribed any helpful
occurrence whereby in an obvious, if accidental, way the
laws of the world were revealed, because they had comprehended something as a deed of the Universe, and after
their own fashion set forth its connexion and peculiar
character. It was religion when they rose above the rude
iron age, full of flaws and inequalities, and sought again the
golden age on Olympus in the joyous life of the gods,
because beyond all change and all apparent evil that results
only from the strife of finite forms, they felt the ever-stirring,
living and serene activity of the World and the World-Spirit.
But when they drew up marvellous and complex genealogies
of the gods, or when a later faith produced a long series of
emanations and procreations, it was not religion. Even
though these things may have their source in a religious
presentation of the relation of the human and the Divine, of
the imperfect and the perfect, they were, in themselves, vain
mythology, and, in respect of science, ruinous mysticism.
The sum total of religion is to feel that, in its highest unity,
all that moves us in feeling is one; to feel that aught single
and particular is only possible by means of this unity; to
feel, that is to say, that our being and living is a being and
living in and through God. But it is not necessary that the
Deity should be presented as also one distinct object. To
many this view is necessary, and to all it is welcome, yet it
is always hazardous and fruitful in difficulties. It is not easy
to avoid the appearance of making Him susceptible of suffering like other objects. It is only one way of characterising
God, and, from the difficulties of it, common speech will
probably never rid itself. But to treat this objective concep-

tion of God just as if it were a perception, as if apart from
His operation upon us through the world the existence of
God before the world, and outside of the world, though for
the world, were either by or in religion exhibited as science
is, so far as religion is concerned, vain mythology. What is
only a help for presentation is treated as a reality. It is
a misunderstanding very easily made, but it is quite outside
the peculiar territory of religion.[16]

From all this you will at once perceive how the question,
whether religion is a system or not, is to be treated. It
admits of an entire negative, and also of a direct affirmative,
in a way that perhaps you scarce expected. Religion is
certainly a system, if you mean that it is formed according
to an inward and necessary connexion. That the religious
sense of one person is moved in one way, and that of another
in another, is not pure accident, as if the emotions formed
no whole, as if any emotions might be caused in the same
individual by the same object. Whatever occurs anywhere,
whether among many or few, as a peculiar and distinct kind
of feeling is in itself complete, and by its nature necessary.
What you find as religious emotions among Turks or Indians,
cannot equally appear among Christians. The essential oneness of religiousness spreads itself out in a great variety of
provinces, and again, in each province it contracts itself, and
the narrower and smaller the province there is necessarily
more excluded as incompatible and more included as characteristic. Christianity, for example, is a whole in itself, but
so is any of the divisions that may at any time have appeared

[16] An interesting comparison with Spinoza may be suggested at
this point. For the earlier thinker, intellectual love of the Divine
Substance is in contrast to the imaginative representations of ordinary
religion. For Schleiermacher the highest region, not the lower, is
religion, though he strenuously denies that religion is to be called
knowledge. Hegel, with his contrast between the *Begriff* of the
philosopher and the *Vorstellung* of the plain man, sides rather with
Spinoza. Cf. p. 112 n.

in it, down to Protestantism and Catholicism in modern times. Finally, the piety of each individual, whereby he is rooted in the greater unity, is a whole by itself. It is a rounded whole, based on his peculiarity, on what you call his character, of which it forms one side. Religion thus fashions itself with endless variety, down even to the single personality.

Each form again is a whole, and capable of an endless number of characteristic manifestations. You would not have individuals issue from the Whole in a finite way, each being at a definite distance from the other, so that one might be determined, construed, and numbered from the others, and its characteristics be accurately determined in a conception? Were I to compare religion in this respect with anything it would be with music, which indeed is otherwise closely connected with it. Music is one great whole; it is a special, a self-contained revelation of the world. Yet the music of each people is a whole by itself, which again is divided into different characteristic forms, till we come to the genius and style of the individual. Each actual instance of this inner revelation in the individual contains all these unities. Yet while nothing is possible for a musician, except in and through the unity of the music of his people, and the unity of music generally, he presents it in the charm of sound with all the pleasure and joyousness of boundless caprice, according as his life stirs in him, and the world influences him. In the same way, despite the necessary elements in its structure, religion is, in its individual manifestations whereby it displays itself immediately in life, from nothing farther removed than from all semblance of compulsion or limitation. In life, the necessary element is taken up, taken up into freedom. Each emotion appears as the free self-determination of this very disposition, and mirrors one passing moment of the world.

.   .   .   .

RELIGION AND MORALITY.

Seers of the Infinite have ever been quiet souls. They abide alone with themselves and the Infinite, or if they do look around them, grudge to no one who understands the mighty word his own peculiar way. By means of this wide vision, this feeling of the Infinite, they are able to look beyond their own sphere. There is in religion such a capacity for unlimited many-sidedness in judgment and in contemplation, as is nowhere else to be found. I will not except even morality and philosophy, not at least so much of them as remains after religion is taken away. Let me appeal to your own experience. Does not every other object whereto man's thinking and striving are directed, draw around him a narrow circle, inside of which all this highest for him is enclosed, and outside of which all appears common and unworthy? The man who only thinks methodically, and acts from principle and design, and will accomplish this or that in the world, unavoidably circumscribes himself, and makes everything that does not forward him an object of antipathy. Only when the free impulse of seeing and of living is directed towards the Infinite and goes into the Infinite, is the mind set in unbounded liberty. Religion alone rescues it from the heavy fetters of opinion and desire. For it, all that is is necessary, all that can be is an indispensable image of the Infinite. In this respect it is all worthy of preservation and contemplation, however much, in other respects, and in itself, it is to be rejected. To a pious mind religion makes everything holy, even unholiness and commonness, whether he comprehends it or does not comprehend it, whether it is embraced in his system of thought or lies outside, whether it agrees with his peculiar mode of acting or disagrees. Religion is the natural and sworn foe of all narrow-mindedness and of all one-sidedness.

These charges, therefore, do not touch religion. They rest

upon the confusion between religion and that knowledge which belongs to theology. It is a knowledge, whatever be its value, and is to be always distinguished from religion. Just as inapplicable are the charges you have made in respect of action. Something of this I have already touched upon, but let us take a general glance at it in order to set it entirely aside, and to show you exactly what I mean. Two things must be carefully distinguished. In the first place, you charge religion with causing not infrequently in the social, civil, and moral life, improper, horrible, and even unnatural dealings. I will not demand proof that these actions have proceeded from pious men. I will grant it provisionally. But in the very utterance of your accusation, you separate religion and morality.[17] Do you mean then that religion is immorality, or a branch of it? Scarcely, for your war against it would then be of quite another sort, and you would have to make success in vanquishing religion a test of morality. With the exception of a few who have shown themselves almost mad in their mistaken zeal, you have not yet taken up this position. Or do you only mean that piety is different from morality, indifferent in respect of it, and capable therefore of accidentally becoming immoral? Piety and morality can be considered apart, and so far they are different. As I have already admitted and asserted, the one is based on feeling, the other on action. But how, from this opposition, do you come to make religion responsible for action? Would it not be more correct to say that such men were not moral enough, and had they been, they might have been quite as pious without harm? If you are seeking progress—as doubtless you are—where two faculties that should be equal have

---

[17] Schleiermacher's claim is that, while distinguishing religion and morality, he does not separate them. Their point of union, however, is to found, not by direct inspection, but indirectly by following each up into that "inner unity of life and being" which is the home of feeling, and from which moral action issues autonomously.

become unequal, it is not advisable to call back the one is advance. It would be better to urge forward the laggard.

Lest you should think I am merely quibbling, consider that religion by itself does not urge men to activity at all.[18] If you could imagine it implanted in man quite alone, it would produce neither these nor any other deeds. The man, according to what we have said, would not act, he would only feel. Wherefore, as you rightly complain, there have been many most religious men in whom the proper impulses to action have been wanting, and morality been too much in the background, who have retired from the world and have betaken themselves in solitude to idle contemplation. Religion, when isolated and morbid, is capable of such effects, but not of cruel and horrible deeds. In this way, your accusation can be turned into praise.

However different the actions you blame may be, they have this in common, that they all seem to issue immediately from one single impulse. Whether you call this special feeling religious or not, I am far from disagreeing with you when you so constantly blame it. Rather I praise you the more thorough and impartial you are. Blame also, I pray you, not only where the action appears bad, but still more where it has a good appearance. When action follows a single impulse, it falls into an undue dependence, and is far too much under the influence of the external objects that work upon this one emotion. Feeling, whatever it be about, if it is not dormant, is naturally violent. It is a commotion, a force to which action should not be subject and from which it should not proceed. Quiet and discretion, the whole impress of our

[18] An unqualified assertion of the quietistic nature of religion *per se*. We must connect this with Schleiermacher's early association with the Moravians, and the influence of the theology of the Brethren, as well as with his intense aversion to a utilitarian view of piety. Morality which stands in need of the props supplied by religion is no true morality, and to make religion the handmaid of morals is to degrade it.

nature should give action birth and character, and this is as much required in common life as in politics and art. But this divergence could only come because the agent did not make his piety sufficiently evident. Wherefore, it would rather appear that, if he had been more pious he would have acted more morally. The whole religious life consists of two elements, that man surrender himself to the Universe and allow himself to be influenced by the side of it that is turned towards him is one part, and that he transplant this contact which is one definite feeling, within, and take it up into the inner unity of his life and being, is the other. The religious life is nothing else than the constant renewal of this proceeding. When, therefore, anyone is stirred, in a definite way, by the World, is it his piety that straightway sets him to such working and acting as bear the traces of commotion and disturb the pure connexion of the moral life? Impossible. On the contrary, his piety invites him to enjoy what he has won, to absorb it, to combine it, to strip it of what is temporal and individual, that it may no more dwell in him as commotion, but be quiet, pure, and eternal. From this inner unity, action springs of its own accord, as a natural branch of life. As we agreed, activity is a reaction of feeling, but the sum of activity should only be a reaction of the sum of feeling, and single actions should depend on something quite different from momentary feeling. Only when each action is in its own connexion and in its proper place, and not when, dependently and slavishly, it corresponds to one emotion, does it exhibit, in a free and characteristic way, the whole inner unity of the spirit.

Consequently your charge does not touch religion. And, if you are speaking of a morbid state of it, you are speaking of what is quite general and is not in any way original to religion nor specially seated in it, and from which consequently nothing is to be concluded against religion in particular. Religion is, of course, finite, and therefore subject to imperfections; but it must be apparent to you that, in a healthy state, man cannot be represented as acting from religion or being driven to action by religion, but piety and morality form each a series by itself and are two different functions of one and the same life. But while man does nothing from religion, he should do everything with religion. Uninterruptedly, like a sacred music, the religious feelings should accompany his active life.

.   .   .   .

Nature the Vestibule of the Divine Temple.

We have now, I hope, firm ground beneath us. We have attached ourselves to that moment, which is never directly observed, but in which all the different phenomena of life fashion themselves together, as in the buds of some plants blossom and fruit are both enclosed.[19] When, therefore, we have asked where now among all it produces is religion chiefly to be sought, we have found only one right and consistent answer. Chiefly where the living contact of man with the world fashions itself as feeling. These feelings are the beautiful and sweet-scented flowers of religion, which, after the hidden activity opens, soon fall, but which the Divine growth ever anew produces from the fulness of life. A climate of paradise is thus created in which no penuriousness disturbs the development, and no rude surrounding injures the tender lights and fine texture of its flowers. To this I would now conduct you, your vision having been purified and prepared.

First of all,[20] then, follow me to outward nature, which

[19] The "mystical" moment in which sense and object are one; see note [9].

[20] All that is finite is a manifestation of the Infinite. But we can behold the Infinite more perfectly in certain forms of the finite than in others. Consequently, Schleiermacher now draws a series of concentric circles, each revealing the Infinite more adequately than the

is to many the first and only temple of the Godhead.[21] In virtue of its peculiar way of stirring the heart, it is held to be the inmost sanctuary of religion. At present, however, this outward nature, although it should be more, is little else than the outer court, for the view with which you next oppose me is utterly to be repudiated. The fear of the powers which rule in nature, which spare nothing, which threaten the life and works of man, is said to give the first feeling of the Infinite, or even to be the sole basis of religion. Surely in that case you must admit, that if piety came with fear it must go with fear.

·　　·　　·　　·　　·　　·　　·　　·

MAN MUST FIND GOD FIRST IN HIMSELF.

But is it so easy to find original in nature the love and resistance, the unity and peculiarity, whereby it is a Whole for us? Just because our sense tends in quite another direction, is there so little truly religious enjoyment of nature. The sense of the Whole must be first found, chiefly within our own minds, and from thence transferred to corporeal nature. Wherefore the spirit is for us not only the seat of religion but its nearest world. The Universe portrays itself in the inner life, and then the corporeal is comprehensible from the spiritual.[22] If the mind is to produce and sustain

last. These are—Nature, the Individual's inner life, Humanity, History, and, beyond all these, further forms of the Infinite's self-manifestation which religious presentiment (*Ahnung*) can dimly perceive. The "circles" are successively described in the brief extracts which follow.

[21] First Circle. The *sublime* rather than the *beautiful* in nature is regarded as of importance for religion. Anomalies in the course of the natural world are meant to suggest to us the existence of a higher law or system in which they disappear.

[22] Second Circle. Once more we come upon the principle that what is felt and contemplated in religion is the Infinite as individualised.

"In himself that man first finds God and in his own relation to the world around him. In his own mind he discovers a sense of The Whole and transfers it to Nature around him, so that he unifies nature and gives it a soul, yet not in man alone as a solitary individual but in love that his experience is fully realised. we find ourselves in others."

religion it must operate upon us as a world and as in a world.

Let me reveal a secret to you that lies almost hidden in one of the oldest sources of poetry and religion. As long as the first man was alone with himself and nature, the Deity ruled over him and addressed him in various ways; but he did not understand, and answered nothing. His paradise was beautiful, the stars shone down on him from a beautiful heaven, but there awoke in him no sense for the world. Even from within, this sense was not developed. Still his mind was stirred with longing for a world, and he collected the animal creation before him, if perhaps out of them a world might be formed. Then the Deity recognised that the world would be nothing, as long as man was alone. He created a helpmate for him. At length the deep-toned harmonies awoke in him, and the world fashioned itself before his eyes. In flesh of his flesh, and bone of his bone, he discovered humanity. In this first love he had a foretaste of all love's forms and tendencies—in humanity he found the world. From this moment he was capable of seeing and hearing the voice of the Deity, and even the most insolent transgression of His laws did not any more shut him out from intercourse with the Eternal Being.

The history of us all is related in this sacred legend. All is present in vain for those who set themselves alone. In order to receive the life of the World-Spirit, and have religion, man must first, in love, and through love, have found humanity.[23] Wherefore, humanity and religion are closely

In this *Address* Schleiermacher appears to take an ambiguous view of personality. It was, throughout, a characteristic of his thought to lay stress on individuality; accordingly, on the one hand, each self is regarded as an indispensable reflection of the Infinite. On the other hand, the conclusions on the subject of personal immortality arrived at in the final paragraphs are at best dubious.

[23] Third Circle. The life of the individual is incomplete without the wider world of society. Though Schleiermacher gave some

and indissolubly united. A longing for love, ever satisfied and ever again renewed, forthwith becomes religion. Each man embraces most warmly the person in whom the world mirrors itself for him most clearly and purely; he loves most tenderly the person who he believes combines all he lacks of a complete manhood. Similarly the pious feelings are most holy that express for him existence in the whole of humanity, whether as blessedness in attaining or of need in coming short.

Wherefore, to find the most glorious elements of religion, let us enter upon the territory where you are in your peculiar, your most loved home. Here your inner life had its birth, here you see the goal of all your striving and doing before your eyes, and here you feel the growth of your powers whereby you are evermore conducted towards it. Humanity itself is for you the true universe, and the rest is only added in so far as it is related to it or forms its surroundings. Even for me, this point of view suffices.

. . . .

INDIVIDUALITY.

From these wanderings through the whole territory of humanity, pious feeling returns, quickened and educated, into its own Ego, and there finds all the influences that had streamed upon it from the most distant regions. If, on returning with the consecration of intercourse with the world still fresh upon us, we give heed how it is with us in this feeling, we become conscious that our Ego vanishes, not only into smallness and insignificance, but into one-sidedness, insufficiency, and nothingness. What lies nearer to mortal man

prominence to the idea of the kingdom of God, to him the individual is primary, the society secondary. In particular, we miss from the *Reden* the thought that religion must view humanity as organised for a great moral end, to be realised in them and through them by God.

than unaffected humility ? . . . You not only find at times all
the manifold degrees of human powers within you, but when
self-love is quite submerged in sympathy, all the countless
mixture of human tendencies that you have ever seen in the
characters of others appears simply arrested impulses of your
own life.   There are moments when, despite all distinction of
sex, culture, or environment, you think, feel, and act as if you
were really this or that person.   In your own order, you have
actually passed through all those different forms.   You are a
compendium of humanity.   In a certain sense your single
nature embraces all human nature.[24]   Your Ego, being
multiplied and more clearly outlined, is in all its smallest and
swiftest changes immortalised in the manifestations of human
nature.   As soon as this is seen, you can love yourselves with
a pure and blameless love.   Humility, that never forsakes
you, has its counterpart in the feeling that the whole
of humanity lives and works in you.   Even contrition is
sweetened to joyful self-sufficiency.   This is the completion of
religion on this side.   It works its way back to the heart, and
there finds the Infinite.   The man in whom this is accomplished, is no more in need of a mediator for any sort of
intuition of humanity.   Rather he is himself a mediator for
many.

But there is not merely the swinging of feeling between the
world and the individual, in the present moment.   Except as
something going on, we cannot comprehend what affects us,
and we cannot comprehend ourselves, except as thus pro-
gressively affected.   Wherefore, as feeling persons, we are
ever driven back into the past.   The spirit furnishes the chief
nourishment for our piety, and history immediately and

[24] The importance which Schleiermacher attached to individuality
is seen in this emphatic passage.   This is a subject which received
still further attention in his ethics, in which he argues that each
person acquires moral value only in so far as he expresses human
nature with independence and idiosyncrasy.

especially is for religion the richest source.[25] History is
not of value for religion because it hastens or controls in any
way the progress of humanity in its development, but because
it is the greatest and most general revelation of the deepest
and holiest. In this sense, however, religion begins and ends
with history. Prophecy and history are for religion the same
and indistinguishable, and all true history has at first had a
religious purpose, and has taken its departure from religious
ideas.

What is finest and tenderest in history, moreover, cannot
be communicated scientifically, but can only be comprehended
in the feeling of a religious disposition. The religious mind
recognises the transmigration of spirits and souls, which to
others is but graceful fiction, as, in more than one sense, a
wonderful arrangement of the Universe for comparing the
different periods of humanity according to a sure standard.

RELIGION AS THE SENSE OF THE INFINITE.

Some prominent emotions of religion connected with nature
and humanity, I have now sketched in vague outline. I have
brought you to the limits of your horizon. Here is the end
and summit of religion for all to whom humanity is the whole
world. But consider that in your feeling there is something
that despises these bounds, something in virtue of which you
cannot stay where you are. Beyond this point only infinity
is to be looked into. I will not speak of the presentiments
which define themselves and become thoughts which might
by subtilty be established, that humanity, being capable of
motion and cultivation, being not only differently manifested
in the individual, but here and there really being different,

[25] Fourth Circle. Humanity must be viewed not only as it is, but
in its process of becoming; and this is History. The stamp of
Romantic influence on this passage is plain.

cannot possibly be the highest, the sole manifestation of the unity of spirit and matter. As the individual is only one form of humanity, so humanity may be only one form of this unity. Beside it many other similar forms may exist, bounding it and standing over against it.[26] But in our own feeling we all find something similar. The dependence of our earth, and therefore of the highest unity it has produced, upon other worlds, has been impressed upon us both by nature and by education. Hence this ever active but seldom understood presentiment of some other marriage of spirit and matter, visible and finite, but above humanity, higher and closer and productive of more beautiful forms.[27] But any sketch that could be drawn would be too definite. Any echo of the feeling could only be fleeting and vague. Hence it is exposed to misconception, and is so often taken for folly and superstition.

This is sufficient reference to a thing so immeasurably far from you. More would be incomprehensible. Had you only the religion that you could have! Were you but conscious of what you already have! Were you to consider the few

[26] In these words, it has very plausibly been argued, Schleiermacher is suggesting, or at least playing with, the idea that there may be some truth in the instinct which pleads that mankind cannot be the sole, or the highest, form of spiritual existence with which the boundless material universe is peopled. May not, he seems to ask, the angels and world-spirits of which the history of religion is so full, be but stages on the way to the Infinite, ever more perfect forms of the union of the Infinite and the finite? (Cf. Aquinas, p. 16.) In his *Glaubenslehre* (§ 43) his final conclusion on the subject of angels is stated thus: "The one doctrine we can formulate regarding angels is that the question whether they exist ought not to have any influence on our action, and that revelations of their existence are no longer to be looked for."

[27] Otto (the son of Albrecht) Ritschl thinks that there is a veiled reference in these words to the Person of Christ. What Schleiermacher appears to have in his mind, however, is not a single figure, but rather a multiplicity of possible examples.

religious opinions and feelings that I have so slightly
sketched, you would be very far from finding them all
strange to you. Something of the same kind you must have
had in your thoughts before. But I do not know whether to
lack religion quite, or not to understand it, is the greater
misfortune. In the latter case also it fails of its purpose, and
you impose upon yourselves in addition.

Two things I would specially blame in you. Some things
you select and stamp as exclusively religious, other things
you withdraw from religion as exclusively moral. Both you
apparently do on the same ground. Religion with you is
the retribution which alights on all who resist the Spirit
of the Whole, it is the hatred everywhere active against
haughtiness and audacity, the steady advance of all human
things to one goal.[28] You are conscious of the feeling that
points to this unfailing progress. After it has been purified
from all abuses, you would willingly see it sustained and extended. But you will then have it that this is exclusively
religion, and you would exclude other feelings that take their rise
from the same operation of the mind in exactly the same way.

How have you come to this torn off fragment? I will tell
you. You do not regard it as religion but as an echo of
moral action, and you simply wish to foist the name upon it
in order to give religion the last blow. What we have agreed
to acknowledge as religion does not arise exclusively in the
moral sphere, not at least in the narrow sense in which you
understand the word. Feeling knows nothing of such a
limited predilection. If I direct you specially to the sphere
of the spirit and to history, it does not follow that the moral
world is religion's Universe. In your narrow sense of it the
moral world would produce very few religious emotions. The
pious man can detect the operation of the World-Spirit in
all that belongs to human activity, in play and earnest, in

[28] *I.e.* you recognise the presence in history of an eternal and
purposive government of all human things.

19

smallest things and in greatest. Everywhere he perceives enough to move him by the presence of this Spirit, and without this influence nothing is his own. Therein he finds a Divine Nemesis that those who, being predominantly ethical or rather legal, would, by selecting from religion only the elements suited to this purpose, make of it an insignificant appendage to morals, do yet, purify religion as they may, irrecoverably corrupt their moral doctrine itself and sow in it the seed of new errors. When anyone succumbs in moral action, it sounds well to say it is the will of the Eternal, and that what does not succeed through us will sometime, by others, come to pass. But if this high assurance belonged to moral action, moral action would be dependent on the degree of receptivity for this assurance in each person at any moment. Morality cannot include immediately aught of feeling without at once having its original power and purity disturbed.[29]

With all those feelings, love, humility, joy, and the others that I pictured as the undulation of the mind between the two points of which the world is one, and your Ego the other, you deal in another way. The ancients knew what was right. They called them all piety. For them those feelings were an essential part of religion, the noblest part. You also recognise them, but you try to persuade yourselves that they are an essential section of your moral action. You would justify these sentiments on moral principles, and assign them their place in your moral system. But in vain, for, if you remain true to yourselves, they will there neither be desired nor endured. If action proceed directly from the emotions of love or affection, it will be insecure and thoughtless. Moral action should not proceed from such a momentary influence of an outward object. Wherefore your doctrine of morals, when it is strict and pure, acknowledges no reverence except

[29] For otherwise the autonomy of the moral will would be invaded by the entrance of motives drawn from other sources than reverence for the right as such.

for its own law. Everything done from pity or gratitude it condemns as impure, almost as selfish.[30] It makes light of, almost despises, humility. If you talk of contrition, it speaks of lost time being needlessly increased. Your own feeling must assure you that the immediate object of all these sentiments is not action. They are spontaneous functions of your deepest and highest life, coming by themselves and ending by themselves. Why do you make such an ado, and begging for grace for them, where they have no right to be? Be content to consider them religion, and then you will not need to demand anything for them except their own sure rights, and you will not deceive yourselves with the baseless claims which you are disposed to make in their name. Return them to religion : the treasure belongs to it alone. As the possessor of it, religion is for morality and all else that is an object of human doing, not the handmaid, but an indispensable friend and sufficient advocate with humanity. This is the rank of religion, as the sum of all higher feelings.

That it alone removes man from one-sidedness and narrowness I have already indicated. Now I am in a position to be more definite. In all activity and working, be it moral or artistic, man must strive for mastery. But when man becomes quite absorbed, all mastery limits and chills, and makes one-sided and hard. The mind is directed chiefly to one point, and this one point cannot satisfy it. Can man, by advancing from one narrow work to another, really use his whole power? Will not the larger part be unused, and turn, in consequence, against himself and devour him? How many of you go to ruin because you are too great for yourselves? A superfluity of power and impulse that never issues

---

[30] This is the ethical rigorism of Kant in its severest form. Kant taught that an action is good only when done from a good motive, while this motive must never be derived from the sphere of natural inclination, but always and only from the good will itself ; that duty is duty only as done exclusively for duty's sake.

in any work, because there is no work adequate, drives you aimlessly about, and is your destruction.

To resist this evil would you have those who are too great for one object of human endeavour, unite them all—art, science, life, and any others you may know of? This would simply be your old desire to have humanity complete everywhere, your ever-recurring love of uniformity. But is it possible? Those objects, as soon as they are attended to separately, all alike strive to rouse and dominate the mind. Each tendency is directed to a work that should be completed, it has an ideal to be copied, a totality to be embraced. This rivalry of several objects of endeavour can only end by one expelling the others. Nay, even within this one sphere, the more eminent a mastery a man would attain, the more he must restrict himself. But if this pre-eminence entirely occupy him, and if he lives only to attain it, how shall he duly participate in the world, and how shall his life become a whole? Hence most virtuosos are one-sided and defective, or at least, outside of their own sphere, they sink into an inferior kind of life.

The only remedy is for each man, while he is definitely active in some one department, to allow himself, without definite activity, to be affected by the Infinite. In every species of religious feeling he will then become conscious of all that lies beyond the department which he directly cultivates. The Infinite is near to everyone, for whatever be the object you have chosen for your deliberate technical working, it does not demand much thought to advance from it to find the Universe. In it you discover the rest as precept, or inspiration, or revelation. The only way of acquiring what lies outside the direction of the mind we have selected, is to enjoy and comprehend it thus as a whole, not by will as art, but by instinct for the Universe as religion.

Even in the religious form these objects again fall into rivalry. This result of human imperfection causes religion to appear dismembered. Religion takes the form of some peculiar receptivity and taste for art, philosophy, or morality, and is consequently often mistaken. Oftener, I say, it appears thus than freed from all participation in one-sidedness, than completed, all-embracing. Yet this complete form of religion remains the highest, and it is only by it that, with satisfactory result, man sets alongside of the finite that he specially concentrates on, an Infinite; alongside of the contracting endeavour for something definite and complete, expansive soaring in the Whole and the Inexhaustible. In this way he restores the balance and harmony of his nature, which would be lost for ever, if, without at the same time having religion, he abandon himself to one object, were it the most beautiful, most splendid. A man's special calling is the melody of his life, and it remains a simple, meagre series of notes unless religion, with its endlessly rich variety, accompany it with all notes, and raise the simple song to a full-voiced glorious harmony.

If then this, that I trust I have indicated clearly enough for you all, is really the nature of religion, I have already answered the questions, Whence do those dogmas and doctrines come that many consider the essence of religion? Where do they properly belong? And how do they stand related to what is essential in religion? They are all the result of that contemplation of feeling, of that reflection and comparison, of which we have already spoken.[31] The con-

[31] This is the first indication of a view which came to possess ever greater prominence and influence in Schleiermacher's system. Doctrinal propositions, he holds, are not judgments about what is objectively known, but only descriptions of pious states of consciousness. Doctrines, accordingly, are not religion, but the secondary products of reflection upon religion. An application of this principle may be seen in the closing section of this *Address*, where he discusses the doctrines of God and immortality, and argues that they possess but a secondary and inferior value, since they belong to the sphere of ideas rather than to feeling and immediate consciousness.

ceptions that underlie these propositions are, like your
conceptions from experience, nothing but general expressions
for definite feelings.   They are not necessary for religion
itself, scarcely even for communicating religion, but reflection
requires and creates them.   Miracle, inspiration, revelation,
supernatural intimations, much piety can be had without the
need of any one of these conceptions.   But when feeling is
made the subject of reflection and comparison they are
absolutely unavoidable.   In this sense all these conceptions
do certainly belong to the sphere of religion, and indeed
belong without condition or the smallest limit to their
application.

.   .   .   .

The Personality of God and Immortality.

Remember, in the first place, that any feeling is not an
emotion of piety because in it a single object as such affects
us, but only in so far as in it and along with it, it affects us
as revelation of God.[32]   It is, therefore, not an individual or
finite thing, but God, in whom alone the particular thing is
one and all, that enters our life.   Nor do we stand over
against the World and in it at the same time by any one
faculty, but by our whole being.   The Divine in us, therefore,
is immediately affected and called forth by the feeling.   Seeing then that I have presented nothing but just this immediate and original existence of God in us through feeling,
how can anyone say that I have depicted a religion without
God?   Is not God the highest, the only unity?   Is it not
God alone before whom and in whom all particular things
disappear?   And if you see the world as a Whole, a Universe,

[32] Cf. note [1].   To interpret this passage rightly we must allow for
Schleiermacher's contention that religion is interested not so much in
the objective reality of God as in His subjective presence.   Pious
feeling, he sometimes seems to say, might almost be said to *be* God.

can you do it otherwise than in God? If not, how could you distinguish the highest existence, the original and eternal Being, from a temporal and derived individual? Otherwise than by the emotions produced in us by the world we do not claim to have God in our feeling, and consequently I have not said more of Him.

If you will not admit that this is to have God, and to be conscious of Him, I can neither teach nor direct you further. How much you may know I do not judge, for it does not at present concern me, but in respect of feeling and sentiment, you would be for me godless. Science, it is true, is extolled as giving an immediate knowledge about God, that is the source of all other knowledge : only we are not now speaking of science, but of religion. This way of knowing about God which most praise and which I also am to laud, is neither the idea of God as the undivided unity and source of all, that is placed by you at the head of all knowledge ; nor is it the feeling of God in the heart, of which we boast ourselves. It lags far behind the demands of science, and is for piety something quite subordinate. It is an idea compounded from characteristics, from what are called attributes of God. These attributes correspond to the different ways in which the unity of the individual and the Whole expresses itself in feeling. Hence I can only say of this idea, what I have said of ideas generally, in reference to religion, that there can be much piety without it, and that it is first formed when piety is made an object of contemplation.

Yet this idea of God, as it is usually conceived, is different from the other ideas before adduced ; for though it seeks to be the highest and to stand above all, God, being thought of as too like us, as a thinking and willing Person, is drawn down into the region of opposition. It therefore appears natural that the more like man God is conceived, the more easily another mode of presentation is set over against it. Hence we have an idea of the Highest Being, not as personally thinking and willing, but exalted above all personality, as the universal, productive, connecting necessity of all thought and existence.[33]

Nothing seems to me less fitting than for the adherents of the former view to charge with godlessness those who, in dread of this anthropomorphism, take refuge in the other, or for the adherents of this latter view to make the humanness of the idea of God a ground for charging the adherents of the former with idolatry, or for declaring their piety void.

It matters not what conceptions a man adheres to, he can still be pious.[34] His piety, the Divine in his feeling, may be better than his conception, and his desire to place the essence of piety in conception, only makes him misunderstand himself. Consider how narrow is the presentation of God in the one conception, and how dead and rigid in the other. Neither corresponds to its object, and thus cannot be a proof of piety, except in so far as it rests on something in the mind, of which it has come far short. Rightly understood, both present, at least, one element of feeling ; but, without feeling, neither is of any value. Many believe in and accept a God presented in conception, and yet are nothing less than pious ; and in no case is this conception the germ from which their piety could ever spring, for it has no life in itself. Neither conception is any sign of a perfect or of an imperfect religion, but perfection and imperfection depend upon the degree of cultivation of the religious sense. As I know of nothing more that could bring us to an understanding on this subject of conceptions, let us now go on to consider the development of the religious sense.

[33] On the possibility of a personal Absolute, see the argument of Lotze, Selection XII.

[34] In a later explanation Schleiermacher points out that his purpose here is to urge that as belief in the existence of a personal God does not necessarily connote real piety, so belief in an impersonal God does not necessarily exclude it.

As long as man's whole relation to the world has not arrived at clearness, this feeling is but a vague instinct, the world can appear to him nothing but a confused unity.[35] Nothing of its complexity is definitely distinguishable. It is to him a chaos, uniform in its confusion, without division, order, or law. Apart from what most immediately concerns the subsistence of man, he distinguishes nothing as individual except by arbitrarily cutting it off in time and space. Here you will find but few traces of any conceptions, and you will scarcely discern to which side they incline. You will not set much value on the difference, whether a blind fate, only to be indicated by magic rites, exhibits the character of the Whole, or a being, alive indeed, but without definite characteristics, an idol, a fetich, one, or, if many, only distinguishable by the arbitrarily appointed limits of their sphere.

As we advance the feeling becomes more conscious. Circumstances display themselves in their complexity and definiteness. The multiplicity of the heterogeneous elements and powers, by whose constant and determined strife phenomena are determined, becomes more prominent in man's consciousness of the world. In the same degree the result of the contemplation of this feeling changes. The opposite forms of the idea stand more distinctly apart. Blind fate changes into a higher necessity, in which, though unattainable and unsearchable, reason and connexion rest. Similarly, the idea of a personal God becomes higher, but at the same time divides and multiplies, each power and element becomes animate, and gods arise in endless number. They are now

---

[35] Man's religious sense of the Whole, we learn here, advances through the following stages :—the Infinite (of which the finite is the manifestation) is felt *first* as a confused chaos (Fetichism), *next* as an inharmonious multiplicity (Polytheism), and, *finally*, as a unity in variety, as system (Theism). How this feeling mirrors itself in idea or thought is another and a secondary question. On the historical order here stated, cf. p. 319 n.

distinguishable by means of the different objects of their activity, and different inclinations and dispositions. A stronger, fairer life of the Universe in feeling you must acknowledge is here exhibited. It is most beautiful when this new won complexity and this innate highest unity are most intimately bound together in feeling, as, for example, among the Greeks, whom you so justly revere. Both forms then unite in reflection, one being of more value for thought, the other for art; one showing more of the complexity, the other of the unity. But this stage, even without such a union, is more perfect than the former, especially if the idea of the Highest Being is placed rather in the eternal unattainable necessity than in single gods.

Let us now mount higher where opposing elements are again united, where existence, by exhibiting itself as totality, as unity in variety, as system, first deserves its name. Is not the man who perceives existence both as one and as all, who stands over against the Whole, and yet is one with it in feeling, to be accounted happier in his religion, let his feeling mirror itself in idea as it may? There as elsewhere, then, the manner in which the Deity is present to man in feeling is decisive of the worth of his religion, not the manner, always inadequate, in which it is copied in idea. Suppose there is someone arrived at this stage who rejects the idea of a personal God. I will not decide on the justice of the names you are accustomed to apply to him, whether Pantheist or Spinozist. This rejection of the idea of a personal Deity does not decide against the presence of the Deity in his feeling. The ground of such a rejection might be a humble consciousness of the limitation of personal existence, and particularly of personality joined to consciousness. He might stand as high above a worshipper of the twelve gods whom you would rightly name after Lucretius, as a pious person at that stage would be above an idolater.

But we have here the old confusion, the unmistakable sign

of defective culture. Those who are at the same stage, only not at the same point, are most strongly repudiated. The proper standard of religiousness, that which announces the stage to which a man has attained, is his sense for the Deity. But to which idea he will attach himself depends purely on what he requires it for, and whether his imagination chiefly inclines towards existence and nature or consciousness and thought.

You will not, I trust, consider it blasphemy or incongruity that such a matter should depend on the direction of the imagination.[36] By imagination I do not mean anything subordinate or confused, but the highest and most original faculty in man. All else in the human mind is simply reflection upon it, and is therefore dependent on it. Imagination in this sense is the free generation of thoughts, whereby you come to a conception of the world; such a conception you cannot receive from without, nor compound from inferences. From this conception you are then impressed with the feeling of omnipotence. The subsequent translation into thought depends on whether one is willing in the consciousness of his own weakness to be lost in the mysterious obscurity, or whether, first of all, seeking definiteness of thought, he cannot think of anything except under the one form given to us, that of consciousness or self-consciousness. Recoil from the obscurity of indefinite thought is the one tendency of the imagination, recoil from the appearance of contradiction in transferring the forms of the finite to the Infinite is the other.

Now, cannot the same inwardness of religion be combined with both? Would not a closer consideration show that the two ways of conceiving are not very wide apart? But the pantheistic idea is not to be thought of as death, and no effort

[36] Imagination means here not capricious fancy, but that ideal faculty in man which reaches out beyond the immediate datum of sense, and creates the object as a whole, furnishing us, *e.g.*, with the conception of the world as a unity.

is to be spared to surpass in thought the limits of the persona,
idea.

So much I have thought it necessary to say, not so much
in explanation of my own position, as to prevent you from
thinking that all are despisers of religion who will not accept
the personality of the Highest Being as it is usually set forth.
And I am quite convinced that what has been said will not
make the idea of the personality of God more uncertain for
anyone who truly has it; nor will anyone more easily rid
himself of the almost absolute necessity to acquire it, for
knowing whence this necessity comes. Among truly religious
men there have never been zealots, enthusiasts, or fanatics for
this idea. Even when timidity and hesitation about it is
called atheism, truly pious persons will leave it alone with
great tranquillity. Not to have the Deity immediately
present in one's feeling has always seemed to them more
irreligious. They would most unwillingly believe that anyone could in point of fact be quite without religion. They
believe that only those who are quite without feeling, and
whose nature has become brutish, can have no consciousness
of the God that is in us and in the world, and of the Divine
life and operation whereby all things consist. But whosoever
insists, it matters not how many excellent men he excludes,
that the highest piety consists in confessing that the Highest
Being thinks as a person and wills outside the world, cannot
be far travelled in the region of piety. Nay, the profoundest
words of the most zealous defenders of his own faith must
still be strange to him.

The number who would have something from this God,
that is alien to piety, is only too great. He is to give an
outward guarantee of their blessedness and incite them to
morality.[37] They want to have it before their eyes. They

[37] Schleiermacher has here in view the Kantian tenet that the
existence of God must be postulated in order to secure (even though it
be in a future life) the combination of virtue and happiness.

would not have God working on man by freedom, but in the
only way in which one free being can work on another, by
necessity, by making Himself known either by pain or by
pleasure. But this cannot incite us to morality. Every
external incitement is alien to morality, whether it be hope
or fear. To follow it where it concerns morality is unfree,
therefore unmoral. But the Highest Being, particularly
when he is thought of as free, cannot wish to make freedom
itself not free, and morality not moral.

This now brings me to the second point, to immortality.[38] I
cannot conceal that in the usual manner of treating this subject there is still more that seems to me inconsistent with the
nature of piety. I believe I have just shown you in what
way each one bears in himself an unchangeable and eternal
nature. If our feeling nowhere attaches itself to the individual, but if its content is our relation to God wherein all
that is individual and fleeting disappears, there can be nothing
fleeting in it, but all must be eternal. In the religious life
then we may well say we have already offered up and disposed of all that is mortal, and that we actually are enjoying
immortality. But the immortality that most men imagine
and their longing for it, seem to me irreligious, nay, quite
opposed to the spirit of piety. Dislike to the very aim of
religion is the ground of their wish to be immortal. Recall
how religion earnestly strives to expand the sharply cut outlines of personality. Gradually they are to be lost in the
Infinite that we, becoming conscious of the Universe, may as
much as possible be one with it. But men struggle against
this aim. They are anxious about their personality, and do
not wish to overstep the accustomed limit, or to be anything
else but a manifestation of it. The one opportunity that

---

[38] A later explanation informs us that what the author is discussing
here is whether the hope of immortality is so essential to a pious
direction of the mind that the two stand or fall together. Cf.
note [33].

death gives them of transcending it, they are very far from
wishing to embrace. On the contrary, they are concerned as
to how they are to carry it with them beyond this life, and
their utmost endeavour is for longer sight and better limbs.
But God speaks to them as it stands written, "Whosoever
loses his life for My sake, the same shall keep it ; and whosoever keeps it, the same shall lose it." The life that they
would keep is one that cannot be kept. If their concern is
with the eternity of their single person, why are they not as
anxious about what it has been as about what it is to be?
What does forwards avail when they cannot go backwards?
They desire an immortality that is no immortality. They are
not even capable of comprehending it, for who can endure the
effort to conceive an endless temporal existence? Thereby
they lose the immortality they could always have, and their
mortal life in addition, by thoughts that distress and torture
them in vain. Would they but attempt to surrender their
lives from love to God! Would they but strive to annihilate
their personality and to live in the One and in the All!
Whosoever has learned to be more than himself, knows that
he loses little when he loses himself. Only the man who
denying himself sinks himself in as much of the whole
Universe [39] as he can attain, and in whose soul a greater and
holier longing has arisen, has a right to the hopes that death
gives. With him alone it is really possible to hold further
converse about the endlessness to which, through death, we
infallibly soar.

This, then, is my view of these subjects. The usual conception of God as one single being outside of the world and
behind the world is not the beginning and the end of religion.
It is only one manner of expressing God, seldom entirely pure
and always inadequate. Such an idea may be formed from
mixed motives, from the need for such a being to console and

[39] A striking instance of the older pantheistic language which
Schleiermacher had gradually come to discard.

help, and such a God may be believed in without piety, at least in my sense, and I think in the true and right sense. If, however, this idea is formed, not arbitrarily, but somehow by the necessity of a man's way of thinking, if he needs it for the security of his piety, the imperfections of his idea will not cumber him nor contaminate his piety. Yet the true nature of religion is neither this idea nor any other, but immediate consciousness of the Deity as He is found in ourselves and in the world.[40] Similarly, the goal and the character of the religious life is not the immortality desired and believed in by many—or what their craving to be too wise about it would suggest—pretended to be believed in by many. It is not the immortality that is outside of time, behind it, or rather after it, and which still is in time. It is the immortality which we can now have in this temporal life; it is the problem in the solution of which we are for ever to be engaged. In the midst of finitude to be one with the Infinite and in every moment to be eternal is the immortality of religion.[41]

References.—The most useful English account of Schleiermacher's thought is probably to be found in Adams Brown's *The Essence of Christianity* (1902), chap. v., where a good bibliography is given. The student should not fail to read the admirable introduction which Dr. Oman has prefixed to his translation of the *Reden* ; it contains also a sketch of Schleiermacher's life. Cf. too the works by Pfleiderer,

---

[40] No better description of religion, as Schleiermacher conceived it, is to be found in the *Addresses.*

[41] It has already been said that the theological influence of Schleiermacher was epoch making. In the first place, he revived in theology the art of systematic thinking ; secondly, he drew firmly the distinction between religion and dogma, between piety and the theory of it, and to this distinction he was the first to give full effect in the construction of a system of doctrine ; thirdly, he insisted that religion is an *historical* phenomenon, and that apart from history its meaning cannot be understood. For the various schools of theological thought which trace their chief impulse to Schleiermacher, see Pfleiderer, *Development of Theology since Kant* ; Frank, *Geschichte der neueren Theologie* ; and Kattenbusch, *Von Schleiermacher zu Ritschl.*

Frank, and Kattenbusch, mentioned in the last note, and very specially Lichtenberger's *History of German Theology in the Nineteenth Century* (T. & T. Clark, 1889). For more detailed study of the *Reden*, see A. Ritschl, *Schleiermachers Reden über die Religion*; Lipsius, "Schleiermachers Reden" (in *Jahrbücher für prot. Theol.* 1875)—very important; Huber, *Die Entwicklung des Religionsbegriffs von Schleiermacher*; R. Otto's reprint of the first edition, with notes; Gaston Frommel, *Études de Théologie Moderne*; and Kirn's valuable article "Schleiermacher" in Hauck's *Realencyclopädie für protestantische Theologie und Kirche*; also E. Brunner, *Die Mystik und das Wort* (1924).

[The remainder of the page consists of handwritten marginal notes, partially legible:]

Comments:

Is it right to base religion on feeling? He does stress emotion at every point. Intuitive element in his feeling. Deeply moving awareness of infinite as ethical. Idea of conception now as he begins to describe them — yet starts the. Increasingly passes from Pantheism to Theism. Distinction doesn't matter. Isn't our "Experience" of something. Where is Obj. Truth? His personal attitude to you. Doesn't it boil down to psychological states. Discovery in plenary revelation, mere "na-yet" in the concreteness in plenary word of. place of sin.

Immediate self...

Ritschl made room for revelation.
Dislike of doctrine: exaltation of "Experience"
Speculation intellectualization of ethical movement.
A reaction against the emotional types of theology.
Barth never ceases to attack Ritschl as sublimation matter.
If we emphasize areas too much, pious people will rebel.
Interpretation of Religion p. 232.

Haikus:—
Is it true to say with the theories of Experience
that religious belief is consequent upon religious experience
Is it true to say with rationalism that religious experience is
consequent on a priori act of belief; the truth being rather
that the deepest of all religious experiences is just the experience
of believing.

IX.

GOD SEEN IN THE BEAUTIFUL.

Cousin (1792–1867).

An " argument " for Theism based on man's delight in the beauties of nature, and his sentiment of pure admiration for nobility of virtuous human deeds and characters, would seem to lie at hand parallel to the arguments from Truth and Goodness. Yet not only has its admission to an independent position been very rare, but recognition has been faint and hesitating even when rejection has been avoided, both among theologians and philosophers.[1] Meanwhile, many poets and artists have been religious in their own way, and a gulf has opened between philosophy and science, as representing knowledge and ethics on the one hand, and poetry and the arts as seeking the worship of the Beautiful on the other. If only Beauty could be established as co-ordinate with the True and the Good, it would seem as if there would not be much difficulty about the inference to Theism in the one case being as valid as in the others.

In illustration of this, the most effective reference would be to such poets and artists as have explicitly explained their religion. We were inclined to resort to Wordsworth as a poet in whom the love of Beauty was a potent factor for religion, and who gave close attention to the genesis and development of this sentiment in his own personal history. From the *Prelude*, where this autobiography is given, and from certain other poems, the " argument " could be exhibited copiously. But it is more congruous with our other selections to resort to a philosophical work, and we give the leading passages of the argument as set forth by Cousin.

[1] For some account of such treatment as is found in English writers, see Caldecott, *Philosophy of Religion*, p. 56 and pp. 187–196.

Victor Cousin's lectures at the Sorbonne formed a prominent feature in the philosophical teaching at the French Universities during the first half of the nineteenth century; Renan, for example, always acknowledged their influence on himself. They were chiefly critical and historical, his own views being what is known as eclectic,—selected from various systems. The most vigorous expression of them is in the volume entitled *Du Vrai, Du Beau, et Du Bien*, made up in 1853 from lectures actually delivered more than thirty years before.

In the section on *Le Beau*, Cousin is chiefly occupied in establishing the datum that Beauty is a specific quality of things and persons, giving rise to a specific sentiment in the beholder; from this he moves to the inference that there is a supreme Beauty which is an attribute of the Divine Being.

He commences with a reference to the history of the subject:—

It is the eighteenth century which has introduced, or rather has restored, to philosophy those researches on the Beautiful and on Art which were so familiar to Plato and Aristotle, but which had been slighted by the Schoolmen,[2] and had remained almost foreign to the great philosophers of the seventeenth century.

Of course, no one would look to the Empirical School for the revival of this noble branch of philosophy. Neither Locke nor Condillac allowed a single chapter for it, nay, not

---

[2] Cousin was familiar with the Schoolmen, and his epithet "slighted" is accurate. The recognition of Beauty was not wholly missing in the comprehensive mind of Aquinas, and what he says shows discernment, but he does not bring it to the front for Theism. The Beautiful and the Good, he says, are identical as to subject-matter, for both are founded upon Form, and therefore both receive our praise; but they differ in their reference: the Good is related to desire, that is good which we desire, and it moves us as a final cause; while the Beautiful is related to Knowledge,—*pulchra dicuntur quæ visa placent*,—and it moves as a formal cause (*S. Th.* pt. i. q. v. art. iv.). But even here he does not give it an article to itself, but is treating it in the article *De Bono*. And Thomists are not accustomed to bring it into separate evidence.

even a page. Their successors treated it with the same disdain ; since they did not find it easy to bring it under their
system, the most convenient course was to ignore it. It is
true that Diderot was enthusiastic for the Beautiful and
for its expression in Art, even to the possession of flashes of
genius in this direction; but in his head everything fermented
but nothing ripened, as Voltaire said. Hints upon it appear
in his writings,—ingenious enough, but often contradictory ;
and there are no principles, all is but transitory impression ;
he cannot make up his mind what the ideal is, he is satisfied
with a crude and affected naturalness such as we expect from
the author of *L'Interprétation de la nature*, the *Père de famille*,
the *Neveu de Rameau*, and *Jacques le Fataliste*. Diderot is
a materialist in art as he is in philosophy; he is of his
age and school, with a tincture of poetry, sensibility, and
imagination. It was worthy of the Scottish school, and
of Kant, that they both gave to the Beautiful a place
in their teaching.[3]

[3] In English philosophy Shaftesbury (d. 1713) was the great
exception to the contemners of Æsthetic ; in the Scottish School,
Hutcheson (d. 1746) made it prominent, and ensured for it respect
by the succeeding leaders of the School, Reid, Adam Smith, Stewart.
It was this side of philosophy that Burke chose for his mental refresh-
ment (*On the Sublime and Beautiful*). In Germany, Kant was led
by the place Æsthetic had won in the University curriculum to
endeavour to treat it on a level with Logic and Ethics, and devised
a Third Critique (of Judgment) accordingly. But the effect of his
treatment was too subjectivist to satisfy himself, and he widened
out that Critique into a consideration of Teleology in general (see the
Selection on Kant). Later, Hegel, Lotze, and von Hartmann made
important contributions. A living philosopher, B. Croce, has gone so
far as to make Æsthetic the principal feature of his philosophy. His
treatment is not easy to comprehend, and he has found no eminent
followers. But as he himself finds in his conception no springing
ground for Theism his procedure, interesting as it is, hardly contributes to the purpose of these selections. Quite directly to our
purpose, however, is the treatment of Æsthetic by Lord Balfour.
Besides sporadic treatment in various publications, Lord Balfour's

They studied it both in the mind and in nature, but they did not even approach the difficult question of its expression by human genius. We propose to treat the subject in its whole extent, and to offer at least an outline of a regular and complete theory of Beauty and of Art.

The Beautiful can be studied in two ways : either outside ourselves, *i.e.* in itself and in the objects, whatever they may be, which offer an image of it ; or else in the spirit of man, in the faculties which grasp it, in the ideas or the sentiments which it excites in us. Now the true method which should be familiar to you to-day is that of proceeding from the study of man to the study of things.[4] Our starting-point will therefore be a psychological analysis : we shall study the soul in presence of the Beautiful, and thence proceed to the consideration of the Beautiful in itself and in its objects.

The results of the inquiry as to the Datum are :

In the Soul.—Agreeableness of sensations is an accompaniment of the higher sentiment, but it is not indispensable, though disagreeableness must be absent. But the truly Beautiful has its source in Reason, it is of universal scope, and before it all men are in accord : it is ideal and absolute. As a sentiment it must not be confounded with desire, which implies deficiency. It is a specific sentiment, giving a pleasure of its own, austere in tone. It becomes a stimulus to the

Gifford Lectures (1914) treat of the Theistic bearing of the Beautiful side by side with that of Truth and the Good. He examines it especially by the light of Evolution in External Nature, in Morals, and in History, and asks whether survival-value can be regarded as completely accounting for it. His thesis is that "our only choice lies between a naturalistic and a theistic setting," and his decision is emphatic for Theism.

[4] The wording reminds us that our selection is from a course of lectures. Cousin was one of those who boldly carried rhetorical art into their academic teaching : his free employment of oratory extended his influence over circles far wider than his university classes, and contributed to the revival of a spiritualistic philosophy in French thought during the middle of the nineteenth century.

play of imagination, which, again, reacts on the sentiment. But it is imagination, under the control of Reason, which imposes upon it unity, harmony of parts, just proportion, measure, simplicity. Taste is the full appreciation of the Beautiful ; Art is Taste set in action. The kinds of Æsthetic sentiment are two : the Beautiful and the Sublime.[5]

In objects.—Utility gives no clue to Beauty. Adjustment of means to ends goes further, but is inadequate. Proportion is a condition of it, and must be present : order, and unity in variety, similarly. The kinds of objective Beauty are three : Physical, Intellectual, Moral. These culminate in Moral or Spiritual Beauty. Beyond all actual Beauty is the Beauty which is Ideal. He resumes :

All the forms of the Beautiful which we have enumerated and related to one another constitute what we designate actual Beauty. But beyond these is another order, Ideal Beauty.[6] The Ideal resides neither in the individual nor in a collection of individuals. Nature or experience provides the occasion of our conceiving it, yet Beauty is essentially a distinct thing. The man who has once conceived it finds

[5] The reader would do well to call into his service, before taking into account this aspect of mind and nature and its capacity for constituting a broad basis for Theism, other terms than the two which have been selected in treatises on Æsthetic. Some terms of a technical kind were required, and the *Beautiful* and the *Sublime* have passed into recognised use. But it is not meant that the varied richness of languages should be reduced to these, and in the religious reference we should resort to all the wealth which poetic diction offers to us. Æsthetic Theism ponders over the soul as it rejoices in God, is satisfied, marvels, is glad, gives honour, sings praises, delights daily in His name, walks in the light of His countenance. It thinks of the glory of the Lord, of the splendour of His majesty, of His fair beauty ; of His judgments as more to be desired than gold, as sweet, as loved exceedingly, as the soul's delight. We ought to spend a few moments with the Psalmists, and with, say, Milton, in order to be in a position to appreciate the spirit which animates those for whom the religious sentiment is, primarily, the adoration and the love of God.

[6] This is how Cousin states the Theistic inference, though his statement includes affirmation of ideality in the datum.

all natural figures, beautiful as they may be, only images of a Beauty which is not realised in them. Show me a noble action, and I will imagine an action more noble still. The Belvidere Apollo can be criticised in more points than one. The Ideal recedes as we approach it; its last term is in the Infinite, that is to say, in God; or to express it better still, the true and absolute Ideal is no other than God Himself.

As we have found God to be the principle of all things, He must be the principle of perfect Beauty, and consequently of all those natural forms of Beauty which express it with more or less of imperfection. He is the principle of the Beautiful, both as Author of the physical, and as Father of the intellectual and the moral worlds.

It is simply to be a slave of the senses and of appearances if a man stops at the movements, forms, sounds, and colours, which by their harmonious combinations produce the Beauty of the visible universe, and fails to conceive behind this scene, magnificent and well ordered as it is, the author of order, the Geometer, the Artist supreme.

The physically Beautiful serves as an envelope for the intellectually and morally Beautiful. The intellectually Beautiful, that splendour of the True, what else can be its principle, if not that which is the principle of all Truth? Moral Beauty, as we shall see farther on, comprises two distinct elements, equally but differently beautiful, Justice and Charity, respect for men and love of men. He who expresses in his conduct Justice and Charity accomplishes the noblest of works; the good man is in his way the greatest of Artists.

But what are we to say of Him who is the substance of Justice and the inexhaustible source of Love? If our nature is noble, what must be the nobility of the Author of our nature? His justice and His kindness are everywhere, within us and outside us. His justice is that moral order which no human law has made, but which all human laws strive to express, which persists and maintains itself in the world by its own force. When we look into ourselves our conscience attests the Divine justice in the peace and satisfaction which accompany virtue through all the troubles and distractions which are the inexorable penalties of vice and crime. How often and with what ever fresh eloquence we celebrate the untiring solicitude of Providence, its benefits everywhere evident in the most minute as in the most superficial phenomena of nature, easily forgotten by us only because of their very familiarity, but filling us in moments of reflection with admiration and gratitude, and proclaiming a surpassing Divinity, abounding in love for all His creatures.

Thus God is the principle of all the three orders of the Beautiful which we have distinguished—physical, intellectual, and moral.

Further, it is in God that the Beautiful and the Sublime, those great forms of the Beautiful which we have found spread abroad in all the three orders, combine. God is perfect Beauty: for what object can better satisfy all our faculties, Reason, Imagination, Sentiment? He presents to our Reason the most elevated Idea beyond which there is nothing, to our Imagination the most attractive Contemplation, to our Sentiment an object supremely lovely. He is therefore perfectly the Beautiful; but is He not also the perfect Sublime? If He extends the horizon of our thought, it is to confound us in the abyss of His magnificence. If the soul expands before the spectacle of His goodness, does it not at the same time feel awe when it thinks on His justice, as it stands before the soul with no less clearness than His goodness? God is both gentle and awful. At the same time that He is life, light, movement, and all the ineffable grace in visible and finite nature, He is also called the Eternal, Invisible, Infinite, Immeasurable, the absolute Unity and Being of beings. These august attributes, as certainly as the tender graces of Beauty, must produce in our soul in the very highest degree that sombre emotion we call the Sublime.　Yes, God is for us the type and the source of these two great forms, because He is also an enigma which we cannot penetrate, and yet the clearest key we can find to all other enigmas.　Beings finite as we are can grasp nothing which is free from limits, yet we can explain nothing without reference to that which is free from limits altogether.　By our own nature we have some idea of the infinite nature of God, by the void which is in us we lose ourselves in the being of God.　Thus forced to have recourse to Him in order to explain anything at all, and always driven back upon ourselves under the weight of His infinitude, we experience at times, or even in a single moment, for the Deity who at once raises us and overwhelms us, a sentiment irresistibly attracting us ; which yet also causes a stupor, not to say an insurmountable terror, which He alone can pacify because He alone is the unity of the Sublime and the Beautiful.[7]

[7] As examples of the refusal to allow Beauty to be conjoined with Duty as basis for Theism, we may take two great writers who were themselves endowed highly with the faculty of Taste:—

Martineau (*Types of Ethical Theory*, bk. i. branch i.) : "(In Greek ethics) the notion of Duty retreats into the background, and in its place they investigate the *Highest Good*, a more comprehensive object, including, along with Morality, Beauty also and Wisdom, a combination which, though fitted to dignify and adorn it (Morality), misses its peculiar and paramount *authority*, and changes it from a matter of universal obligation into the monopoly of philosophers."

Newman (*Grammar of Assent*, pt. i. chap. v. § 1) : "As we have naturally a sense of the beautiful and graceful in nature and Art, though tastes proverbially differ, so we have a sense of duty and obligation, whether we all associate it with the same actions in particular or not.　Here, however, Taste and Conscience part company ; for the sense of beautifulness, as indeed the Moral Sense, has no special relations to persons, but contemplates objects in themselves. . . . And, further, taste is its own evidence, appealing to nothing beyond its own sense of the beautiful or the ugly, and enjoying the specimens of the beautiful simply for their own sake ; but conscience does not repose on itself, but vaguely reaches forward to something beyond self, and

Thus the absolute Being who is at once absolute unity and absolute variety is necessarily the final reason, the primary foundation, the fulfilled ideal of all Beauty. In Him we have that Eternal Beauty of which Deotima had glimpses, and which she thus depicts to Socrates in the *Symposium* : [8]—

dimly discerns a sanction higher than self for its decisions, as is evidenced in that keen sense of obligation and responsibility which informs them. And hence it is that we are accustomed to speak of conscience as a voice, a term which we should never think of applying to the sense of the Beautiful."

[8] The insistence on τὸ καλόν permeates Plato's treatment of the Highest Good: in the *Republic* and *Phædo* it is very definitely marked ; in the *Symposium* it rises to its highest point in the discussion which is closed with the splendid passage here cited.

It is hardly fair to any writer to place any utterance in close proximity to this classical pæan in praise of the Beautiful. But lest it should appear that for appreciation of this aspect of Theism we have to resort either to the Greek or the French mind, we append three citations from a very different quarter, the great Calvinist divine, Jonathan Edwards (d. 1758). In his treatise on the *Religious Affections* (pt. iii. § 2) : "Men do not first see that God loves them and then see that He is lovely ; but they first see that God is lovely, and that Christ is excellent and glorious, and their hearts are captivated with this view, and the exercises of their love are wont from time to time to begin here ; and then, consequentially, they see God's love and favour to them. In the love of the true saint God is the lowest foundation." And "the first foundation of a true love for God is that whereby He is in Himself lovely or worthy to be loved, in the supreme loveliness of His nature. This is certainly what chiefly makes Him amiable. What chiefly makes a man or any creature lovely is his excellency ; and so what chiefly renders God lovely, and must undoubtedly be the chief ground of true love, is His excellency. God's nature or divinity is infinitely excellent ; yea, it is infinite beauty, brightness, and glory itself. But how can that be true love of this excellent and lovely nature, which is not built on the foundation of its true loveliness ? How can that be true love of beauty and brightness, which is not for beauty and brightness' sake ? " And " true saints have their minds, in the first place, inexpressibly pleased and delighted with the sweet ideas of the glorious and amiable nature

"Eternal Beauty, ungenerated and imperishable, exempt from decay as from increase, which is not beautiful in one point of view and unlovely in another, not beautiful only in fair weather, in certain places, in certain relations; not beautiful for some persons, but forbidding for others; Beauty which has neither sensible figure, nor countenance, nor hands, nor anything corporal; which is neither any particular thought nor any particular science; which resides in no being different from itself, whether animal, earth or sky, or any other thing; which is absolutely identical with itself and invariable, in which all other beautiful things participate, yet in such manner that their birth or their destruction bring to it neither diminution nor increase nor any mode of change. . . . To arrive at this Perfect Beauty, we must begin with the forms of beauty we see down here, and, with our eyes fixed on the Beauty Supreme, unceasingly raise ourselves as we pass, so to speak, through all the degrees of the scale, from a single beautiful bodily form to two such forms, from two to all the others, from beautiful bodily forms to beautiful sentiments, from beautiful sentiments to noble knowledge; until from knowledge to knowledge we arrive at a perfected knowledge, which has no other object than the Beautiful itself, and we end by knowing it in its own nature. O my dear Socrates, continued the stranger from Mantinea, it is the spectacle of the Eternal Beauty which alone can give value to this life of ours. . . . What would not be the destiny of a mortal to whom it might be given to contemplate Beauty without alloy in its purity and its simplicity, clothed no longer in human flesh and human colours, and all those perishable and vain charms; but per-

of the things of God. And this is the spring of all their delights and the cream of all their pleasures : it is the joy of their joy."

And it was a German contemporary, Winckelmann (d. 1768), who wrote : "I cast my eyes down before Beauty, as did those to whom the Highest appeared, believing that I saw the Highest in this vision."

mitted to see it in reality, in its own perfect form, Beauty Divine ! "

References.—Sully, in *Encyclopœdia Britannica,* eleventh edition ; Bosanquet, *History of Æsthetic* (1891) ; Croce, *Encyclopœdia Britannica,* fourteenth edition ; recent expositions and criticisms of Croce by J. A. Smith, Wildon Carr, Carritt, and Collingwood.

X.

RELIGION AS SOCIOLOGY.

AUGUSTE COMTE (1798–1857).

THE existence of National religions is so familiar a fact that the student of history feels some surprise when he finds how much of Theology is written with only the individual believer in immediate view. He finds the individual placed on a Bench of Judgment, and allowed plenary power of hearing and determining the cause, and deciding whether a man should be religious, and of what kind his religion should be. Knowing as historian the incalculable variations which distinguish individuals from one another, he is obliged to seek some presumption underlying the surface; this he finds in the supposition of an ideal manhood at the centre of each individual life, by virtue of which both thought and feeling and ethical principle enjoy supreme authority, and are presumably invariable in all men. This presumption he finds alike in the Theology which is Rationalist and that which is Ethical, and he finds that it underlies also a great part of the Theology of Christianity. But he is surprised, because the religions he has been studying present themselves rather as the outcome of tribal and national life and thought. They bear signs of complexity which suggest that their genesis is due to the operation of many minds carried on through many generations; and the sanction by which they operate upon individuals does not act directly within the individual's own convictions so much as through the influence of the tribe or nation to which he belongs. Explanations of religion, therefore, seem to him to move in some other region than that of interpretation of fact; they seek power to explain religion by carrying thought away into an ideal region. He is quite prepared, accordingly, when presently there appears an attempt to account for religion without rising into any ideal region at all; to treat it as a natural phenomenon explained adequately when it is adequately described. Such an attempt, inspired by the sense of the sufficiency of fact as seen in the nineteenth century, is sure to pay small regard to the individual, who as an isolated being is so very far from being a fact; and therefore the student of history finds it quite natural when presently the world is offered a theory of religion as the expression and product not of the individual at all, but of society. Such Sociological theories are now before the world; for these the best theory for an introductory study is, we think, that of Auguste Comte. There may be other thinkers who have included the Social factor, and have really a more profound or more accurate estimate of its character and its function; but Comte looms prominently as one who took his stand upon it, as he understood it, and made it the corner-stone of his system. Defective as his sociology may be, it is at least deep enough and wide enough to give us a platform from which we may survey the problem of Religion as a fabric constructed by mankind as a Society.

Before studying Comte's theory it must be noted that it is Sociological in two aspects : (1) Society is the *Subject* of religion : it is man in Society who believes and worships : it is mankind which produces religious beliefs, ceremonies, institutions ; and (2) it is Society which is also the *Object* of religion : it is mankind which is believed in and worshipped, which is the goal of action, and the supreme object both of thought and of veneration. We shall not be introducing an unjustifiable prejudice, we trust, in saying that it is in the first of these aspects that Comte's system is of permanent value to the philosophy of religion, as contributing a theory which has won a place among leading theories. In the second aspect his position amounts to a denial that religion is concerned with a something beyond and above the believing community, and therefore he might have been content to call it an Ethics or a Sociology rather than a Religion. How far his appeal to the Social *subject* carries with it his positivist restriction of the *object* of worship must be left to the judgment of students after seeing Comte's position stated by himself.

Comte's two principal works are his *Cours de Philosophie Positive* (1830–1842), and his *Système de Politique Positive* (1851–1854). In the latter, which we take as a fair development from the former (against the view of J. S. Mill and Harriet Martineau, but in agreement with Lewes, Harrison, and John Morley), he expounds his view of Social Order and Social Progress. The elements of Social Order (volume ii.) he takes to be Religion, Property, the Family, Language, Social organisation, and Social functions. He commences, therefore, with Religion as the primary element in Social Order. We print from Frederic Harrison's translation (Longmans' edition, 1875, out of print). The selected passages are from chapter i. pp. 7–22, 51–53, 53–56, 58–66.

THE GENERAL THEORY OF RELIGION; OR THE POSITIVE THEORY OF HUMAN UNITY.

Religion, originally Spontaneous, then Inspired, and afterwards Revealed, has at length found its ground in Demonstration. In its full maturity it must satisfy at once the feelings, the imagination, and the reason, as each of these was in turn the source of one of its three earlier forms. But over and above this it must govern directly the active powers of Man,—powers which neither Fetichism, nor even Polytheism, nor least of all Monotheism, could adequately control. Now that its ultimate requirements are ascertained, and its preliminary phases are completed, a sound general theory of Religion is possible, which could not begin so long as narrow views and exclusive sympathies prevailed. The aggregate of the history of the race supplies us now with materials amply sufficient for this task. For the three provisional systems of religion are so contrasted with each other, that the leading features they all contain in common will go to make up the ultimate system; whilst the law by which these systems have supplanted each other will give to that ultimate system its true characteristics. To this general Theory of Religion, therefore, the first chapter of this volume will be devoted; and thus our abstract study of the

social system will start with a systematic inquiry into
that institution, which forms the universal basis of all
society.[1]

In the first place, we must remedy the want of clearness
and precision which hangs over the term *Religion*. Very
careful thinkers are perpetually mixing up its essential purpose with its temporary means. Its main function, in fact,
is far from being determined; and Religion is referred at
one time to the feelings, at another to the intellect. Besides,
the constant use of this term in the plural number shows
that its primary meaning has never been exactly understood.

Throughout this treatise the term Religion will be used
to express that state of complete harmony peculiar to human
life, in its collective as well as in its individual form, when

[1] In these opening sentences we find the outline of Comte's psychology of religion, and of his history also. The psychology is, that
Feeling, Imagination, and Reason must all combine. The history is
guided by his famous " Law of the Three Stages," which he applies
to religion as to all other departments of life.

In the first stage (Theological) Feeling predominated, and imagination gave man Fetichism, then Polytheism, then Monotheism ; in the
second (Metaphysical) Reason came to the front, and, starting from
Monotheism, which was personal, set up abstractions, *e.g.* the Infinite,
Substance, First Cause; then came Comte's opportunity to relinquish
all these, and in the third Stage (Positive) to insist that the time had
come for seeing that facts and their connexions suffice for Religion as
for all the rest of Man's life. The "positive" is the actual, useful,
certain, precise, as opposed to the negative, vain, dubious, indefinite ;
it is also the relative as opposed to the absolute. In this stage he
claims that all the psychological factors operate in due proportion.
It should be remembered that Comte is not reproaching mankind
for the defects of the two earlier stages : he hopes that he is leading
thought forward. For criticism of this " Law," see especially
E. Caird's *Social Philosophy of Comte* ; and for a defence, Lévy Bruhl
(translated 1903). The other key to Comte's Philosophy is his
Classification of the Sciences, culminating in Sociology. See
note [6].

all the parts of Life are ordered in their natural relations to each other. This definition, which alone embraces equally all the different phases of Religion, applies equally to the heart and to the intellect, for both of these must concur to produce any true unity of life. Religion therefore gives a natural harmony to the soul exactly analogous to that which Health gives to the Body. The union of the moral and the physical nature is so close, and the relation which these two states hold to one another is so intimate, that we may regard the Harmony of the Soul as virtually embracing the health of the Body. Such a notion would be quite in accordance with the practice of the primitive theocracies, in which every direction respecting health was attributed to a religious sanction. The gradual separation of the two sets of rules, as to moral and physical health, was only a passing consequence of the natural dissolution which the ancient systems underwent. But since in the definitive System of Life the connexion of these two institutions will be much increased, it will be more appropriate for Religion in that system to assume this comprehensive authority over all life than it was in primitive times.[2]

This definition excludes the use of the plural; it makes it as impossible to speak of several religions as of several healths. In each case, moral or physical, there are only different degrees in the attainment of the true harmony. The natural development of the human race, like that of

[2] This is his definition. From this it is obviously idle to ask whether or not we have religion, or whether or not there is an object of religion; for in this sense religion is identical with what we have in our mind, and the object of religion is just what we find when all the factors of our mind are in operation; just that, and nothing more. Whatever Humanity ultimately thinks and feels *is* its religion; and conversely, whatever ultimate object of thought and feeling it discovers and venerates is the object of its religion. *La théorie générale de la religion se confond pour Auguste Comte avec la théorie positive de l'unité humaine.* (Brunetière.)

the entire animal series, exhibits as a whole a Harmony which grows more and more complete in proportion as it rises into the higher types. But the character of this unity remains always the same, in spite of all the irregularities through which it may actually be worked out.[3]

The sole distinction which must be constantly maintained is that which relates to the two different phases of our life, individual and collective. Although more and more closely connected, these two forms will never be united in one, and each implies a special quality in religion. To establish a state of complete unity, its task must consist both in *regulating* each personal life, no less than in *combining* different individual lives. Still, however important this distinction is, it must not affect the intimate relation which these two Functions of Religion bear to each other. The conception of their thorough agreement is the first general notion required by the Positive theory of Religion, which never could be reduced to system at all, if these two great ends of human existence did not coincide in fact.[4]

In truth, the natural convergence between them springs from the radical identity of the various elements of these two forms of life. The personal and the social life of man can only differ seriously, in extent or duration, or it may be in rate of speed, never in principle nor in object, and

[3] Religion, not Religions. This anticipates Comte's statement of National Religions as preparatory for the Universal religion, their obvious office while Nations occupied the scene in preparation for the unified Human race.

[4] To Comte it is fundamental that there is harmony between the welfare of the Individual and that of Society ; he refers this homogeneous character to the nature of man as essentially social. The term *Altruism* is Comte's own, as is *Sociology*. Those who are aware how difficult it is to get a new word into currency will see that the adoption of two leading terms in our present vocabulary indicates the extent of the influence which Comte has exercised. Comte said that he learnt his Altruism from Hume, Adam Smith, and Gall.

consequently not in means. This would be far from being the case with a race inherently unsocial in nature, in which the unity of the individual life and the harmony of collective life might require conditions very distinct and even opposed. Such is the case, in fact, with many of the carnivorous species, where the unity of the personal powers depends upon an habitual state of mere selfishness, as we had occasion to explain in the former volume. Man, on the other hand, more than any other of the social animals, tends more and more to realise a unity strictly unselfish, one, moreover, which is not so easy to attain as the unity of selfishness, but which is superior in completeness and also in permanence. In his instance, for we need now consider no other, to *regulate* and to *combine* invariably require conditions essentially the same.[5]

[5] In his zeal for Sociology, Comte made no separate sphere for Psychology—regarding the individual mind as not a phenomenon which gives rise to a Science ; and yet there are places where the Individual crops up somewhat awkwardly for him. In his attempt to regard religion as *regulating* the individual experience and as *combining* the individuals into a unity, he seems to be in confusion, for the individuals seem to have some independent status and value, and the total unity seems to be a combination of them. Wundt, for example, thinks that Comte did not get beyond the view of "the revolutionary moralists of the previous century, to whom Society was a sum of individuals governed by an authority which reconciles conflicting interests" (*Ethical Systems*, chap. iv.). But Sidgwick considered that Comte was more successful in suppressing all trouble from the part of Egoism (*History of Ethics*, p. 255). Höffding also takes Comte to have suppressed the individual both in politics and in religion (*History of Philosophy*, vol. ii.). Le Bon takes Comte as an instance of the Latin disdain of liberty in contrast with Spencer (*Psychologie de Socialisme*, tr. 1899). If we distinguish between Comte's intention and his accomplishment, we shall not be surprised to find the Individual making difficulties for him at times, especially as his later view of human nature is so highly charged with that individualistic phenomenon, Feeling. It is very difficult to read in any but an individualistic sense the paragraphs next following, where the combination of men is treated of, effected as it is by means of Veneration, Affection, Attach-

With respect to the intellect, this natural coincidence
between the individual and the social form of unity shows
itself especially when we consider that the differences
amongst individuals are not greater than those between the
successive states through which each mind passes under the
various conditions, external and internal, which affect it.
Every doctrine capable of thoroughly regulating any single
understanding becomes, thereby alone, capable of gradually
combining other minds. The number of these can only
affect the greater or less rapidity with which the agreement
is effected. This natural test has been the true source of
that innate confidence which different reformers in philosophy have felt in the ultimate ascendancy over mankind of
their own system,—a system invested with full sanction in
their own minds by virtue of this personal experience.
The firmness of their own convictions gave them positive
proof that their doctrines would find ultimate acceptance
amongst men.

But the agreement natural to these two functions of
religion, the individual and the social, is still more direct
and obvious in the sphere of Feeling than in that of Thought.
I have already shown in Biology how in all the races
capable of social life the predominance of those feelings
which combine several individuals is also the best adapted
to regulate each individual separately. The personal efficiency of every animal race, not adapted for social existence,
can, indeed, only result from a full and habitual subordination of the nature to some self-regarding instinct. Hence
moral harmony is with them ordinarily very imperfect and
very uncertain, owing to the natural antagonism between the
various selfish instincts, each of which requires imperatively

ment, Benevolence, and Love, of which the Individual is the seat. In
his later life Comte was inclining to lay more stress on the Individual;
as is seen in his devising an Ethics beyond Sociology, though he did
not live to work it out.

to be gratified. True control over all the affections, to be complete and at the same time permanent, can only be formed, and certainly can only be developed, by the uniform subordination of all these personal feelings to the feelings which relate to society. This is the ground on which such a harmony is possible in its full measure to man alone.

In the sphere of the activity the same connexion between combining and regulating is a consequence of that tendency to converge which we perceive both in the inclinations which determine our conduct and in the opinions which modify it. The activity of every social animal can only be maintained so long as it remains considerate towards others. With the races not capable of social life, action is always devoid of unity, and is too inconsistent to permit any real provision. It is only capable of control when the various instincts are concentrated into a single passion, and that is only possible in very inferior animals.[6]

[6] Man's place in the Cosmos is quite clear to Comte; he is the highest of beings; the human race and its welfare give the highest term in the Statical order of the Universe, the highest attainment of Progress. This is simply on the *positive* ground that we know of nothing beyond Mankind; that all else is fictional, and need no longer occupy attention. This position of Man in the hierarchy of being is expressed on the side of knowledge by Comte's order of the Sciences, which proceeds from Mathematics to Astronomy, thence to Physics, and onward to Chemistry, Biology, and Sociology.

In his later work Comte, finding that there is a lower and a higher range in Sociology, draws out Ethics and Religion, and sets them up as the ultimate spheres of knowledge. (For criticism of his scheme of the Sciences, with a counter-scheme, see Spencer's *Essays*; for preference for Comte's, Mill's *Comte and Positivism*; and Lévy Bruhl; and for further criticism, Professor K. Pearson, *Grammar of Science*.)

Comte is free from the trouble caused to some minds by the consideration that Man is a creature dwelling in a corner of space: the dimensions of the habitation do not for him affect the worth of the inhabitant.

Comte's Positivism is therefore not to be described by the term *Agnosticism* if we take "knowledge" as he means it; he is quite

Now that the intimate connexion between these two Functions of Religion has been established, we shall be free to employ in turn either one or the other to explain the unity of man. Their essential agreement is, no doubt, only fully developed under the final form of Positive Religion, towards which the highest members of the human family are gradually tending. During the transitional era of Theology one Function was supreme over the other, according as the prevalent belief was more or less social in its character. Polytheism was much more capable of combining than of regulating; whereas Monotheism only combined men so far as it succeeded in regulating their lives. Still these temporary differences only brought out in stronger light the natural agreement between the two functions of Religion; for each thus becomes the collateral support of the other.

This leading idea forms the starting-point of a general theory of Religion. It shows a natural agreement between the two permanent conditions which are equally characteristic of a state of harmony. It now becomes necessary to continue the task by one which is more difficult, and for which the ground is less prepared, namely, the examination of the two conditions, the one external, the other internal, the complete harmony of which alone makes it possible to regulate or to combine.

To constitute any true religious state there must be a concurrence of two primary elements; the one objective and essentially intellectual, the other subjective and essentially moral. Thus Religion exerts an influence at once over the understanding and the feelings, neither of which separately

satisfied with what knowledge can give, its object is positive and real in his sense. It is Agnostic to those who hold that Metaphysics and Theology carry us beyond the Natural Sciences. As to the term "Naturalism," the current use too often implies the absence of reference to Mind or Spirit: in that sense Positivism is quite in opposition to it.

would suffice to establish a true unity either for individual or collective life. On the one hand, it is requisite that our minds should conceive a Power without us, so superior to ourselves as to command the complete submission of our entire life. But, on the other hand, it is equally indispensable that our moral nature should be inspired within by one affection, capable of habitually combining all the rest. These two essential conditions naturally tend to work as one, since the sense of submission to a Power without necessarily seconds the discipline of the moral nature within; and this in turn prepares the way for the spirit of submission.

The extreme difficulty which the mental condition of modern times presents to unity leads us frequently to suppose it possible only in the field of morals. It is, no doubt, only in the moral nature that any agreement at all is consistently sustained in the midst of the prevailing anarchy. But the too obvious imperfection of this as a basis of Order, public or private, is a very good proof of the inherent weakness of this principle by itself, either to combine or to regulate.

Even if the nature of the human brain permitted, more completely than it does, the supremacy of the higher instincts, still their constant ascendancy would not establish any true unity within us, especially in the sphere of action, without an objective basis without us, which the intellect only can supply. So long as this belief in an external Power remains incomplete or unsteady, the loftiest emotions are no check against infinite extravagance and profound disagreement. What would be the consequence of supposing the life of man entirely independent of the external world? In this preposterous hypothesis not only would the activity of our race be at once deprived of any substantial object, but the benevolent emotions also would at the same time lose all character of consistency, and would ultimately be wasted in barren and aimless effusion.

In order, then, to regulate or to combine mankind, Religion must, in the first instance, place man under the influence of some external Power possessed of superiority so irresistible as to leave no sort of uncertainty about it. This great principle of social science is at bottom merely the full development of that primary notion of sound Biology—the necessary subordination of every Organism to the Environment in which it is placed. At the opening of the century this truth, of the close dependence of organism on environment, remained still completely misunderstood by the most eminent thinkers. Its gradual acceptance forms the principal advancement in science during our times, although till now it has not been viewed in a manner sufficiently systematic. For its right conception it should, in the first place, be confined to the Vegetative existence, the primary basis of all the higher types of life. Here it is impossible to mistake that the continued operation of the surrounding conditions is, in three ways, indispensable to every being—first, in furnishing the materials of food; secondly, in exciting the vital power; thirdly, in regulating its exercise. Now the same external influences apply alike to the strictly Animal life, in which the powers of sensation and motion are equally determined by the force without. Lastly, passing to the higher functions of man, we find them also equally dependent on the external world, either as supplying sustenance or stimulus, or as regulating the action of the brain. Thus man's Moral nature, besides that it rests upon the two lower functions of life, is, no less than they are, directly under the limitations of the world without. A sound theory of Biology thus furnishes the Positive theory of Religion with a foundation wholly unassailable, for it proves the general necessity for the constant supremacy of an external Power as a condition of unity for man, even in his individual life.

At the same time this reasoning drawn from Biology is

useful as proving that the moral conditions required by the
state of unity are of more importance than the intellectual.
In fact, the intellectual must be always more or less completely fulfilled in all races of animals capable of comprehending the first conditions of their life. For the unvarying
dependence of the being on its environment has nothing of
an accidental character about it, and does not admit at any
moment of the slightest doubt. This truth so completely
forms part of the life of every organism that it would
require a greater intellectual effort to reject it than to
acquiesce in it. Even in the human species the most
presumptuous dreamer could never seriously go so far as to
deny in direct terms a subjection to the World without, by
which his daily conduct is determined. On the other hand,
the moral conditions of true unity, though not less indispensable than the intellectual conditions, are such as are by
their very nature more liable to collapse. This moral
nature, indeed, is so little an essential element of living
beings as to be absolutely wanting in a great number of
races. Without doubt it is always found wherever there is
a capacity for social existence. But as collective life can
only be developed in a high form, in our own kind, it is
only in man that Religion can control the feelings in such a
way as to lead to real action. Yet the requisite intellectual
belief in a dominant Power may be distinctly seen in some
of the higher animals. Thus, though the importance of the
moral unity is not less than that of intellectual, it presents
greater difficulties to a scientific explanation, and none, in
fact, has been given by any school of theologians or meta-
physicians.

That we may understand this more clearly, let us for the
moment recall the point of view which more or less prevailed
until the very recent period when Biology sufficiently
established that the Benevolent Affections were a real part of
human nature. On that assumption moral unity could

only exist as the result of an egoistic principle. Now the
utter inefficiency of any such influence as a regulating
force has been sufficiently shown. The feeling of dependence on a Power without cannot really supply its place.
However deep this conviction may be, it inspires at most
an enforced resignation, if the Power without is one which
obviously offers an insuperable resistance. But this painful
moral condition is far removed from a true discipline of the
feelings, which must always be free, to possess real vitality.
The difference is seen at once when we compare the moral
condition of the dog in a domestic state with that of the lion
in captivity. Although long experience inspires the wild
brute with a passive sense of resignation, moral unity does
not exist within him. He gives way in turn to impotent
struggles and to ignoble torpor. On the other hand, the
moral life of the dog becomes direct and continuous the
moment that he has learnt to submit his egoistic cravings
to his sympathetic instincts. The contrast is yet clearer
between the ancient slave and the modern proletary.
Although in material matters both present a personal
existence, whether active or passive, nearly the same, the
liberty of the workman renders him alone capable of true
moral unity, for it permits free action to his benevolent
feelings. The bitterest circumstance of ancient slavery to all
the higher spirits must have been the impossibility of living
truly for others, all their tasks being compulsory, or at any
rate supposed to be so. It is, moreover, evident that an
habitual belief in a subjection to an external Power is far
from sufficing to establish unity in man, although it is indispensable for it to a certain degree. For when this sense
of dependence becomes too intense it prevents even the
discipline of the affections, which is the result of the spontaneous action of the altruistic instincts. The happiness and
the dignity of every animate being require, therefore, the
constant action and reaction of an acknowledged external

Power without, with free play for the Sympathetic Instincts within.

To complete our estimate of the second condition necessary to religion, its Moral unity, we must regard it as the principal means of establishing indispensable harmony with the first, or Intellectual unity. This is by its nature invariable, at least in all essential laws; and thus the mutual agreement between them must in the main be due to the moral element, which alone can dispose the being to voluntary submission. We have hitherto not properly distinguished submission from a degrading servility, for want of a sound moral theory. Of the three organs of the brain devoted to the altruistic instincts, as we have seen in the former volume, the religious sentiment depends principally on the intermediate one, that of *Veneration*. This is the disposition which accords best with feelings of devotion towards a superior Power. But beside the vital reaction of this intermediate organ upon the two extremes which surround it, these also must share directly, although in a less degree, in originating that composite feeling of which Religion is the product. In fact, to make submission complete, *Affection* must unite with respect; and this combination of feelings is, indeed, effected spontaneously by the sense of gratitude, which has its origin in the union of dependence and respect. This relation at first seems limited to the most special of the sympathetic instincts, that which we especially call *Attachment*. But it extends also to the highest organ of the altruistic feelings, that of universal *Benevolence*, on which the complete unity of the affections more especially depends. To this end it is enough that the same disposition be observed in the external Power, which by its superiority demands our submission. This similarity of feeling between the external Power and those subject to its influence has nothing of the fortuitous about it; it is a consequence of the thorough universality of the benefits conferred. This is such that no one of the various beings whose submission is supposed can claim them for itself exclusively. In the second place, the profound respect inspired by the Supreme Power awakens also a mutual sentiment of benevolence in all who join in devotion to the same great Object. This last characteristic again of the religious spirit leads us to comprehend a further attribute of the external Power. We must suppose in fact that the Supreme Power admits of a real attachment on our part, an idea which presumes in it a faculty by which its natural Goodness controls the exercise of its Authority. By this further condition of the religious state we get a more complete union between its two principal conditions : Conviction and Affection. This existed very thoroughly in the earliest form of human religion ; but in later forms the desire of satisfying this want tended to retard the establishment of the final phase of Unity, as will be hereafter explained.

Having thus completed our systematic analysis of the religious emotion we can better do justice to the sagacity, deep although empirical as it was, which in spite of the difficulty of his task guided the original author of the true theory of the brain. Gall, when his genius led him to suppose the organ of veneration to be the proper seat of the religious instincts, fell into important error only in that he regarded as simply moral a disposition which is in the same degree intellectual.[7] But this philosophical misconception, though not of great importance in Biology, leads in Sociology to immense aberration. By withdrawing attention from the objective base of human Unity, it renders any real history of the entire range of Religion impossible ; for it overlooks the

[7] The reference to Gall reminds us of Comte's weakness for Phrenology ; but this is, as Wundt says, only an "external" matter. Mill regarded it as Comte's substitute for the Introspection which, as used by French contemporaries at least, he rejected. Comte had no affinity for Materialism : behind neither of the two parallel series, physical and mental, was there any metaphysical substance.

unfailing source of all varieties in Religion, that is, that we are ever modifying our views respecting the order of the external World. The result is that this vicious assumption leads us to regard as Absolute, conceptions which are Relative by their very nature.

The religious state, therefore, has for its basis the permanent combination of two conditions equally essential—Love and Belief; these, though profoundly distinct, must conspire to one natural end. Each of them, beside that it is itself indispensable, adds to the other an element, without which its complete efficacy would not be exerted. Such is the instability of our cerebral organisation that Belief would not be perfect without Love, however high might be the degree of demonstration reached. But, conversely, the best heart would fail in due Love for any external Power, whose very existence admitted of continual doubt. And thus, whilst Love stimulates Conviction by overcoming pride, Conviction prepares the way for Love by counselling submission.[8]

These are, broadly, the respective parts which fall to the feelings and to the reason in that supreme task of human skill—the formation by a series of efforts, at first instinctive and then systematic, of some principle of Unity to govern the active life of man, individual or collective. Harmony in the moral sphere results from the subjection of the egoistic to the altruistic feelings; mental unity is derived from the predominance of an external Order over us. On the one hand, all our instincts are concentrated under one Affection, which alone can reduce them to order; on the other hand, all our

[8] The later stage in which Comte wrote the *Polity* is marked by its dominant reference to Feeling, which had been almost ignored in the *Philosophy* : in the development the great Positivist becomes almost a Mystic. In fact, Comte, Positivist as he was, showed a remarkable appreciation of true Mysticism : he says of the Mystics of the fourteenth and fifteenth centuries, "Their first empirical efforts prepared the way for the more comprehensive and systematic agency of Positivism.'

ideas group themselves round the contemplation of Force external to us. At the same time this Economy of external nature furnishes us with a direct guide to Action, which consists in accepting this order of nature with dignity, or in modifying it with wisdom. Our being is thus knit together, within and without, by a complete convergence both of the Feelings and of the Thoughts, towards that Supreme Power which controls our Acts. At that point there arises *Religion* in its true sense, that is, a complete unity, whereby all the motives of conduct within us are reduced to a common object, whilst our conduct as a whole submits with freedom to the Necessity imposed by a power without. The mere composition of this admirable word will henceforth serve to suggest the leading idea of this theory ; it recalls the fact of two states of unity in succession ; the first, the combination of the powers within ; the second, the connexion with the Force without. This is the issue in which terminates the grand dualism of positive Thought between the organism and its environment ; or rather between Man and the World ; or, better still, between Humanity and the Earth.

But in order to complete the fundamental conception of Unity, we must further suppose that the state of harmony requires for its maintenance the continuous union of the two principal elements, affective and speculative. Now, notwithstanding their natural affinity, the harmonious action of Thought and Feeling must often be disturbed by the tempests which arise in the complicated system of human existence, individual and collective. Sometimes this goes so far as to change for a time the natural state of coalition into one of antagonism more or less violent. This struggle between the Intellect and the Heart is the principal feature of all the great revolutions, whether in the individual or in society. The greatest of these revolutions is specially distinguished by that unmeasured anarchy, both mental and moral, which tortures the West of Europe, since the irrevocable collapse of the last provisional system. Thus the natural co-operation of Love with Faith does not affect a complete equilibrium, but a state of continuous movement, tending ever by the law of its action to a better union. The degree of completeness, to which by successive steps this combination of the elements of our nature may be brought, will be treated in this work as the chief measure of perfection attained by man. Human nature then, individual as well as collective, tends to grow more and more religious, however strange such a law may seem to our present ideas.

Having now sufficiently examined, first, the twofold Function of Religion, secondly, the two Conditions which united form its Basis, to complete the theory of Religion in the abstract, it remains to define the leading Elements of which it is composed.

The third branch of the inquiry into Religion, to analyse its Elements, has fewer difficulties than the second, to determine its Conditions; and follows from it. Since Religion deals at once with the Intellect and the Heart, it must always consist of an intellectual part and of a moral part. The former constitutes the *dogma*, properly so called, which explains the aggregate of that external Order to which our unity is necessarily subordinate. In accordance with the principle of classification by means of increasing dependence, this order of nature will require explanation, first by Cosmology, then by Biology, lastly by Sociology. The Supreme Power is thus sufficiently manifested by this ascending series of conceptions; and we proceed in due course from the first portion of Religion to the second, and follow the same cardinal rule of progression from the World Without to that Within.[9] The Intellect having been reduced to order, order must be established also in the Heart. From the reign of

[9] The object being the World, we have the advantage of the whole chain of the Sciences to tell us what the object is. Metaphysics Comte repudiates, of course.

Faith we pass to that of Love. Such, at least, is the chain of systematic reasoning by which Philosophy would constitute a final state of human unity, collective and social. Still in Society, as with each one of us, the ordinary and spontaneous course of development is the reverse. Naturally, we proceed from the internal to the external, from Love to Faith.

Without stopping to consider the difference between these, the objective and the subjective methods, we may note that the two essential portions of Religion remain always widely distinguished. The only proper subdivisions of Doctrine are due to the succession, both in logic and in science, of the three grand stages of Philosophy,—Cosmology, Biology, and Sociology. But indispensable though these be for purposes of classification, we must never lose sight of the fundamental Unity of the whole Economy of Nature, which Religion comprehends always as a whole. This is not the same with the moral part of Religion, in which the radical distinction between feelings and acts requires a separation of the component Elements.

Love must alike control Feelings and influence Acts. But these two direct duties of the governing Principle of life must not be confounded; since the former relates only to the internal, the latter relates also to the external World. In their widest extension these two functions furnish Religion, the first, with its *worship* properly speaking; the second, with its *government*, moral as well as political.[10] Viewing Religion as a whole, both are necessarily subordinate to the *doctrine* which supplies them at once with the conditions and the laws by which Worship must control the feelings and Government the conduct, private and public. Nevertheless in its turn Affection, with its twofold domain, reacts powerfully upon Conviction, with its single domain; and ever recalls Thought to the subjective end, which its objective spirit is constantly forgetting.

[10] Worship is the expression of Feeling: Government is the expression of ordered Activity.

Such, systematically viewed, are the constituent parts of Religion, which, undertaking to reduce human life to unity, brings within its sphere the three chief sides of our nature, Thought, Feeling, Action. In commencing with the first it is especially objective; the second is mainly subjective; the last partakes equally of both characters. This progression of ideas from the external to the internal serves as a crucial example of true scientific classification. The Doctrine thus forms the groundwork for the Worship, and the Worship for the Government. This, the natural arrangement of the three elements, shows the propriety of the universal rule that a religion must be characterised by its worship. The worship, which holds a middle place, is dependent on the doctrine, and instrumental to the government, and thus is entitled in principle to represent them both. Taking the worship and the government together, we have the true twofold division of Religion into the sphere of Faith and that of Love. Taking, on the other hand, the worship with the doctrine, we have another combination, that of the theoretic element and of the practical element. Although the latter analysis of Religion is in accordance with the custom of instruction, the former analysis is much more valuable for purposes of teaching. The principal practical distinction is due to the fact that human action, individual or collective, relates sometimes to our external condition; sometimes to our own physical, intellectual, or moral nature. Now this threefold internal sphere, the human, the necessary object of our highest activity, is the special field of Worship understood in its fullest sense. If we are to regard Religion as composed of two elements only, we must therefore take it as a combination of Worship and Government. The other combination of Worship with Doctrine has been mentioned only to bring out more clearly the natural fitness of the second element of Religion, the Worship, to represent both. But the analysis which I finally choose as the best to express the true series of parts, is that which makes Religion to consist of three essential elements, Doctrine, Worship, and Government. Thus Religion in its complete form resumes in itself the entirety of man's real existence, and is equally scientific, æsthetic, and practical. It thus combines in their sources the three great creations of man, Philosophy, Poetry, and Politics. This universal Synthesis begins by giving system to the study of the True; next it idealises the instinct for the Beautiful; and, finally, it realises the attainment of the Good.[11]

This completes the Theory of Religion in the abstract; its Functions, its Nature, and its component Elements having each been duly considered. But the great subject of Religion will hardly be sufficiently worked out, unless by an explanation of the general Character of the true unity. Taking the three orders of ideas together, we shall be in a position to show what is the synthetic method best adapted to attain the double End of religion, to supply its two primary Conditions, and to develop all its essential Elements. This task naturally forms the leading purpose of the present chapter, which will serve as a basis common to all subsequent inquiries into the problems of society. My preceding remarks are designed only to secure a systematic basis for this all-important construction.

The importance and the difficulty of this scientific demonstration appear more strongly when we see that even this would be insufficient without a justification from history. The true Religion could not have come into existence without a preparation of vast length, scarcely yet concluded even amongst the first of the nations. The principle which governs the final state of Synthesis would be but very imperfectly defined, unless we were to follow up our direct analysis of it, by a general sketch of the provisional phases,

[11] Here Comte sets himself in accord with the threefold analysis of the Object of Religion as the True, the Beautiful, and the Good. (Cf. the Selection from Cousin.)

22

which prepared the way for the complete attainment of Unity.

At first sight it might appear that this double method of inquiry trenches upon the subjects of the two volumes which are to succeed—one of which will embrace the actual course of the development of mankind, the other the true character of the final system. Further consideration, however, will show that this is quite in accordance with the regular connexion of the various branches of Sociology, as stated in the Introduction to this volume, and in the whole of the General View. What I am about to do is only to give special importance in this, the chief statical theory, to the law stated therein,—the law of constant subordination of the study of Progress to that of Order. The evolution of man can result only from the continuous development of the fundamental organism—Humanity, and this may be defined in the natural type, assumed, in the first instance, to be complete. Thus a statical treatment of the subject will serve as a universal basis for the dynamical explanation reserved for the third volume; wherein will be drawn out the necessary course of progress through which the human race had to pass in its path to Unity. The same is true of the relation of this volume to the concluding volume. In fact, the Future of mankind can only exhibit the state of Order most conformable to our nature, the germ of which was contained in the earliest state. This is therefore the place to consider the general Character of the final system; whilst my fourth volume will treat its ultimate expansion, upon the termination of my volume upon History, or its indispensable preparation.

This outline of the plan of this work will, I hope, show that the course adopted does not involve any real repetition. The method which I am here employing for Religion will be followed in the consideration of all the essential elements of the social system, such as the Family, Language, etc., the subjects of the following chapters.[12]   Each of these will be treated here with reference first to the general Elements of its fundamental constitution ; secondly, to the gradations necessary for its complete realisation.   The next two volumes will treat : the one the actual course which this Development has taken ; the other, the normal Type which that development will finally assume.   Thus the statical basis I now commence will facilitate the working out of both these subjects, though it will not render them superfluous.

This distinction in method is, lastly, to reduce it to system ; an illustration of the contrast between the concrete and the abstract which, far from being absolute, admits of various degrees.   In this volume each essential Element of the great organism is studied separately from the rest, first in its own nature, and then in its historical development.   On the other hand, in social Dynamics, the study will always be concerned with the whole of these different elements together, so as to show first their general evolution, and then their ultimate harmony.   Thus all the leading subjects of the social science will be treated first separately without references to time, secondly, in combination and in order of succession.   The treatise when complete will have considered Society, first as existing in space, then as existing in time, but so as not to involve the errors either of repetition or of anticipation. This great principle of logic applies to every case where statical study can be contrasted with the dynamical.   It bears a strong analogy to the relation drawn by Bichat between the primary theory of the Organism and the direct theory of Life.   The constant use of this method, which in subsequent chapters does not require to be justified, will give no serious difficulty to readers who are duly prepared.

[12] Here Religion is taken as parallel with Family and Language as Social phenomena.   Max Müller, Matthew Arnold, and Jowett were fond of using the genesis of Language as a parallel to the genesis of religion.

Abstract Anatomy, when treating of the vital properties of the various tissues and the evolution of each, is not encroaching on the proper sphere of Physiology, where the tissues are treated only as combined in organs properly so called.   In the same way, in social Statics the study in the abstract of the existence of each primary element, and its development as a whole, leaves to social Dynamics its special task, that of combining into a whole these varying conceptions, and thereby determining the character of the successive phases of Humanity.

.   .   .   .

Comte then proceeds to examine the Basis of Religion, the order within and without, Man and the World.   The study of the order of Nature occupies the Intellect of Man, and gives the Intellectual basis of religion : this awakens Emotion, or rather it fosters and directs what would spontaneously arise, and we have the Moral basis.

We pass now to a brief statement of how the conception of Humanity itself becomes the conception of the *object* of Religion.

The Positive Belief thus attains its true unity both objectively and subjectively by that which is only a necessary consequence of its own normal evolution.   The laws of thought in fact lead to the grouping of all the laws of nature round that aggregate Being which is the direct controller of man's destiny; submitting itself to the conditions to which it exists, but modifying them by its own wisdom.   When such a point is reached, this belief becomes thorough—in harmony with the affections ; for it directs towards this Great Being, whose property is sympathy, all the homage which is due to the beneficent control of the Order of nature.[13]   This Being, it is true, vast and relatively

[13] It is of the first importance to notice this. Comte uses the expression "Order of Nature"; and when we ask what this means to him, his answer is quite anthropocentric. All kinds of natural phenomena outside Human Nature are stages of being leading up to

eternal as it is, has not really created the materials which in its sagacious activity it employs, nor the laws by which its results are determined. But an absolute view of facts is still less natural to the feelings than it is to the mind. The Order of nature is certainly so imperfect that its benefits are only dispensed to us in an indirect way, by means of the loving ministry of that active and intelligent Being, but for whom our existence would be scarcely tolerable. Now this belief alone would justify us in offering the whole of our dutiful feelings of gratitude to Humanity; even although there did exist a still higher Providence, the source of all the powers of our common mother. The consensus of positive philosophy essentially excludes this last hypothesis. But, strictly speaking, this particular problem has become just as idle with respect to the Heart as it is for the Head; or rather it implies similar risks to both. Our true intellectual wants, both theoretical and practical, are satisfied by the simple understanding of the general Order of nature to which we have to submit, and which we are enabled to modify. If the authorship of it were indeed within the reach of our under-standings, we should still be right in abstaining from the search after its creation; for our duty is to reserve the whole force of our speculative powers for their true task, the perpetual improvement of our condition, and of our nature. It is the same with the moral question, and that in a still higher degree. Our gratitude, whether in our individual or collective capacity, for the benefits which we receive from the Order of nature, should be restricted to their immediate Author; and this is one whose existence and whose activity are constantly before our eyes. Thus regulated, our gratitude would inspire in us that high moral improvement which this tribute of duty involves. Even supposing that our general

Humanity, and placed more or less completely at the disposal of Humanity; so that it is frequently a convenient ellipsis to say the order of Man when we mean the whole order of Nature.

parent, Humanity, were to find in the Order of nature a
Providence still higher than its own, yet it would not belong
to us to offer up our worship to that Providence directly.
Nay, such a great violation of moral continuity, apart from
its manifest injustice, would prove at once contrary to the
main object of our worship, for it diverts us from the act of
direct adoration, which is alone thoroughly natural to our
emotional nature.   The intermediate religion which we see in
its decline, has shown only too distinctly how serious this
danger is, since the thanksgivings it addressed to an
imaginary Being for the most part were simply acts of
ingratitude towards Humanity, the only real author of the
benefits received.   In a word, our gratitude should be
awakened by productions, not by materials ; which latter have
hardly ever a value worthy of our praises.   Even in the
Order of realities it is of still greater importance to the heart
than it is to the intellect, that no essential intermediate
element in the series should be passed over.   It is even more
necessary to preserve our affections from working towards a
chimerical object than it is to preserve our thoughts, now
that their true object has become visible.   If the adoration
of imaginary powers was morally indispensable so long as the
true Great Being was unknown, now that its existence is
proved manifest, it would only serve to turn us from the one
Worship which is capable of improving us.   Those, therefore,
who strive to prolong it in our day are unconsciously turning
it against its legitimate purpose, which was to regulate for a
time the expansion of our higher feelings under the Regency
of God, during the long minority of Humanity.[14]

[14] Comte's grounds for taking Humanity as the object of Religion
are here briefly outlined.   Laying it down as a preliminary that,
whether it is satisfactory to us or not, there is no object beyond,
"by the consensus of positive philosophy," he proceeds to claim for
Humanity that it does really satisfy our Intellect, our Emotions, and
our Moral needs ; and that it is therefore qualified to take the place

Thus real Faith harmonises entirely with true Love directly that the Positive Doctrine is complete, and is reduced to a system. The unity of man rests solely on a sound general conception of our condition and our nature. A deeper study of the great universal Order reveals to us at length the ruling power within it of the true Great Being, whose destiny it is to bring that Order continually to perfection by constantly conforming to its laws, and which thus best represents to us that system as a whole. This undeniable Providence, the supreme dispenser of our destinies, becomes in the natural course the common centre of our affections, our thoughts, and our actions. Although this Great Being evidently exceeds the utmost strength of any, even of any collective, human force, its necessary constitution and its peculiar function endow it with the truest sympathy towards all its servants. The least amongst us can and ought constantly to aspire to maintain and even to improve this Being. This natural object of all our activity, both public and private, determines the true general character of the rest of our existence, whether in feeling or in thought, which must be devoted to love, and to know, in order rightly to serve, our Providence by a wise use of all the means which it furnishes to us. Reciprocally this continued service, whilst strengthening our true unity, renders us at once happier and better. The last result which is its property is that it finally incorporates us into the Great Being, in the development of which we have had a part to bear.

hitherto occupied by the ideas of God put forward by Theology and, later, by Metaphysics, which are now discharged from further service by the enlightened Positivist. The use of the term "Positive" in this sense Comte took over from the French Socialist, St. Simon, with whom he had associated himself for some years. Within Humanity Comte assigns the first place to Woman as the more highly endowed with the primary quality, Feeling. Unsparing criticisms of Humanity as object of Worship abound in the controversial literature which the claim has evoked. Cf. the references at end of this Selection.

Then follows Comte's view of what he means by Humanity :

Such, then, is the general spirit of the true religion which I have already indicated in my General View of Positivism. I must reserve for the fourth volume its direct and special explanation, having prepared the way for it in the third by an historical basis as the ground of a comparative judgment. I must, however, still more accurately define the fundamental conception which crowns the entire system of positive thought ; and I must still further set forth the composite and relative character of the highest existence we know.

This vast and eternal organism is peculiarly distinguished above all others by reason of its being formed of separable elements, each of which is conscious of its own co-operation, and consequently can give or withhold it, at least so far as its co-operation is direct. Its essential attributes as well as its necessary conditions are both alike the consequence of this partial independence ; for it admits of combination on a great scale, but at the same time of profound antagonism. In a word, the chief superiority of the Great Being consists in this, that its organs are themselves beings, individual or collective. All the functions belonging to it, whether those of the affections, of the intellect, or the activity, are therefore ultimately exercised by certain individuals whose free inter-vention is indispensable, although the refusal of any single individual will generally be compensated by the assent of others. But to illustrate this point we will now consider separately the two existences belonging to each individual human unit, which in the General View were considered together, without any difficulty thereby arising.

The Supreme Power is the continuous result of all the forces capable of voluntarily taking part in the amelioration of the race, even without excepting our worthy helpmates amongst the animals. Each individual member of this great whole has two successive existences, the one objective, and

always transitory, in which he serves directly the Great
Being by using the entire series of the previous labours of
our race ; the other subjective, and of its essence perpetual,
in which his service is indirectly prolonged by the results
which he leaves to his successors. Strictly speaking, scarcely
any man becomes an organ of Humanity until his second life
has begun. The first really forms nothing but a trial of his
worthiness for the final incorporation, which ordinarily
should not be recognised until the objective existence has
been completely ended. Thus the individual is not yet a real
organ of the Great Being, though he aspires to become so by
his services as a distinct being. His relative independence
exists only in his first life, during which he remains
immediately subject to the Order of nature, to the laws of
matter, of life, and of society. Once incorporated with the
Supreme Being he becomes truly inseparable from it.
Thenceforth he is removed from the influence of all physical
laws, and remains only subject to the higher laws which
directly govern the development of Humanity.

It is by means of this passage to a subjective life that the
chief extension of the great organism is maintained. Other
beings increase only by the law of the renovation of their
elements, by the preponderance of absorption over exhalation.
But besides this source of expansion, the Supreme Power
increases especially, by virtue of the subjective eternity to
which its worthy objective servants rise. Thus the subjective
existences are necessarily more and more in preponderance,
both in number and in duration, in the total composition of
Humanity. It is on this ground that its power always
exceeds that of any collection of individuals. Even the
insurrection of almost the entire living population against the
combined subjective influence of the past, would not prevent
the evolution of the race from following its course. Those
servants of Humanity who remained loyal could easily overcome this revolt, by basing their efforts upon the old

principles, which, in spite of anarchy, would be left in all
hearts and intellects from the labours of all former generations, they only being the genuine successors. In a word,
the living are always more and more ruled by the dead.
But to meet the metaphysical error which would result from
too abstract a conception, we must never lose sight of the
real nature of this preponderance of the subjective organs of
Humanity. Each subjective organ is the product of a
previous objective existence, and it requires the alliance of
another objective existence for its exercise. Thus man serves
Humanity as a being during his life strictly so called, and as
an organ after his death, which finally transforms his objective
into a subjective life. In his first existence he freely receives
and spontaneously employs the resources of all kinds
accumulated by the Great Being. In the second, if his
personal office has been worthily filled, he takes part in the
work of directing the continual use of the collective material of
mankind. His individuality is at once the essential condition,
and yet the principal danger of his objective co-operation; for
the problem is, how to place the egoism which is unavoidable
under the guidance of the altruism which is indispensable.
When his service has become subjective, the constant ascendancy of the sociable over the personal faculties is a spontaneous consequence. For, not only is Humanity composed
only of existences capable of assimilation, but it assimi-
lates only from each that portion of his life which is
capable of being incorporated, and rejects every individual
shortcoming.

In this general sketch I cannot hope to explain entirely,
even to minds already well prepared, the most extensive and
most difficult of the positive conceptions, the sum of the
whole system of real doctrine. Still it will be proper to
define exactly this, the essential centre of the true religion.
All the rest of this treatise will illustrate still further this
radical notion, and show its application in a manner more or

less explicit. The last volume will complete the theory as the general basis of the final system.

It is obvious that it is the leading characteristic of the true religion, that everything in it relates to Humanity. But the composite nature of the Great Being produces a difficulty which, whilst applying chiefly to the worship, affects the doctrine, and even the regimen. In fact this centre of human unity seems incapable of receiving any personal representation. This point, which will be hereafter dealt with, I will at once endeavour to clear up.

This objection is removed by reflecting on the nature of the true Supreme Being. Although it is really composed of subjective existences, it can act directly only by means of objective agents. These are individual beings, of the same nature as itself, though less eminent, and not so permanent. Each of these personal organs becomes therefore capable of representing the Great Being in many ways, when duly incor-porated therein. Thus the veneration of men of real great-ness forms an essential part of the veneration of Humanity. Even during his objective life, each of them forms a sort of personification of the Great Being. It is, however, essential to this representation that they be conceived as free from the serious imperfections which often obscure the best characters. The variety of the individual types, and the connexion be-tween their social duties, make this essential point of concep-tion easy; especially when a sound education enables the true qualities of Humanity to be universally understood.[15]

[15] We have here Comte's doctrine of "Subjective Humanity," best known through its component doctrine of Subjective Immortality and familiar in English literature especially through George Eliot's ex-pression of sympathy. Each individual in the present life plays a part which Comte dignifies with the term *objective* existence: on his decease he bequeaths his record as a contribution to the common stock. This common record is Humanity, and in his contribution to it the indi-vidual finds immortality. But this total Humanity requires a sub-jective side, *i.e.* a *subject* by whom it is to be maintained in objective

Now he exhibits Humanity as the Object of Religion.

I have now adequately set forth the only system of human Unity which thoroughly fulfils all its conditions. To complete my sketch, I must consider this system, first, as regards the object of religion, and then as regards its composition.

The object aimed at by religion is twofold : it is the unity of the individual, and the unity of the society. Now, in both of these it is easy to see that the Synthesis which

existence : the thoughts of the living as repositories of the total record are considered to constitute this *subject*. In this office all are not equally competent to bear the record, but there are individuals of high gifts who are representative personifications of great stretches of the past experience of the Race ; hence his Priests of Humanity, his Calendar of Great Men ; and here also comes in one of his peculiar aberrations, his assignment of special function in this respect to Woman, whom he does not hesitate to designate Guardian Angels for men ; without, however, assigning any personages for a similar beneficent function for women themselves.

In setting up this view of Humanity as the object of religious worship, we find Comte's *positivism* give way. The Ideal element invades his closed circle. For he distinguishes between worthy men and unworthy ; the latter drop back into non-existence ; in the permanent Humanity which is worshipful, only those secure their immortality who have in some way deserved remembrance and gratitude. There is an Election to life, though it operates spontaneously and not by the fiat of an overruling Power ; the result is the same as that of ultra-Calvinism, though the reference to Divine control is absent ; or it is parallel with the limitation of Salvation to the Church ; and the Positivist Society of Comte has been described as *une laïcization du Catholicisme.* On the other hand, men like Littré repudiated this development ; J. S. Mill deemed it "ridiculous" and "ludicrous" ; and Morley (*Encyclopædia Britannica*) regards it as a fantastic decoration, crowning what he considers to be Comte's real merit, his humanitarian sympathy and philanthropic utilitarianism. As Comte presents his system of Worship, the appearance is given of a revival of at least the mood and habit of that First Stage which he had declared to belong to primitive man, but now finds to be still indispensable at the culmination of human Progress.

has Humanity for its base is the only one that is complete and durable; for it is the only one in true conformity with our nature.

No other principle could establish an equal degree of harmony between the three essential elements of our existence. When everything refers to Humanity, the affections, the intellect, and the activity at once assume their natural relations. The activity, directly devoted to the service of the Great Being, is kept in due subordination to the feelings. At the same time the intelligence fully accepts its true office, that of enlightening the activity. Thus the heart is supreme both over the mind and the character, in a way far more simple and systematic than under any other mode.

And from this harmony of the whole, harmony of the parts equally results; whereby the different powers of our various faculties are confirmed and developed.

It establishes the discipline of the affection when it secures a direct and continual appeal to the nobler instincts; which although, in themselves, the less active, are at once the most delightful to experience, and the most capable of a great expansion. Without doubt this form of discipline implies a constant struggle against the ascendancy of the personal instincts. But this conflict within would be far more desperate, and far less capable of conclusion, under a system of personal gratification. For beside the constant effort to repress the benevolent emotions, it would be necessary to restrain the antagonism of the various lower inclinations. Even when one of the personal instincts had succeeded in effectively crushing the benevolent within, the energy of the individual would still fail in the vain task of resisting the world without, against which the ascendancy of egoism necessarily forms a permanent rebellion. On the contrary, the altruistic system of discipline, .which holds a continual rein upon the personal instincts, is the only one destined to true success in the task. Beside the important

help which the world without supplies, it is far from requiring the sacrifice of personality, but requires only its
due subordination to sociability. The religion of Humanity
ennobles indeed our lower instincts; even whilst training
them to discipline. For the cares of every description,
required day by day for the preservation of the individual,
find in this religion a sanction, as the means which enables
each to accomplish better his social duties; so long as they
are not pushed beyond the natural limits, which men are
too ready to neglect. Sound religion especially condemns
all habitual austerities; which, however respectable in
intention, would lessen the general force of every servant of
Humanity, and hamper the exercise of his ordinary duties.
It must be said also for the system of altruism, that not
only does it sanction all reasonable regard for the person,
but it largely assists such regard when treated in the whole;
for it does much to strengthen the physical health, as several
physicians have judiciously remarked. The entire freedom
from anxiety, and the sweet sense of expansiveness, which
invariably follow the active cultivation of the nobler feelings,
have a direct part in producing a balance in the physical
nature. When I come to develop further the connexion in
the nervous system, as indicated in the preceding volume,
between the vegetative organs of our body and the emotional
region of the brain, I shall reduce to a system this unques-
tionable reaction, and found thereon new modes of improving
the mutual influence of the moral and the physical nature.

With respect to intellectual harmony, it might at first
sight appear that the altruistic system was not favourable
to it, if we argue hastily from the long insurrection of the
mind against the heart in modern Europe. But this dis-
astrous conflict is far from implying a permanent incompatibility between the two; for it is the reason itself which
has discovered a regular method of conciliation, by carrying
the positive study of the external world to the point at

which Belief becomes the immediate fellow-worker with Affection. The Religion of Humanity arose originally as nothing but a system of philosophy, with no other object but that of founding a real and durable harmony, throughout the entire series of our positive notions, whether logical or scientific. If it recalls the intellect to the due control of the heart, whilst respecting its freedom, it does so after amply satisfying all the reasonable demands which the intellect has put forth in its struggle for freedom in modern times. Indeed, the indispensable preponderance of the heart, far from restraining the legitimate exercise of the speculative faculties, strengthens and improves them whilst subjecting them to discipline. Thus preserved from wasting itself in hopeless problems and idle disquisitions, our entire capacity for meditation or contemplation is free to satisfy our true speculative wants, whether to organise our knowledge or to extend it. Logical harmony is finally established upon the direct agreement between the objective and the subjective method, in accordance with the twofold nature of the Positive Unity, which is at the same time within and without the individual mind. For, objectively, the Great Being is as much external to each of us as another real existence, whilst subjectively we form part of it, at least in hope. This Unity co-ordinates in their natural way all our scientific theories; since the social order evidently supposes an anterior vital order, and that in turn supposes a pre-existent material order. The altruistic system directly recalls our intelligence to the constant pursuit of the most valuable and most difficult speculations; though without neglecting the lower studies, which are not less indispensable both for method and for doctrine. Lastly, this continued exercise of the reason harmonises perfectly with the free play of the imagination. Art is profoundly incorporated with the essence of the religion of Humanity; it serves to idealise and ennoble its doctrine, its worship, and even its discipline. When devoted to the animated expression of our highest feelings, which alone are capable of habitual expression, this idealisation in Art will form the intellectual exercise best adapted to the sum of our composite nature. Our religion sanctions its assiduous cultivation by all in unison, as the means of moral improvement, which, though indirect, is full of power. It supplies the mind with the best mode of preserving it from, or correcting in it, that unloveliness inherent in all scientific speculations, however carefully we seek to purge them from the spirit of vainglory.

Turning finally to the activity, it is evident that the altruistic system is more capable than any other of giving it grandeur. Practical life necessarily eluded the grasp of all the provisional systems of religion, by reason of the reality which is the characteristic of action. On the contrary, it was from the practical life that the Positive principle first arose, and was then extended to the contemplative, and lastly to the affective life. Under the true religious discipline, the activity forms the connecting link between belief and affection, as being the object of the former and the result of the latter. The smallest actions are ennobled when they are referred to Humanity. The reaction which they exert over the moral nature naturally seconds the familiar expansion of the good feelings; for an intimate connexion necessarily exists between all kinds of progress. It is only thus that *to live for others* can really become for all the supreme happiness; since the ordinary labours of each are thus essentially destined for the good of others, so that each servant of Humanity may attain to happiness when he feels that he is filling his own duty worthily. But beside that each in his vocation will be naturally working towards this common end, there will be cultivated in all the same spirit of eagerness to help forward the work of general advancement. Although the grander services in this Cause require systematic organs, each joins himself to this supreme part of human life, taking thought first towards himself, then towards others. Thus the activity which has its source originally in the affections, tends at length to awaken the affections. At the same time it forms the best means of regulating the intellect; for it ever impels the intellect to study the Order of nature with a view to bring it to perfection.

On all three sides it thus appears, even looking to personal unity alone, how blessed a thing to us is that external Necessity which imposes on us the altruistic discipline as the sole basis of a harmony at once real and stable; for this discipline for others becomes the sole guarantee of true happiness for any individual. A rational philosophy sanctions and perpetuates those vague yearnings that arose in the last provisional system of religion, and marks as the highest boons that man can know the three grand conditions of all social life—*Love, Faith, Hope.* The first of these forms the inward impulse of unity; the second supplies us with its external basis; the last, closely connected with the activity, becomes at first the result, and then the stimulant of each of the other two. This simple order seems indeed disturbed on occasions of anarchy in public or private life; and it would then appear that Hope only is left behind; without which indeed any life is impossible. But a more careful study shows us how, even in these cases, Hope is then dependent on an earlier system of Affection and Belief, a discipline of life which insensibly remains after its foundations have been removed. Besides, the too common tendency to despair in nations or in men proves how much, in such exceptional cases, Love and Faith are indispensable to Hope. In every case, however, the union of these three qualities is the distinctive mark of our true unity, be it affective, speculative, or active. As Order is gradually restored in the West, it will be felt, even better than it was felt in the Middle Age, how completely these three essential conditions of all

23

public good furnish also the chief sources of our individual happiness.

If it be admitted that the Religion of Humanity alone can adequately produce any true personal unity, its superiority is still clearer when we turn to social unity. For its power to restore harmony in society is a consequence of its Principle of affection and its Basis of speculation; both of which tend equally to reunite men universally in the same feeling and in the same belief. Both the Positive theory of human nature and the historical analysis of human progress forbid us to look to any other system of discipline as being able to establish any practical communion of Love and Faith amongst all the members of the human race. Children of the same Great Being, we all become at first His objective servants in life, and then His subjective organs after death. The communion of this vast whole is far from being confined to the present: Intellect and Feeling combine in comprehending in the same circle, the entire sum of the Past, the entire sum of the Future of mankind; the Past being the source, the Future being the aim, of the vast consensus of Man. It is this spirit of *continuity*, or communion between successive generations in time, which is more characteristic of the true Religion even than the *solidarity* or union of the whole living race now contemporary in space. It is here that we gather most distinctly the true purpose of our objective existence in life; which is, to transmit, improved to those who shall come after, that increasing heritage we received from those who went before. Thus regarded as a whole, the service of Humanity appears to be in its essence truly gratuitous. Each generation is bound to restore freely to the succeeding that which itself has freely received from the preceding. The improvement which it adds to the sum total itself forms never more than a trifling fraction of the worth of the whole; and it is, moreover, a constantly decreasing fraction. We must extend this notion of the collective transmission of each age to the personal co-operation of each individual. In stating, in the second chapter of this volume, the Positive theory of wages, I shall be able to show that wages never recompense the essential part of the service given, but merely the material part. Every act of human labour uses up certain material which require to be continually renewed, whether to replace the provisions consumed, or to restore the instruments worn out. Wages form the fund whence this twofold restoration takes place, and have no relation with the service given: a service that could only be recompensed worthily by means of complete reciprocity between the producer and him who enjoys his product. This notion, which is already recognised for all the higher social functions, is extended by the Religion of Humanity to real labour of every kind. The new view of labour will tend to remove those moral evils of industry, the result of the egoist system; evils which would seriously embarrass the altruistic system also, were it to suffer appeals to the selfish instincts in place of steadily restraining them.

Such is the social affinity of the true Religion, that every durable association of men has always spontaneously tended towards this form of union. It is only the higher Feelings which can unite men; and common interests have never secured permanent bonds of community, even in small spheres. We thus find everywhere that consecration of individual efforts under the sanction of an ultimate purpose in human good, at once collective and continuous. Thus arose the notion which, widened by successive generalisation, has gradually led up to the conception and sentiment of the Great Being. Even where the association has only destruction as its object, it still rests on mutual attachment; only this attachment is then limited to a special population. At the same time this military activity is directly opposed to moral unity; because it constantly arouses feelings of enmity towards the greater part of the human race. For this reason it is still more necessary for the heart than for the head to conceive the community of mankind as coextensive with the entire race. Any sense of national antagonism between the different servants of Humanity is totally incompatible with true conception of, and certainly with true feeling for, the Great Being. Nevertheless the Order of nature is such as always to prevent any absolute empire in the altruistic system. For the broadest sense of union can never extend beyond the limits of our race, except to such of the animal races as can really be associated with us. Outside the circle of this vast confederacy, whose destiny it is to improve the earth as its domain, our planet possesses a variety of animate beings who cannot be assimilated. Towards them our activity will always remain one of destruction, and no sophistry should blind us to the reality of this cruel necessity we acknowledge. This bond of Unity in a common attachment must therefore always remain a relative conception; although it is true that its sphere is continually widening. Even when our personal have been thoroughly subordinated to our sociable faculties, the egoism imposed by facts on the totality of Man must forbid the feelings of Love to embrace all Nature. Necessary as such limits to Love may be, they should in no way impair our enthusiasm; whilst we ought fairly to admit their force, as a good check on indulgence in absolute ideas. We can only regret that the imperfections natural to the Order of nature bar us from unlimited expansion of affections, which of themselves would desire to embrace all things alike in their Love.

To complete our view of the social efficacy of the true Synthesis, we must turn to its power to unite without coercing. For a sound conception of the Great Being makes the independence no less sacred than the co-operation of the members; both are equally necessary to the essential service, since the parts performed by an aggregate are impossible without individual organs. It can only be an unintelligent, and even a narrow, view of social duty which can ever lead an honest social reformer to undervalue personal liberty. The supposed antagonism between individual liberty and social combination comes from a crude attempt to found an altruistic Unity, with only one mental and moral condition. These socialist visionaries thought only of the solidarity of living men, and forgot the continuity of ages. We need apprehend little from this misconception, which is directly contrary to the ideas and the feelings which characterise the systematic Religion of Humanity. As regards the Great Being, the subjective service after death constantly becomes more and more important, compared with the objective service in life. Now subjectivity invariably supposes individuals as its authors; and their free co-operation alone can endue them with an aggregate influence. Far from lowering the freedom of the individual, the Positive religion sanctifies and develops it afresh; for it supplies it with a noble destination. This freedom is a condition indispensable to personal dignity; it is in no less degree indispensable to every service of society, which any form of oppression would paralyse. True co-operation ought always to be wholly voluntary; allowance being made for the motives which cause it to be withheld. In a word, the altruist regimen supposes and produces the spirit of trust, as it exacts and increases the habit of responsibility. On the other hand, it directly sanctions every real form of superiority, be it natural or be it acquired; for it devotes on system the strong to the service of the weak. Far from breaking up and subdividing Power, whether spiritual or temporal, the Religion of Humanity habitually concentrates Power, to enable it better to fulfil its social function. In its judgment on the Past, it gives the amplest honour to the illustrious characters, each of whom has done so much to influence the destinies of men. The Positive Religion inspires all the servants of the Great Being with a sacred zeal to represent that Being as fully as possible. It invokes the veneration of all towards every truly worthy individual. The full acceptance of this Religion alone can check that spirit of blindness or of envy which in our day would seek to crush out the real inequalities which exist amongst men, instead of turning the inequalities to account. A healthy sense of individual merit should invariably sustain our Positive morality, and dispose us to combat all those miserable attempts to discredit the power of individuals—a power for ever consecrated to the service of the Great Being.

This closes the general treatment. The remainder of chapter i. is occupied with detailed exposition of the three elements of religion, Doctrine, Worship, and Discipline; and with his Theory of the history of Religion. The latter shows in a summary way the Law of the Three Stages at work, preparatory to its full treatment in vol. iii. Comte concludes the chapter in the tone of one who has achieved a great result, and in 1855 he expressed his feeling as to what he had accomplished: "Je puis maintenant espérer que les âmes vraiment religieuses, disposées à la synthèse par la sympathie, sauront bientot surmonter les discordances dogmatiques pour encourager le seul effort de notre siècle envers la religion universelle."

References.—In support of Sociological theory, with or without special reference to Comte: Lévy Bruhl, *La Philosophie d'Auguste Comte* (tr. 1903); Guyau, *L'Irreligion de l'Avenir*; Swinny, art. "Positivism" in *Encyclopædia of Religion and Ethics* (T. & T. Clark); Durkheim, especially *Elementary Forms of the Religious Life* (1915); Ames, *Psychology of Religious Experience* (1910); Irving King, *Development of Religion* (1910); Cornford, *From Religion to Philosophy* (1912). In opposition: E. Caird, *Social Philosophy of Comte* (1885); Balfour, *Foundations of Belief* (1895); R. Mackintosh, *From Comte to Benjamin Kidd* (1899); Webb, *Group Theories of Religion* (1916). For the Sociological character of Christian Theology, see the *Selections* from Schleiermacher and Ritschl.

XI.

AGNOSTICISM.

MANSEL (1820–1871).

HENRY LONGUEVILLE MANSEL comes before us as a conspicuous example of those thinkers who find in Revelation a refuge from the incapacities of Reason. His unsparing criticism of man's rational powers is deduced from the fundamental principle of his master in philosophy, Sir William Hamilton (who interpreted Kant in a strictly subjectivistic sense; see Hamilton's *Discussions*, and cf. *supra*, p. 206, n. 29), that the Infinite cannot be known, because to know is to condition, and what is conditioned is finite. We cannot think an object without discriminating it from all else; every object, therefore, is relative to other objects. We cannot think an object without distinguishing it from ourselves; every object, therefore, is relative to the thinking subject. In other words, knowledge is relative and limited by its very nature; terms like Absolute and Infinite signify nothing that can be known; and it follows that the object of religion is utterly inaccessible to thought.

In his Bampton Lectures (1858), entitled *Limits of Religious Thought*, Mansel argued powerfully from these premises that a demonstrable Theology is impossible. Still, he contended, this gives rationalism no right to cast stones at orthodoxy, for the fundamental concepts of Reason with which every religious philosophy works are equally infected with radical contradiction. Nay, he goes further, and, out-stripping Kant in the fervour of his agnosticism, holds that neither human logic *nor* human ethics are applicable to the Divine Being, while "Personality," as a mere reflection of our limited consciousness, is absolutely incompatible with an infinite nature. Religious belief, whether intellectual or moral, is necessarily a tissue of contradictions, our only solace being the presence of like antinomies in any scheme of unbelief. Nevertheless, we are told that, casting ourselves on Revelation, "it is our duty to think of God as personal; and it is our duty to believe that He is infinite."

This sudden and inconsequent resort to Revelation drew steady and severe criticism of Mansel's views from a multitude of controversial writers. Philosophical sceptics declined to be forced into acceptance of Revelation; Christian theologians declined to abandon Reason. It is obvious that any such theory as Mansel's makes Revelation impossible; for God could not, *ex hypothesi*, make Himself intelligible to minds such as ours are. We have no knowledge, and we can have no knowledge, of any language He might use. Mansel, it is clear, was operating with a negative and spurious conception of the Infinite, which he regarded not as inclusive, but as exclusive, of the finite and its relations. Presuppositions of this kind make impossible from the outset any real unity of God and man, whether of knowledge or of will.

The passages which we have cited below are taken from the Bampton Lectures III. and IV.

THE RELIGIOUS INCAPACITY OF REASON.[1]

The results, to which an examination of the facts of consciousness has conducted us, may be briefly summed up as follow:—Our whole consciousness manifests itself as

---

[1] Throughout this passage, in which Mansel sets himself to prove the essentially self-contradictory nature of the basal conceptions of rational theology, we must mark closely the notions he is analysing. His Absolute, *e.g.*, is a purely negative idea; it denotes that which has no relation to anything else, and as applied to God, involves Acosmism. And his Infinite is equally negative; for as the simply unlimited it excludes all that is finite. Once define the terms so, and inevitable antinomies crowd upon you. Mansel was apparently unwilling to recognise that on this subject an altogether different line of argument can be developed, that, namely, which construes Infinite and finite, Absolute and relative, as inseparable correlatives for thought, intrinsically bound up together, "one of the two giving us

subject to certain limits, which we are unable, in any act
of thought, to transgress.[2] That which falls within these
limits, as an object of thought, is known to us as *relative*
and *finite*. The existence of a limit to our powers of
thought is manifested by the consciousness of *contradiction*,
which implies at the same time an attempt to think and an
inability to accomplish that attempt. But a limit is
necessarily conceived as a relation between something within
and something without itself ; and thus the consciousness of
a limit of thought implies, though it does not directly
present to us, the existence of something of which we do
not and cannot think. When we lift up our eyes to that
blue vault of heaven, which is itself but the limit of our own

the constant and ontological ground, the other the phenomenal
manifestation." Idealism has elaborated the conception of an Absolute
which embraces the relative as a living element of itself, an Infinite
which fills the finite with meaning, and takes it up organically into its
own nature, a Cause which is not so much first in time, as rather the
eternal ground of all changes and events. Mansel would probably
have urged that we cannot *think* these ideas ; but this means only that
we cannot picture them to our imagination, not that their content is
not genuinely rational.

Herbert Spencer accepted from Mansel the purely relative theory of
knowledge on which this argument is based, and carried it to its logical
results. See *First Principles*, chap. iv.

Huxley (*Essay on Agnosticism*, 1889) said that it was Hamilton's
Philosophy of the Unconditioned (from which Mansel drew) which early
in life "stamped on his mind the strong conviction that . . . the
limitation of our faculties, in a great number of cases, renders real
answers to such questions not merely actually impossible, but
theoretically inconceivable."

On the whole subject of agnosticism, especially in its religious
aspect, the student should refer to Professor Flint's exhaustive work,
Agnosticism (Blackwood, 1903).

[2] This is criticised with much acuteness and persistence by Idealistic
thinkers, who urge that knowledge of a limit is implicitly knowledge of
that which is beyond the limit. Cf., *e.g.*, J. Caird's *Introduction to the
Philosophy of Religion*, chap. i.

power of sight, we are compelled to suppose, though we cannot perceive, the existence of space beyond, as well as within it; we regard the boundary of vision as parting the visible from the invisible. And when, in mental contemplation, we are conscious of relation and difference, as the limits of our power of thought, we regard them, in like manner, as the boundary between the conceivable and the inconceivable; though we are unable to penetrate, in thought, beyond the nether sphere, to the unrelated and unlimited which it hides from us. The *Absolute* and the *Infinite* are thus, like the *Inconceivable* and the *Imperceptible*, names indicating, not an object of thought or of consciousness at all, but the mere absence of the conditions under which consciousness is possible.[3] The attempt to construct in thought an object answering to such names, necessarily results in contradiction,—a contradiction, however, which we have ourselves produced by the attempt to think,—which exists in the act of thought, but not beyond it,—which destroys the conception as such, but indicates nothing concerning the existence or non-existence of that which we try to conceive. It proves our own impotence, and it proves nothing more. Or rather it indirectly leads us to believe in the existence of that Infinite which we cannot conceive, for the denial of its existence involves a contradiction no less than the assertion of its conceivability. We thus learn that the provinces of Reason and Faith are not coextensive,—that it is a duty, enjoined by Reason itself, to believe in that which we are unable to comprehend. . . .[4]

[3] When estimating the real worth of Mansel's argument we must not forget that these difficulties are the same after revelation as before, unless it confers upon man wholly new faculties, which Mansel does not suppose it to do.

[4] Is it legitimate for Mansel to use such a phrase at all ? How can Reason enjoin any positive duty towards an Infinite which Reason itself enables us to prove to be a mere subjective negation ?

It is our duty, then, to think of God as personal; and it is our duty to believe that He is infinite. It is true that we cannot reconcile these two representations with each other, as our conception of personality involves attributes apparently contradictory to the notion of infinity.[5] But it does not follow that this contradiction exists anywhere but in our own minds, it does not follow that it implies any impossibility in the absolute nature of God.[6] The apparent contradiction, in this case, as in those previously noticed, is the necessary consequence of an attempt on the part of the human thinker to transcend the boundaries of his own consciousness. It proves that there are limits to man's power of thought, and it proves no more.

The preceding considerations are equally conclusive against both the methods of metaphysical theology described in my last lecture, that which commences with the Divine to reason down to the human, and that which commences with the human to reason up to the Divine. For though the mere abstract expression of *the infinite*, when regarded as indicating nothing more than the negation of limitation, and therefore of conceivability, is not contradictory in itself, it becomes so the instant we attempt to apply it in reasoning to any object of thought. A thing—an object—an attribute —a person—or any other term signifying one out of many possible objects of consciousness, is by that very relation necessarily declared to be finite. An infinite thing, or object, or attribute, or person, is therefore in the same moment

---

[5] On the alleged incompatibility of Infinity and Personality, cf. Selection from Lotze, *infra*, pp. 368 ff.

[6] If this is seriously meant, and we can actually criticise the imperfect and inconsistent conceptions of our own mind by reference to the absolute nature of God, in which such inconsistencies are resolved in a deeper harmony, then a rational Theism is not from the nature of things impossible, and Mansel's theory of nescience is undermined.

declared to be both finite and infinite. We cannot, therefore, start from any abstract assumption of the Divine infinity to reason downwards to any object of human thought. And, on the other hand, if all human attributes are conceived under the conditions of difference, and relation, and time, and personality, we cannot represent in thought any such attribute magnified to infinity, for this again is to conceive it as finite and infinite at the same time. We can conceive such attributes, at the utmost, only *indefinitely*; that is to say, we may withdraw our thought, for the moment, from the fact of their being limited, but we cannot conceive them as *infinite*, that is to say, we cannot positively think of the absence of the limit, for the instant we attempt to do so the antagonist elements of the conception exclude one another and annihilate the whole. . . .

There are two modes in which we may endeavour to contemplate the Deity—the one negative, based on a vain attempt to transcend the conditions of human thought and to expand the religious consciousness to the infinity of its Divine Object; the other positive, which keeps within its proper limits, and views the object in a manner accommodated to the finite capacities of the human thinker. The first aspires to behold God in His absolute nature; [7] the second is content to view Him in those relations in which He has been pleased to manifest Himself to His creatures. The first aims at a *speculative* knowledge of God as He is, but, bound by the conditions of finite thought, even in the attempt to transgress them, obtains nothing more than a tissue of ambitious self-contradictions, which indicate only

[7] One of the most vulnerable points in Mansel's argument shows here. An Absolute, which is by definition out of all relation, cannot enter into cognisable relations with us; nor can we, with minds such as ours, apprehend His self-manifestation. But his conclusion is merely an inference from his definition, and affects no one who rejects that definition.

what He is not. The second, abandoning the speculative knowledge of the infinite as only possible to the Infinite Intelligence itself, is content with those *regulative* [8] ideas of the Deity which are sufficient to guide our practice but not to satisfy our intellect; which tell us, not what God is in Himself, but how He wills that we should think of Him. In renouncing all knowledge of the Absolute, it renounces at the same time all attempts to construct *à priori* schemes of God's Providence as it ought to be; it does not seek to reconcile this or that phenomenon, whether in nature or in revelation, with the absolute attributes of Deity, but confines itself to the actual course of that Providence as manifested in the world, and seeks no higher internal criterion of the truth of a religion than may be derived from its analogy to other parts of the Divine government.[9]

[8] In an interesting note Mansel points out that his usage of the terms *speculative* and *regulative* in this connexion is the exact opposite of Kant's. Kant (*Critique of Pure Reason*, p. 394, Meiklejohn's trans.) held that the ideas of the absolute or unconditioned, which reason supplies, are merely regulative in their function, *i.e.* they enable us to organise our experience by giving direction and systematic unity to the work of the understanding, though they really do not give us a knowledge of ultimate being, but only point the way. Their use, accordingly, is regulative or heuristic, not speculative or constitutive. Mansel prefers to reverse this terminology, and to say that the *finite* conceptions are regulative, the *infinite* speculative, and therefore worthless : " In the philosophy of religion, the true regulative ideas which are intended to guide our thoughts are the finite forms under which alone we can think of the infinite God." Cf. *supra*, p. 209, note [32].

[9] So Butler in his *Analogy of Religion, natural and revealed, to the constitution and course of nature*. But it may be noted that Mansel pushed the elder thinker's argument a great many steps further, finding complete difference where Butler had rejoiced to find analogy. Butler's argument is, in brief, that whatever difficulties there may be in the proof of revelation, equal difficulties meet us in the proof of natural religion. But for Mansel the difficulties are not in the world, they are in our mind, and flow from a radical

Guided by this, the only true Philosophy of Religion, man is content to practise where he is unable to speculate. He acts as one who must give an account of his conduct; he prays, believing that his prayer will be answered. He does not seek to reconcile this belief with any theory of the Infinite; for he does not even know how the Infinite and the Finite can exist together. But he feels that his several duties rest upon the same basis; he knows that, if human action is not incompatible with Infinite Power, neither is human worship with Infinite Wisdom and Goodness, though it is not as the Infinite that God reveals Himself in His moral government, nor is it as the Infinite that He promises to answer prayer.

disqualification for knowledge of Divine things inherent in the very structure of our faculties. And as, in his opinion, every religious philosophy, believing or unbelieving, is under the same logical disability, he recommends us to take refuge in Revelation.

A survey of the literature of speculative theology during the last forty years is enough to show how many have taken Mansel's negative counsel to distrust Reason, without accepting his positive substitute for it.

The close affinity between Mansel's scheme of thought and that of Pascal or Newman is obvious. A modern and lighter rendering of the same thesis is given in W. H. Mallock's pleasantly written *Religion as a Credible Doctrine* (1903). Points of contact with it are also to be found in A. J. Balfour's *Foundations of Belief* (1895), though in the latter case we find likewise a partial approach to the general position of Kant, and even, in some respects, of Hegel. Above all, the student should compare Herbert Spencer's *First Principles,* the book which has conveyed Mansel's agnostic views to an even wider circle than he himself reached. For criticism of Spencer, see Edward Caird's *Evolution of Religion* (2 vols., 1892); Iverach, *Theism in the Light of Present Science and Philosophy,* Lect. IX.; and James Ward, *Naturalism and Agnosticism.*

XII.

THE PERSONALITY OF GOD.

LOTZE (1817–1881).

HERMANN LOTZE, the latest of the great philosophers of Germany, stands as a realist in line with Leibnitz and Herbart. That is to say, he sets out from the presupposition of individualism or monadism, though his inquiry into the idea of causality leads him ultimately to a spiritual Monism, or the doctrine of one universal Substance in which all things live and act, and their relation to which explains their unity and mutual influence.   Lotze's theory of knowledge must in strictness be placed beside that of Kant.   He teaches the purely phenomenal range of cognition ; yet this is more than balanced by the metaphysical assumption—which he makes on the strength of the faith inherent in knowledge—that things, in order to be centres of action and to be experienced by us, must share in varying degrees the quality of selfhood, must be modes, that is, of the absolute Substance which enjoy their own states.   Thus the genuine affinity of reality and intelligence is reaffirmed, and the objectivity of knowledge is saved.   His system of philosophy was obviously built up with a constant polemical reference on the one hand to Hegelianism, and on the other to the materialistic dogmas promulgated by the science of his day. In view of Hegelianism, he protests against the sacrifice of the individual's spiritual needs and instincts to any exclusively abstract and intellectual considerations whatsoever.   Urging that in any case human thought can never constitute reality, but at best represent it inadequately, he reasserts and vindicates the part played by *feeling*,—the ethical, æsthetic, and religious demands of the spirit,—alike in the structure of experience and our estimate of its meaning.   As against materialistic science, while defending with eager conviction the mechanical view of nature even in the domain of organic life, he argues that the function of mechanism in the universe is entirely subordinate, and "must be regarded philosophically as the instrument of purpose." His system may therefore be described as a teleological idealism, which ultimately rests for him upon judgments of worth, in which ethics and religion, and even the interpretative work of knowledge, take their rise. "It is only the Good which has in itself the complete right to be, and this is recognised in a judgment or postulate of value, which carries us beyond the merely intellectual region into the domain of feeling." His Theism is uncompromising, and the one infinite real Being to which his ontological inquiries conduct is viewed unambiguously as personal.

The extract we have given is a masterly defence of the position that the Absolute combines in itself the attributes of Infinitude and Personality, and it will be seen that the argument follows thoroughly original lines. It is taken from Bk. ix. chap. iv. of his *Microcosmus* (Eng. trans. by Miss E. E. C. Jones, 2 vols., 1886). Modelled on the pattern of Herder's *Ideen*, this work, published 1856–1864, and described by himself as an "attempt at an anthropology," contains a psychology elaborated in close connexion with physiological results and with the progress of culture, and in its later sections develops the author's ideas on cosmology and religious philosophy—all presented in an attractive and semi-popular style. Lotze's views on questions of religious belief are set forth with admirable conciseness also in his *Outlines of the Philosophy of Religion*, notes of his later Lectures, of which two versions are published in English (by G. T. Ladd, Boston, 1886, and F. C. Conybeare, 1892). An added touch of reality is given to Lotze's disquisitions by his genuine eminence in psychology, a sphere in which he is best known by his brilliant and original doctrine of "local signs" (in the perception of space), and his assertion of the basal importance of feeling as a factor in mental life.

IMPERSONAL FORMS OF THE SUPREME BEING.

EGO AND NON-EGO—OBJECTIONS TO THE POSSIBILITY OF THE PERSONALITY OF THE INFINITE.

Two distinct series of attributes through which man tries to comprehend the being of God recall to us the two impulses from which arose the notion of God and belief in Him. Metaphysical attributes of Unity, Eternity, Omnipresence, and Omnipotence determine Him as the ground of all finite reality; ethical attributes of Wisdom, Justice, and Holiness satisfy our longing to find in that which has supreme reality, supreme worth also.[1] We have no need to give a complete account of these attributes, or to touch doubtful questions as to their reciprocal limits; the only really important point for us is to reach a conviction as to the mode of existence that is to give a definite form to this essence of all perfection, determining also at the same time the special significance of several of the attributes referred to. If these reflections, which are now struggling to a conclusion, were allowed once more to run into the prolixity of systematic completeness, it would be easy to develop from the preceding investigations as to the nature of existence the answer which we should have to give to this last question as to the nature of that Infinite which we have there discovered. But just because it is easy for the reader to supply this transition, we will regard the goal to which it would lead, the notion of a Personal God, as being already reached, and endeavour to defend this against doubts as to its possibility, as being the only logical conclusion to which our considerations could come.

The longing of the soul to apprehend as reality the Highest Good which it is able to feel, cannot be satisfied by or even consider any form of the existence of that Good except Personality. So strong is its conviction that some living Ego, possessing and enjoying Self, is the inevitable presupposition, and the only possible source and abode of all goodness and all good things, so filled is it with unspoken contempt for all existence that is apparently lifeless, that we

[1] The proof that what is real and what has worth are one, or as he elsewhere expresses it, the proof of the undivided unity of the *world of forms* and the *world of values* is for Lotze the ultimate, and perhaps insoluble, problem of philosophy. Cf. the Selection from Ritschl.

24

always find the myth-constructing beginnings of religion busied in transforming natural to spiritual reality; but never find them actuated by any desire to trace back living spiritual activity to unintelligent Realness as to a firmer foundation. From this right path the progressive development of reflection turned off for a time. With increasing cosmic knowledge, it grew more clear what must be required in the notion of God, if He were not only to contain in Himself all that is greatest and most worthy, but also to contain it after such a fashion as to appear at the same time as the creative and formative ground of all reality; and, on the other hand, in more refined observation of spiritual life, the conditions became clear to which in us finite beings the development of personality is attached; both trains of thought seemed to combine in showing that the form of spiritual life is incompatible with the notion of the Supreme Being, or that the form of personal existence is incompatible with the notion of the Infinite Spirit. And there arose attempts to find more satisfying forms of existence for the Highest Good in ideas of an Eternal World-Order, of an Infinite Substance, of a Self-developing Idea,[2] and to depreciate the form of personal existence which had previously seemed to the unsophisticated mind to be the only one that was worthy. . . .

There is given at this point a brief examination of the three typical impersonal forms of the Supreme Being to which he has just referred. On this follows his independent exposition. It is objected, he says, that

. . . An Ego (or Self, *Ich*) is not thinkable without the contrast of a Non-Ego or Not-Self; hence personal existence cannot be asserted of God without bringing even Him down to that state of limitation, of being conditioned by something

[2] The reference is to the systems of Fichte, Schelling, and Hegel.

not Himself, which is repugnant to Him.[3] The objections that speculative knowledge makes to the personality of God fall back upon this thought; in order to estimate their importance, we shall have to test the apparently clear content of the proposition which they take as their point of departure. For unambiguous it is not; it may be intended to assert that what the term Ego denotes can be comprehended in reflective analysis only by reference to the Non-Ego; it may also mean that it is not conceivable that this content of the Ego should be experienced without that contrasted Non-Ego being experienced at the same time; finally, it may point to the existence and active influence of a Non-Ego as the condition without which the being upon which this influence works could not be an Ego.

The relations which we need in ideation for making clear the object ideated, are not in a general way decisive as to its nature; they are not conditions of the possibility of the thing as they are for us conditions of the possibility of its presentation in idea.[4] But the special nature of the case before us seems to involve something which is not generally included—for it is just in the act of ideation that Selfhood (*Ichheit*) consists, and hence what is necessary for carrying out such an act is at the same time a condition of the thing.

[3] What is here in view is apparently the formulation of this objection by Strauss (*Die christl. Glaubenslehre,* i. p. 504), "Personality is that selfhood which shuts itself up against everything else, which it thereby excludes from itself; the Absolute, on the other hand, is the comprehensive, the unlimited, which excludes nothing from itself but just the exclusivity which lies in the conception of personality." (It has been truly said by Ritschl that this idea of the Absolute is simply that of space.) The same line is taken by Mansel and Spencer, so that for them the conception of personality is a portion of our knowledge with which the Unknowable—inconsistently enough—is *known* to be in contradiction.

[4] It is a favourite and, perhaps, in some of its developments, a dubious principle of criticism with Lotze that movements of our thought must always, as such, be distinguished from real processes of Being. Cf. *Metaph.* i. p. 95.

Hence the first two interpretations which we gave of the proposition referred to seem to run together into the assertion that the Ego has significance only as contrasted with the Non-Ego, and can be experienced only in such contrast. Whether we agree with this assertion will depend in part upon the significance attached to the words used. We see in the first place that at any rate Ego and Non-Ego cannot be two notions of which each owes its whole content only to its contrast with the other; if this were so they would both remain without content, and if neither of them apart from the contrast had a fixed meaning of its own, not only would there be no ground for giving an answer one way or the other to the question which of the two members of the contrast should take the place of the Ego and which that of the Non-Ego, but the very question would cease to have any meaning. Language has given to the Ego alone its own independent name, to the Non-Ego only the negative determination which excludes the Ego without indicating any positive content of its own. Hence every being which is destined to take the part of the Ego when the contrast has arisen, must have the ground of its determination in that nature which it had *previous to* the contrast, although before the existence of the contrast it is not yet entitled to the predicate which in that contrast comes to belong to it.[5] Now if this is to remain the meaning of the term, if the being is to be Ego only at the moment when it is distinguished from the Non-Ego, then we have no objection to make to this mode of expression, but we shall alter our own. For it is

[5] We may illustrate this by the correlative pair of concepts, *right* and *left*. These directions are what they are independently of our comparing them, otherwise when we did compare them we should have no ground for deciding which was which. So the *Ego* and *Non-Ego* are distinct realities before they are contrasted by reflective thought, and the contrast is only possible on the ground of their previous distinction.

our opponents' opinion and not ours that personality is to be found exclusively where, in ideation (or presentation), Self-consciousness sets itself as Ego in opposition to the Non-Ego; in order to establish the selfhood (*Selbstheit*) which we primarily seek, that nature is sufficient in virtue of which, when the contrast does arise, the being becomes an Ego, and it is sufficient even before the appearance of the contrast. Every feeling of displeasure or of dislike, every kind of self-enjoyment (*Selbstgenuss*), does in our view contain the primary basis of personality, that immediate self-existence which all later developments of self-consciousness may indeed make plainer to thought by contrasts and comparisons, thus also intensifying its value, but which is not in the first place produced by them.[6] It may be that only the being who in thought contrasts with himself a Non-Ego from which he also distinguishes himself, can say *I* (Ich) to himself; but yet in order that in thus distinguishing he should not mistake and confound himself with the Non-Ego, this discriminating thought of his must be guided by a certainty of self which is immediately experienced by a self-existence which is earlier than the discriminative relation by which it becomes Ego as opposed to Non-Ego. A different consideration has already (cf. i. p. 241 *seq.*) led us by an easier path to the same result, and we may refer the reader to this passage for explanation and completion of what is said here. The discussion referred to showed us that all self-consciousness rests upon the foundation of direct sense of self,[7] which can

[6] *I.e.* the basal characteristic of the Self, which makes it to be a Self and is the foundation of all later development, is not a mere intellectual intuition, but a feeling of interest, of pleasure and pain which is absolutely unique, immediately experienced, and incommunicable. The absence of this from such a definition as Spinoza's marks the difference between the personal and impersonal systems.

[7] The supreme instance of what is with Lotze a fundamental principle, namely, that it is in direct Perception, whether inner or outer that we are in immediate contact with Reality.

by no means arise from becoming aware of a contrast with the external world, but is itself the reason that this contrast can be felt as unique, as not comparable to any other distinction between two objects. Self-consciousness is only the subsequent endeavour to analyse with the resources of cognition this experienced fact—to frame in thought a picture of the Ego that in cognition apprehends itself with the most vivid feeling, and in this manner to place it artificially among the objects of our consideration, to which it does not really belong. So we take up our position with regard to the first two interpretations of the proposition of which we are speaking,—thus, we admit that the Ego *is thinkable* only in relation to the Non-Ego, but we add that it *may be experienced* previous to and out of every such relation, and that to this is due the possibility of its subsequently becoming thinkable in that relation.

But it is not these two interpretations but the third that is most obstructive to that faith in the Personality of God which we are seeking to establish. In one form, indeed, in which it sometimes occurs we need not make it an object of renewed investigation; for we may now consider it as, in our view, established that no being in the nature of which self-existence was not given as primary and underived, could be endowed with selfhood by any mechanism of favouring circumstances however wonderful. Hence we may pass over in complete silence all those attempts which think to show by ill-chosen analogies from the world of sense how in a being as yet selfless an activity originally directed entirely outwards is, by the resistance opposed to it by the Non-Ego (comparable to that which a ray of light encounters in a plane surface), thrown back upon itself and thereby transformed into the self-comprehending light of self-consciousness.[8]

[8] Lotze, it is obvious, is thinking of Fichte, and his well-known theory of the *Anstoss* or shock of collision (with the Non-Ego) in which self-consciousness arises. Cf. Prof. Pringle-Pattison, *Hegelianism and Personality*, p. 53.

In such ideas everything is arbitrary, and not a single feature of the image employed is applicable to the actual case which it is intended to make clear : that outgoing activity is an unmeaning imagination, the resistance which it is to meet with is something that cannot be proved, the inference that that activity is by that resistance turned back along the path by which it came is unfounded, and it is wholly incomprehensible how this reflection could transform its nature, so that from blind activity it should turn into the selfhood of self-existence.

Setting aside these follies which have influenced philosophic thought to an unreasonable extent, we find a more respectable form of the view which we are combating occupied in proving that though that self-existence cannot be produced by any external condition in a being to which it does not belong by nature, yet it could never be developed even in one whose nature is capable of it, without the co-operation and educative influences of an external world.   For [it is held] (i.) that from the impressions which we must receive from the external world, there comes to us not only all the content of our ideas, but also the occasion of all these feelings in which the Ego, existing for self, can enjoy self without as yet being conscious of a relation of contrast to the Non-Ego. (ii.) That all feeling [9] must be conceived as (in some definite form of pleasure or displeasure) interested in some definite situation of the being to which it belongs, some particular phase of its action and its passion; but that neither is passion possible without some foreign impression which calls it forth, nor activity possible without an external point of attraction which guides it, and at which it aims.   (iii.) That

[9] "Feeling" is here used more narrowly than in the older English meaning, in which it includes not only pleasure and pain, but sensations, *e.g.* of colour and sound.   The allocation of the term "feeling" to the whole pleasure and pain side of life, and to that only, is now accepted in German and English psychology.

in any single feeling the being which is self-existent is only
partially self-possessing; that whether it has self-existence
truly and completely depends upon the variety of the external
impulses which stimulates by degrees the whole wealth of its
nature, making this wealth matter of self-enjoyment; that
thus the development of all personality is bound up with
the existence and influence of an external world, and the
variety and succession of those influences; and that such
development would be possible even for God only under
similar conditions.

It is not sufficient to lessen the weight of this objection
by the assertion that this educative stimulation is necessary
only for finite and changing beings, and not for the nature
of God, which, as a self-cognisant Idea, eternally unchangeable, always possesses its whole content simultaneously.
Though this assertion grazes the truth, yet in this form it
would be injurious in another respect to our idea of God,
for it would make the being of God similar to that of an
eternal truth,—a truth indeed not merely valid, but also
conscious of itself. But we have a direct feeling of the wide
difference there is between this personification of a thought
and living personality; not only do we find art tedious
when it expects us to admire allegorical statues of Justice
or of Love, but even speculation rouses our opposition forthwith, when it offers to us some self-cognisant Principle of
Identity, or some self-conscious Idea of Good, as completely
expressing personality. Either of these is obviously lacking
in an essential condition of all true reality in the capacity
of *suffering*. Every Idea by which in reproductive cognition
we seek to exhaust the nature of some being, is and remains
nothing more than the statement of a thought-formula by
which we fix, as an aid to reflection, the inner connexion
between the living activities of the Real; the real thing
itself is that which applies this Idea to itself, which feels
contradiction to it as disturbance of itself, and wills and

attempts as its own endeavour the realisation of the Idea. The only living subject of personality is this inner core, which cannot be resolved into thoughts, the meaning and significance of which we know in the immediate experience of our mental life, and which we always misunderstand when we seek to construe it; hence personality can never belong to any unchangeably valid truth, but only to something which changes, suffers, and reacts.[10] We will only briefly point out in passing the insurmountable difficulties which the attempt to personify Ideas thus would encounter if there were any question of determining the relation between the Ideas so personified and the changing course of the world; it would immediately appear that these could as little do without the additions necessary to transform them into suffering and acting beings as the World-Order to which we have before referred.

Yet the transference of the conditions of finite personality to the personality of the Infinite is not justified. For we must guard ourselves against seeking in the alien nature of the external world, in the fact that it is *Non*-Ego, the source or the strength with which it calls out the development of the Ego; it operates only by bringing to the finite mind stimuli which occasion the activity which that mind cannot produce from its own nature.[11] It is involved in the notion

[10] A good instance of Lotze's intense realism. Elsewhere (*Metaph.* Eng. trans. vol. i. p. 89 ff.) he refuses to make Law a separate entity superior to things, and assigns it reality only *in* things and their actions ; similarly, he argues here that no universal truth can ever constitute personality, for the truth itself has existence only *in* and *through* personal life. The Absolute is not only Intellect but Will.

[11] Here, and in what follows, he is arguing that external stimuli are essential for the development of human personality, not *quâ* personality, but *quâ* limited personality, which does not contain within itself the conditions of its existence. Personality, that is, as we experience it, is only realised through the consciousness of difference from something other than itself. In the case of the Absolute this

of a finite being that it has its definite place in the whole, and thus that it is not what any other is, and yet that at the same time it must as a member of the whole in its whole development be related to and must harmonise with that other. Even for the finite being the forms of its activity flow from its own inner nature, and neither the content of its sensations nor its feelings, nor the peculiarity of any other of its manifestations, is given to it from without; but the incitements of its action certainly all come to it from that external world to which, in consequence of the finiteness of its nature, it is related as a part, having the place, time, and character of its development marked out by the determining whole. The same consideration does not hold of the Infinite Being that comprehends in itself all that is finite, and is the cause of its nature and reality; this Infinite Being does not need—as we sometimes, with a strange perversion of the right point of view, think—that its life should be called forth by external stimuli, but from the beginning its concept is without that deficiency which seems to us to make such stimuli necessary for the finite being, and its active efficacy thinkable. The Infinite Being, not bound by any obligation to agree in any way with something not itself, will, with perfect self-sufficingness, possess in its own nature the causes of every step forward in the development of its life. An analogy which though weak yet holds in some important points, and is to some extent an example of the

qualification falls away, and therefore also the need for external stimuli. The importance of this line of reasoning can hardly be exaggerated, for it makes clear that those who object to conceiving the Supreme Power as Personal include as essential in their idea of personality what is really to be excluded as irrelevant. Cf. Campbell Fraser's *Philosophy of Theism* (Gifford Lectures, Second Series), pp. 149, 150 ; Illingworth, *Personality Human and Divine*, chaps. ii.–iv. This argument has recently been subjected to an extremely acute and suggestive criticism by J. E. M'Taggart in his *Studies in Hegelian Cosmology.*

thing itself, is furnished to us by the course of memory in the finite mind. The world of our ideas, though certainly called into existence at first by external impressions, spreads out into a stream which, without any fresh stimulation from the external world, produces plenty that is new by the continuous action and reaction of its own movements, and carries out in works of imagination, in the results reached by reflection, and in the conflicts of passion, a great amount of living development—as much, that is, as can be reached by the nature of a finite being without incessantly renewed orientation, by action and reaction with the whole in which it is comprehended; hence the removal of these limits of finiteness does not involve the removal of any producing condition of personality which is not compensated for by the self-sufficingness of the Infinite, but that which is only approximately possible for the finite mind, the conditioning of its life by itself, takes place without limit in God, and no contrast of an external world is necessary for Him.

Of course there remains the question what it is that in God corresponds to the primary impulse which the train of ideas in a finite mind receives from the external world? But the very question involves the answer. For when through the impulse received from without there is imparted to the inner life of the mind an initiatory movement which it subsequently carries on by its own strength, whence comes the movement in the external world which makes it capable of giving that impulse? A brief consideration will suffice to convince us that our theory of the cosmos, whatever it may be, must somehow and somewhere recognise the actual movement itself as an originally given reality, and can never succeed in extracting it from rest.[12] And this indication

[12] Here also we have a principle which constantly recurs in Lotze's discussions, and is of profound significance for the interpretation of modern psychology and metaphysics as a whole, namely, that we have not to ask how being and reality—including change—are made, but

may suffice for the present, since we wish here to avoid increasing our present difficulties by entering upon the question as to the nature of time. When we characterise the inner life of the Personal God, the current of His thoughts, His feelings, and His will, as everlasting and without beginning, as having never known rest, and having never been roused to movement from some state of quiescence, we call upon imagination to perform a task no other and no greater than that which is required from it by every materialistic or pantheistic view. Without an eternal un-caused movement of the World's Substance, or the assumption of definite initial movements of the countless world-atoms, movements which have to be simply recognised and accepted, neither materialistic nor pantheistic views could attain to any explanation of the existing cosmic course; and all parties will be at last driven to the conviction that the splitting up of reality into a quiescent being and a movement which subse-quently takes hold of it, is one of those fictions which, while they are of some use in the ordinary business of reflection, betray their total inadmissibility as soon as we attempt to rise above the reciprocal connexion of cosmic particulars to our first notions of the cosmos as a whole.

The ordinary doubts as to the possibility of the personal existence of the Infinite have not made us waver in our con-viction. But in seeking to refute them, we have had the feeling that we were occupying a standpoint which could only be regarded as resulting from the strangest perversion of all natural relations. The course of development of philosophic thought has put us who live in this age in the position of being obliged to show that the conditions of personality which we meet with in finite things, are not lacking to the Infinite;

to explain them as given; not to create the world, but to understand it. This principle may be found admirably exemplified in James Ward's article on Psychology in the *Encyclopædia Britannica*, and in the psychological works of Professor Stout.

whereas the natural concatenation of the matter under discussion would lead us to show that of the full personality which is possible only for the Infinite a feeble reflection is given also to the finite;[13] for the characteristics peculiar to the finite are not producing conditions of self-existence, but obstacles to its unconditioned development, although we are accustomed, unjustifiably, to deduce from these characteristics its capacity of personal existence. The finite being always works with powers with which it did not endow itself, and according to laws which it did not establish,—that is, it works by means of a mental organisation which is realised not only in it but also in innumerable similar beings. Hence in reflecting on self, it may easily seem to it as though there were in itself some obscure and unknown substance—something which is in the Ego though it is not the Ego itself, and to which, as to its subject, the whole personal development is attached. And hence there arises the questions—never to be quite silenced—What are we ourselves? What is our soul? What is our self—that obscure being, incomprehensible to

---

[13] This is a further step in the argument. The Infinite is not only personal, but is the sole example of full and perfect personality. The qualities of limitation which, as some hold, constitute the very definition of personality, are really disabilities and imperfections, which, far from contributing to reveal, only conceal and hamper the development of true personal life. Cf. Ritschl, *Justification and Reconciliation* (Eng. trans. pp. 226–238), where this argument is practically reproduced, and see the closing words of this extract. Lotze was always in too complete sympathy with the instincts of piety to hold ambiguous language on the question of the personality of God. How close this sympathy was may be gathered from the three propositions in which he sums up what he designates "the characteristic convictions of every religious mind":

(1) Moral laws embody the will of God.
(2) Individual finite spirits are not products of nature, but are children of God.
(3) Reality is more and other than the mere course of nature, it is a kingdom of God (*Outlines of Phil. of Rel.*, Eng. trans. p. 159).

ourselves, that stirs in our feelings and our passions, and never rises into complete self-consciousness? The fact that these questions can arise shows how far personality is from being developed in us to the extent which its notion admits and requires. It can be perfect only in the Infinite Being which, in surveying all its conditions or actions, never finds any content of that which it suffers or any law of its working, the meaning and origin of which are not transparently plain to it, and capable of being explained by reference to its own nature. Further, the position of the finite mind, which attaches it as a constituent of the whole to some definite place in the cosmic order, requires that its inner life should be awakened by successive stimuli from without, and that its course should proceed according to the laws of a psychical mechanism, in obedience to which individual ideas, feelings, and efforts press upon and supplant one another. Hence the whole self can never be brought together at one moment, our self-consciousness never presents to us a complete and perfect picture of our Ego—not even of its whole nature at any moment, and much less of the unity of its development in time. We always appear to ourselves from a one-sided point of view, due to those mental events which happen to be taking place within us at the time,—a point of view which only admits of our surveying a small part of our being; we always react upon the stimuli which reach us, in accordance with the one-sided impulses of this accidental and partial self-consciousness; it is only to a limited extent that we can say with truth that *we* act; for the most part action is carried on in us by the individual feelings or groups of ideas to which at any moment the psychical mechanism gives the upper hand. Still less do we exist wholly *for ourselves* in a temporal point of view. There is much that disappears from memory, but most of all individual moods, that escape it by degrees. There are many regions of thought in which while young we were quite at home, which in age we can only bring before our minds as alien phenomena; feelings in which we once revelled with enthusiasm we can now hardly recover at all, we can now hardly realise even a pale reflection of the power which they once exercised over us; endeavours which once seemed to constitute the most inalienable essence of our Ego seem, when we reach the path along which later life conducts us, to be unintelligible aberrations, the incentives to which we can no longer understand. In point of fact we have little ground for speaking of the personality of finite beings; it is an ideal, which, like all that is ideal, belongs unconditionally only to the Infinite, but like all that is good appertains to us only conditionally and hence imperfectly.

The more simple content of this section hardly needs the brief synoptical repetition in which we now proceed to gather up its results and to add them to those already reached.

(*a*) Selfhood, the essence of all personality, does not depend upon any opposition that either has happened or is happening of the Ego to a Non-Ego, but it consists in an immediate self-existence which constitutes the basis of the possibility of that contrast wherever it appears. Self-consciousness is the elucidation of this self-existence which is brought about by means of knowledge, and even this is by no means necessarily bound up with the distinction the Ego from a Non-Ego which is substantially opposed to it.

(*b*) In the nature of the finite mind as such is to be found the reason why the development of its personal consciousness can take place only through the influences of that cosmic whole which the finite being itself is not, that is, through stimulation coming from the Non-Ego, not because it needs the contrast with something *alien* in order to have self-existence, but because in this respect, as in every other, it does not contain in itself the conditions of its existence. We do not find this limitation in the being of the Infinite; hence for it alone is there possible a self-existence, which needs neither to be initiated nor to be continuously developed by

something not itself, but which maintains itself within itself
with spontaneous action that is eternal and had no beginning.

(c) Perfect Personality is in God only, to all finite minds
there is allotted but a pale copy thereof; the finiteness of the
finite is not a producing condition of this Personality, but a
limit and a hindrance of its development.

References.—*The Philosophy of Lotze,* by Professor Henry Jones,
1895; *La Métaphysique de Hermann Lotze,* by Henri Schoen, 1902;
Personality Human and Divine, 1894, and *Reason and Revelation,*
1902, by J. R. Illingworth; the article "Lotze" in the *Encyclopædia Britannica* by J. T. Merz, with references in vol. ii. of his
Scientific Thought in the XIXth Century; and cf. a pamphlet published by Professor H. Gardiner under the title *Lotze's Theistic Philosophy,* and an article in the *Critical Review* for July 1902, entitled
"Lotze's Philosophy and its Theological Influence," by H. R.
Mackintosh. Cf. also the Selection from Ritschl. The influence of
Lotze has been considerable on Professor Ward of Cambridge, Professor (Seth) Pringle-Pattison of Edinburgh, Professor Davidson of
Aberdeen, Dr. J. Lindsay, the Oxford essayists who contributed to the
volume entitled *Personal Idealism* (1902), and on Professors Royce,
Howison, and Bowne in the United States. For a masterly discussion,
on lines that recall Lotze, see Father Dalgairns' paper, "The Personality of God," in the *Contemporary Review,* vol. xxiv. p. 321. Cf.
also A. Fairbairn, *Philosophy of the Christian Religion;* the numerous
works of Professor Eucken, of Leipzig, e.g. *Der Wahrheitsgehalt der
Religion;* Dr. Galloway's *Studies in the Philosophy of Religion,*
especially p. 249 ff.; Principal Iverach, *Theism,* Deems Lecture
(1907); and J. W. Schmidt-Japing, *Lotzes Religionsphilosophie in
ihrer Entwicklung* (1925).

XIII.

ETHICAL THEISM.

W. R. SORLEY (1855–   ).

IN the theistic literature of recent years, Professor W. R. Sorley's *Moral Values and the Idea of God* (Gifford Lectures) has come to fill a high place. It may be doubted whether a stronger defence of ethical theism has ever been made. Not merely is the book noteworthy as a sustained argument, marked by original power and rare clarity, but the view it expounds of the general nature of ethical cognition is throughout in singularly close touch with moral experience.

Professor Sorley argues for theism as the only creed which can give us a worthy and intelligible theory of the universe. For him appreciations of moral worth have as much truth as judgments of perception ; they are equally valid of being other than, and in that sense beyond, our minds. Accordingly, they form part of the data of metaphysics, and our conceptions of ultimate reality cannot afford to overlook the fact of the consciousness of obligation. Thus an argument is carried on from point to point which supplies a reasoned justification for using ethical ideas in ontological construction, shows how they can be used legitimately, and considers what effect they have on our final view of the world. In conclusion, it is held that no theory except theism, as an interpretation of the universe implying purpose and freedom, does justice to the actual relationship, discovered through experience, between moral values and the world we know. If the truth of our objective judgments of existence is to be harmonised with our equally objective judgments of value, it can be done only

25

by regarding the same self-conscious Divine Spirit as the source and ground of both.

The following brief summary of the author's reasoning in his own words may be inserted here: " My argument . . . was founded not on the moral order by itself but on its relation to the order of existing things. Since existence and value belong to the same universe they must have the same ultimate ground. The order of nature and of finite minds, as we know them, do not, however, manifest ethical values with any exactness or purity; in their existing nature they are out of harmony with the moral order. But harmony may be reached if it is allowable to assume purpose in the world and freedom in man. Nature can then be regarded as an appropriate medium for the realisation of values by minds finite but free. The harmony is a relation which stands in need of realisation ; and the purpose of realising it requires consciousness in the ground of reality as a whole. This ground or principle of reality will therefore involve the will to goodness as well as intelligence and power ; and this is what we mean by God " (*Moral Values*, 479 f.).

The lectures, it is plainly stated, do not take into account that range of experience known as " the facts of the religious consciousness." But it would perhaps not be difficult to mark out, at all events approximately, the lines on which the theistic view here set forth might be extended to cover what the greatest among believing men have felt and known. In another place Professor Sorley has offered this description of what religion is : " In all its forms, it is an attitude in which the individual soul seeks and experiences some kind of harmony with a power which transcends the visible world and is for the experient supreme."

Towards the close of his book, the author gives much importance to the postulate of personal immortality as strictly vital to any view for which the cosmos is reasonable. Not happiness but goodness is the aim of human life, and opportunities for realising goodness are not limited as are those of gaining knowledge or of the cultivation of beauty. But to reject immortality is to be confronted with an irreconcilability between the objective moral order and the order of actual existence. Values have been won through the struggles and pains of time ; " and if," we are told, " free minds, when perfected, are to pass away, even for absorption in God, these values are lost."

Our extracts are taken from the third edition, pp. 446–449, 456–468, and 486–495.

THEISM

As we have seen, neither pluralism nor monism is able to give an interpretation of reality in which both the moral order and the order of nature are adequately recognised.[1] The failure of the latter theory was mainly due to its refusal to admit the ideas of purpose and of freedom into its account. And its rejection of these ideas was due to the requirements of its theory rather than to an unprejudiced study of the facts. We have found that, even if experience does not compel us to admit the reality of purpose in nature and of individual freedom, at least it does not exclude these ideas, and it justifies our acceptance of them as postulates in the formation of a comprehensive view of reality as a whole.

We must therefore return to the point which was reached in examining the moral argument. The result of that examination had about it—I am willing to admit—a certain air of paradox. If we were asked to state the strongest objection to the theistic view of the world which is felt at the present time, we should reply without hesitation that it lies in the existence and power of evil in the world. The dilemma of Epicurus is still with us : If God wishes to prevent evil but cannot, then he is impotent ; if he could but will not, he is malevolent ; if he has both the power

[1] Sorley's treatise is concerned with the relation of the moral order to the order of existence and causation, and it should be noted carefully that his argument for theism is founded, as he says, "not on the moral order by itself but on its relation to the order of existing things."

and the will, whence then is evil ? If the world had been
so constructed that only good appeared in it and no evil,
then (it is supposed) the theistic interpretation might hold,
but it fails to account for a world like this of mingled good
and evil.   The paradox of which I have been guilty
consists in taking this very fact of evil and founding upon
it a theistic argument.   Had everything in the world been
harmonious, had there been no discord, pain, or evil, had
all actual events brought forth moral values and been
examples of moral law, then it might have seemed as if, in
our explanation of the universe, we need not go beyond
this one universal law, at once natural and moral, which
would be displayed by all things at all times.   Now such
an explanation will not fit our world, just because of the
discord between nature (including man) and morality.
But the moral order, as well as the order of nature, is of
the essence of reality ; [2] and they can be harmoniously
united in one universe only when nature is understood, not
merely in its present appearance but as working out a
purpose—that purpose being or including the making of
moral beings.   To repeat what has been already said, " If
we do not interpret the world as purposive, our view of it
cannot find room for both the natural order and the moral
order.   If we do interpret it as purposive, we must attribute
an idea and purpose of good to the ground of the world " :
that is to say, our view will be an ethical theism.   If the
purpose be the production of finite selves who will freely
realise goodness, we have a point of view from which it is
possible to explain, in general terms, both the slow stages
and frequent lapses in their moralisation, and also the

[2] The fundamental thesis of the book is that values are objectively
real, and that our interpretation of the universe must take them into
account ; in particular, that the order of reality embraces the moral
order of the world and is " the order of that one mind whose purpose
nature and man are slowly fulfilling."

nature of the medium in which this moralisation has to be achieved. Epicurus's dilemma has made an assumption in formulating its alternatives. It regards goodness as something that can be produced by compulsion. It overlooks the possibility that the will to goodness means the creation of beings who will achieve goodness freely, and whose freedom needs experience of all sorts of circumstances that it may develop into secure harmony with the moral order.

If we look at the theistic interpretation of reality from this point of view, we shall see that certain modifications have to be made in that doctrine of the unity of the world which led to and was expressed in the monistic theory. In the first place, the time-process as a whole, that is to say, the course of the world or system of nature, will have to be regarded as purposive. Taking it at any moment, we cannot say that it is perfect or a complete expression of a divine meaning: that divine meaning can only be gathered from its course as a whole, or from insight into the purpose which determines its course as a whole. And, in the second place, the finite individuals, in whom the spiritual nature of reality is manifested, must be acknowledged as agents in the accomplishment of the world-purpose, as possessing a real though limited power of initiative, and therefore a certain measure of independence. The time-process is the means whereby this freedom and independence are made contributory to complete ethical harmony or unity.

This ethical unity, be it noted, could not be arrived at in any other way, if the view is correct that the realisation of moral values requires freedom. At the same time, the attainment of this ethical unity, just because it requires freedom, involves in its process a certain modification of the doctrine of the actual unity of the universe. It is impossible to take any and every particular situation or event, especially those involving human factors, and to say " here the divine is manifested," or " the perfection of the universe **required** just this act ; anything else would have been inconsistent with the completeness of the whole." Yet in this way the monist must interpret things. In practice, he may be as ardent as any reformer in discussing the good and evil of conduct in contemplation, and in preferring good to evil ; but, looking at the matter as a philosopher, he must regard the event as inevitable : anything else would have contradicted the nature of things, which is also the nature of God : to regret it or wish it undone is to quarrel with that which alone is—to sin against the holy ghost of logic. Now, unity of this sort is inconsistent with a due appreciation of the moral aspect of reality. The ethical unity of the universe is a unity to be attained.[3] It does not belong in its completeness to any particular stage of the time-process, but only to its realised purpose. In its working out ethical unity requires a very real diversity, for it needs the co-operation of free individuals. We cannot identify these individuals with God or refer each action of theirs to the divine nature as its cause. As possessing in himself the purpose, or an idea of the purpose, of the whole time-process, God must be regarded as transcending the process itself ; as communicating freedom to the individual minds whose being depends upon his, he must be regarded as transcending them also, for their actual volitions may be alien to his nature ; and we may have to interpret this transcendence as self-limitation.[4]

. . . .

[3] True as this is, the religious mind is occupied rather with the *reality* of the ideal, in God. Acknowledging that the way of theism is not from the categorical imperative alone, Sorley does not enter upon the revelation of God which men have found in nature and art, and supremely in historical revelation.

[4] The idea of divine self-limitation emerges for religious thought also at other points; *e.g.* in the concept of creation, and, some have held, incarnation. Sorley urges that the idea is sound, " if we mean

How then are we to conceive the world in the light of the idea of God ? We have discarded the pantheistic answer to the question, which identifies the world with God ; and we have equally rejected the deistic view which regards God as being external and aloof. But the positive conception is more difficult to define. It must be something intermediate between the two impossible extremes. Neither identity on the one hand, nor complete distinction on the other hand, will satisfy our quest for a view of the relation of the world to God. It would seem, therefore, that we are forced to adopt a principle of selection amongst the facts of the world ; and selection is an awkward business and hard to apply without arbitrariness, still harder to apply without the appearance of arbitrariness. Yet arbitrariness must be avoided. We may not say, " I see God's hand here, in the providence that saved my fall, when ruin encompassed others ; but I cannot see it there, where misfortune awaited myself." If there is to be selection it must be in accordance with a definite principle, and that principle must be well grounded.

Where can we find a guiding principle ? Is there anywhere in the world a standard for discriminating the divine from that which is not divine, so that we may lay hold of the standard, and by means of it get a point of view from which reality as a whole may be seen as a revelation of God ? If there is any such, we must find it in one or other of the realms into which we have found the real in our experience to divide itself—in the realm of nature and its laws, or in that of finite selves and their wills, or in that of intrinsic values. But the first will not serve, for we have seen that imperfection clings to it. For the same reason the second region—that of finite selves—is an insecure guide ; and besides, we have attributed to these selves a

by infinite that which is not limited by anything other than its own nature."

freedom which is inconsistent not indeed with their dependence upon God, but with their being regarded as a
true mirror of the divine nature.[5]   There remains then the
realm of values—an ideal realm, very imperfectly realised
in our experience, and only incompletely conceived in our
consciousness.   It is possible for us to mistake the true
meaning of these ideal values ; but the possibility of error
does not affect the validity of truth when discovered.   The
values are there, and in our apprehension of them we have
at least a guide which gives us a principle for selecting
between the worthy and the unworthy, and enables us to
attain a certain insight into the purpose of the whole.

Is it a misleading instinct which has led men almost
uniformly to use the adjective " divine " in speaking of
these higher values—of beauty and truth and goodness ? [6]
The poets and artists have used this language in speaking
of beauty ;   and though they may not have meant to
convey a dogma by it, they intended it to express their
admiration of what was highest.   The philosophers have
often employed similar language, when their theory
allowed them to see more in the world than mechanical
law and to regard the quest for truth as of greater significance than dialectical dispute.   And to the moralist it
has often been almost an axiom that goodness and God
mean the same thing.   Of the other values I will not speak,
for my topic is the moral values and their bearing on our
interpretation of reality.

Now of the moral order of the universe we have discovered that it does belong to the order of reality, and

[5] Selves are thus given a substantive existence and not merely an
adjectival relation to the Absolute.   They are real with a measure
of independence as being charged with the discovery and realisation
of values, and nature is a fit medium for this their task.

[6] Otto would plead for another unique higher value, viz. " the
holy," with which we are in living contact in religion.   See Selection
XVI.

further that it cannot be fitted into a pantheistic conception of that order. Its distinction from, and yet intricate relation to, the natural order, and its implication of freedom in the lives which it claims to rule, forbid the easy solution that the All is simply One. But if the moral order is not altogether sundered from the natural order, if the universe is really a universe and not a multiverse, then we must hold that the moral order is the order of that one mind whose purpose nature and man are slowly fulfilling. Here, therefore, we have a key to the theistic interpretation of the world. The moral order expresses the divine nature ; and things partake of this nature in so far as they conform to that order or manifest goodness.

This gives us the principle of which we are in search. The theistic universe is fundamentally ethical. The central point in our idea of God is not the pantheistic conception of a substance of infinite attributes or an Absolute free from all determinations ; [7] nor is it the deistic conception of an external Creator or First Cause. Neither " Own Cause " nor " First Cause " will be our conception, but—if we must speak of cause at all—then it will be Final Cause. And Final Cause must mean the purpose of realising goodness. The difficulty of the conception of Creation is mixed up with the difficulty of the relation of the time-process as a whole to ultimate reality ; and with that difficulty I am not making any attempt to deal. [8] But the notion of Creation involves a more essential

[7] Spinoza and Bradley may be supposed to be in view here. Sorley on the whole is unfriendly to the term "the Absolute," as out of keeping with the theistic view of the world. If "the Absolute" means the sum-total of reality—as it does for monism—it cannot be equated with "God" as theism interprets that name, for there are elements in the world which, as they now are, cannot be regarded as manifesting the divine nature.

[8] For Sorley's view of the time-process as a whole, and its ontological status, see his article in *Mind* for 1923, pp. 145–159, entitled

point than the idea either of a beginning *in* time or of a beginning *of* time. It involves the idea of God as the ground or support of the world—not merely its beginning —for without him it could not at any moment exist.[9] For this reason, while we may not see God in each natural event, we must yet look through nature to God and see his mind in its final purpose.

I have already spoken of nature as the medium for the production and perfection of goodness in finite minds. This interpretation we may give—indeed, we must give —if we accept the moral and the natural orders as belonging together. But it does not follow that it will explain everything in nature. It would be too proud an assumption to assert that the whole of nature, of which we know only the barest fragment, has no other purpose than this one which concerns ourselves. Omniscience is a foible against which the modest philosopher should be on his guard. What other purposes than this there may be in the wealth of worlds which people space, or even in the small world known to ourselves, we cannot tell; and, except as a matter of speculative interest, it does not concern us to know. On such questions the only safe attitude is one of provisional agnosticism. But these doubtful issues do not interfere with our interpretation of our own consciousness and the world which environs it. The certainty of the moral law is not affected by anything that lies hidden among the unexplored recesses of the starry heavens.

The same conception of purpose, which guides the theist

" Time and Reality." There he argues that the whole process in time—in which, according to absolute monism, "the finite is pushed out into apparent reality only that it may get pushed back again" —can only be saved from meaninglessness if the finite brings back to its source a value gained from its adventure in time.

[9] In theology the idea of "creation out of nothing" has been used as an indispensable symbol of this sheer dependence of the world on God.

in the explanation of the world of nature, must serve him also in the interpretation of the realm of finite spirits. They too must be interpreted through their purpose, and this purpose will be, as before, the realisation of goodness. But there is this difference. Nature is a medium only; *through* it the end is to be reached. But minds are not a mere medium : it is *in and by* them that values are to be realised. They must themselves attain these values and not merely receive them. To nature we can ascribe no power or freedom of its own ; each of its operations must be regarded as prescribed for it. But finite spirits themselves either contribute to working out the world-purpose or else oppose their wills to it.

The question of freedom has been already discussed, and the validity of the idea defended. And I may now venture to express the opinion that it is essential to the theistic interpretation of reality. So many theists are convinced determinists, that this statement may have an appearance of arrogance. Yet no other view seems to me really open. If there is no freedom in man's volition, and each act is rigidly determined by his inherited disposition and his environment, then it is plain that every act of man is really caused by that being who is the author at once of his nature and of the world in which he lives. To his Creator, and only to his Creator, it ought to be imputed. And, if this is so, we are left without any kind of hypothesis by which to explain the preference of the worse to the better course, or to render that preference consistent with the goodness of God. On the determinist theory, as on the assumption of freedom, man and nature may be purposive, and in the end harmony may be established and goodness triumph. But, on the former theory, we can think of no reason why goodness should not have been established from the outset, or why men should have been formed with dispositions that led them to sin. The evil in the world has to be referred to God as its author; and ethical theism falls to the ground.

If ethical theism is to stand, the evil in the world cannot be referred to God in the same way as the good is referred to him; and the only way to avoid this reference is by the postulate of human freedom. This freedom must be a real freedom, so that it may account for the actual choice of evil when good might have been chosen.[10] We have therefore to face the inference that there is a limitation of the divine activity; that things occur in the universe which are not due to God's will, though they must have happened with his permission, that is, through his self-limitation. Nor does this view justify the objection that we are making the divine nature finite; for, if it is conceived as limited, it is not limited by anything outside itself. Rather we may say that a higher range of power and perfection is shown in the creation of free beings than in the creation of beings whose every thought and action are predetermined by their Creator.

On the other hand, individual freedom is not, and cannot be, unlimited; otherwise each free being would require a world of his own, and there would be no universe. And clearly man's freedom is restricted by the conditions both of heredity and of environment. The range of his selection is limited by the experience which gives content to his life, as well as by the inherited tendencies which are his from the beginning of his career. These afford ample opportunity for freedom in the development of his activity, but not unrestricted openings for any and every

---

[10] The conception of " original sin," as asserted not merely by theologians but (in essence) by such a philosopher as Kant, is a suggestion that we do justice to the whole fact and meaning of sin only when we describe it as both free and necessary—a dire and universal entanglement of human life for which we nevertheless judge ourselves responsible.

kind of life. A man cannot at will choose to be a mathematician, an artist, a statesman, or even a millionaire. But there is one form of activity which is never closed, and that is the realisation of moral values ; one choice before every man, the choice of good or evil.

This is the limitation of human freedom which applies to man as a part of nature ; and it is such that the line which nature restricts least, and leaves most open to free determination, is that concerned with the production and increase of moral values. But the more important aspect of the limitation remains. Man's freedom must surely be limited from the side not of nature only, as the medium in which it is exercised, but also of God. How then are we to conceive this limitation without man being altogether absorbed by God ? The world as a time-process has a certain unity through natural law, but this law fails to cover or to account for the volitions of free minds ; it has a further unity in the moral order, but this unity is still an ideal and never in our experience completely realised. Its full unity must therefore come from the fact that it is a purposive system, in which nature is the medium of moralisation, and finite minds are the agents who, in free alliance and free struggle, work out this unity in achieving their own perfection. The purpose exists eternally in the divine mind, and the time-process is the scene on which finite minds bring it about. Their agency must, therefore, be somehow directed—or, as the theologians say, over-ruled—towards the attainment of this end.

But may not the time-process end, after all, simply in confusion, perhaps in disaster, and its purpose fail ? This is, indeed, a suggestion that has found a place in many theologies, which have imagined a hostile spirit—a prince of this world—who, although of lower rank and power, can yet frustrate the designs of the Supreme Mind by his implacable enmity. This is only one of the ways in which the unity of nature and morality is denied. It presents a vivid picture of the world-struggle, but no solution of the universal problem, beyond denying that there is a true universe. Short of this supposition, and on the lines of our own reflexion, may it not be imagined that the world-plan meets only with partial success tempered by partial failure, that multitudes of finite spirits fail for ever to realise the good that is in their power ? Freedom is a dangerous gift, and is the danger only to the recipient ? In conferring this gift on finite beings may not the Supreme Mind have called into existence a power which he can no longer control, in the only way in which free spirits can be controlled ?

This suggestion, again, cannot be refuted by conclusive argument. It is less violent and imaginative than the previous suggestion, but it is equally inconsistent with any view of a complete unity of the universe. My argument has been all along that, ultimately, the unity of the universe must be conceived as ethical ; and this conception would bring moral discord into the heart of things. Can we regard the Supreme Mind as having so little foresight as to be unable to see the result of his own purpose ? It has usually been maintained that this must be so, if free will be admitted. It is said that foreknowledge is inconsistent with freedom, so that, if men are free, their volitions cannot be foreseen even by divine intelligence, and God must be frequently taken by surprise by their actions. This view calls for examination, for it seems to me that it tends to misinterpret the nature of free activity, and that it assumes that divine and human foreknowledge follow the same method.

A man's free actions proceed from himself, that is, from his character. But what is his character ? It is not simply a combination of distinct factors whose growth may be traced separately. None of these factors has any reality except in the unity of the conscious life ; and this unity is not open to the inspection of an observer. The latter's knowledge of another self is always external and therefore incomplete. He is thus liable to surprises, not because an incalculable force may irrupt here and there into the otherwise orderly processes of volition, but because there is something within the circle of a man's character and dispositions that can never be adequately known to another, and that something is its centre. But God's knowledge need not be external, like that of the human observer. To him man's mind must be known from within, and, at the same time, without the obscurity and imperfection with which the man knows himself.

Even this, it may be urged, does not show that a choice which is truly spontaneous can be foretold. Such a choice implies a real possibility of opposites, a real absence of predetermination, so that it could not be foretold even by complete knowledge from within of a man's character. Perhaps this is so. But it does not follow that divine foreknowledge works by the same method as human anticipation. It need not be of the nature of an inference from character as the cause to action as the effect. We can conceive another way, though its use is not open to us. The event which we perceive is never strictly instantaneous ; it has a certain duration, very short, indeed, but not infinitesimal. This is our time-span, and in it we see at a glance what is really a succession. If this time-span were considerably enlarged, we should have immediate knowledge of a longer series, for example, of a succession of actions in which a resolution is made and carried out. Within the time-span differences of past and future do not interfere with immediacy. Why then should not all time be seen as one by an infinite intelligence ? Assuming that God's knowledge is not limited to a finite span of the time-process, the whole course of the world's history will be

seen by him in a single or immediate intuition. The
question how a particular event, such as the action of a
man, comes about—whether by free will or by mechanical
necessity—will make no difference to the immediacy of
that intuition. What we call foreknowledge will be just
knowledge ; past and future, equally with present, lie open
to the mind of infinite time-span.

For this reason it appears to me that freedom is not
related to foreknowledge in the same way as it is to
predetermination. Universal determination contradicts
freedom ; universal knowledge does not. And we cannot
suppose that God, to whose view all time lies open, would
call into existence spirits whose activity would frustrate
his purpose in their creation.[11]

Apart, therefore, from solutions which limit either the
power or the knowledge or the goodness of God, the theistic
world-view must maintain not only that the moral purpose
of the universe is eternally present in the mind of God, but
also that it will attain actual fulfilment in the finite minds
through whom it is being worked out. And for this reason
God must be regarded as not far off from each individual
spirit. In what way this divine providence, direction, or
overruling actually operates is a problem which philosophy
cannot undertake to solve without assistance from that
range of experience which I have not taken into account—
the facts of the religious consciousness.[12]

[11] Even those who were unable to give whole-hearted assent to
this impressive argument might still contend that the certainty
both of freedom and of universal divine foreknowledge are native to
religious faith, and insist on being retained, even at the cost of an
insoluble antinomy.

[12] It is, however, a legitimate but difficult question whether apart
from religious experience the ethical facts themselves can be fully
recognised and appreciated. If, *e.g.*, the independence of moral
beings has been *communicated* by the divine will, and thus is rooted
in a dependence on God which is not merely past but present, does

But one result emerges. I have said before, and the
assertion followed from the preceding argument, that, in
interpreting the world, theism has to proceed by selection
when it seeks in the world or in men traces of the divine.
The principle of selection cannot be anything else than the
moral order which has been taken as the ground from
which we must explain the course of the world. In all
goodness we must see the manifestation of the divine
purpose, in all evil a temporary failure in its realisation.
In so far as men strive for its realisation they are ethically
at one with God ; in so far as they lose sight of this end they
are ethically at variance with him. And this principle is
not arbitrary ; it follows directly from the position given
to the moral order and from the way in which the order
of nature and finite minds is related thereto. The old
moralists who explained " conscience " as meaning " knowledge with God," may have given a fanciful derivation of
the word. But the idea which prompted the derivation
was not far wrong. In the moral consciousness we have
some apprehension of the value which gives meaning to the
world and which has been interpreted as a divine purpose ;
and in moral practice we co-operate towards the fulfilment
of this purpose.

The theistic view of the world which I have been considering is definitely an ethical view. It was led up to by an
inquiry into the facts of value in the world and by the
conception of a moral order of the world ; and it issues in
a view which finds the moral purpose of the world to be
the purpose of a Supreme Mind, and which regards finite
minds as attaining unity with this Supreme Mind, not by
the absorption of their individuality but by the perfecting

not this cast some new light on the meaning of freedom as such ?
Is it in the end possible to sever ethics from religion without destroy-
ing the distinctive character of ethics itself ?

of their character in co-operating with the divine purpose.
Other values than the ethical have dropped out of sight in
the course of the argument.   Yet the general view which
has been reached might be extended so as to cover them
also.   Wherever there is intrinsic worth in the world, there
also, as well as in moral goodness, we may see a manifestation of the divine.   God must therefore be conceived as
the final home of values, the Supreme Worth—as possessing the fulness of knowledge and beauty and goodness and
whatever else is of value for its own sake.

This view has not been put forward on account of its
religious importance.   That is a side of things which I have
hardly ventured to touch.   It is given as an interpretation
of reality which takes equal account of existents and laws
and moral values.   And, as such, it is neither inadequate
to cover the facts of experience, as any naturalistic theory
is, nor does it betray the hopeless incongruity on fundamental points which we find both in pluralism and in
monism.   At the same time, it is not contended that the
view solves all questions or that it does not raise problems
of its own.   The solutions it gives are for the most part
general ; they offer a principle of explanation rather than
an explanation of each event in detail.   If particulars
can be explained by it, it is mostly by the help of the
religious consciousness which claims a more intimate
apprehension of God than morality can offer.   And the
conception of a unity which is not yet but is to be realised,
and which when realised will be ethically complete, though
individualities remain distinct, raises speculative problems.
Is God the Absolute ? it may be asked ; and if not, is he
not therefore finite, so that the universe is incompletely
unified by the idea of God ?   It may be answered that, if
by the Absolute is meant the sum-total of reality, then
there are real events and real beings which do not, as we
see them, manifest the divine nature, so that God and the

Absolute will not be identical. But there is nothing out-side God in the sense of being fully independent of his being and will. The independence of finite beings is a restricted independence communicated by the divine will. If we conceive God as unable to limit himself in this way, then this conception also limits his power. It appears to me that the idea of the self-limitation of God involves no greater difficulty than the idea of the manifestation or appearance of the Absolute in things and persons. And, on the most rigid theory of the Absolute, the diversity of its appearances must be admitted—even if they are held to be only the appearance of diversity. These questions, however, call for further discussion. . . .

THE IDEA OF GOD.

The perplexities connected with the ideas of infinity and absoluteness are inevitable for any explanation of the relation between finite beings and the ground of reality as a whole, though they appear in their most pointed form in elucidating the doctrine of ethical theism. Here they are part of the difficulty of conceiving the co-existence and co-activity of God and man in the same universe. They are problems of form, however, rather than of content, and their solution does not supply us with a positive idea of God. This positive idea has to be arrived at from the nature of reality as known to us—the reality which is inter-preted through the idea of God. Reality, as we have found, includes certain values of which we have a more or less adequate apprehension ; and the realm of nature, or of causation, can be interpreted as belonging to the same universe as the realm of values only by regarding it as instrumental towards the discovery and production of values by finite minds. On this view the idea of the ground of reality, or God, is reached through the idea of value.

Here, therefore, the idea of value is fundamental. Even the attributes of intelligence and power (although postulated on other grounds also) will, from this point of view, be held to belong to the divine nature because of their implication in the idea of value and their necessity for its realisation. The term " perfection," which means value or worth at its highest point, is therefore more appropriate in speaking of God, and more significant of his positive nature, than either the term " infinite " or the term " absolute." [13]

If we conceive God as simply infinite being, then our idea of him is reached by the denial of a characteristic of finite beings ; and we have only a negative idea of God.[14] But if we conceive him as the perfect being, our idea is positive, it means that certain qualities known to us are present in him in their fulness. To this line of argument also objections have been taken. Just as the idea of God as infinite is a negative idea got by denying the limitations of finite beings, so it has been argued that the positive idea of God as perfect is founded upon the observation of certain qualities actually belonging to finite persons ; so that the whole procedure, in the first place, is anthropomorphic, an inference from man to God, and in the second place, so far as it has any validity at all, is only analogical, while the difference between God and man is so great that the validity of any analogy must be of the slightest.

A short consideration of these objections will bring out the true nature of the idea. Our idea of God is properly called anthropomorphic when it is arrived at by an inference from or modification of human qualities. In this way if the reasoner starts from the power, goodness, and intelligence of man and argues that God must therefore be

[13] See p. 393 above, note 7.
[14] By some modern writers the term " unconditioned " has been put forward as conveying in a more adequate form the meaning to which " infinite " points.

powerful, good, and intelligent, only in a higher, indeed an infinite degree, then the procedure is anthropomorphic, and we may say that man is making God after his own image. There may be apologies for this procedure, for at least it is true that there is no higher object immediately known to man than the human mind, and it is therefore more reasonable to hold that God is like man than that he resembles other created things. But it is not the procedure that has been adopted in this book. We have not argued that God is good because we find goodness in man, but that he is good because we find the idea of goodness to be valid for that universal order which we are trying to understand. And we speak of his wisdom and his power, not because man has some share of these qualities, but because they are implied in that conception of the world as purposive which is necessary to explain the relation of the order of nature to the moral order. This method of argument is not anthropomorphic, any more than are arguments concerning causal processes or mathematical relations. The latter depend on our apprehension of certain objective connexions just as the former proceeds from our ideas of objective moral values. The knowledge in both cases is due to our power of knowing, but this does not make it anthropomorphic, for it is a knowledge of relations and of values whose validity is independent of their manifestation in human beings.[15]

But when we try to understand the way in which goodness or wisdom or power belongs to God, we are dependent upon our knowledge of the manifestation of these qualities in finite persons. To this extent our knowledge of the divine attributes rests upon our knowledge of human qualities. From knowledge of the latter we get some

[15] The above explanation is of vital significance for our estimate of Sorley's general argument, and failure to allow for it has occasionally led to misapprehension of his exact line of reasoning.

indication of the way in which moral and other values belong to personality ; while their connexion with the limitations of human personality marks off the features which are peculiar to their realisation in man.[16]   Man is a spiritual being, but he is a spirit immersed in matter, restricted in time and space, and sensuous as well as spiritual.   Human virtues are the excellences of a being with this double nature ; sensuous in his impulses, spiritual in the ideals which are open to him.   The moral value which the virtue expresses may have a more or less close connexion with the sensuous basis of man's character, and the virtue accordingly may be less or more akin to the realisation of the same value in a being who is purely spiritual and therefore not subject to the restrictions of a sensuous and material nature.   Courage, for instance, and temperance are human virtues which we cannot attribute in anything like their human form to the divine nature, for they postulate obstacles on the part of sense or of impulse to moral performance.   The meaning of these virtues lies mainly in the control of unruly desires or impulses.   In other virtues the factor of positive worth is more prominent, and they can be understood without reference to the restrictions of their human embodiment.   This is most true in the case of wisdom and of love, which express the fundamental characteristics of the values of truth and goodness.

Even here the inference from the human manifestation to the divine is limited by the analogy of the spirit of man to the spirit of God.   Wisdom, regarded as a divine attribute, does not imply the human method of knowledge with its precarious advance from step to step and its restricted range.   But it does involve all knowledge, though the method of divine apprehension will differ from the human.   All the truth must be God's, as has been

[16] Cf. the Selection from Lotze above, p. 369 ff.

said, intuitively or without the discursive process by which the human understanding mostly works ; so that truth may be said to belong to his nature, whereas for man it is something to be attained. Something similar holds true when we speak of the love of God. By moralists love has been regarded as the crowning feature of the virtuous life, and theologians have reached no more profound definition than that God is love. Can it be said that the two qualities—the human love and the divine—are only connected by an uncertain analogy ? It is true that love, as used of God, does not connote all that it habitually does in its human manifestations, while on the other hand it must at the same time connote much more. But it does in both cases mean the will to the good of others and the will to communion with them. The good which love seeks is not in either case merely happiness, but rather, in the first place, the realisation in each person of the values of which he is capable. And the communion which love seeks will be facilitated by agreement as to the values most cherished. Love is possible as a one-sided relation only ; but the communion in which it finds satisfaction is a reciprocal relation. Communion with God is therefore possible only when man's nature is purged from lower desires and his affection set on the things that are more excellent. Only the pure in heart can see God and hold communion with him. Thus the love of God is a will to the good of men which has as its end the communion of man with God, and it is manifested in the secular process whereby the soul is turned from things of sense to spiritual interests and is thus fitted for citizenship in the kingdom of God.

It is in the light of the idea of God, as thus sketched, that we must seek to understand the co-activity of God and man in the world. The world has been spoken of as

revealing a divine purpose, and man, who is also purposeful
has been regarded as working out or opposing that purpose.
How far is " purpose " used in the same sense when we
thus bring the divine and the human together ?   For any
finite mind, and in any limited system, the purpose implies
an end which is outside the actual process ; the idea of the
end determines the conscious activity ; but the end itself
lies beyond the action, at the close of the temporal process.
Now, reality as a whole can have nothing outside it, its
purpose must be within itself ; and of reality as a whole
God is the ground or reason, so that his purpose and
activity cannot be limited by time or space.   Thus conceived, the divine purpose must be held to be free from
that distinction between means and attainment which
characterises finite purposes.   Two marks, however,
remain which are common to purpose in both its kinds.
The first of these is consciousness ; the purpose implies
insight and determination by reason or wisdom.   The
second is value ; the whole is somehow good, either goodness realised or goodness sought.   In the practical life of
morality this good has to be striven for by continuous
effort and is achieved only by successive approximations.
In this respect, therefore, human and divine purpose are
differentiated.   But even in human life there are experiences in which this limitation is less obtrusive than it is in
morality.   In contemplation and in artistic enjoyment
the temporal element may almost disappear from consciousness, so that these kinds of life have often seemed to the
philosopher or to the artist to approach most nearly to
the divine.* Perhaps we can have no better analogue
of the eternal life.[17]

* See a symposium on " Purpose and Mechanism," *Proceedings of
the Aristotelian Society*, 1912, especially pp. 251–255.

[17] It may perhaps be inquired whether this slight disparagement
of the temporal element, and the consequent denial that the dis-

In this way the human consciousness may be regarded as in touch with the divine. On the other hand the divine purpose, although conceived as in itself free from time and change, cannot be shut off from the process in which it receives temporal fulfilment. This temporal process is in some way its manifestation. Creation, emanation, reproduction, appearance are terms which have been used to indicate the nature of this manifestation. None of them gives any explanation of the origin of the finite from the infinite, or can claim to be more than a metaphor. Behind them, and unanswered by them, lies the question of the way in which we are to conceive the divine purpose as working. Do the decrees of God determine from eternity all that each man does and attains ? Does the divine nature draw after it as a necessary consequence the whole history of the world ? Does it reproduce itself by an inevitable process in each temporal event ? The question is put in different ways, but it has seemed to many thinkers that, however put, the answer must be the same. Whether they have preferred to speak of creation, or of emanation, or of appearance, the concept of causation has ruled their thought. No room has been left for the freedom of the finite ; ultimately, all activity has been referred to God, or to the fundamental reality, however named. The relation of divine and human agency, therefore, no longer presents any problem, for human activity is explained as merely a necessary consequence of the divine nature or divine decree.

A real problem arises when we recognise that finite

tinction between means and attainment ought to be carried up into the divine purpose, is in harmony with the plea for the positive status of time in reality referred to in p. 393 above, note [8]. If any event or series of events in time is in point of fact the means to the realisation of a cosmic end, must it not be recognised as such, even by the divine thought ?

spirits are not merely reproductions of or channels for the divine activity but themselves genuinely purposeful and active. God is contemplated as communicating freedom to men that they may attain the values which only free beings can realise and enjoy. Men are free to work out their purposes, and, at the same time, there is a divine purpose in the world which human history fulfils and to which the environment of nature is subordinate. Here God and man meet. The divine purpose is that values should be realised in man's nature, and it can be attained only by man making this purpose his own. Hence the possibility of co-operation and also of conflict ; and through the latter arise the sense of estrangement and need of atonement that mark the religious consciousness. How is the agency of both God and man to be conceived without an arbitrary dualism which treats God as if he were simply one member in a finite interaction ?

One way of dealing with the difficulty would be to mark off separate spheres for the divine activity and the human. And this often seems to be the purport of traditional distinctions, such as that between the natural and the supernatural, or between the realms of nature and of grace. The whole region of common life—our dealings with nature and our ordinary social relations—would in this way be assigned to the guidance of man's free will ; but, beyond these, a region would be recognised in which the human soul is in contact with the highest. In the presence of God he will be powerless—clay in the hands of the potter, who makes one vessel to honour and another to dishonour. This is the realm of grace ; and in it the divine spirit acts upon man irresistibly, choosing him for sonship and training him for communion with God, or else passing him by and leaving him " to the freedom of his own will." But it is not possible thus to split up man's life into two separate regions. The ordinary affairs of common life

are affected by the deepest things of the spirit ; the soul of
man is a unity, though its divine flame may burn feebly
in the earthly air. Even the theological ethics, which
enforces the distinction between supernatural grace and
natural virtue, holds that that grace influences the whole
nature of man. Nor can we be content to explain the
unequal distribution of grace by a simple appeal to the
divine good pleasure, without any regard to man's response.
To do so would annul man's freedom at the centre of his
being. In meeting and welcoming the divine grace man's
spirit is not passive but responsive ; and the divine influence
comes as a gift and not by compulsion. " Behold, I stand
at the door and knock," * said the Master. Entry is craved,
not forced. And there is a secret shrine prepared for his
advent :

> This sanctuary of my soul
> Unwitting I keep white and whole,
> Unlatched and lit, if Thou should'st care
> To enter or to tarry there.

Here accordingly the theological doctrine of irresistible
grace is relinquished.[18] The spirit of God is conceived as

---

* Rev. iii. 20—quoted in this connexion by Professor Pringle-
Pattison, *The Idea of God*, p. 292.

[18] Yet it may reappear in a different form — a form which repudiates unconditionally the idea of the divine personal influence
(which is what " grace " means) as an infinite quasi-mechanical
force acting as it were in a straight line, and yet seeks to express the
overmastering power of the love of God. The constraint of duty and
affection towards another man may be felt to be such that, although
acting with conscious freedom, the agent truly says : " I can no
other." And this may hold true, *in sensu eminenti*, of the felt appeal
of the divine goodness—an appeal in and through which divine power
or grace is energising. In the highest religious experience of
obedient faith the contrast of grace and freedom vanishes—except
in so far as the initiative is with grace—and to divide the ground
between God and man is seen to be vain. But when man will not

working in and through the spirit of man, but in such a way as not to destroy human freedom. So long as we regard the divine influence as a quasi-mechanical force such a conception is impossible. But it is no longer so when we apply to the problem the idea of God as love. Love works through freedom. Compulsion or threats interfere with freedom ; but in love spirit appeals to spirit in virtue of their fundamental affinity. The soul may be immersed in routine without thinking of the deeper things in life, or it may assert its lower interests and remain deaf to the call of God. But that call is to its essential nature and spiritual destiny ; and, if the call is answered, the soul finds its freedom in fulfilling the divine purpose.

make God's purpose his own, grace and freedom become opposites, and we are left with the enigma of a relation between them in which the divine purpose is *not* being fulfilled.

References.—Professor Sorley's other writings should be consulted, especially his *Ethics of Naturalism* (1885) and *Recent Tendencies in Ethics* (1904). See also W. R. Matthews, *Studies in Christian Philosophy* (1921), and *God in Christian Thought and Experience* (1930).

XIV.

PLURALISM AND THEISM.

JAMES WARD (1843–1925).

The Realm of Ends, 1911.

IN facing the high problem of Theism those who follow
the *à posteriori* road have the choice between taking as
their primary datum the Physical or the Mental order,
or both taken together on various terms.   In the last
hundred years the successes of Physical Science have drawn
interest prominently in that direction, and the literature
which sets forth its significance has been extensive.   But
for this Selection we offer an important Argument to
Theism from the mental datum, to replace that of Paul
Janet in our earlier editions by one which has appeared
since his day

The prominence of Pluralism upon a psychological basis
is largely due to one who was an original psychologist
himself and the master of a vivacious expository style,
William James :   endowed also with an indomitable
courage which led him to extend the range of mental life
needing consideration both to the recesses of sub-conscious-
ness and to the open field of the experiences covered by the
term " Mysticism."   Led by William James these enlarge-
ments of the field of Mind have been worked upon
abundantly, and have provided new material for the
examination of Theism.   But a deeper psychology than
that of James has been needed, and has been supplied, and
it is this which is offered in brief summary by this extract
from the writings of James Ward.   Additional value
attaches to it from the fact that Ward's work embodies
results which bring into action some of the leading ideas
of the comprehensive philosophies of Leibniz, Kant,

Herbart, Lotze, and Wundt, which operated, with due criticism and modification, in the thought of Ward.

It was appropriate that further resort to the primacy of mentality should have been made by Ward, the first Professor of " Mental Philosophy " at Cambridge. A lifetime of study, teaching, and writing had resulted in a presentation of Psychology which has been acclaimed as the highest level of exposition of the Science, and has given a new lustre to the succession of British psychologists, distinguished as that succession has been.

As the title of Ward's constructive volume shows, he regarded the world of Mind as essentially Teleological, a " Realm of Ends." Its ultimate constituents are taken to be living and conscious individual minds, acting selectively ; manifestly a plurality, but also seen to be working together as an interacting whole. But when Psychology has made its report we are invited by Ward to stand back, as it were, and ask both whence ? and whither ? as to the units and as to the interconnexion. And to do this with the age-long concept of Theism, in some form or other, in our minds. In the words of Professor Dawes Hicks, who knew well what he was saying, " Ward threw his entire strength into the attempt to show that Theism can be sustained."

Our extract from this masterly argument is Ward's own summary of what he conceived himself to have accomplished in application to (i) method of treatment of the problem ; (ii) the character of the Theistic conception ; (iii) the relation of Deity to the World ; and (iv) the justification for a further resort to Faith as coadjutor with Reason in this supreme quest.[1]

Positive Results Attained.

And now to state succinctly the positive results we seem to have attained. They may be gathered up under

[1] The full scope of the constituent minds and the fact of their interaction must be kept in view throughout Ward's writings. A neglect to do this by Professor Muirhead led Ward to protest, " I am not and never have been a pluralist " (*Replies to Criticisms*, in 3rd ed. p. 495) ; meaning, of course, that he dissociated himself from the extreme positions of the rigorous Pluralists, Herbart and William James.

four heads relating to Method or standpoint, to God or the One, to the World or the Many, and to Faith in the Unseen.

I. As to method—we have started from what we are, cognitive and conative subjects ; and from where we are—so to say *in mediis rebus*—in a world consisting to an indefinite extent of other like subjects. No speculation, no dialectic, no ontological deduction, is needed to reach this position ; and without it all these alike are impossible. But beginning thus, we are led both on theoretical and on practical grounds to conceive a more fundamental standpoint than this of the Many, namely, that of the One that would furnish an ontological unity for their cosmological unity and ensure a teleological unity for their varied ends, in being—as it has been said—" the impersonated Ideal of every mind " [2]—the One, as ultimate source of being and ultimate end of their ends. But though we can conceive this standpoint, we cannot here attain to it or see the world from it. It is there, like their centre of gravity for the inhabitants of a planetary ring, but the aspect of the world from thence is more than we can conceive. Attempts to delineate this have been really but projections of our own eccentric and discursive views : creative synthesis as human implies aspects, creative intuition as divine is beyond them. The result of all attempts to begin with the One is only to lower our idea of the world, not to raise our idea of God. His *modus operandi,* if even this phase is allowable, in creating, conserving, and ruling the world is beyond us.

II. As to God from the point of view of man, then, we can only regard him as Spirit, as possessing intelligence and will, and so as personal. But while we must admit such attributes carried to their limit to be beyond us, we cannot regard God as absolute in such wise as to deprive

[2] Howison, *Limits of Evolution,* 2nd ed. p. xiv.

ourselves of all personality or initiative.[3]   How God created the world, how the One is the ground of the Many, we admit we cannot tell ; but since it is from the Many as real that we start we are forced to say that creation implies limitation ; otherwise the world could be nothing. Such theism would be acosmism.   But while we have to maintain that in determining the world—his world—God also determines himself, it would be absurd to suppose that in thus determining himself he, so to say, diminishes himself.   Such determination may be negation, nay must be, to be real at all ; but it is not abnegation.   God does not transform, differentiate, or fractionate himself into the world, and so cease to be God.   Such theism would only be pantheism, which is truly but atheism.[4]   But now, finally, if the world, though God's world, the expression and revelation of himself, is yet not God, if though he is immanent in it, he is also as its creator transcendent to it, surely the greater the world—the greater the freedom and capacity of his creatures—the greater still is he who created and sustains and somehow surely overrules it all. Oriental servility and *à priori* speculation have made God synonymous with an " Infinite and Absolute " that leaves room for no other and can brook none.   To express dissent from this view, the unfortunate term " finite God," devised by those who uphold the view, has been accepted from them by its opponents.   As used by the former, it implies and was meant to imply imperfection and de-

---

[3] Ward's Personalist conclusion as to Theism is one of the marks of his affinity with Lotze.   They agree in contemplating Deity as a knowing and experiencing Subject, active and loving His " world of self-determining free agents."

[4] Here Ward delivers us from the cold breath of Spinoza's famous saying, *Determinatio negatio est* (Ep. 50).   This cannot be accepted if it means that the One is broken up or dissolved into the Many. This would give us Pantheism, and so, in result, no Theism at all, as Ward points out.

pendence, to place God in line with the Many and to deny his transcendent supremacy. So understood a finite God is a contradiction, of course. But the term " finite God," as accepted by the latter, means for them all that God *can* mean, if God implies the world and is not God without it : it means a living God with a living world, not a potter God with a world of illusory clay, not an inconceivable abstraction that is only infinite and absolute, because it is beyond everything and means nothing, an ἀπειρόθεος as Thomas Davidson, I believe, called it.[5]

III. And now as to this living world, of which God is the ground, this realm of ends which he respects because it is his end—it is, we say, a world of self-determining, free agents, severally intent on attaining more good, or at least on retaining the good they have. We note three main characteristics—contingency in part, stability in part, and progress in part—all involved in experience as epigenetic. There is contingency, for a common *modus vivendi* is still to seek ; there is stability, for all effectual co-operation is conserved as good ; and there is progress, so long as the ills we have or the goods we know not of prompt to further efforts. But goods we know not of are ideal ; and ideal ends are only possible on the plane of rational life : the brutes at least leave well alone, and species as soon as they are adjusted to their

[5] The concept of Deity as finite, but with limitation induced by and from himself, is an interesting phase of recent philosophy of religion in Britain and America. It can be traced back to Hume and Mill, but gained its vogue from William James. It received an early welcome at Oxford : Bishop Gore was attracted by it (Bampton Lectures, 1891) ; and Rashdall made it prominent (*Personal Idealism*, p. 390 ff.). A long and closely argued adverse criticism has been made by Archbishop D'Arcy, *Proceedings* of the Aristotelian Society, 1917, followed up by a vigorous defence by Dr. F. C. S. Schiller in the same volume. Here Ward rejects it as " very inaccurate " in its usual statement ; but he acknowledges some force in it when the problem of Evil has to be confronted (*Realm of Ends*, p. 316).

27

environment remain stationary, so long at least as that
remains unchanged. Such a stationary state may be
possible where progress is due solely to the *vis a tergo* of
actual physical ills ; it is impossible, even though these
should cease, once the Good as an ideal has loomed in
sight, and begun as a *vis a fronte* to draw spirits onwards.
But it has taken untold ages to accomplish that finite
amount of progress which the pressure of material want
promotes ; can we then expect the indefinite progress
that spiritual possibilities open up will be easily or speedily
achieved ? Compared with the interval between the
lowest forms of merely animal life and the highest, the
interval between civilised man and man in the infancy of
the race, is vast ; and yet, so far as we can judge, the time
it has occupied is correspondingly brief. The greater
definiteness and steadiness of purpose that intelligence
brings and the permanent tradition that social co-operation
makes possible have then unquestionably accelerated the
rate of progress on the whole.

But now struggles of a new order arise through this
very progress itself. Moral evils spring up and grow
apace in the rich soil of worldly prosperity ; for the intelligence and social continuity that make nobler ideals
possible can also subserve the ends of selfishness, injustice,
and oppression. Thus the greatest enemy of mankind is
man : so it has always been, so it may long continue to be.
Yet here too there has been progress ; and the vision of a
new era, when righteousness shall cover the earth as the
waters cover the sea, evokes the lip-service of multitudes
and the life-devotion of a few. But time, that tries all
things, will assuredly bring more and more to take the
lesson to heart that

" Man must pass from old to new,
From vain to real, from mistake to fact,
From what once seemed good to what now proves best,"

But why, we ask, must the lesson be so slowly learnt ? Because to be effectually learnt, it must be learnt by heart, every jot and tittle of it by actual living experience. Advanced to the plane of social intercourse and rational discourse, man has sought out many inventions, preferring at first what looks easy to what seems arduous, what looks near to what seems remote, what looks tangible to what seems visionary. This we call worldly wisdom. The more all its schemes are found to fail, the more clearly will stand out the one straight and narrow way—at first so hard to find and still so hard to ascend—that verily leads to life. As from geology we learn of species after species that have disappeared in the process of adjusting organism to environment ; so in history we learn from the rise and fall of empire after empire that only righteousness exalteth a nation and that those that pursue evil perish. It is thus in the light of evolution that the mystery of evil becomes clearest. God is the creator of the world, we say : his end can only be the Good—no other is even conceivable. But in a world created for the Good there can be no inherent, no ineradicable evil. The process of evolution must then in itself be good, the one way possible to actual good for creatures that are created to achieve it. And if again we ask why the way is so long and the progress so devious and so slow, we can but sup- pose it is so because only so can the progress be thorough and the way assuredly the best ; this we may well believe is why "the mills of God grind slowly and grind exceeding small." Only after proving all things can we hold fast to that which is good.[6]

[6] For Ward's treatment of the problem of Evil reference must be made to the various points at which it comes to be dealt with in his writings. The present volume includes three lectures upon it : Evil and Pessimism ; Evil and Optimism ; Moral Evil and Moral Order. In the text above, the sentence, " In a world created for the

But now—and this leads on to our last head—does this not come near to saying, it may be asked, that the best of all possible worlds is a world without God ? is it not practically atheism, in short ? and if not that, still, if the world is left severely alone to work out its own salvation, what have we but the God-forsaken world in which the so-called deists are said to have believed ? Not atheism, certainly, for faith in God as the ground of the world affords us an assurance, which we could not otherwise have, that complete harmony and unity, the good of all in the good of each, is really attainable, nay, will verily be attained. Whereas, if we stop at a plurality of finite selves in interaction, we have no guarantee, cannot even reasonably expect, that such a totality will ever attain to perfect organic unity. Nor does the theism to which pluralism points leave no place for God *in* the world ; it is then not deism : creation, if we think, we shall see can be conceived only as continuous presence.* If God is the ground of the world at all he is its ground always as an active, living, interested Spirit, not as a merely everlasting, changeless, and indifferent centre, round which it simply whirls. Still God's action in the world must be for us as inscrutable as his creation of it : indeed there is no reason why we should attempt to discriminate between them. In calling God transcendent we seek only to express that duality of subject and object which we take as fundamental to all spiritual being, not to suggest that his relation to the world must be thought under the category of external causation, like the interaction of object with object. This is obviously inadequate. Nor is the relation of God to the world comparable to the interaction of one finite subject

Good there can be no inherent, no ineradicable evil," stands out with impressive force.

* Cf. above, Lect. xii. pp. 260 f.

with another ; for between them there is no such dependence as that which connects them both with God. We
trench upon the mystical when we attempt to picture this
divine immanence, " closer to us than breathing and nearer
than hands and feet." It is this which stirs the " cosmic
emotion " of poets like Wordsworth, Goethe, Browning,
and Tennyson, to this that the inward witness of the
spirit refers which is the essence of religious experience
everywhere. In both there opens out in varying degrees of
clearness and certainty

> " The true world within the world we see,
> Whereof our world is but the bounding shore."

This is the unseen world, the world not realised, in which
faith moves.[7]

IV. In keeping with the great principle of continuity,
everywhere displayed in the working out of the world's
evolution, we have found this faith foreshadowed in the
upward striving that is the essence of life. Consider
for a moment the development of the senses. The first
clear response is to mechanical contact, and we have as
the first specific sense, the sense of touch. From this is
presently differentiated the sense of hearing, when objects
not yet present to actual touch give premonitions of their
proximity by the vibrations they set up : hearing is thus
the faith of touch. As hearing to touch so smell stands

---

[7] Here Ward comes in sight of Mysticism. He affirms that " the
essence of religious experience " everywhere rests upon the internal
Witness of the Spirit—the same phrase as that adopted by T. H.
Green at Oxford, in his intimate colloquies with his pupils at Balliol
forty years before Ward's lectures. This is the type of the experiences which Ward in his closing pages assigns to Faith as not included in the area covered by Reason with which his Gifford Lectures
deal. These are experiences which are due to no vain or presumptuous rival of Knowledge, but to a legitimate outcome of man's
central nature, capable of acting in concord with Reason, and giving
us the final synthesis we need.

to taste : it is a foretaste that further extends the objective range. A freckle or pigment-spot is all that light at first produces ; but when its hints are *heeded* and the pigmented retina that first arose is furnished by the organism's own prophetic efforts with directing muscles, it exchanges its passive sight for active vision, and opens out a vastly wider objective world.   In keeping with all this is the place of faith on the higher plane where it contrasts with intellectual sight : it is like a new sense that brings us face to face with an unseen world.   What does this mean ? Let us go back a step.   Here as everywhere—in its highest as in its lowest form—faith is striving and striving is faith.   The whole conscious being is concerned : there is not merely the cognition of what is, there is also an appreciation of what it is worth, a sense of the promise and potency of further good that it may enfold ; there is a yearning to realise this ; and there is finally the active endeavour that such feeling prompts.   It is through this faith that man is where he is to-day, through it that mountains have been removed and the unattainable verily attained.   More life and fuller achieved by much toil and struggle, an ascent to higher levels, not movement along the line of least resistance—this is the one increasing purpose that we can so far discern, when we regard the world historically as a realm of ends in place of summarising it scientifically under a system of concepts.

And how do we stand now ? That the present world and progress on the plane of the present world do not and never will meet our highest needs—about this there is little question.   But where in what is, in what we have so far attained, can we discern those eternal values that point upwards and beyond this present world ?   Surely in all that we find of the beautiful and sublime in this earth on which we dwell and the starry heavens above it ; in all that led men long ago to regard nature as a cosmos ; in

all that is best and noblest in the annals of human life ;
in these very needs themselves that the seen and temporal
fail to meet ; and above all, in that nascent sense of the
divine presence which constitutes the truly religious life,
and converts faith into the *substance* of things hoped for,
the *evidence* of things not seen. But now a third question
at once suggests itself. Faith on the lower levels was
justified by its results : can we here too apply this test
of success or failure ? The founder of Christianity at any
rate did not hesitate to appeal to it :—" Beware of false
prophets. Ye shall know them by their fruits : do men
gather grapes of thorns or figs of thistles ? " And, in fact,
this is the test that is and will be applied ; for, as I have
already said, however much in theory men consider pre-
misses, in practice they consider only results.

A powerful practical argument in favour of religious
faith might be worked out on the following lines :—first
we might point to its *universality* : no race of mankind is
wholly without that feeling of dependence on the supernatural and mysterious, which, as Schleiermacher thought,
is the common characteristic of religious emotion. Next
we might point to its *survival* ; no race has yet outgrown it.
There have been periods of religious decline, no doubt ;
but they have sooner or later involved moral and intellectual
decadence as well. And in these days when faith is said
to be waning, we find that "things are in the saddle and ride
mankind," and whither that tends history has made only
too clear. Hitherto—in keeping with the judgment by
results—such times have been followed by periods of
revival and awakening ; and there are happily signs of
such in our own day. Lastly we might point to the
advance of religion that has usually accompanied the
increase of morality and intelligence ; nay, we might
show that religion has largely furthered such advance.
And here by way of contrast I may refer briefly to a strange

prophet, whose writings are at this moment exciting the keenest attention—I refer to Nietzsche. As the struggle for existence and the survival of the fittest have brought man to the highest place as the paragon of animals, so in time they will lead, he teaches, to a yet higher being, the *Uebermensch* or Over-man. But this higher man, he foretells, will reject the existing morality of liberty, equality, and fraternity, founded on the golden rule of benevolence and brotherly love—the morality of slaves as he contemptuously names it. The new morality will be the morality of heroes, that is, egoists : might will be right. As man now subjugates the lower animals to his own ends, so the Over-man will exploit feebler men and—as it has been sarcastically put—rise on stepping-stones of *their* dead selves to higher things. In short, a race is to appear, so Nietzsche and others would have us believe, that is to try the experiment of life wholly on the lines of what is called " modern thought " and wholly without faith in God or a world to come. I do not think the growing Nietzsche cult will last long or in the end do harm. If the terrible experiment must be tried * we may safely anticipate the result : it will be Hobbes's state of nature over again ; till the world retraces its steps.

It will be said, perhaps :—" The regenerate Christian is already an *Uebermensch*, no longer ' natural man,' but ' spiritual ' in the Pauline sense ; nor is his experience fairly described as subjective belief in God ; it is actual love of God and conscious communion with him." We have no right to question this ; though we must admit that such inward conviction of the reality of religious experience is, for *the purposes of our discussion*, to be classed as faith, not as knowledge, in so far as it is—epistemologically, though not psychologically—subjective, incommunicable,

* When writing this sentence (in 1902) I feared, like many, that the experiment *would* be tried, and it has been !

and objectively unverifiable. In so far, however, as he lets his light shine and men see his good works, the religious man affords practical evidence of the worth of his faith. With enough of such light, the justification of faith would be sure.[8]

One final question, among the many that suggest themselves, I must not wholly omit. We have been contemplating the universe as a realm of ends. If we were asked what is the end of this realm of ends we might answer rightly enough that its end can only be itself ; for there is nothing beyond it, and no longer any meaning in beyond. It is the absolutely absolute. Still within it we have distinguished the One and the Many, and we have approached it from the standpoint of the latter. In so doing we are liable to a bias, so to say, in favour of the Many : led to the idea of God as ontologically and teleologically essential to their completion, we are apt to speak as if he were a means for them. Those who attempt to start from the standpoint of the One betray a bias towards the opposite extreme. The world, on their view, is for the glory of God : its ultimate *raison d'être* is to be the means to this divine end. Can we not transcend these one-sided extremes and find some sublimer idea which shall unify them both ? We can indeed ; and that idea is Love. But here again we trench on the mystical, the ineffable, and can only speak in parables. Turning to Christianity as exhibiting this truth in the purest form we know, we find it has one great secret—dying to live, and one great mystery—the incarnation. The love of God

[8] Ward admits the fact of experiences of the religious type which are " subjective (epistemologically), incommunicable, and objectively unverifiable." But he does not include these within the orbit of his rational method, unless they find expression in good works in the objective world. Some such term as Faith is required to designate them, and we must make a synthesis of such Faith with Reason when we make our complete account of Religion.

in creating the world implies both. *Leiblichkeit ist das
Ende aller Wege Gottes,* said an old German theologian.
The world is God's self-limitation, self-renunciation might
we venture to say ?   And so God is love.   And what must
that world be that is worthy of such love ?   The only
worthy object of love is just love : it must then be a world
that can love God.   But love is free : in a ready-made
world then it could have no place.   Only as we learn to
know God do we learn to love him : hence the long and
painful discipline of evolution, with *its* dying to live—
the converse process to incarnation—the putting off the
earthly for the likeness of God.   In such a realm of ends
we trust " that God is love indeed, and love creation's final
law."   We cannot live or move without faith, that is clear.
Is it not then rational to believe in the best, we ask ; and
can there be a better ?

THE COSMOLOGY OF THEISM.

It will be well to recall what theism as such in any case
implies, viz. that the initial state, from which pluralism
seeks to start as a fact, finds in God its ground and reason.
The bare existence of reality in the plural, it may be
argued, seems no more to demand a ground than its bare
existence in the singular.   But when the Many, regarded as
existentially independent of each other, are found to be
mutually complementary, conspiring, as it were, to realise
an intelligible organic whole, then the presence from the
first of an underlying unity suggests itself.   Why should the
Many tend towards one end unless they had in the One
their source ?   Otherwise, the further we attempt to
regress must we not allow that the more inconceivable a
supreme end becomes ? *   Those who decline to accept
theism may either leave such questions unanswered,

* Cf. Lect. IX. p. 197.

centuries before Hegel was born. Up to this point the reconciliation of pluralism and theism seemed possible, but here the disagreement threatens to be radical : an evolution that is essentially dialectical demands more than pluralism, resting on the *prima facie* evidence of experience, can accept ; while evolution as epigenesis seems even more clearly to conflict with the ideas of theism generally current. We come in fact upon the old problem of " fixed fate, free-will, fore-knowledge absolute " ; intractable as it has proved, we must needs try to discuss this problem with open minds.[10]

References.—Psychological Principles (1918) ; *Naturalism and Agnosticism* (4th ed. 1906) ; *Realm of Ends,* or *Pluralism and Theism* (3rd ed. 1919) ; *Essays* (ed. Sorley and Stout, 1927). Cf. art. by Professor Dawes Hicks, *Hibbert Journal* (October 1925) ; *Memoir*, by Mrs. O. Ward Campbell, in the volume of *Essays*.

---

[10] Ward then proceeds to consider the bearing of his Theism upon the problems of Freedom and Evil.

XV.

RELIGION AS JUDGMENTS OF WORTH.

RITSCHL (1822—1889).

ALBRECHT RITSCHL, who may be described as the chief and, perhaps, the most interesting figure in the world of theology for the past twenty-five years, deserves a place in a volume like this, mainly on account of his reasoned and impressive attempt to work out a new theological method. To some extent he may be said to have built upon the foundations of Kant and Schleiermacher, and in his later years the influence of Lotze upon his thinking was easily traceable. Early in his intellectual development, too, Ritschl had come into sympathetic contact with nearly all the tendencies which have helped to mould the higher thought of the age ; he is indeed to a great degree an " epitome and reflection " of the chief spiritual movements of his generation, though never ceasing to preserve an extremely vigorous independence of mind. Ritschlianism has a claim to general consideration for the function it continues to discharge, in a time of intellectual transition, as a missionary theology with a special attractiveness for minds that have been nourished upon science.

The most salient characteristics of the Ritschlian system, viewed on its philosophical side, are the exclusion of metaphysics from theology, the effort to dispense with speculative Theism, the all but exclusively practical conception of religion, and the strongly marked antithesis which is set up between religious and theoretical knowledge. All these features are obviously only different applications of a single principle. While Ritschl is at one with Schleiermacher in contending that the theologian must take his stand upon the Christian experience, and find his materials in the consciousness of redemption which is present in believing men, yet he is resolute in emphasizing the fact that in the interpretation of Christianity we must recur at every point to the definite historical revelation given in the person of Jesus Christ. Not subjective experience, but revelation, thus realised objectively in a fact of history, is the basal element in Christianity.

The extracts from the great work on *Justification and Reconciliation*, which we have given below, are chiefly designed to put before the reader Ritschl's theory of religious knowledge as a system of value-judgments. In a well-known passage he divides judgments into two classes—*theoretical judgments*, which predicate certain relations of the object as it exists in its own nature, and *value-judgments*, which affirm its *value* or *worth* for the percipient Self, according to the pleasure or pain it excites. The former enter into science and philosophy, the latter into ethics, æsthetics, and religion. It is essential to observe that no adherent of this theory, in any of its forms, would concede that value-judgments are less objectively valid or certain than those assigned to the theoretical class : it is only claimed that the mind reaches a persuasion of their truth by a different avenue. And it is contended, from the same point of view, that no propositions should be given a place in theology except those which have a distinctively moral and religious interest—in other words, to take the aptest illustration for our purpose, no Theistic proof can be regarded as either cogent or apposite which does not rest at bottom on the ultimate notion of *worth*.

Sympathetic discussion of these topics in the past few years has had for its main object to dispel the air of subjectivity and caprice which at first seemed to attach to value-judgments, the real validity of which had been prejudiced by certain inconsiderate expressions used in the first expositions of the theory. But it is increasingly felt that Ritschl, aided by the large and enthusiastic school which rapidly gathered round him, has done a very real service to religious thought by the force and persistency with which he has urged the truth that the apprehension of spiritual realities is spiritually conditioned, even though his conception of the significance of spirit may seem unduly narrow. He has done this by proclaiming that faith and science appeal to different interests and capacities in the mind of man, and that "nothing worth the proving can be proven."

Our extracts are taken from the Introduction and the fourth chapter of *The Christian Doctrine of Justification and Reconciliation* (a translation of vol. iii. of the original work, containing Ritschl's own dogmatic system, and edited by Mackintosh and Macaulay, T. & T. Clark, 2nd ed. 1902).

GOD NOT A METAPHYSICAL CONCEPTION.

From Introduction.

There are no sufficient grounds for combining a theory of things in general with the conception of God. That is done, however, when Aristotle gives the name God to the idea of the highest end which he postulates as winding up the cosmic series of means and ends, and so as an expression of the unity of the world. This conjunction of the two forms the content of the teleological argument for God's existence constructed by Scholastic theology. We have a similar case in the cosmological argument. It exhibits a metamorphosis of the Neoplatonic view of the world, which rests merely upon the idea of things and their causal connexion. Now in religion the thought of God is given. But the religious view of the world, in all its species, rests on the fact that man in some degree distinguishes himself in worth from the phenomena which surround him and from the influences of nature which press in upon him.[1] All religion is equivalent to an explanation of the course of the world—to whatever extent it may be known—in the sense that the sublime spiritual powers (or the spiritual power), which rule in or over it,

---

[1] This is the fundamental value-judgment which, for Ritschl, lies at the basis of all religion. The objection has been urged, not quite unreasonably, that such a view puts the world rather than God into the place of primary importance as a religious incentive. (Cf. Orr, *The Ritschlian Theology and the Evangelical Faith*, 1897, p. 70 ff.) Religion has the appearance of a weapon at which man has grasped in the struggle for existence,

conserve and confirm to the personal spirit its claims and its independence over against the restrictions of nature and the natural effects of human society. Thus the thought of God, when by the word is understood conscious personality, lies beyond the horizon of metaphysic, as metaphysic is defined above.[2] And both these proofs for God's existence, whose construction is purely metaphysical, lead not to the Being the idea of which Scholastic theology receives as a datum from Christianity, but merely to conceptions of the world-unity which have nothing to do with any religion. This use of metaphysic, consequently, must be forbidden in theology, if the latter's positive and proper character is to be maintained.

THE FUNDAMENTAL MOTIVE OF RELIGION.

From Chapter IV.

In every religion what is sought, with the help of the superhuman spiritual power reverenced by man, is a solution of the contradiction in which man finds himself, as both a part of the world of nature and a spiritual personality claiming to dominate nature.[3] For in the former *rôle* he is a part of nature, dependent upon her, subject to and confined by

[2] Founding upon a narrow and strained interpretation of Aristotle's language, Ritschl defines metaphysics as the systematic investigation of the regulative conceptions of knowledge. In other words, he identifies metaphysics with epistemology, and thus ignores the data for metaphysical thought which are yielded, *e.g.*, by ethics and æsthetics.

[3] This definition of religion, let it be remembered, is meant to be "neither a statement of the common characteristics of all religions, nor a determination of the universal ideal of religion, but a description of the tendency which in all religions finds more or less adequate expression." Garvie, *The Ritschlian Theology*, 2nd ed. 1902.

other things; but as spirit he is moved by the impulse to maintain his independence against them. In this juncture, religion springs up as faith in superhuman spiritual powers, by whose help the power which man possesses of himself is in some way supplemented and elevated into a unity of its own kind which is a match for the pressure of the natural world.[4] The idea of gods, or Divine powers, everywhere includes belief in their spiritual personality, for the support to be received from above can only be reckoned on in virtue of an affinity between God and men. Even where merely invisible natural powers are regarded as Divine, they are conceived in a way analogous to that in which man distinguishes himself from nature. For the rest, the ease with which definite stupendous natural phenomena, whether beneficent or destructive, are personified, proves that it is in the spiritual personality of the gods that man finds the foothold which he seeks for in every religion. The assertion [5] that the religious view of the world is founded upon the idea of a whole certainly holds true of Christianity: as regards the other religions it must be modified thus far, that in them what is sought is a supplementary addition to human self-feeling or to human independence over against and above the restrictions of the world. For in order to know the world as a totality, and in order himself to become a totality in or over it, by the help of God, man needs the idea of the oneness of God, and of the consummation of the world in an end which is for man both knowable and realisable. But this condition is fulfilled in Christianity alone.

. . . .

[4] *I.e.* it is constituted a self-enclosed and independent personal life, a spiritual unity or whole, which, in contrast to the multiplicity of the world of things, is *sui generis*.

[5] *Vide* Lotze, *Microcosmus* (English translation), vol. ii. p. 577.

THE PECULIAR CHARACTER OF RELIGIOUS KNOWLEDGE.

How, then, is *religious knowledge* related to theoretical or philosophical knowledge?[6] This question, indeed, has already been raised by the very fact of Greek philosophy; still, much more tangible and comprehensive reasons for raising it are to be found in the mutual relations of Christianity and philosophy. Accordingly, it is best that we should limit the question to Christianity in so far as it is a religion, intelligible as such from the characteristics noted above. The possibility of both kinds of knowledge mingling, or, again, colliding, lies in this, that they deal with the same object, namely, the world.[7] Now we cannot rest content with the amiable conclusion that Christian knowledge comprehends the world as a whole, while philosophy fixes the special and universal laws of nature and spirit. For with

---

[6] It is because they are unanimous in using the idea of value-judgments, as the feature by which scientific is to be differentiated from religious knowledge, that the members of the so-called Ritschlian school, amid much free and even wide internal divergence, may rightly be viewed as a strong and distinctive "movement" in present-day theology. Among the more prominent members of the school may be named Harnack, the well-known Church historian of Berlin, Kaftan, Herrmann, Reischle, Loofs, Bornemann, and Häring. Already there are signs that the company of Ritschl's disciples must sooner or later part into a "Right" and a "Left" wing, as happened in the case of Hegelianism, according as the separate members of the party approach or diverge from the expression which the Christian faith has received in the historic creeds. See the works cited above, and cf. also Ecke, *Die theologische Schule Albrecht Ritschls*, 1897, pp. 67–130.

[7] On this point Ritschl wavered. The "amiable conclusion" with which, he says, "we cannot rest content," was once his own, and is expressed in the first edition (1874) of the work from which we are quoting. Finally, though with curious and inconsistent reversions to his earlier standpoint, he came to adhere to the view set forth in the sentences which follow.

this task every philosophy likewise combines the ambition to
comprehend the universe under one supreme law. And for
Christian knowledge, also, one supreme law is the form under
which the world is comprehensible as a whole under God.
Even the thought of God, which belongs to religion, is
employed in some shape or other by every non-materialistic
philosophy. Thus no principle of discrimination between the
two kinds of knowledge is, at least provisionally, to be found
in the object with which they deal.

Now, in order to elicit the distinction between the two
from the realm of the subject, I recall the twofold manner in
which the mind (*Geist*) further appropriates the sensations
aroused in it. They are determined, according to their value
for the Ego, by the feeling of pleasure or pain.[8] Feeling is
the basal function of mind, inasmuch as in it the Ego is
originally present to itself. In the feeling of pleasure or
pain, the Ego decides whether a sensation, which touches the
feeling of self, serves to heighten or depress it. On the other
hand, through an idea the sensation is judged in respect of
its cause, the nature of the latter, and its connexion with
other causes ; and by means of observation, etc., the knowledge of things thus gained is extended until it becomes
scientific. The two functions of spirit mentioned are always

---

[8] In assigning so great, and so direct, an importance to the feeling of
pleasure and pain Ritschl shows clearly the influence of Lotze. Cf.
the latter's unequivocal declaration (*Outlines of a Philosophy of Religion*, Conybeare's translation, p. 123) : "What we mean by *value* in
the world lies wholly in the *feeling* of *satisfaction* or of *pleasure* which
we experience from it." Later discussions have led to the drawing of
a necessary line of distinction between the *feeling* of worth and the
judgment of worth. The most careful treatment of the whole subject
is to be found in Reischle, *Werturteile und Glaubensurteile*, Halle,
1900. Cf. three articles by Professor Garvie in the *Expositor* for 1903,
under the title "The Value-Judgments of Religion," and a paper "On
the Judgment of Value," in J. Orr's *Ritschlianism : Expository and
Critical Essays*, 1903.

in operation simultaneously, and always also in some degree mutually related, even though it be in the inverse ratio of prominence. In particular, it must not be forgotten that all continuous cognition of the things which excite sensation is not only accompanied, but likewise guided, by feeling.[9] For in so far as attention is necessary to attain the end of knowledge, will, as representing the desire for accurate cognition, comes in between; the proximate cause of will, however, is feeling as expressing the consciousness that a thing or an activity is worth desiring, or that something ought to be put away. Value-judgments therefore are determinative in the case of all connected knowledge of the world, even when carried out in the most objective fashion. Attention during scientific observation, and the impartial examination of the matter observed, always denote that such knowledge has a value for him who employs it. This fact makes its presence all the more distinctly felt when knowledge is guided through a richly diversified field by attention of a technical or practical kind.

But even if we have made up our mind that religious knowledge in general, and therefore Christian knowledge too, consists of value-judgments, such a definition is as lacking in precision as it would be to describe philosophical knowledge contrariwise as disinterested. For without interest we do not trouble ourselves about anything. We have therefore to distinguish between *concomitant* and *independent* value-judgments. The former are operative and necessary in all theoretical cognition, as in all technical observation and combination. But all perceptions of moral ends or moral hindrances are *independent* value-judgments, in so far as they excite moral pleasure or pain, or, it may be, set

[9] This seems to cast some doubt on the impartial objectivity even of scientific study. But elsewhere Ritschl corrects this impression by insisting on the difference between the feeling of interest in knowledge as such, and interest in particular conclusions.

in motion the will to appropriate what is good or repel the
opposite. If the other kinds of knowledge are called "disinterested," this only means that they are without these
moral effects. But even in them pleasure or pain must be
present, according as they succeed or fail. Religious knowledge forms another class of independent value-judgments.
That is, it cannot be traced back to the conditions which
mark the knowledge belonging to moral will, for there exists
religion which goes on without any relation whatever to the
moral conduct of life. Besides, in many religions, religious
pleasure is of a purely natural kind, and is independent of
those conditions which lift religious above natural pleasure.
For only at the higher stages do we find religion combined
with the ethical conduct of life. Religious knowledge moves
in independent value - judgments, which relate to man's
attitude to the world, and call forth feelings of pleasure or
pain, in which man either enjoys the dominion over the
world vouchsafed to him by God, or feels grievously the lack
of God's help to that end.[10] This theory is almost more
easily intelligible if it be tested by religions which possess
no moral character. Orgiastic worships represent contending natural feelings with extraordinary intensity, and with
abrupt changes, in virtue of their recognition of the value
which the identity of the Godhead with the vegetation as
it decays and again revives, has for the man who modifies
his attitude towards the world of nature in sympathy with
the Godhead which he adores. The peculiar nature of religious value-judgments is less clear in the case of religions of
an explicitly ethical character. Nevertheless, in Christianity
we can distinguish between the religious functions which
relate to our attitude towards God and the world, and the

---

[10] In this *locus classicus* we should note that the religious value-
judgment is viewed as being primarily, not upon God, but on the world
and our attitude to it. This order has generally been reversed by
Ritschl's followers. Cf. p. 432, note [1].

moral functions which point directly to men, and only indirectly to God, Whose end in the world we fulfil by moral service in the Kingdom of God. In Christianity, the religious motive of ethical action lies here, that the Kingdom of God, which it is our task to realise, represents also the highest good which God destines for us as our supramundane goal. For here there emerges the value-judgment that our blessedness consists in that elevation above the world in the Kingdom of God which accords with our true destiny. This is a religious judgment, inasmuch as it indicates the value of this attitude taken up by believers towards the world, just as those judgments are religious in which we set our trust in God, even when He condemns us to suffering.

In its day the Hegelian philosophy represented theoretical knowledge as not merely the most valuable function of spirit, but likewise the function which has to take up the problem of religion and solve it. To this Feuerbach opposed the observation that in religion the chief stress falls upon the wishes and needs of the human heart.[11] But as the latter philosopher also continued to regard professedly pure and disinterested knowledge as the highest achievement of man, religion, and especially the Christian religion—which he held to be the expression of a purely individual and therefore egoistic interest, and a self-delusion in respect of its object, God—was by him declared to be worthless, as compared not merely with the knowledge of philosophic truth, but also with purely moral conduct. But an interest in salvation in the Christian sense, when rightly understood, is incompatible with egoism. Egoism is a revolt against the common tasks of action. Now, people might say that faith in God for our salvation, and a dutiful public spirit towards our fellows, have nothing to do with one another, and that therefore

[11] In his *Das Wesen des Christentums*, which appeared in 1841, and some years later was translated into English by George Eliot.

there is no conceivable reason why religion, as a rule, should not be egoistic. But in Christianity, precisely, faith in God and moral duty within the Kingdom of God *are* related to one another. As a rule, therefore, it is impossible that Christian faith in God should be egoistic. On the other hand, theoretical knowledge in itself, as has been shown, is not disinterested; but moral conduct is still less so. For in the latter domain the vital point is that one realises as one's own interest the interest of others to whom the service is rendered. The moral disposition can nowhere strike root save in such motives. It is true that, contrary to the rule, faith in God may be combined with egoistic arrogance towards others. But the same danger attaches to both of the other kinds of activity which have been compared. It is possible for one occupied with theoretical knowledge to be vain and haughty, and for one devoted to the moral service of others to be tyrannical or sycophantic.

Scientific knowledge is accompanied or guided by a judgment affirming the worth of impartial knowledge formed by observation. In Christianity, religious knowledge consists in independent value-judgments, inasmuch as it deals with the relation between the blessedness which is assured by God and sought by man, and the whole of the world which God has created and rules in harmony with His final end. Scientific knowledge seeks to discover the laws of nature and spirit through observation, and is based on the presupposition that both the observations and their arrangement are carried out in accordance with the ascertained laws of human cognition. Now the desire for scientific knowledge carries with it no guarantee that, through the medium of observation and the combination of observations according to known laws, it will discover the supreme universal law of the world, from which, as a starting-point, the differentiated orders of nature and spiritual life, each in its kind, might be explained, and understood as forming one whole.

On the contrary, the intermingling and collision of religion and philosophy always arises from the fact that the latter claims to produce in its own fashion a unified view of the world.[12] This, however, betrays rather an impulse, religious in its nature, which philosophers ought to have distinguished from the cognitive methods they follow. For in all philosophical systems the affirmation of a supreme law of existence, from which they undertake to deduce the world as a whole, is a departure from the strict application of the philosophic method, and betrays itself as being quite as much an object of the intuitive imagination, as God and the world are for religious thought. This is the case at all stages and in all forms of Greek philosophy, especially in those forms in which the ultimate universal grounds of existence, through which the universe is interpreted, are identified with the idea of God. In these cases the combination of heterogeneous kinds of knowledge—the religious and the scientific—is beyond all doubt; and it is to be explained by the fact that philosophers, who, through their scientific observation of nature, had destroyed the foundations of the popular faith, sought to obtain satisfaction for their religious instincts by another path. In a certain respect, too, they were able to follow this tendency with especial confidence, so far as they succeeded in making out the unity of the Divine Being to be the ground of the universe. But in another respect they failed to satisfy the essential conditions of the religious view of the world, partly in so far as they surrendered the personality of the Godhead thus identified with the ground of the world, partly because they had to give up the active influence of a personal God upon the world. Nor, under these circumstances, could any worship be deduced from the idea of God. Thus the collision of Greek philosophy with the popular faith was twofold,

[12] Here an old, and what Ritschl considers a superseded, view persistently endeavours to reassert itself. Cf. p. 453, note [7].

and in both respects inevitable. For one thing, the actual observation of nature and her laws is incompatible with the religious combination of popular views of nature and the idea of God. Further, the rigidly unified view of the world held by philosophers is incompatible with the religious view of the world which is only loosely developed in Polytheism. But the real force of the latter incompatibility is to be found in the fact that, under the guise of philosophic knowledge, what was really only the religious imagination has been operative in designing the general philosophic view of the world, the supreme principle of which is never proved as such, but always merely anticipatively assumed.

.   .   .   .

AN ILLUSTRATION FROM LUTHER.[13]

That religious knowledge consists of value-judgments is brought out in a felicitous way by Luther in his *Larger Catechism*, in the explanation of the First Commandment : "Deus est et vocatur, de cuius bonitate et potentia omnia bona certo tibi pollicearis, et ad quem quibuslibet adversis rebus ac periculis ingruentibus confugias, ut deum habere, nihil aliud sit, quam illi ex toto corde fidere et credere. . . . Haec duo, fides et deus, una copula coniungenda sunt." In these sentences are expressed various truths, of which the theology of the schools both earlier and later has taken no account, and which its modern successors combat even yet. Knowledge of God can be demonstrated as religious knowledge only when He is conceived as securing to the believer such a position in the world as more than counterbalances

[13] In this paragraph we find an admirable illustration of the Ritschlian theory of religious knowledge. God, to the religious man, is not a mere philosophical notion, but an intensely practical reality. Whether Ritschl and his school are right in their interpretation of Luther's theology is an interesting and hotly disputed point.

its restrictions. Apart from this value-judgment of faith, there exists no knowledge of God worthy of this content. So that we ought not to strive after a purely theoretical and "disinterested" knowledge of God, as an indispensable preliminary to the knowledge of faith. To be sure, people say that we must first know the nature of God and Christ ere we can ascertain their worth for us. But Luther's insight perceived the incorrectness of such a view. The truth rather is that we know the nature of God and Christ only in their worth for us.

.   .   .   .

IS THE IDEA OF GOD APPREHENSIBLE BY SCIENCE?

When we mark the attitude taken up by the human spirit towards the world of nature, two analogous facts present themselves. In theoretical knowledge, spirit treats nature as something which exists for it; while in the practical sphere of the will, too, it treats nature as something which is directly a means to the realisation of the common ethical end which forms the final end of the world. The cognitive impulse and the will both take this course without regard to the fact that nature is subject to quite other laws than those which spirit obeys, that it is independent of spirit, and that it forms a restraint on spirit, and so far keeps it in a certain way in dependence on itself. Hence we must conclude either that the estimate which spirit, as a power superior to nature, forms of its own worth—in particular, the estimate which it forms of moral fellowship, which transcends nature—is a baseless fancy, or that the view taken by spirit is in accordance with truth, and with the supreme law which is valid for nature as well. If that be so, then its ground must lie in a Divine Will, which creates the world with spiritual life as its final end. To accept the idea of God in this way is, as Kant observes, practical faith, and not an act of theoretical cognition. While, therefore, the Christian religion is thereby proved to be in harmony with reason, it is always with the reservation that knowledge of God embodies itself in judgments which differ in kind from those of theoretical science.[14]

The meaning, therefore, of this moral argument for the necessity of the thought of God differs altogether from the aim of the other arguments; and for that reason the success it attains surpasses that of the others. The cosmological and teleological arguments are intended to show that the conception of God—necessary to complete the circle of knowledge—is similar in kind to the results of science. A truth which for religious faith is certain is thus proved, it is held, to be at the same time the result of scientific cognition as it advances from observation to observation and crystallises into conclusions, and should be set up as the criterion of theological science. But this method ends in failure, partly because neither argument takes us beyond the limits of the world, partly because their pretended results, even if they were correct, differ from the Christian conception of God in this, that they fail to

[14] The question at issue in this important paragraph may be stated thus : Can science furnish the idea of God ? Two conflicting strains of thought, which we take to be indicative of the transition through which Ritschl's mind was passing, may be differentiated here. On the one hand, he still clings to the belief that it is possible to construct a valid theoretical proof of God's existence on the lines of Kant's moral argument, in the sense that the Christian idea of God supplies a unifying principle which science can accept as rationally accounting for the coexistence of nature and spirit. On the other hand, he is growingly certain that the idea of God "can be represented only in value-judgments," and that science, therefore, as such, is incapable of recognising or apprehending it. The first line of argument was attractive, because it seems to vindicate the right of theology to the name of science ; the second still more so, because it brings into relief the fact that spiritual knowledge is wholly dependent on faith.

express His worth for men, and in particular His worth for men as sinners. On the other hand, while Kant regards practical faith in God, conceived as endowed with the attributes which Christianity ascribes to Him, as necessary to complete our knowledge of the world, yet he does not posit this idea—which is an object merely of practical faith, and cannot be proved apart from such faith—as a conception which is theoretical or rational in the sense of general science. On the contrary, he maintains it in its original and specific character. Now it is the duty of theology to conserve the special characteristic of the conception of God, namely, that it can only be represented in value-judgments.[15] Consequently it ought to base its claim to be a science, when looked at in itself, on the use of the method described above, and, when looked at in its relation to other sciences, by urging that, as Kant was the first to show, the Christian view of God and the world enables us comprehensively to unify our knowledge of nature and the spiritual life of man in a way which otherwise is impossible. When we have once got a true conception of this point, a review of the moral constitution of man, based upon the principles of Kant, will serve as the *ratio cognoscendi* of the validity of the Christian idea of God when employed as the solution of the enigma of the world.

References.—The student should consult the books which have been cited in the notes. In addition the following will be found useful :— Stählin, *Kant, Lotze, Albrecht Ritschl*, English translation, 1889 ; Swing, *The Theology of Albrecht Ritschl*, 1901 ; Pfleiderer, *Development of Theology in Germany and Great Britain* ; Adams Brown, *The Essence*

---

[15] This sentence may be called the theological motto of Ritschlianism. The question still awaiting solution is whether, even if we grant that judgments of science and judgments of faith spring from different and equally valid interests, the unity of the mind does not necessarily compel us to hold that they *must* be combined in our final view of things.

of Christianity, 1902, chap. vii. (with an excellent bibliography) ; and various articles in the *American Journal of Theology*, and *Zeitschrift für Theologie und Kirche.* Cf. also J. K. Mozley, *Ritschlianism* (1909), and G. Halliday, *Facts and Values* (1914). There are many points of contact between Ritschlian thought and that set forth in Sabatier's *Esquisse d'une Philosophie de la Religion d'après la Psychologie et l'Histoire*, English translation, 1897 (*Outlines of a Philosophy of Religion, based on Psychology and History*).

XVI.

THE NUMINOUS.

RUDOLF OTTO (1859-   ).

IN 1917 there was issued a book, known to English readers
as *The Idea of the Holy*, which has been described as " probably at once the most significant and the most provocative
work on religion which has appeared in our generation."
It was distinguished by an unusually keen sense for the
originality of religion and its forms of feeling and intuition.   The author was Professor Rudolf Otto, occupant
of a theological chair at Marburg, and till then chiefly
known in this country by his earlier work, *Naturalism and
Religion*.   Wide travel and research in various religions
had given him a right to speak with special knowledge.
The sub-title of the new volume on the Holy (*das Heilige*)
was " an inquiry into the non-rational factor in the idea
of the Divine and its relation to the rational."   Its conclusions have no little affinity with those reached by Mr.
Marett, of Oxford, in his *Threshold of Religion*.

According to Otto, there is that in Deity which intrinsically is other than the rational and ethical.   When God
is spoken of as " holy," the adjective contains a certain
non-rational element, irreducible and indefinable, but
capable of being isolated and scrutinised.   For this element
he coins the word " numinous," from the Latin *numen* ;
and he argues that the Holy, as conceived by Christian
Theism, is made up compositely of the numinous *plus*
factors of a rational and moral kind.   The numinous is
closely akin to the sublime, which in Kantian phrase
" schematises " it.   The pages quoted below, in the admirable translation of Professor Otto's book by Professor
J. W. Harvey, are taken from the first six chapters, and give

a delicate yet vigorous analysis of the numinous itself as well as of the effects in feeling which are evoked or liberated by its presence to the human mind. It is felt as a Mystery that both daunts and fascinates.

Throughout stress is laid on the point that religion is neither morals nor mere intellectual belief, but a thing by itself in the sense that what constitutes it is a particular sort of elements or " moments " of feeling. Such feeling, however, is no mere emotion arising subjectively ; it is called forth by, and apprehends, an enigmatic and overwhelming Presence belonging to another world than this. From the first there is a peculiar awareness of the Divine (this is different in quality from every other kind of recognition), which gradually unfolds its content ; but this awareness is such that it can be expressed, not in concepts proper, but exclusively in analogies and symbols. The Divine cannot be demonstrated as real ; it can only be pointed to.

Following Kant in his usage, Otto claims that there is an *à priori* knowledge of the Holy as a specific category of value. It comes with experience, but not out of it ; sense-impressions are its occasions, but not its source. Further, in the complex category of the Holy, not only are both the non-rational element of sacro-sanctity and the rational element of moral goodness purely *à priori*, but their conjunction is so too. The actual inward relationship of the two sides may not come to light till far on in man's religious development, but once it has been recognised, knowledge of its truth comes into the mind with the certitude of first-hand insight, although no logical necessity for the conjunction can be discerned. *A priori* knowledge is not innate knowledge ; this last all possess, the former all *may* possess, if touched by the right stimulus. It is plain that here difficult questions are emerging, both concerning the existence of any religious *à priori* as such and the intricate theory of its inner structure which Otto propounds.

Much of the psychological and theological impressiveness of Otto's book lies in the richness of illustrative material he has drawn from different religions, and above all from the religion of the Bible. Thus he later brings the conception of the numinous to bear on ideas of sin and atonement, and we are shown, in this reference and others, the slow ethicising of the numinous in history, from Moses through prophecy to Christ—where "ethicising" means incorporating the ethical, not merging in it. The Holy, he repeatedly urges, however it may come to be shot through with conceptual and moral factors, never loses its primordial nucleus of formidable and alluring mystery. Morals and rationalising do not between them cover the whole field of religion.

At a still later point Otto treats of the faculty or power native to man by which the presence of the Holy, with its numinous ingredient, is detected. This faculty he names "divination" (here casting back to the religious philosophy of Fries, a contemporary of Kant, in which Otto finds the most solid basis for theology), and insists that such special insight is not in fact within the reach of every normal mind, but belongs only to those whose spirit has been touched from above. The *numen* and the prophet are correlative. Yet although it needs to be awakened, the power of divination is there, and, given the fit conditions, it signals the nearness of the Holy. Before the Holy we are both awed and exalted, abased and yet allured, convinced of our own worthlessness, yet through contact and communion filled with a new sense of worthiness. " By each new obeisance of spirit I mount to His feet."

Otto's orderly and luminous arrangement of facts, too often presented as a confused mass, is of special value. Yet the great importance of his book does not lie here, or in any display of new data, so much as in its disclosure of the unsuspected meaning of data long familiar and precious to the religious mind itself. He contends for a specific and irreducible element in devout experience ; an element which, from certain points of view, seems to make religious experience parallel to our experience of the external world, in the sense that in both cases alike we are confronted by the *given*, and are in contact with an objective reality not ourselves. The response of religion, far from being an auto-suggestive process in the mind, is made to certain definite stimuli—" certain features of the living world," as it has been put, " which have a quite peculiar effect upon us and cannot be ignored." They represent a higher sphere impinging on our life. Otto, that is to say, proceeds upon the basal assumption that every

29

religion claims to be, not only a state of mind in the worshipper, but the apprehension of a Reality which is independent of man's reaction to it and could on no other terms possess for him a real significance.

THE RATIONAL AND THE NON-RATIONAL.

Chapter I.

By rational otto means the conceptual idea.

It is essential to every theistic conception of God, and most of all to the Christian, that it designates and precisely characterises Deity by the attributes Spirit, Reason, Purpose, Good Will, Supreme Power, Unity, Selfhood. The nature of God is thus thought of by analogy with our human nature of reason and personality; only, whereas in ourselves we are aware of this as qualified by restriction and limitation, as applied to God the attributes we use are "completed," *i.e.* thought as absolute and unqualified. Now all these attributes constitute clear and definite *concepts* : they can be grasped by the intellect; they can be analysed by thought; they even admit of definition. An object that can thus be thought conceptually may be termed *rational*.[1] The nature of deity described in the attributes above mentioned is, then, a rational nature; and a religion which recognises and maintains such a view of God is in so far a "rational" religion. Only on such terms is Belief possible in contrast to mere *feeling*. And of Christianity at least it is false that "feeling is all, the name but sound and smoke "—where "name" stands for conception or thought. Rather we count this the very mark and criterion of a religion's high rank and superior value—that it should have no lack of *conceptions*

[1] The restricted, psychological sense in which "rational" is used ought to be noted. It means that of which clear and defined conceptions can be formed.

about God ; that it should admit knowledge—the knowledge that comes by faith—of the transcendent in terms of conceptual thought, whether those already mentioned or others which continue and develop them.[2] Christianity not only possesses such conceptions but possesses them in unique clarity and abundance, and this is, though not the sole or even the chief, yet a very real sign of its superiority over religions of other forms and at other levels. This must be asserted at the outset and with the most positive emphasis.[3]

But, when this is granted, we have to be on our guard against an error which would lead to a wrong and one-sided interpretation of religion. This is the view that the essence of deity can be given completely and exhaustively in such " rational " attributions as have been referred to above and in others like them. It is not an unnatural misconception. We are prompted to it by the traditional language of edification, with its characteristic phraseology

[2] This emphatic protest must not be forgotten by critics of Otto. He holds both things : that the ascent of religion is marked by the ever more perfect fusion of the numinous and the rational or ethical, and that none the less to rationalise and moralise religion completely would be to destroy it *as* religion. (The *rational* aspect of the idea of God is worked out in his book, *Kantisch-Fries'sche Religionsphilosophie*[2], 1921.)   Otto does not take it as an essential part of his task to show how the two disparate elements in the Holy, the numinous and the rational, actually come together and unite.   But he is clear that their union, " the moralisation of the idea of God," is in no sense the elimination of the numinous or its supersession by something else, but its being completed and charged with a new content.   On p. 47 of *The Idea of the Holy* the interpenetration of the non-rational with the rational elements of the religious consciousness, " like the inter-weaving of warp and woof in a fabric," is illustrated by the suffusion of personal affection by the sex instinct.

[3] Otto has a special competence in judging of the relative values of historical religions. His writings on Indian Mysticism take a high place.

non-rational
means what
doesn't belong
to idea or
concept

and ideas ; by the learned treatment of religious themes
in sermon and theological instruction ; and further even
by our Holy Scriptures themselves. In all these cases the
" rational " element occupies the foreground, and often
nothing else seems to be present at all. But this is after
all to be expected. All language, in so far as it consists
of words, purports to convey ideas or concepts—that is
what language means ; and the more clearly and un-
equivocally it does so, the better the language. And hence
expositions of religious truth in language inevitably tend
to stress the " rational " attributes of God.

But though the above mistake is thus a natural one
enough, it is none the less seriously misleading. For so ·
far are these " rational " attributes from exhausting the
idea of deity, that they in fact imply a non-rational[4] or
supra-rational Subject of which they are predicates. They
are " essential " (and not merely " accidental ") attributes of that subject, but they are also, it is important to
notice, *synthetic* essential attributes. That is to say, we
have to predicate them of a subject which they qualify,
but which in its deeper essence is not, nor indeed can be,
comprehended in them ; which rather requires comprehension of a quite different kind. Yet, though it eludes
the conceptual way of understanding, it must be in some
way or other within our grasp, else absolutely nothing
could be asserted of it. And even Mysticism, in speaking of
it as τὸ ἄρρητον, the ineffable, does not really mean to imply
that absolutely nothing can be asserted of the object of
the religious consciousness ; otherwise, Mysticism could

---

[4] By " non-rational " is meant, not the merely incoherent and
contradictory, but that which lies beyond the frontier of logical
thought, and in which the finite mind is confronted with a limit.
" Extra-rational " is the sense. Ideas on the rational side which
form analogous parallels to non-rational elements Otto calls
" schemata," and the use of them " schematisation."

exist only in unbroken silence, whereas what has generally been a characteristic of the mystics is their copious eloquence.

Here for the first time we come up against the contrast between Rationalism and profounder religion, and with this contrast and its signs we shall be repeatedly concerned in what follows. We have here, in fact, the first and most distinctive mark of Rationalism, with which all the rest are bound up. It is not that which is commonly asserted, that Rationalism is the denial, and its opposite the affirmation, of the miraculous. That is manifestly a wrong or at least a very superficial distinction. For the traditional theory of the miraculous as the occasional breach in the causal nexus in nature by a Being who himself instituted and must therefore be master of it—this theory is itself as massively " rational " as it is possible to be. Rationalists have often enough acquiesced in the possibility of the miraculous in this sense ; they have even themselves contributed to frame a theory of it ;—whereas anti-Rationalists have been often indifferent to the whole controversy about miracles. The difference between Rationalism and its opposite is to be found elsewhere. It resolves itself rather into a peculiar difference of *quality* in the mental attitude and emotional content of the religious life itself. All depends upon this : in our idea of God is the non-rational overborne, even perhaps wholly excluded, by the rational ? Or conversely, does the non-rational itself preponderate over the rational ? Looking at the matter thus, we see that the common dictum, that Orthodoxy itself has been the mother of Rationalism, is in some measure well founded. It is not simply that Orthodoxy was dissipated in doctrine and the framing of dogma, for these have been no less a concern of the wildest mystics. It is rather that Orthodoxy found in the construction of dogma and doctrine no way to do justice to the non-rational aspect of its subject. So far from keeping the non-rational element in religion alive in the heart of the religious experience, orthodox Christianity manifestly failed to recognise its value, and by this failure gave to the idea of God a one-sidedly intellectualistic and rationalistic interpretation.

This bias to rationalisation still prevails, not only in theology but in the science of comparative religion in general, and from top to bottom of it. The modern students of mythology, and those who pursue research into the religion of " primitive man " and attempt to reconstruct the " bases " or " sources " of religion, are all victims to it. Men do not, of course, in these cases employ those lofty " rational " concepts which we took as our point of departure ; but they tend to take these concepts and their gradual " evolution " as setting the main problem of their inquiry, and fashion ideas and notions of lower value, which they regard as paving the way for them. It is always in terms of concepts and ideas that the subject is pursued, " natural " ones, moreover, such as have a place in the general sphere of man's ideational life, and are not specifically " religious." And then with a resolution and cunning which one can hardly help admiring, men shut their eyes to that which is quite unique in the religious experience, even in its most primitive manifestations. But it is rather a matter for astonishment than for admiration ! For if there be any single domain of human experience that presents us with something unmistakably specific and unique, peculiar to itself, assuredly it is that of the religious life.[5] In truth the enemy has often a keener

[5] The question whether there are uniquely religious values, or whether what we call religious values are not just ethical values referred to Ultimate Reality, has been much debated. Otto at least seems right in trying to explain adequately the distinction made throughout history between objects with a religious character and

vision in this matter than either the champion of religion or the neutral and professedly impartial theorist. For the adversaries on their side know very well that the entire " mystical unrest " has nothing to do with " reason " and " rationality."

And so it is salutary that we should be incited to notice that Religion is not exclusively contained and exhaustively comprised in any series of "rational" assertions ; and it is well worth while to attempt to bring the relation of the different " moments " of religion to one another clearly before the mind, so that its nature may become more manifest.

This attempt we are now to make with respect to the quite distinctive category of the holy or sacred.

" NUMEN " AND THE " NUMINOUS."

Chapter II.

" Holiness "—" the holy "—is a category of interpretation and valuation peculiar to the sphere of religion. It is, indeed, applied by transference to another sphere—that of Ethics—but it is not itself derived from this. While it is complex, it contains a quite specific element or " moment," which sets it apart from " the Rational " in the meaning we gave to that word above, and which remains inexpressible — an ἄρρητον or *ineffabile*—in the sense that it completely eludes apprehension in terms of concepts. The same thing is true (to take a quite different region of experience) of the category of the beautiful.

objects without it. Religious objects, he would say, are such as arouse a kind of overmastering awe which stands wholly by itself and cannot be analysed into simpler factors, but is a unique and immediate datum of experience. Such awe is relative to a numinous Reality or Presence comparable to nothing except itself.

Now these statements would be untrue from the outset if "the holy" were merely what is meant by the word, not only in common parlance, but in philosophical, and generally even in theological usage. The fact is we have come to use the words *holy, sacred* (heilig) in an entirely derivative sense, quite different from that which they originally bore. We generally take "holy" as meaning "completely good"; it is the absolute moral attribute, denoting the consummation of moral goodness. In this sense Kant calls the will which remains unwaveringly obedient to the moral law from the motive of duty a "holy" will; here clearly we have simply the *perfectly moral* will. In the same way we may speak of the holiness or sanctity of Duty or Law, meaning merely that they are imperative upon conduct and universally obligatory.[6]

But this common usage of the term is inaccurate. It is true that all this moral significance is contained in the word "holy," but it includes in addition—as even we cannot but feel—a clear overplus of meaning, and this it is now our task to isolate. Nor is this merely a later or acquired meaning; rather, "holy," or at least the equivalent words in Latin and Greek, in Semitic and other ancient languages, denoted first and foremost *only* this overplus : if the ethical element was present at all, at any rate it was not original and never constituted the whole meaning of the word. Any one who uses it to-day does undoubtedly always feel "the morally good" to be implied in "holy"; and accordingly in our inquiry into that element which is separate and peculiar to the idea of the holy it will be useful, at least for the temporary purpose of

---

[6] Here the question is passed over whether, say, the categorical imperative of duty may not itself have numinous quality, which induces awesome reverence. Passages are to be found in Otto, too, which suggest something of the kind and lead us to ask whether, for him, moral experience is rational or non-rational.

the investigation, to invent a special term to stand for "the holy" *minus* its moral factor or "moment," and, as we can now add, minus its "rational" aspect altogether.[7]

It will be our endeavour to suggest this unnamed Something to the reader as far as we may, so that he may himself feel it. There is no religion in which it does not live as the real innermost core,[8] and without it no religion would be worthy of the name. It is pre-eminently a living force in the Semitic religions, and of these again in none has it such vigour as in that of the Bible. Here, too, it has a name of its own, namely, the Hebrew "qādôsh," to which the Greek ἅγιος and the Latin *sanctus*, and, more accurately still, *sacer*, are the corresponding terms. It is not, of course, disputed that these terms in all three languages connote, as part of their meaning, *good, absolute goodness*, when, that is, the notion has ripened and reached the highest stage in its development. And we then use the word "holy" to

[7] The numinous and the Holy, it must be observed, are not equivalents. The numinous is an element *within* the Holy; it is that in the Holy which is non-rational and non-moral. The student will inquire whether the numinous factor in the Holy is represented by Otto as the fundamental one, or as ranking as of equal importance with what is moral and rational.

[8] Otto manifestly intends to hold the balance evenly between the rational and ethical elements on the one hand and the non-rational on the other, so that in the final development what is religious is always ethical, and what is ethical is always religious. Yet passages occur (more frequently perhaps in his later book of essays, *Aufsätze das Numinose betreffend*) which apparently teach that something wholly non-moral in type is the *deepest* thing in all religion, even the highest. We must ask whether the danger of ending in a superstitious mystical awe rather than a childlike faith is wholly averted. Also whether "rational" and "non-rational" factors, if externally isolated from each other in principle as Otto isolates them, can ever be livingly united. The question persists: Can we be satisfied to regard it as merely one more idiosyncrasy of religion, that the two sides thus confront each other indifferently; is there no essential tie between the mystery and the rational form?

translate them. But this "holy" then represents the gradual shaping and filling in with ethical meaning, or what we shall call the "schematisation," of what was a unique original feeling-response, which can be in itself ethically neutral and claims consideration in its own right. And when this moment or element first emerges and begins its long development, all those expressions (*qādôsh*, ἅγιος, *sacer*, etc.) mean beyond all question something quite other than "the good." This is universally agreed by contemporary criticism, which rightly explains the rendering of *qādôsh* by "good" as a mistranslation and unwarranted "rationalisation" or "moralisation" of the term.

Accordingly, it is worth while, as we have said, to find a word to stand for this element in isolation, this "extra" in the meaning of "holy" above and beyond the meaning of goodness. By means of a special term we shall the better be able, first, to keep the meaning clearly apart and distinct, and second, to apprehend and classify connectedly whatever subordinate forms or stages of development it may show. For this purpose I adopt a word coined from the Latin *numen*. *Omen* has given us *ominous*, and there is no reason why from *numen* we should not similarly form a word *numinous*. I shall speak then of a unique "numinous" category of value and of a definitely "numinous" state of mind, which is always found wherever the category is applied. The mental state is perfectly *sui generis* and irreducible to any other ; [9] and therefore, like every absolutely primary and elementary datum, while it admits of being discussed, it cannot be strictly defined. There is only one way to help another to an understanding of it. He must be guided and led on by consideration and discussion of the matter through the ways of his own mind,

[9] Otto does not strictly mean that it cannot be analysed ; the next chapter of his book, indeed, is headed "The Elements in the Numinous."

until he reach the point at which " the numinous " in him [10] perforce begins to stir, to start into life and into consciousness. We can co-operate in this process by bringing before his notice all that can be found in other regions of the mind, already known and familiar, to resemble, or again to afford some special contrast to, the particular experience we wish to elucidate. Then we must add : " This *X* of ours is not precisely *this* experience, but akin to this one and the opposite of that other. Cannot you now realise for yourself what it is ? " In other words, our *X* cannot, strictly speaking, be taught, it can only be evoked, awakened in the mind ; as everything that comes " of the spirit " must be awakened.

THE ELEMENTS IN THE " NUMINOUS." [11]

From Chapter III.

Creature-Feeling.

The reader is invited to direct his mind to a moment of deeply felt religious experience, as little as possible qualified

[10] It has been urged that Otto uses the term " numen " for the external reality, and " the numinous " for the state of mind evoked by it. But this is too simple. In his usage " the numinous " designates both things : the object of the religious response—the Something More which is the object of wonder and longing in all piety—and the response itself in terms of feeling. The divine reality is numinous, and the devotee feels numinously towards it. If ambiguity sometimes results, at all events the double reference of the word saves Otto's book from being merely psychology, and makes it a singularly fresh contribution to the philosophical and phenomenological study of the essence and values of religion.

[11] As the numinous is, on Otto's showing, a simple and original *datum*, not a construct, we are justified in saying that what he discusses in this section is not so much the numinous apprehension itself, as rather " certain emotional states within which the numinous can be detected as an element."

by other forms of consciousness. Whoever cannot do this, whoever knows no such moments in his experience, is requested to read no further; for it is not easy to discuss questions of religious psychology with one who can recollect the emotions of his adolescence, the discomforts of indigestion, or, say, social feelings, but cannot recall any intrinsically religious feelings. We do not blame such a one, when he tries for himself to advance as far as he can with the help of such principles of explanation as he knows, interpreting " Æsthetics " in terms of sensuous pleasure, and " Religion " as a function of the gregarious instinct and social standards, or as something more primitive still. But the artist, who for his part has an intimate personal knowledge of the distinctive element in the æsthetic experience, will decline his theories with thanks, and the religious man will reject them even more uncompromisingly.

Next, in the probing and analysis of such states of the soul as that of solemn worship, it will be well if regard be paid to what is unique in them rather than to what they have in common with other similar states. To be *rapt* in worship is one thing; to be morally *uplifted* by the contemplation of a good deed is another; and it is not to their common features, but to those elements of emotional content peculiar to the first that we would have attention directed as precisely as possible. As Christians we undoubtedly here first meet with feelings familiar enough in a weaker form in other departments of experience, such as feelings of gratitude, trust, love, reliance, humble submission, and dedication. But this does not by any means exhaust the content of religious worship. Not in any of these have we got the special features of the quite unique and incomparable experience of solemn worship. In what does this consist ?

Schleiermacher has the credit of isolating a very im-

portant element in such an experience. This is the "feel
ing of dependence." But this important discovery of
Schleiermacher is open to criticism in more than one
respect.

In the first place, the feeling or emotion which he really
has in mind in this phrase is in its specific quality not a
"feeling of dependence" in the "natural" sense of the
word. As such, other domains of life and other regions
of experience than the religious occasion the feeling, as a
sense of personal insufficiency and impotence, a consciousness of being determined by circumstances and environment.
The feeling of which Schleiermacher wrote has an undeniable analogy with these states of mind : they serve
as an indication to it, and its nature may be elucidated by
them, so that, by following the direction in which they
point, the feeling itself may be spontaneously felt. But
the feeling is at the same time also qualitatively different
from such analogous states of mind. Schleiermacher
himself, in a way, recognises this by distinguishing
the feeling of pious or religious dependence from all
other feelings of dependence. His mistake is in making
the distinction merely that between "absolute" and
"relative" dependence, and therefore a difference of
degree and not of intrinsic quality.[12] What he overlooks
is that, in giving the feeling the name "feeling of dependence" at all, we are really employing what is no more than
a very close analogy. Any one who compares and contrasts the two states of mind introspectively will find out,
I think, what I mean. It cannot be expressed by means
of anything else, just because it is so primary and elementary
a datum in our psychical life, and therefore only definable

[12] Schleiermacher, we may surmise, would have stressed the word
"absolute," arguing that absoluteness cannot be simply a matter
of degree.

through itself.[13]   It may perhaps help him if I cite a well-known example, in which the precise "moment" or element of religious feeling of which we are speaking is most actively present.   When Abraham ventures to plead with God for the men of Sodom, he says (Gen. xviii. 27) : " Behold now, I have taken upon me to speak unto the Lord, which am but dust and ashes."   There you have a self-confessed "feeling of dependence," which is yet at the same time far more than, and something other than, *merely* a feeling of dependence.   Desiring to give it a name of its own, I propose to call it " creature-consciousness " or creature-feeling.   It is the emotion of a creature, abased and overwhelmed by its own nothingness in contrast to that which is supreme above all creatures.

It is easily seen that, once again, this phrase, whatever it is, is not a *conceptual* explanation of the matter.   All that this new term, " creature-feeling," can express, is the note of self-abasement into nothingness before an over-powering, absolute might of some kind ; whereas every-thing turns upon the *character* of this overpowering might, a character which cannot be expressed verbally, and can only be suggested indirectly through the tone and content of a man's feeling-response to it.   And this response must be directly experienced in oneself to be understood.[14]

We have now to note a second defect in the formulation of Schleiermacher's principle.   The religious category

[13] It has been doubted whether " creature-feeling," according to Otto the primary reflection or effect in self-feeling of contact with the *numen*, can be thus taken as a primary and unanalysable human emotion, and is not rather complex in structure, possibly indeed in part dependent for its quality on an antecedent *idea* of God.

[14] Otto may here be charged with taking refuge in the inscrutable, but his general description of course holds true of every simple and primary apprehension, *e.g.* of a colour-sensum or a bodily sensation. How should we describe beauty or hunger to one who had never felt it ?

discovered by him, by whose means he professes to determine the real content of the religious emotion, is merely a category of *self*-valuation, in the sense of self-depreciation. According to him the religious emotion would be directly and primarily a sort of *self*-consciousness, a feeling concerning one's self in a special, determined relation, namely, one's dependence. Thus, according to Schleiermacher, I can only come upon the very fact of God as the result of an inference, that is, by reasoning to a cause beyond myself to account for my " feeling of dependence." But this is entirely opposed to the psychological facts of the case. Rather, the " creature-feeling " is itself a first subjective concomitant and effect of another feeling-element, which casts it like a shadow, but which in itself indubitably has immediate and primary reference to an object outside the self.[15]

But this object is just what we have already spoken of as " the numinous." For the " creature-feeling " and the sense of dependence to arise in the mind the " numen " must be experienced as present, a " numen præsens," as in the case of Abraham. There must be felt a something "numinous," something bearing the character of a " numen," to which the mind turns spontaneously ; or (which is the same thing in other words) these feelings can only arise in the mind as accompanying emotions when the category of " the numinous " is called into play.

The numinous is thus felt as objective and outside the self. We have now to inquire more closely into its nature and the modes of its manifestation.

[15] There is much to be said for the position that in Schleiermacher's argument " feeling " is no mere emotion, from which the divine Object is *inferred*, but a mode of immediate apprehension or dim cognition. Otto himself, though he might seem to refer religion solely to the " function " of feeling, certainly is no subjectivist ; the numinous experience, he insists, has an afferent or cognitive as well as an emotional aspect.

MYSTERIUM TREMENDUM.

From Chapter IV.

The Analysis of " Tremendum."

We said above that the nature of the numinous can only be suggested by means of the special way in which it is reflected in the mind in terms of feeling. " Its nature is such that it grips or stirs the human mind with this and that determinate affective state." We have now to attempt to give a further indication of these determinate states. We must once again endeavour, by adducing feelings akin to them for the purpose of analogy or contrast, and by the use of metaphor and symbolic expressions, to make the states of mind we are investigating ring out, as it were, of themselves.

Let us consider the deepest and most fundamental element in all strong and sincerely felt religious emotion. Faith unto Salvation, Trust, Love—all these are there. But over and above these is an element which may also on occasion, quite apart from them, profoundly affect us and occupy the mind with a well-nigh bewildering strength. Let us follow it up with every effort of sympathy and imaginative intuition wherever it is to be found—in the lives of those around us, in sudden, strong ebullitions of personal piety and the frames of mind such ebullitions evince, in the fixed and ordered solemnities of rites and liturgies, and again in the atmosphere that clings to old religious monuments and buildings, to temples and to churches. If we do so, we shall find we are dealing with something for which there is only one appropriate expression, *mysterium tremendum*. The feeling of it may at times come sweeping like a gentle tide, pervading the mind with a tranquil mood of deepest worship. It may pass

over into a more set and lasting attitude of the soul,
continuing, as it were, thrillingly vibrant and resonant,
until at last it dies away and the soul resumes its
"profane," non-religious mood of everyday experience.
It may burst in sudden eruption up from the depths of
the soul with spasms and convulsions, or lead to the
strangest excitements, to intoxicated frenzy, to transport,
and to ecstasy. It has its wild and dæmonic forms and can
sink to an almost grisly horror and shuddering. It has its
crude, barbaric antecedents and early manifestations, and
again it may be developed into something beautiful and
pure and glorious. It may become the hushed, trembling,
and speechless humility of the creature in the presence of
—whom or what ? In the presence of that which is a
Mystery inexpressible and above all creatures.

It is again evident at once that here, too, our attempted
formulation by means of a concept is once more a merely
negative one. Conceptually "mysterium" denotes
merely that before which the eyes are held closed, that
which is hidden and esoteric, that which is beyond conception or understanding, extraordinary and unfamiliar.
The term does not define the object more positively in its
qualitative character. But though what is enunciated in
the word is negative, what is meant is something absolutely and intensely positive. This pure positive we can
experience in feelings, feelings which our discussion can
help to make clear to us, in so far as it arouses them actually
in our hearts.

1. The Element of Awefulness.

To get light upon the positive " quale " of the object of
these feelings, we must analyse more closely our phrase
mysterium tremendum, and we will begin first with the
adjective.

" Tremor " is in itself merely the perfectly familiar and

30

" natural " emotion of *fear*. But here the term is taken, aptly enough but still only by analogy, to denote a quite specific kind of emotional response, wholly distinct from that of being afraid, though it so far resembles it that the analogy of fear may be used to throw light upon its nature. There are in some languages special expressions which denote, either exclusively or in the first instance, this " fear " that is more than fear proper. . . .

In my examination of Wundt's Animism I suggested the term " Scheu " (dread) ; but the special " numinous " quality (making it " *awe* " rather than " *dread* " in the ordinary sense) would then of course have to be denoted by inverted commas. " Religious dread " (or " awe ") would perhaps be a better designation. Its antecedent stage is " dæmonic dread " (cf. the horror of Pan) with its queer perversion, a sort of abortive offshoot, the " dread of ghosts." It first begins to stir in the feeling of " something uncanny," " eerie," or " weird." It is this feeling which, emerging in the mind of primeval man, forms the starting-point for the entire religious development in history. " Dæmons " and " gods " alike spring from this root, and all the products of " mythological apperception " or " fantasy " are nothing but different modes in which it has been objectified. And all ostensible explanations of the origin of religion in terms of animism or magic or folk-psychology are doomed from the outset to wander astray and miss the real goal of their inquiry, unless they recognise this fact of our nature—primary, unique, underivable from anything else—to be the basic factor and the basic impulse underlying the entire process of religious evolution.[16] . . .

[16] Welcome emphasis is here laid on the truth—so often missed— that religion begins with religion, not with something else. So far from ideas of gods being the imaginative creation of fears excited by the inexplicable, they sprang from a vague primordial perception of

Though the numinous emotion in its completest development shows a world of difference from the mere " dæmonic dread," yet not even at the highest level does it belie its pedigree or kindred. Even when the worship of " dæmons " has long since reached the higher level of worship of " gods," these gods still retain as " numina " something of the " ghost " in the impress they make on the feelings of the worshipper, namely, the peculiar quality of the " uncanny " and " awful," which survives with the quality of exaltedness and sublimity or is symbolised by means of it. And this element does not disappear even on the highest level of all, where the worship of God is at its purest.[17] Its disappearance would be indeed an essential loss. The " shudder " reappears in a form ennobled beyond measure where the soul, held speechless, trembles inwardly to the furthest fibre of its being. It invades the mind mightily in Christian worship with the words : " Holy, holy, holy " ; it breaks forth from the hymn of Tersteegen :

> " God Himself is present :
> Heart, be stilled before Him :
> Prostrate inwardly adore Him."

The " shudder " has here lost its crazy and bewildering note, but not the ineffable something that holds the mind. It has become a mystical awe, and sets free as its accompaniment, reflected in self-consciousness, that " creature-

"Something quite apart," wholly other than this world ; something which, imaged as gods or demons, was later used to explain odd and strange facts.

[17] No part of Otto's argument has aroused more vehement dissent. An awe-inspiring element, he affirms, is present in the object even of the highest and purest faith ; and what love casts out is slavish fear, not fear as such. " We can sometimes detect, even in the teaching of Jesus, notes still vibrating which seem to suggest a trace of that weird awe and shuddering dread before the mysteries of the transcendent of which we have already spoken " (*Idea of the Holy*, p. 87). The *daunting* aspect of the numinous remains to the end.

feeling" that has already been described as the feeling of personal nothingness and abasement before the awe-inspiring object directly experienced.

The referring of this feeling of numinous "tremor" to its object in the numen brings into relief a "property" of the latter which plays an important part in our Holy Scriptures, and which has been the occasion of many difficulties, both to commentators and to theologians, from its puzzling and baffling nature. This is the ὀργή (orgé), the Wrath of Yahweh, which recurs in the New Testament as ὀργὴ θεοῦ, and which is clearly analogous to the idea occurring in many religions of a mysterious "ira deorum." To pass through the Indian Pantheon of Gods is to find deities who seem to be made up altogether out of such an ὀργή; and even the higher Indian gods of grace and pardon have frequently, beside their merciful, their "wrath" form. But as regards the "Wrath of Yahweh," the strange features about it have for long been a matter for constant remark. In the first place, it is patent from many passages of the Old Testament that this "Wrath" has no concern whatever with moral qualities. There is something very baffling in the way it "is kindled" and manifested. It is, as has been well said, "like a hidden force of nature," like stored-up electricity, discharging itself upon any one who comes too near. It is "incalculable" and "arbitrary." Any one who is accustomed to think of deity only by its rational attributes must see in this "Wrath" mere caprice and wilful passion. But such a view would have been emphatically rejected by the religious men of the Old Covenant, for to them the Wrath of God, so far from being a diminution of His Godhead, appears as a natural expression of it, an element of "holiness" itself, and a quite indispensable one. And in this they are entirely right. This ὀργή is nothing but the "tremendum" itself, apprehended and expressed by the aid of a naive analogy from the domain of natural experience, in this case from the ordinary passional life of men. But naive as it may be, the analogy is most disconcertingly apt and striking; so much so that it will always retain its value, and for us no less than for the men of old be an inevitable way of expressing one element in the religious emotion. It cannot be doubted that, despite the protest of Schleiermacher and Ritschl, Christianity also has something to teach of the "Wrath of God."

It will be again at once apparent that in the use of this word we are not concerned with a genuine intellectual "concept," but only with a sort of illustrative substitute for a concept. "Wrath" here is the "ideogram" [18] of a unique emotional moment in religious experience, a moment whose singularly *daunting* and awe-inspiring character must be gravely disturbing to those persons who will recognise nothing in the divine nature but goodness, gentleness, love, and a sort of confidential intimacy, in a word, only those aspects of God which turn towards the world of men. . . .

2. The Element of "Overpoweringness" ("*majestas*").

We have been attempting to unfold the implications of that aspect of the "mysterium tremendum" indicated by the adjective, and the result so far may be summarised in two words, constituting, as before, what may be called an "ideogram," rather than a concept proper, namely, "absolute unapproachability."

It will be felt at once that there is yet a further element which must be added, that, namely, of "might," "power," "absolute overpoweringness." We will take to re-

---

[18] For Otto an "ideogram" is, as it were, a finger-post pointing towards an idea other in kind than itself, a figured illustration hinting at a meaning that eludes precise formulation.

present this the term "majestas," majesty—the more
readily because any one with a feeling for language must
detect a last faint trace of the numinous still clinging to
the word.[19]   The "tremendum" may then be rendered
more adequately "tremenda majestas," or "aweful
majesty."   This second element of majesty may continue
to be vividly preserved, where the first, that of unapproachability, recedes and dies away, as may be seen, for example,
in Mysticism.[20]   It is especially in relation to this element
of majesty or absolute overpoweringness that the creature-
consciousness, of which we have already spoken, comes
upon the scene, as a sort of shadow or subjective reflection of it.   Thus, in contrast to "the overpowering" of
which we are conscious as an object over against the self,
there is the feeling of one's own abasement, of being but
"dust and ashes" and nothingness.   And this forms
the numinous raw material for the feeling of religious
humility.

Here we must revert once again to Schleiermacher's
expression for what we call "creature-feeling," namely, the
"feeling of dependence."   We found fault with this
phrase before on the ground that Schleiermacher thereby
takes as basis and point of departure what is merely
a secondary effect ; that he sets out to teach a consciousness of the religious *object* only by way of an inference from
the shadow it casts upon *self*-consciousness.   We have now
a further criticism to bring against it, and it is this.   By
"feeling of dependence" Schleiermacher means consciousness of *being conditioned* (as effect by cause), and so he

[19] It may reasonably be held here also, as in the case of "creature-
feeling," that the numinous sense of *majestas* is a complex rather
than a simple emotional state.

[20] "Essentially," Otto writes below, "Mysticism is the stressing to
a very high degree, indeed the overstressing, of the non-rational or
supra-rational elements in religion."

develops the implications of this logically enough in his
sections upon Creation and Preservation. On the side
of the deity the correlate to "dependence" would thus be
"causality," *i.e.* God's character as all-causing and all-
conditioning. But a sense of this does not enter at all
into that immediate and first-hand religious emotion which
we have in the moment of worship, and which we can
recover in a measure for analysis ; it belongs on the
contrary decidedly to the *rational* side of the idea of God ;
its implications admit of precise conceptual determination ;
and it springs from quite a distinct source. The difference
between the "feeling of dependence" of Schleiermacher
and that which finds typical utterance in the words of
Abraham already cited might be expressed as that between
the consciousness of *createdness* (Geschaffenheit) and the
consciousness of *creaturehood* (Geschöpflichkeit). In the
one case you have the creature as the work of the divine
creative act ; in the other, impotence and general nothingness as against overpowering might, dust and ashes as
against "majesty." In the one case you have the fact of
having been created ; in the other, the status of the
creature. And as soon as speculative thought has come
to concern itself with this latter type of consciousness—
as soon as it has come to analyse this "majesty"—we are
introduced to a set of ideas quite different from those of
creation or preservation. We come upon the ideas, first,
of the annihilation of self, and then, as its complement, of
the transcendent as the sole and entire reality. These
are the characteristic notes of Mysticism in all its forms,
however otherwise various in content. For one of the
chiefest and most general features of Mysticism is just this
self-depreciation (so plainly parallel to the case of Abraham),
the estimation of the self, of the personal " I," as something not perfectly or essentially real, or even as mere
nullity, a self-depreciation which comes to demand its

own fulfilment in practice in rejecting the delusion of selfhood, and so makes for the annihilation of the self. And on the other hand, Mysticism leads to a valuation of the transcendent object of its reference as that which through plenitude of being stands supreme and absolute, so that the finite self contrasted with it becomes conscious even in its nullity that "I am nought, Thou art all." There is no thought in this of any causal relation between God, the creator, and the self, the creature. The point from which speculation starts is not a "consciousness of absolute dependence"—of myself as result and effect of a divine cause—for that would in point of fact lead to insistence upon the reality of the self ; it starts from a consciousness of the absolute superiority or supremacy of a power other than myself, and it is only as it falls back upon ontological terms to achieve its end—terms generally borrowed from natural science—that that element of the "tremendum," originally apprehended as "plenitude of power," becomes transmuted into "plenitude of being."

This leads again to the mention of Mysticism. No mere inquiry into the genesis of a thing can throw any light upon its essential nature, and it is hence immaterial to us how Mysticism historically arose. But essentially Mysticism is the stressing to a very high degree, indeed the overstressing, of the non-rational or supra-rational elements in religion ; and it is only intelligible when so understood. The various phases and factors of the non-rational may receive varying emphasis, and the type of Mysticism will differ according as some or others fall into the background. What we have been analysing, however, is a feature that recurs in all forms of Mysticism everywhere, and it is nothing but the "creature-consciousness" stressed to the utmost and to excess, the expression meaning, if we may repeat the contrast already made, not "feeling of our createdness " but " feeling of our creaturehood," that is, the consciousness of the littleness of every creature in face of that which is above all creatures. . . .

Sense of Excitement.

3. The Element of " Energy " or Urgency.[21]

There is, finally, a third element comprised in those of " tremendum " and " majestas," awefulness and majesty, and this I venture to call the *urgency* or *energy* of the numinous object. It is particularly vividly perceptible in the " ὀργή " or " Wrath " ; and it everywhere clothes itself in symbolical expressions—vitality, passion, emotional temper, will, force, movement, excitement, activity, violence. These features are typical and recur again and again from the dæmonic level up to the idea of the " living " God. We have here the factor that has everywhere more than any other prompted the fiercest opposition to the " philosophic " God of mere rational speculation, who can be put into a definition. And for their part the philosophers have condemned these expressions of the energy of the numen, whenever they are brought on to the scene, as sheer anthropomorphism. In so far as their opponents have for the most part themselves failed to recognise that the terms they have borrowed from the sphere of human conative and affective life have merely value as analogies, the philosophers are right to condemn them. But they are wrong, in so far as, this error notwithstanding, these terms stood for a genuine aspect of the divine nature— its non-rational aspect—a due consciousness of which served to protect religion itself from being " rationalised " away.

[21] The " numen " which dominates all by " majesty," actively directs and rules all by " energy " which is vital and charged with feeling.

THE ANALYSIS OF "MYSTERIUM."

From Chapter V.

"Ein begriffener Gott ist kein Gott."
("A God comprehended is no God.")

TERSTEEGEN.

We gave to the object to which the numinous consciousness is directed the name "mysterium tremendum," and we then set ourselves first to determine the meaning of the adjective "tremendum"—which we found to be itself only justified by analogy—because it is more easily analysed than the substantive idea "mysterium." We have now to turn to this, and try, as best we may, by hint and suggestion, to get to a clearer apprehension of what it implies.

4. THE "WHOLLY OTHER."

It might be thought that the adjective itself gives an explanation of the substantive; but this is not so. It is not merely analytical; it is a synthetic attribute to it; *i.e.* "tremendum" adds something not necessarily inherent in "mysterium." It is true that the reactions in consciousness that correspond to the one readily and spontaneously overflow into those that correspond to the other; in fact, any one sensitive to the use of words would commonly feel that the idea of "mystery" (*mysterium*) is so closely bound up with its synthetic qualifying attribute "aweful" (*tremendum*) that one can hardly say the former without catching an echo of the latter, "mystery" almost of itself becoming "aweful mystery" to us. But the passage from the one idea to the other need not by any means be always so easy. The elements of meaning implied in "awefulness" and "mysteriousness" are in themselves definitely different. The latter may so far preponderate in the religious consciousness, may stand out so vividly, that in comparison with it the former almost sinks out of sight ; a case which again could be clearly exemplified from some forms of Mysticism. Occasionally, on the other hand, the reverse happens, and the " tremendum " may in turn occupy the mind without the " mysterium."

This latter, then, needs special consideration on its own account. We need an expression for the mental reaction peculiar to it ; and here, too, only one word seems appropriate, though, as it is strictly applicable only to a " natural " state of mind, it has here meaning only by analogy ; it is the word "stupor." *Stupor* is plainly a different thing from *tremor* ; it signifies blank wonder, an astonishment that strikes us dumb, amazement absolute. Taken, indeed, in its purely natural sense, " mysterium " would first mean merely a secret or a mystery in the sense of that which is alien to us, uncomprehended and unexplained ; and so far "mysterium" is itself merely an ideogram, an analogical notion taken from the natural sphere, illustrating, but incapable of exhaustively rendering, our real meaning. Taken in the religious sense, that which is " mysterious " is—to give it perhaps the most striking expression—the " wholly other " (θάτερον, *anyad*, *alienum*), that which is quite beyond the sphere of the usual, the intelligible, and the familiar, which therefore falls quite outside the limits of the " canny," and is contrasted with it, filling the mind with blank wonder and astonishment.[22] . . .

[22] In the foregoing paragraph and the next we have a good illustration of Otto's sustained contention that no commingling of " natural" emotions can ever issue in specifically religious emotion. Professor Edward well points out that the author's explanation of *stupor* is meant to " indicate an emotional state which is not only different in intensity, but different in quality from ' natural ' or non-numinous stupor or amazement." The two can quite well be distinguished by the worshipper, if not by the spectator. Cf. Otto's later observations on " bliss."

In accordance with the laws of which we shall have to speak again later, this feeling or consciousness of the "wholly other" will attach itself to, or sometimes be indirectly aroused by means of, objects which are already puzzling upon the "natural" plane, or are of a surprising or astounding character ; such as extraordinary phenomena or astonishing occurrences or things in inanimate nature, in the animal world, or among men. But here once more we are dealing with a case of association between things specifically different—the "numinous" and the "natural" moment of consciousness—and not merely with the gradual enhancement of one of them—the "natural"—till it becomes the other. As in the case of "natural fear" and "dæmonic dread" already considered, so here the transition from natural to dæmonic amazement is not a mere matter of degree. But it is only with the latter that the complementary expression "mysterium" perfectly harmonises, as will be felt perhaps more clearly in the case of the adjectival form "mysterious." No one says, strictly and in earnest, of a piece of clockwork that is beyond his grasp, or of a science that he cannot understand : "That is 'mysterious' to me."

It might be objected that the mysterious is something which is and remains absolutely and invariably beyond our understanding, whereas that which merely eludes our understanding for a time but is perfectly intelligible in principle should be called, not a "mystery," but merely a "problem." But this is by no means an adequate account of the matter. The truly "mysterious" object is beyond our apprehension and comprehension, not only because our knowledge has certain irremovable limits, but because in it we come upon something inherently "wholly other," whose kind and character are incommensurable with our own, and before which we therefore recoil in a wonder that strikes us chill and numb.* . . .

In Mysticism we have in the "Beyond" (ἐπέκεινα) again the strongest stressing and over-stressing of those non-rational elements which are already inherent in all religion. Mysticism continues to its extreme point this contrasting of the numinous object (the numen), as the "wholly other," with ordinary experience. Not content with contrasting it with all that is of nature or this world, Mysticism concludes by contrasting it with Being itself and all that "is," and finally actually calls it "that which is nothing." By this "nothing" is meant not only that of which nothing can be predicated, but that which is absolutely and intrinsically other than and opposite of everything that is and can be thought. But while exaggerating to the point of paradox this negation and contrast—the only means open to conceptual thought to apprehend the "mysterium"—Mysticism at the same time retains the *positive quality* of the "wholly other" as a very living factor in its over-brimming religious emotion. . . .

These terms, "supernatural" and "transcendent" (literally, supramundane : *überweltlich*), give the appearance of positive attributes, and, as applied to the mysterious, they appear to divest the "mysterium" of its originally negative meaning and to turn it into an

---

* In *Confessions*, ii. 9. 1, Augustine very strikingly suggests this stiffening, benumbing element of the "wholly other" and its contrast to the rational aspect of the numen ; the "dissimile" and the "simile : "

"Quid est illud, quod interlucet mihi et percutit cor meum sine læsione ? Et inhorresco et inardesco. *Inhorresco*, in quantum *dissimilis* ei sum. Inardesco, in quantum similis ei sum."

("What is that which gleams through me and smites my heart without wounding it ? I am both a-shudder and a-glow. A-shudder, in so far as I am unlike it, a-glow in so far as I am like it.")

(*Author's footnote.*)

affirmation. On the side of conceptual thought this is nothing more than appearance, for it is obvious that the two terms in question are merely negative and exclusive attributes with reference to " nature " and the " world " or cosmos respectively. But on the side of the feeling-content it is otherwise ; that *is* in very truth positive in the highest degree, though here too, as before, it cannot be rendered explicit in conceptual terms. It is through this positive feeling-content that the concepts of the " transcendent " and " supernatural " become forthwith designations for a unique " wholly other " reality and quality, something of whose special character we can *feel*, without being able to give it clear conceptual expression.[23]

5. THE ELEMENT OF FASCINATION.

From Chapter VI.

The qualitative *content* of the numinous experience, to which " the mysterious " stands as *form*, is in one of its aspects the element of daunting " awefulness " and " majesty," which has already been dealt with in detail ; but it is clear that it has at the same time another aspect, in which it shows itself as something uniquely attractive and fascinating.

These two qualities, the daunting and the fascinating, now combine in a strange harmony of contrasts, and the resultant dual character of the numinous consciousness, to which the entire religious development bears witness, at any rate from the level of the " dæmonic dread " on-

[23] This insistence on the wholly positive quality of feeling-content, which nevertheless can only be *stated* in negatives (the same point is later made with respect to the fascinating aspect of the *mysterium*), is of great value. But for this positive quality, religion would rightly come to be regarded as but an emotional awareness of the enigmatic, fated to disappear as science extended the range of its explanations.

wards, is at once the strangest and most noteworthy
phenomenon in the whole history of religion. The
dæmonic-divine object may appear to the mind an object
of horror and dread, but at the same time it is no less something that allures with a potent charm, and the creature
who trembles before it, utterly cowed and cast down, has
always at the same time the impulse to turn to it, nay even
to make it somehow his own. The " mystery " is for him
not merely something to be wondered at but something
that entrances him ; and beside that in it which bewilders
and confounds he feels a something that captivates and
transports him with a strange ravishment, rising often
enough to the pitch of dizzy intoxication ; it is the
Dionysiac-element in the numen.[24]

The ideas and concepts which are the parallels or
" schemata " on the rational side of this non-rational
element of " fascination " are Love, Mercy, Pity, Comfort ;
these are all " natural " elements of the common psychical
life, only they are here thought as absolute and in completeness. But important as these are for the experience of
religious bliss or felicity, they do not by any means exhaust
it. It is just the same as with the opposite experience of
religious infelicity—the experience of the ὀργή or Wrath
of God : both alike contain fundamentally non-rational
elements. Bliss or beatitude is more, far more, than the
mere natural feeling of being comforted, of reliance, of the
joy of love, however these may be heightened and en-
hanced. Just as " Wrath," taken in a purely rational or

[24] Otto is here calling attention to that in the religious object which
evokes the longing to be in right relations with it ; it is felt to be
precious for its own sake, not merely as a means. The interesting
suggestion has been made that the two qualities of the numinous, the
daunting and the fascinating, might well have been treated of in
the reverse order, on the ground that the fascinating and attractive
aspect is in itself the stronger and, historically, the more influential.

a purely ethical sense, does not exhaust that profound element of *awefulness* which is locked in the mystery of deity, so neither does " Graciousness " exhaust the profound element of *wonderfulness* and rapture which lies in the mysterious beatific experience of deity. The term " grace " may indeed be taken as its aptest designation, but then only in the sense in which it is really applied in the language of the mystics, and in which not only the " gracious intent " but " something more " is meant by the word. This " something more " has its antecedent phases very far back in the history of religions. . . .

" Eye hath not seen, nor ear heard, neither have entered into the heart of man, the things which God hath prepared for them that love Him." Who does not feel the exalted sound of these words and the " Dionysiac " element of transport and fervour in them ? It is instructive that in such phrases as these, in which consciousness would fain put its highest consummation into words, " all images fall away " and the mind turns from them to grasp expressions that are purely negative. And it is still more instructive that in reading and hearing such words their merely negative character simply is not noticed ; that we can let whole chains of such negations enrapture, even intoxicate us, and that entire hymns—and deeply impressive hymns— have been composed, in which there is really nothing positive at all ! All this teaches us the independence of the positive content of this experience from the implications of its overt conceptual expression, and how it can be firmly grasped, thoroughly understood, and profoundly appreciated, purely in, with, and from the feeling itself.[25] . . .

[25] This emphasis on the verbally negative form of expression by which often the loftiest positive religious meanings are conveyed, has already been noted. Biblical writers frequently show that what is in their minds, of praise or wonder, they feel to be *unspeakable*.

It is not only in the religious feeling of longing that the moment of fascination is a living factor. It is already alive and present in the moment of "solemnity," both in the gathered concentration and humble abasement of private devotion, when the mind is exalted to the holy, and in the common worship of the congregation, where this is practised with earnestness and deep sincerity, as, it is to be feared, is with us a thing rather desired than realised. It is this and nothing else that in the solemn moment can fill the soul so full and keep it so inexpressibly tranquil. Schleiermacher's assertion is perhaps true of it, as of the numinous consciousness in general, namely, that it cannot really occur alone on its own account, or except combined and penetrated with rational elements. But, if this be admitted, it is upon other grounds than those adduced by Schleiermacher ; while, on the other hand, it may occupy a more or less predominant place and lead to states of calm (ἡσυχία) as well as of transport, in which it *almost* of itself wholly fills the soul. But in all the manifold forms in which it is aroused in us, whether in eschatological promise of the coming kingdom of God and the transcendent bliss of Paradise, or in the guise of an entry into that beatific Reality that is " above the world " ; whether it come first in expectancy or preintimation or in a present experience (" When I but *have* Thee, I ask no question of heaven and earth ") ; in all these forms, outwardly diverse but inwardly akin, it appears as a strange and mighty propulsion toward an ideal good known only to religion and in its nature fundamentally non-rational, which the mind knows of in yearning and presentiment, recognising it for what it is behind the obscure and inadequate symbols

It is perhaps an allied sense of the inadequacy of words that so often impels the religious soul to resort to *action* as the only worthy expression of devout feeling. "The Highest," says Goethe, " cannot be spoken."

which are its only expression. And this shows that above
and beyond our rational being lies hidden the ultimate and
highest part of our nature,[26] which can find no satisfaction
in the mere allaying of the needs of our sensuous, psychical,
or intellectual impulses and cravings. The mystics called
it the basis or ground of the soul.

References.—Expositions and criticisms of Otto's views are to be
found scattered through many recent works. The following may
be mentioned as of importance : Edward, *Religious Experience : Its
Nature and Truth*, Lecture III. ; J. Baillie, *The Interpretation of
Religion*, pp. 246–255 ; D. M. Baillie, *Faith in God*, pp. 206–218 ;
Hodgson, *The Place of Reason in Christian Apologetic*, pp. 7 ff. ;
Miall Edwards, *Philosophy of Religion*, pp. 306–309 ; F. K. Schumann,
Der Gottesgedanke und der Zerfall der Moderne, pp. 135–179 ; and
articles by Oman in the *Journal of Theological Studies*, vol. xxv.
(1923–24), pp. 275–286 ; by Kattenbusch in *Die Christliche Welt*
for 1917, Nos. 38 and 39 ; by Heim in *Zeitschrift für Theologie
und Kirche* for 1920, pp. 14–41, and by Traub in the same journal
for 1921, pp. 391 ff. ; by Grin, in *Revue de Théologie et de Philosophie*
for 1922, pp. 42–53 ; and by Tillich in *Theologische Blätter* for 1923,
No. 1 ; and cf. H. R. Mackintosh, *The Christian Apprehension of
God*, chap. vi. See also the author's interesting preface to his
Aufsätze das Numinose betreffend (1923).

[26] The student may ask how this assertion, that the numinous or
non-rational element in consciousness is " the ultimate and highest
part of our nature," is to be harmonised with Otto's initial statement
(p. 450) that it is " the very mark and criterion of a religion's high
rank and superior value " that it should possess clear and abundant
conceptions.

INDEX

483

PRINTED BY MORRISON AND GIBB LIMITED, EDINBURGH AND LONDON